Museum Provision and
Professionalism

Leicester Readers in Museum Studies
Series editor: Professor Susan M. Pearce

Care of Collections
Simon Knell

Collections Management
Anne Fahy

The Educational Role of the Museum
Eilean Hooper-Greenhill

Interpreting Objects and Collections
Susan M. Pearce

Museum Management
Kevin Moore

Museum Provision and Professionalism
Gaynor Kavanagh

Museum Provision and Professionalism

Edited by
Gaynor Kavanagh

London and New York

First published 1994
by Routledge
11 New Fetter Lane, London EC4P 4EE

Simultaneously published in the USA and Canada
by Routledge
29 West 35th Street, New York, NY 10001

Editorial matter © 1994 Gaynor Kavanagh
Individual contributions © 1994 individual contributors

Reprinted 1999

Routledge is an imprint of the Taylor & Francis Group

Typeset in Sabon by Florencetype Ltd, Stoodleigh, Devon

Printed and bound in Great Britain by
TJ International Ltd., Padstow, Cornwall

British Library Cataloguing in Publication Data
A catalogue record for this book is available from the British Library

Library of Congress Cataloging in Publication Data
A catalogue record for this book has been requested

ISBN 0–415–11280–X (hbk)
ISBN 0–415–11281–8 (pbk)

Contents

Figures

Tables

Series preface

Museums are established institutions, but they exist in a changing world. The modern notion of a museum and its collections runs back into the sixteenth or even fifteenth centuries and the origins of the earliest surviving museums belong to the period soon after. Museums have subsequently been and continue to be founded along these well-understood lines. But the end of the second millennium AD and the advent of the third point up the new needs and preoccupations of contemporary society. These are many, but some can be picked out as particularly significant here. Access is crucially important: access to information, the decision-making process and resources like gallery space, and access by children, ethnic minorities, women and the disadvantaged and underprivileged. Similarly, the nature of museum work itself needs to be examined, so that we can come to a clearer idea of the nature of the institution and its material, of what museum professionalism means, and how the issues of management and collection management affect outcomes. Running across all these debates is the recurrent theme of the relationship between theory and practice in what is, in the final analysis, an important area of work.

New needs require fresh efforts at information-gathering and understanding, and the best possible access to important literature for teaching and study. It is this need which the *Leicester Sources in Museum Studies* series addresses. The series as a whole breaks new ground by bringing together, for the first time, an important body of published work, much of it very recent, much of it taken from journals which few libraries carry, and all of it representing fresh approaches to the study of the museum operation.

The series has been divided into six volumes each of which covers a significant aspect of museum studies. These six topics bear a generic relationship to the modular arrangement of the Leicester Department of Museum Studies postgraduate course in Museum Studies, but, more fundamentally, they reflect current thinking about museums and their study. Within each volume, each editor has been responsible for his or her choice of papers. Each volume reflects the approach of its own editor, and the different feel of the various traditions and discourses upon which it draws. The range of individual emphases and the diversity of points of view is as important as the overarching theme in which each volume finds its place.

It is our intention to produce a new edition of the volumes in the series every three years, so that the selection of papers for inclusion is a continuing process and the contemporary stance of the series is maintained. All the editors of the series are happy to receive suggestions for inclusions (or exclusions), and details of newly published material.

Acknowledgements

The publishers and editors would like to thank the following people and organizations for permission to reproduce copyright material:

Timothy Ambrose and Crispin Paine, 'Some definitions of "museum"', reproduced from *Museum Basics*, Routledge, 1993. Museums Association, *The Museums Charter* (1991), reproduced courtesy of the Museums Association, London. Sheldon Annis, 'The museum as a staging ground for symbolic action', from *Museum*, 151, pp. 168–71 © UNESCO 1986. Reproduced by permission of UNESCO. Dr Jeanne Canizzo, 'How sweet it is: cultural politics in Barbados', *MUSE*, Canadian Museums Association, Winter 1987, Volume IV, No. 4, pp. 22–7. Stuart Davies, 'A sense of purpose: re-thinking museum values and strategies', from S. Davies and K. Gee, *Debating the Future of Museums: Two Personal Views*, University of Leeds, 1993. G. Brown Goode, 'The principles of museum administration', *Museums Association Conference Proceedings*, 1895, pp. 69–70. Reproduced by permission of the Museums Association. J. Patrick Greene, 'Museums for the year 2000: a case for continuous revolution', *Museums Journal* 88(4) (1989), pp. 179–80. Reproduced by permission of the Museums Association. Peter Jenkinson, 'Museum futures', *Museums Journal*, July 1993, pp. 22–3. Reproduced by permission of the Museums Association. Mark O'Neill, 'Pierro della Francesca and the trainspotters', from *A New Head of Steam. Industrial History in the Museum* (1992) conference papers published by the Scottish Museums Council. Susan M. Pearce, 'Making up is hard to do', *Museums Journal*, December 1993, pp. 25–7, reproduced by permission of the Museums Association. Neil Postman, 'Museum as dialogue', reprinted, with permission, from *Museum News* 69(5) (1990), pp. 55–8. Copyright © 1990, the American Association of Museums. All rights reserved. Michael Wallace, 'The future of history museums', *History News*, July–August 1989, pp. 5–33. Reproduced by permission of *History News*. Stephen Weil, 'The proper business of the museum: ideas or things', from *Rethinking the Museum and Other Meditations*, Smithsonian Institution, 1990, pp. 43–56. Reproduced by permission of the Smithsonian Institution and the author. Gaynor Kavanagh, 'Visiting and evaluating museums', from *Handbook 1993–94*, pp. 42–6, Department of Museum Studies, University of Leicester, 1993. Reproduced by permission of the author. Museums & Galleries Commission 'The museum scene' (1992), reproduced by permission of the Museums & Galleries Commission, London. Laura Suffield, 'The National Audit Office report on museums: Britain's museums "deliver the product"', *The Art Newspaper*, October 1993. Reproduced by kind permission of *The Art Newspaper*. Barbara Woroncow, 'Public palaces or private places?', *Museums Journal*, December 1992, pp. 27–9. Reproduced by permission of the Museums Association. V. T. C. Middleton, 'Purpose of museums and the special characteristics of independents', from V. T. C. Middleton, *New Visions for Independent Museums in the UK*, The Association for

Independent Museums, 1990. Alan Warhurst *et al.*, 'Higher concerns', *Museums Journal*, July 1992, pp. 27–31. Reproduced by permission of the Museums Association. Gaynor Kavanagh *et al.*, 'Curatorial identity', *Museums Journal*, October 1993, pp. 27–33. Reproduced by permission of the Museums Association. John Murdoch, 'Defining curation', *Museums Journal*, March 1992, pp. 18–19. Reproduced by permission of the Museums Association. Patrick J. Boylan, 'Cross-community curatorial competences', *Museums Journal*, January 1993, pp. 26–9. Reproduced by permission of the Museums Association. Paul DiMaggio, 'The American art director as professional: results of a survey', *Bullet*, 24 June, 1993, pp. 5–9. Reproduced by kind permission of *Bullet* and the author. Mary Klemm, Nicholas Wilson and Monica Scott, 'Museum sector workforce training: an analysis of the workforce in the museum, gallery and heritage sector in the United Kingdom', introduction and objectives, Museums Training Institute, University of Bradford, 1993, reproduced by kind permission of the authors. Marista Leishman *et al.*, 'Image and self-image', *Museums Journal*, June 1993, pp. 30–2. Reproduced by permission of the Museums Association. Charles Phillips, 'Museum director as manager', reprinted by permission of the publisher from *History News*, Vol. 38, No. 3, March 1983, pp. 8–15. Copyright © by the American Association for State and Local History. Phyllida Shaw, 'The state of pay', *Museums Journal* 89(4) (1989), pp. 26–8. Reproduced by permission of the Museums Association. Gaby Porter *et al.*, 'Are you sitting comfortably? Are equal opportunities a luxury?', *Museums Journal*, November 1990, pp. 25–35. Reproduced by permission of the Museums Association. David R. Prince, 'Women and museums', *Museums Journal* 89(2) (1988), pp. 55–61. Reproduced by permission of the Museums Association. Marcia Tucker, 'Common ground', reprinted, with permission, from *Museum News*, July/August 1990. Copyright © the American Association of Museums. All rights reserved. Neil Cossons, 'A new professionalism', *Museums Association Conference Proceedings*, 1982. Reproduced by permission of the Museums Association. Neil Cossons, 'Scholarship or self-indulgence?', reproduced with permission from the *RSA Journal*, Vol. 139, No. 5415, February 1991. Neil MacGregor, 'Scholarship and the public'. This article was first published in *Museum Management & Curatorship*, Volume 9, No. 4, December 1990, pp. 361–6, and is reproduced here with the permission of Butterworth-Heinemann, Oxford, UK, and the author. Stephen Weil, 'The ongoing pursuit of professional status', reprinted, with permission, from *Museum News* 67(2) (1988), pp. 30–4. Copyright the American Association of Museums. All rights reserved. Robert MacDonald, 'Ethics: constructing a code', reprinted, with permission, from *Museum News* May/June 1992, pp. 62–5. Copyright the American Association of Museums. All rights reserved. H. L. Madison, 'Tentative code of museum ethics' (1925) published for the 20th annual meeting of the American Association of Museums. Reproduced by permission of the Museums Association. American Association of Museums, 'Code of ethics for museums' (1991), reproduced by permission of the Museums Association. ICOM, 'Code of professional ethics' (1987), reproduced by permission of ICOM. Museums Association, 'Code of conduct for museum professionals' (1991), reproduced by permission of the Museums Association. Museums & Galleries Commission, 'Setting standards for museums' (1993), reproduced by permission of the Museums & Galleries Commission. Museums & Galleries Commission, 'Registration scheme for museums and galleries in the United Kingdom. Second phase: draft for consultation' (1993), reproduced by permission of the Museums & Galleries Commission. Fred Dunning, 'No objects, no money, no venue, no problem', *Museums Journal*, February 1993, p. 22. Reproduced by permission of the Museums Association. Museums & Galleries Commission, 'Guidelines on disability and quality of service for museums and galleries in the United Kingdom' (1992), reproduced by permission of the Museums & Galleries Commission. Museums Association, 'Code of practice for museum authorities' (amended

1987), reproduced by permission of the Museums Association. Museums & Galleries Commission, 'Quality of service in museums and galleries: customer care in museums – guidelines for implementation' (1993), reproduced by permission of the Museums & Galleries Commission. Penny Spencer *et al.*, 'Feel the width', *Museums Journal*, July 1993, pp. 29–30. Reproduced by permission of the Museums Association. Giulia Ajmone Marsan, 'Measure the ecstasy', *Museums Journal*, July 1993, pp. 27–8. Reproduced by permission of the Museums Association.

Every attempt has been made to obtain permission to reproduce copyright material. If any proper acknowledgement has not been made, we would invite copyright holders to inform us of the oversight.

Introduction

Gaynor Kavanagh

I

This volume of selected readings begins with three different definitions of the word 'museum'. This may seem a rather arid beginning and, in a way, it is. Museum people have struggled in committee after committee, in national and international settings, with ease and with great difficulty to put meaning into the word 'museum'. So why do we need to think about this at all? Can't we just get on with the more interesting bits instead? What about sponsorship deals, the restitution of cultural property, the representation of women, provision for the disabled, contemporary documentation and the politics of museum exhibitions? Why spend time on the rituals of definition? Whoever reads the things once they are published anyway? These questions embody an impatience which is understandable and familiar: so an explanation must be given.

Before I go on, consider how you would define a museum if you had to do so for someone who had absolutely no knowledge of one. Try to get it down to no more than seventy-five words. It is not easy, but it is a revealing exercise. Now look at what you have written. What words have you used? Have you described what a museums does (a definition based on function), what it aims to provide (a definition based on mission), or what it should provide and achieve (a definition based on ideals)? Perhaps your definition is a mixture of these. What have been your priorities – people, collections, profits? Or have you taken a more holistic approach?

This exercise has been part of the teaching module upon which this book is based and it is useful for a number of different reasons. Within a student group, it illustrates the different perspectives that people have of what a museum is or should be. Even within a group of museum professionals, distinct differences of opinion give rise to healthy debate and well-defended arguments. The exercise illustrates how difficult it is to pin a definition down and to provide one with which everyone can be happy.

But to take this back to the beginning, why is this important at all? The answer is clear. Decisions about museums spring from individual and collectively held convictions and assumptions about what a museum is, and by extension what it is not. For example, can a museum be a museum if it has no collections and no commitment to collect? Can a museum be a place which is not open to the public? Obviously, very specific forms of understanding of the word 'museum' underpin *everything* that goes on in them, from the quality of displays to the cleanliness of the cafe. The better the definition, the better the museum, and the more able we can be at making a lucid and convincing case for it.

We can turn to the official definitions and explore these, and a number of characteristics should strike the thinking reader. They are dominated by a functional approach and give little room for inspiration. Frankly, they are not the stuff of which dreams are made. This is a pity because the great museums of our day have been developed because the staff concerned were often dreamers – people with vision, intellectual energy and deep social convictions. The inadequacy of standard museum definitions may explain at least part of the need for modern museums to have 'mission statements', that is, short pithy statements about their ultimate objectives which become the pivot of management decisions – in other word a ticket to a dream, if not a dream itself.

Definitions are also important because, regardless of how generous or accurate they are, they are used for official purposes. In the UK, the Museums Association's definition of what a museum is (and therefore what it is not) has helped the Museums and Galleries Commission to decide whether an organization can be formally registered as a museum. Without this formal status, funding and other advantages are lost. In a similar vein, the Audit Commission used the same definition when considering how the standards of local authority museums might be monitored. It follows that if the definition applied is a good one, administrative use can be very helpful indeed.

But what is not helpful is when a definition is applied without any form of awareness and qualification. It is quite possible to find museums which happily measure up to the definition: they collect, document, preserve, exhibit and interpret material evidence for the public benefit. But what if they do these things badly? What if they collect only one object a year, or within such a narrow range that hugely important material is ignored and lost? What if they document all the new acquisitions on the most up-to-date computer system, but neglect the historic collections and their frail paper records? What if preservation takes the form of radical restoration leaving an object in a shiny-as-new and totally stable condition, but with all its historic evidence lost? What if the collections are exhibited so badly their deterioration is accelerated, or are interpreted in such a way as to insult – directly or indirectly – sectors of a possible museum audience? The definition may have been fulfilled, but it has not taken the museum very far.

It is at this point that far greater knowledge of museums and their potential has to come into play. This will substantially influence the form a museum takes and the degree of success it meets. For some people, the object and the collection are seen as the beginning and end of all museum activity. For others, the public and the service element of provision have been paramount. Another group has centred its concerns on the visitor's capacity and inclination to part with money, thereby keeping the museum financially viable. In their extremes, these are largely incompatible approaches to museum provision and in the past have given rise to divisions and not a little dissent. The arguments run like this:

> objects are in danger from the public, who don't understand them anyway and therefore should be kept as far away from them as possible (the carer's argument);

> but, the public can *benefit* from access to what after all is rightfully theirs and has an infinite capacity to engage with new ideas and meanings (the sharer's argument);

> well, if that is what they want, they will have to be made to pay for it (the business argument).

Thankfully, out of such contradictions a more balanced approach has emerged and taken centre stage. It is evident in the way many museums in the 1990s are being planned and run. This approach is based on a more comprehensive view and sees the interdependence of all museum activities. A cyclical pattern is perceived. Well-researched interesting collections, displayed with imagination, originality and understanding, provide something quite special to visitors, who will find value in the experience of visiting. In turn, visitors are likely to be more willing to support future funding – either directly through admission charges or indirectly through the use of their taxes – if they believe the museum to be providing something worthwhile. Thus the better the museum, the better the response, the better the museum (if it is prepared to listen, watch and learn, of course).

In sum, defining a museum leads us only so far: we need to move further by exploring the convictions people hold and their perceptions of the balance of activities in which a museum is engaged. Museums, especially effective ones, are about so much more than a list of functions, a catalogue of tasks, a recipe book of good practice. They are about conviction, energy, commitment, professionalism and much excitement. They are also about wise management, fair treatment and open dialogue.

II

Historians looking at this book in ten or fifty years' time will note what I have written and the selection of papers I have made, seeing it for what it is: a way of thinking – an ideological view – stuck within its own time period. Whatever we create portrays who we are, when we are and why we are. We are never neutral, nor are we innocent. The evidence is there for all who are prepared to question it. Despite all claims to neutrality, museums – like texts – are saturated with the ideology of their time and place. No museum ever opened without political purpose, however broad-based, or operates now without an agenda encoded in all that it does. Jeanne Cannizzo (1987) expressed this well when she wrote:

> Museums are symbolic structures which make visible our public myths: the stories we tell ourselves about ourselves are institutionalised and materialised in our museums.

Museums differ across time and across culture. If I were somehow to show you a museum in Britain in the 1870s, 1930s and 1970s, you would easily spot the differences and 'read' the evidence of the period. At a surface level, it would be evident how the displays were constructed from very different materials – mahogany cases and elegantly hand-written labels in the 1870s, pegboard and typed labels in the 1930s, cork and hessian and very few labels in the 1970s (many museums were in a minimalist phase then). Other differences would be evident, especially in terms of how – if at all – the public were catered for and how they were expected to behave. But there would be far deeper differences: especially the ways in which the material was grouped and explained, what was included and excluded, and how the visitor was addressed. To take one example: how do you think the approach to an object from another culture's belief system might have varied between these points in time? And how might it be dealt with now?

Cultural and political differences will also make themselves evident in the form the museum takes and the priorities adopted. We invest our own culture in the institutions we create. A museum in, say, the West Midlands, in the United Kingdom, will have a different range of characteristics to one in central Sweden, northern France, California, the Ukraine or the suburbs of Sydney. Should you visit them, you would spot the differences instantly, although sometimes they are difficult to put into words. For example, from my own travels, I am conscious of how museums in Sweden in the 1980s appeared to have greater scope for social comment and political expression than museums in Britain at that time. This had little to do with 'museology' and everything to do with history and politics. Not only did both countries hold different ideas about the concept of free speech, but also at the time Swedish Social Democracy and British Conservative rule under Margaret Thatcher were philosophically poles apart. This was reflected in most forms of cultural expression, not least museums.

Museums around the world are united in as much as they are keeping places for objects, open on a restricted basis to members of the public. But, beyond this, they vary according to such factors as the political and social attitudes of those involved, funding structures, the legal framework and the ideological baggage of the time. Moreover, different countries have developed different forms of museums. For example, the multidisciplined provincial museum is a form of museum created through municipal self-government in nineteenth-century Britain. The museums of regional ethnology with their open-air parks are a form of museum born of the Swedish Romantic movement of the late nineteenth century. The science centres in India, developed in the last two decades, have been created to lift levels of public understanding of science and technology.

In sum, we have to be very wary of talking about museums as if they were a homogenous commodity: they are not. The great potential of 'the museum' lies in the flexibility of the idea and in its potential for continuous development. The idea of keeping objects in a special place, showing them to – and sharing them with – people has not as yet been exhausted, and possibly never will be.

III

Having acknowledged that museums are difficult to define and subject to considerable variety, we must go on to think about how a museum actually works and who it is for. Again, this is not straightforward and we would not be helping ourselves if we were to restrict this to a set formula or a prescriptive statement. Instead, a more flexible approach is necessary.

Museums serve a multitude of purposes and, in particular, play many roles, some of which are rarely even hinted at in a museum's mission statement or development plan. It is a fact of social exchange that for one party, in this instance a museum, to play a 'role' there has to be another party to play a responding 'role', in this case a visitor, curator, expert, donor, politician or critic. The roles museums play are complex, multilayered and constantly changing. They can be shelters from the rain, mortuaries for dead objects, shrines to the memory of wealthy donors (frequently long forgotten), forums for debate, repositories for community archives, centres of scholarship and understanding, instruments of social control, locations for recreation and reflection, sacred spaces where the spirits of the ancestors rest, anchor tenants in urban renewal programmes, lovers' meets or places to lose children. No two people will find exactly the same thing in a museum, or in a museum visit.

Museums work around and through three elements: collections, space and people. The balance varies, but without these three no museum can exist. So how does each of these work?

First, collections: the assumption is that museums hold the material evidence of human experience and the natural world. In part, they do. The collections held in the world's museums and art galleries are extraordinarily important and way beyond any financial valuation. They embody forms of collective consciousness. Think of some of your favourite things in museums: why are they important to you? My list would include the clock mechanism from Wells Cathedral (1392) at the Science Museum, the predella panel at the Ashmolean Museum, Oxford, of *St Nicholas of Bari rebuking the storm* by Bicci Di Lorenzo (1443), a piece of bent metal at the Big Pit Museum in Blaenavon, and most probably the entire contents of Torfaen and Kings Lynn Museums. Why? A mixture of things from personal association to just the sheer joy of the thing. A similar range of thoughts and feelings can be part of the acquisition process. Things have come into museum collections for a whole host of reasons, among which information value and survival are often paramount, although rarely the sole criteria. Other influences include prestige, academic sleuthing, fad and fashion, trade links, power structures and sheer opportunism.

In the creation of collections, museums have helped put an order on things and on thinking by endorsing categories. The world has been tidied up under a hierarchical system of headings and objects are ascribed meaning accordingly. Thirty years ago, a late nineteenth-century dress would have been part of a decorative art collection where its form and design would be the sole points of curatorial interest. Now, it might be found in a social history gallery in a display on sweated labour in the cities, or in a science gallery looking at the development of dyes or sewing machine technology. The categories have shifted because ideas change over time and new questions are asked. The same is true for what is collected.

No museum has ever or can ever collect all that represents human experience or the natural world. Processes of selection have been employed and these have been dictated by ways of defining the world and what is important in it. Museums hold collections which are 'selected samples' of material evidence: someone has chosen what to collect and therefore what to neglect. The silences can be deafening. Museums of technology have collected the tools, but not the memories of those who used them. Museums of costume have collected the clothes of middle-class young women, but not those of the poor, aged or disabled. Museums of art have collected what they can afford and have watched important works disappear from public view. That acquisition works as well as it does has been due in no small part to the careful development of the disciplines within museum practice. The judgements and decisions made rest on the essence of professional curatorial practice – thorough knowledge of the subject and a genuine appreciation of an object's potential role within the museum and its collection.

The care of objects also lies within the politics of the museum, as does public access to them. Museums exist to protect the irreplaceable, yet a system of compromises prevails. Objects need to be properly documented and stored. They have to be retrievable from storage and housed in conditions that minimize deterioration and the risk of damage. But only a proportion of the objects, those judged at the time to be the most important, are in what might be termed optimum condition. The rest enjoy varying degrees of care, determined by the availability of resources. Inevitably, objects considered of fundamental importance get the best treatment and end up in either environmentally controlled stores, or more likely, on display. At the other end of the scale, objects perceived as being of limited immediate value have been known to end up in damp basements, sheds without roofs or in 'open storage' in a field. The choices made will be influenced by the underlying belief in the museum and its central functions.

Museums are also about the organization of space. On a practical level, this is about the allocation and arrangement of space within that made available to the museum as a whole. Choices exist: a new gallery or an education room, a large reception space or shops and toilets, storage and offices in the museum or away from the main site. Choices also exist in the allocation of space to the displays, for example whether social history is crammed into a back room while geology dominates, or the water colour collection has more room than the ceramics (usually a good clue either to the discipline bias of the director or the strengths of the collections). The decisions made will yet again depend upon the purpose of the museum and its priorities. This point can be taken further, with respect to geographic contexts. Think about a museum you know, how it looks from the outside, its relationship to surrounding buildings and its location (proximity to transport systems, centres of population and so on). Museums are found in an extraordinary range of 'spaces', from purpose-built temple-like structures to reused railway stations and ice-rinks. They are found in industrial areas, city centres and in the middle of nowhere; they blend in or stick out like a sore thumb. If you explore these points and put them together, you will find that the practical organization of museum space both inside and out forms a language. Once decoded, it tells us a great deal about why the museum was founded and what its current purposes are.

Sheldon Annis (1986) provides a framework which helps us consider crucial aspects of space in museums. He has argued that museums are a very specific form of expressive medium. The objects placed in them shed their previous meanings, 'the world of their origin', and take up new ones, 'the world of significance created by display'. Unlike a book or a film which hold and bind people to a pre-set unchangeable narrative, people can move around a museum at will and tend to set their own agendas. Annis identified three forms of space a museum offers. The cognitive space is the knowledge-giving part of the museum, planned and designed by the museum's staff. The assumption has been that people enter an exhibition, absorb its messages or a proportion thereof, and leave in some way changed.

We now realize that it is not that simple. Whether people succeed or fail in acquiring new understanding from a museum visit is not necessarily dependent on their intelligence, but on the communication strategy of the museum as a whole and how visitors use the other two spaces the museum provides, the dream space and the pragmatic space.

We all enter dream space on museum visits and find our minds filled with a jumble of images, ideas, thoughts and pieces of music that surface unbidden. Sometimes these are sparked off by the visual appearance of the exhibits, or by a phrase on a label or the actions of fellow visitors. Museums provide a fertile ground for our memories and our willingness to open ourselves up to learning. To take one example of the 'dreaming' space, visitors to a folk museum may see a wooden cradle in a reconstructed eighteenth-century house. Some may pass it by without a glance. Others might be attracted to it and, regardless of the formal interpretation offered, will have thoughts and images provoked by it. A child may want to put a doll in it. A grandfather might think of an old tune about rock-a-byeing babies. Someone who likes working with wood might think about how it was made. An antiques dealer might put a price on it. A woman who has lost a child will see what it is – an empty cradle. This is the dream space: the reaction, the feeling, the image that rises to the surface, irrespective of the display designer's intentions.

The final space identified by Annis is the social or pragmatic space and it is this that links to the third element in museum provision: the visitors. The majority of people who visit museums do so in their free time and of their own free will. They have expectations of the visit and these may not just be associated with improving their understanding of a subject. People come to museums for a host of reasons, central to which is sharing the experience with people they care about and – through the visit – strengthening bonds. People expect to enjoy and get something out of both the museum and the act of being there with someone. This applies even to those who choose just their own company. My experience of visiting the Museum of the Moving Image in London has varied enormously because the four visits I have made have been on my own, with my nephews and with two very different groups of postgraduate students. No doubt the experience and memory of that museum might have varied further had I shared the experience with a famous film actor or someone with impaired mobility.

People set their own agendas when visiting a museum and will choose what they are prepared to be interested in. They can resist the tyranny of museum programming and the 'right' and 'wrong' ways of viewing a gallery. Visitors enjoy discussing the things they know and learning about new ones. Moreover, they will respond if the museum meets them half way, that is, if it anticipates and responds to their needs and interests, and learns from the exchange of views.

We know that museums do not appeal to everyone and that there is a long history of museums ignoring and excluding sectors of the population. We also know that museums have treated visitors as if they were a homogenous group with interchangeable needs, which they are not. The needs and interests of a retired couple without their own transport are not likely to be exactly the same as those of a group of teenagers who do not speak English, a young mum with a toddler and a bag of shopping, a group of executives enjoying a break from a conference, or a postgraduate student undertaking research. Greater understanding of this has led museums to plan some form of variation into the services they offer. However, care has to be exercised to avoid stereotyping – the retired couple could be the world's leading experts on nineteenth-century English tiles, the teenagers could be dedicated archaeologists, the mum could be finishing her doctoral thesis, the executives could be planning a break-in and the student could have some form of learning difficulty.

If the collections are the skeletal system, then the visitors are the life blood of the museum. Their histories and environments are the subjects of museum collections. Their commitment of time, as well as their cash, constructs the museum visit. Their ideas and interests are a constant source of inspiration. Finally, it will be their opinions, along with those not willing – for whatever reason – to visit museums, which will help influence future policy and the shape museums will take – politically, socially and economically.

IV

Museum work has been associated principally with the curator, an academic specializing in a specific collection-related field who can perform all tasks necessary to the museum. In many ways, curatorship remains the heart of museum work. Without collections, a museum does not exist. Good collections and therefore extremely competent curatorship are fundamental to museums and all that they aim to do. But as museums have become more complex and our understanding of all the factors which lead to effective provision has grown more sophisticated, the need for a range of complementary and supplementary skills has been recognized. As a result, an integrated museums profession has developed. In the larger museums, teams of people work side by side: curators, education officers, conservators, exhibition technicians, designers, registrars, gallery assistants and attendants, outreach workers, audience advocates, writers, marketing specialists, security experts and managers. In smaller museums, curators, trained to have a high level of awareness and a good degree of competence in these skill areas, operate to the limits of their own versatility. They often work with freelance specialists. There is now acceptance that effective provision rests on a mix of skills, knowledge and attitudes.

The inclusive nature of the concept of the museum professional in the long run has to be more useful and productive than the narrower and exclusive concept of the museum curator. If pursued to its logical conclusion, it might embrace an even wider range of museum workers: attendants, security staff and clerical workers. The question here is whether non-professional grades should be trained simply to do their jobs or whether there should be genuine opportunities for their professional and personal development within the museum system. In response to this, a number of museums have gone over to an open-grade system which, in theory at least, allows progressive promotion from gallery assistant (formerly attendant) to museum director. Postgraduate museum studies courses are being opened to non-graduate entrants. Similarly, the Museums Association in the UK is expanding its categories of membership to non-professional grades in an effort to broaden the base of its membership.

There is considerable scope for the development of the profession, largely because it is an 'open' one, where appointment to museum positions is not restricted to those already holding a specific qualification or prior membership of a professional body. This contrasts with professions like the law or medicine which are described as being 'closed', because they exercise considerable control over entry qualifications and training. The open nature of the museums profession has meant that people with genuine talent have come into the work, sometimes making a mid-career change. Yet some argue that there is not a museums profession at all, that the absence of national museum curators from membership and involvement with the professional body, the Museums Association, and the fact that many people operate within museums at a quite senior level without a formal museum qualification points not to a profession, but a (very) loosely held together occupational group. Although this is true, the fact is that there is a substantial number of people within the museum workforce who collectively and often consciously express the key characteristics of being a profession:

- They have a high degree of specialist and general knowledge, whether this is about the Iron Age, seventeenth-century clocks, the educational needs of five or fifty year olds or marketing a museum to a specific target audience.
- Through pre-entry and in-service postgraduate training, they also have a high degree of specialist and general knowledge about museums, their various functions and roles. Thus an education officer should know how a collection is catalogued and procedures for monitoring environmental conditions, a curator should know how to conduct an evaluation of a gallery or a SWOT analysis of a marketing campaign.
- There is considerable personal commitment to the ideals of museum provision. Most people do not come into museum work because of the salary, but because they hold passionate beliefs about communicating their subject and working with both collections and the public. It is creative work which attracts and needs creative, imaginative people.
- There is a strong sense of public duty, of serving people and of making better museums so that they can be more accessible and socially useful.
- With this has come a willingness to monitor and control standards of behaviour and performance, for the common good, for example through acceptance and observation of codes of conduct.
- Finally, there is peer group control and collective responsibility exercised through the Museums Association, which seeks to guard standards and encourage improvements in all aspects of museum work.

It is not clear how many people earn their living in museums. Various claims are made, but none can be more than educated guesses. A recent survey conducted by MTI (1993) claims that there are 40,000 people in this sector. (It has to be noted that this figure includes those engaged in the care of historic houses.) The Museums and Galleries Commission has estimated that there are 25,000 people in museum work, and John Myerscough has suggested the figure of 19,000 full-time equivalent staff (FTEs) to be about the mark. Until the Museums and Galleries Commissions database DOMUS (the *Directory of Museum Statistics*), which will hold the statistics gathered through the registration programme, is up and running such figures as we have will have to act simply as guides. The fact is that, at this stage, we simply do not know how many people are engaged in museum work. Even if we had more reliable statistics, they would be likely to exclude a hidden army of people without whom museums could not work: volunteers, trustees, advisors, members of focus groups and reminiscence workshops, teachers, parents, donors, service operatives, contractors, cleaners and catering workers.

V

All those who work in museums, or give their services to them, operate within the legislative and constitutional framework of the museum concerned. A museum does not run itself and, other than in the situation where the director is the sole owner of a private museum, the ultimate decisions are taken by some form of governing body. In the UK there are four main types of museum. The national museums and galleries are constituted through individual Acts of Parliament, Royal Charters or Orders in Council. Most are run by trustee boards, usually of about fifteen people, nominated in accordance with the museum's constitution. They are drawn from those seen as being the 'Great and the Good' and tend to be male, in retirement, with some form of interest or expertise relevant to the museum. This is not always the case, however, for younger men and women with relevant commercial or professional experience are to be found on these boards, albeit in the minority. Most are political appointments: trustees are nominated by a minister through a government department. But other appointments can be made, for example where learned societies, local authorities or the board itself has the power to make nominations.

In contrast, a local authority museum is governed by the full council of its elected members. The detailed business of decision-making is carried out by a specialist committee which deals with museums alongside other matters such as the arts, libraries or recreation. Members or councillors are elected, usually on a party ticket, and have a variety of interests, not necessarily associated with the museum. They come from a whole range of backgrounds, from shopkeepers and teachers to retired farmers: the balance of gender and age is more even than in other forms of museum governance.

A university museum is run by Senate and ultimately by its University Council. Senate is in effect a peer group of academics who conduct university business, of which museums may be a very small part indeed.

Finally, the independent museums are usually companies, limited by guarantee, with charitable trust status. As companies, they are governed by directors, appointed under the museum's Articles of Association, who are bound by both the Companies Acts and the Charities Acts to exercise a duty of care. As with the trustees of other types of museum, they are not paid. The trustees of independent museums, who are technically 'company directors', are usually people drawn from the museum's geographical area and may include elected members from the local authorities and other official bodies. Museum, subject or commercial specialists might serve on these boards.

This speedy summary has had to be given to underline the point that museums are not governed by their professional staff or by their director. There is always an ultimate decision-making body which must endorse and ratify policy, ensure that the museum is managed within legal and constitution requirements, and is financially viable. The collective and individual responsibilities of the board and trustees are set out in whatever document constitutes the museum or the organization of which it is part. Sometimes these are very loosely phrased and the trustee board develops its own rules and approaches.

Trustees of museums are rarely trained into their roles. On appointment, little briefing may be offered about the museum, its background and current agenda. However, whether dominated by peers of the realm, retired generals and civil servants, railway enthusiasts or party members, the relationship of the board to the staff and especially to the director is a critical one. It is here that the ability of the professional to communicate clearly and positively a deep understanding of their museum, its problems and potential is so important. Moreover, the governing body needs to understand museums in general and the broad trends and possibilities they face.

A board which is well equipped with information and feels able to trust the professional judgement of the museum staff can provide insight, fresh ideas and thoughtful decisions. This, in turn, depends upon the board's members being appointed for appropriate reasons, and upon the development of an open and constructive dialogue. Most governing bodies work on the principle of delegating authority to the director and through the director to the staff. In their deliberations, they deal only with the development of broad policy proposed by the staff, matters which fall outside current policy or are deemed to be specifically within their field of decision-making, and legal and financial issues.

Awareness of both the difficulties and the potential of the relationship of the governing body to the museum and the needs of those who act as trustees has led to recommendations. In particular, the Museums and Galleries Commission has recommended some form of induction for the trustees of national museums, and the Museums Association has developed a code of practice for museum authorities and guidelines for museum trustees.

The whole issue of how museums are governed in the UK has been under-researched. The documents covering the decisions boards make, with the exception of local authorities, are rarely in the public domain. Although those peers and MPs who serve on museum boards may speak about them in the Houses of Parliament and thus have their speeches recorded in *Hansard*, in the main the experience of being a museum trustee – as crucial as it is – goes without much note outside the boardroom.

VI

However a museum is governed, there has to be a firm grasp of the standards the museum must reach in all areas of its activities. At one time, it was sufficient that a museum monitored and reported once a year on the exhibitions held, the number of visitors, and the museum's income and expenditure. Outside advice might be taken as and when problems occurred. But there was very little, if any, pressure to provide evidence of how well or badly the museum was doing. Today, the situation is very different. Museums operate to standards which have been carefully worked out and relate to most areas of their activities. There are both internal and external mechanisms to ensure that the level of the museum's activities is at least maintained and, ideally, improved.

The internal mechanisms largely spring from good practice in the management of the museum's affairs. A well-thought-out and researched business plan, directed at imaginatively set and viable goals, will include systems of performance indicators. These make clear what is expected in each area of the museum's activities, from acquisition and documentation to carparks and cafeterias. They will be linked to a review programme and set within a time frame to allow effective monitoring. Performance may be further linked to the appraisal of staff within the museum. The problem with many forms of performance review in museums is that much of it relates to those matters which can be indicated by an assessment of quantity, rather than quality – how many people visited a new exhibition, rather than what they made of it. But as museums become more experienced in the assessment of performance, the indicators used and the analysis of the evidence gathered have become increasingly sophisticated and hence more helpful. Moreover, it has been recognized that the promotion of museum standards requires an investment in museum staff (especially in terms of training), an open and confident system of management and an atmosphere where trust exists.

A good proportion of the standards set are designed by the museums themselves and relate to their medium- and long-term strategies. Most, however, come from outside the museum and are either advised by a professional body, or are in the UK a requirement made by a formal authority such as the Museums and Galleries Commission or the Department of National Heritage.

The Museums and Galleries Commission's Registration Scheme set down a set of standards a museum must reach before it could be formally registered. The details are in this volume. The Commission has also drawn up sets of standards for the care of certain types of collections such as archaeological ones, as well as guidelines, for example on customer care. The Museums Association has a *Code of Practice for Museum Authorities* (currently under review) which lays down the fundamentals of good practice. In America, museums can undergo rigorous assessment through the American Association of Museums scheme for Accreditation, and take detailed specialist advice through the Museum Assessment Programs. Most countries have agencies and specialists who can advise and support museums and help them achieve the standards sought.

There are both problems and possibilities in the measurement of museum standards. The problems stem from an inflexible unimaginative approach, where standards are simple formulae or prescriptive views of museum practice. Concern for standards can become close to being a management obsession with data, which occupies the time and energy needed for other tasks. In the long run, little in terms of true improvement can be generated through such an approach. The possibilities lie in seeing it all as a means of strengthening facilities and services, through learning from experience. Those museums which are successfully using systems to measure their performance are choosing to be very specific about the areas in which they are used and the terms in which they are expressed. Part of the success depends upon not losing sight of the museum's overall purpose and holding onto a vision of what the museum might be in the future.

VII

There are no guarantees as to the future of museums. The majority of the national museums and a good proportion of the main local authority and university museums in the UK were founded in the second half of the nineteenth century; the substantial proportion of independent museums have been founded since 1960. We are used to them being there, and to being part of the fabric of our society. Museums have changed both to serve the needs of different generations and to meet the agendas of the day. Popular education, wartime propaganda, urban renewal, tourism, academic trends, curatorial fads and fancies, educational reform, political necessity – to name but a few and to varying degrees – have been served by museums, indeed have made and shaped museums. No doubt, the malleability of the concept of museums will ensure that they will keep on changing.

If we were somehow to glimpse a museum in fifty years' time, would we recognize it? No doubt the technology and the educational programmes would be out of this world. The exhibitions programmes would be on subjects not recognized as 'display worthy' at the moment. But would there be collections of extraordinary things? Hopefully, yes, because without them such places would not and could not be museums. Hopefully, too, the objects museum professionals care for and are acquiring now will have survived sufficiently well to be, not just of use, but real sources of information and inspiration.

Beware: there are a lot of assumptions here. I am assuming that society will progress and continue to want museums, and that people associated with museums will always want to learn and improve museum practice. I am assuming that people will still think that looking at things in museums is a worthwhile way of spending their time and that politicians will continue to tolerate, if not support, museums. You can write your own thesis or theory about the future of museums – but when you do, do not forget the biggest assumption of all: that there will be peace. Museums have been in the front line of many wars, and have been damaged and destroyed by them. Those which have been safe have been used for wartime and warlike purposes. The ultimate threat to the future of museums is war, because it destroys everything that makes them possible: people, living cultures, the best of our material heritage and, above all, hope.

VIII

The papers in this volume spring from recommended reading for the course on museum provision and professionalism, given as part of the programme for the masters' degree and postgraduate diploma in museum studies at the University of Leicester. There are seven sections:

> The museum: some definitions
> Thinking about museums
> Museums UK
> The museums profession
> Professionalism
> Codes of ethical conduct
> Institutional standards

Quite clearly, a lot of ground is covered here. It would be possible to create a volume of comparable size on at least six of the sections listed above. Therefore, some discipline has had to be exercised in the selection of the material. Preference has been given to work which is insightful and thought-provoking, or which in some ways summarizes either a situation or a school of thought. Even at the time of compiling this volume, some of the formal papers are subject to review and the reader should check whether more up-to-date versions of some of this material exist, for example relating to museum registration in the UK. I have introduced each paper with a brief note printed in italics.

Given the nature of the subject, it was difficult not to allow material from the UK to dominate the selection, although some material relating to the US has been included. There is much that needed to be included about the museum situation in the US and Canada, Australia and New Zealand, and of course Europe. However, space was at a premium: future volumes could redress this balance. A short reading list is given at the end.

Part 1
The museum: some definitions

1

Some definitions of 'museum'
Timothy Ambrose and Crispin Paine

It is important to know exactly what we mean when we use the word 'museum'. But, even so, definitions do not come easily and most need some qualification. The concept of a 'museum' is in a continuous state of development. It is modified by the politics of the museum's situation, the content of its collections and the audiences it aims to serve. However, a number of what might be called 'working definitions' are in existence and these guide our thinking by reminding us of the fundamental features that distinguish a museum from other types of institutions and practices.

THE ICOM DEFINITION

'A non-profit-making, permanent institution, in the service of society and its development, and open to the public, which acquires, conserves, researches, communicates and exhibits, for the purposes of study, education and enjoyment, material evidence of man and his environment.'

THE MUSEUMS ASSOCIATION (UNITED KINGDOM) DEFINITION

'A museum is an institution which collects, documents, preserves, exhibits and interprets material evidence and associated information for the public benefit.'

"Institution" implies a formalised establishment which has a long-term purpose. "Collects" embraces all means of acquisition. "Documents" emphasises the need to maintain records. "Preserves" includes all aspects of conservation and security. "Exhibits" confirms the expectation of visitors that they will be able to see at least a representative selection of the objects in the collection. "Interprets" is taken to cover such diverse fields as display, education, research and publication. "Material" indicates something that is tangible, while "Evidence" guarantees its authenticity as the "real thing". "Associated information" represents the knowledge which prevents a museum object being merely a curio, and also includes all records relating to its past history, acquisition and subsequent usage. "For the public benefit" is deliberately open ended and is intended to reflect the current thinking, both within our profession and outside it, that museums are the servants of society.

THE AMERICAN ASSOCIATION OF MUSEUMS DEFINITION

'A non-profit permanent, established institution, not existing primarily for the purpose of conducting temporary exhibitions, exempt from federal and state income taxes, open to the public and administered in the public interest, for the purpose of conserving and preserving, studying, interpreting, assembling, and exhibiting to the public for its instruction and enjoyment objects and specimens of educational and cultural value, including artistic, scientific (whether animate or inanimate), historical and technological material. Museums thus defined shall include botanical gardens, zoological parks, aquaria, planetaria, historical societies, and historic houses and sites which meet the requirements set forth in the preceding sentence.'

This paper first appeared in T. Ambrose and C. Paine (eds) (1993) Museum Basics, *London: Routledge, p.8.*

2

The Museums Charter
Museums Association

Most formal definitions of 'museums' stress the functional aspects of museum provision. Few are invested with any form of ideal or vision: the 'doing' predominates. Such definitions help us define the activities of museums yet rarely their perceived social, cultural or political purposes. Individual museums have redressed this by devising 'mission statements', that is, short summaries of their ultimate goals. In these, philosophy dominates over function, dreaming over doing, thinking over reacting. This is an important task. Arguably, there has to be space in museum work for vision and hope; moreover there has to be opportunity for the contemplation of horizons broader than the next acquisition or the reorganization of the stores.

In 1991, the Museums Association published its Museums Charter *to act as a reminder of the factors essential for 'the creation of a modern and dynamic museum scene'. This was aimed principally at opinion formers and politicians, but is an indicator of the concern currently held by museum professionals in the UK.*

Ultimately we as citizens must determine the value we place upon one of the essential hallmarks of a civilized country: an educated and informed society. A strong and dynamic museum culture that is accessible and of benefit to all members of society is integral to this achievement. This principle should underpin national and local government policies for museums.

Museum provision should remain varied and flexible, allowing for the differing needs of every type of museum, whether independent, local authority maintained, co-operative venture, national or regional. However, the present patchwork system of provision is highly unsatisfactory. It fails to provide adequate support for museums and does not allow them to realize the full potential of their collections. A national duty of stewardship is implicit in the public's right of access to the national heritage.

The Museums Association considers the following eight factors essential for the creation of a modern and dynamic museum scene.

Public right to museums

Museum collections are a fundamental national resource to which everyone has a right of access. Central and local government should take appropriate measures to ensure that no sector is prevented from enjoying this right.

Education

Museum collections represent unparalleled opportunities for education, recreation and inspiration. The full learning potential of all museums must be recognized and realized.

Protection of the heritage

Museums should be able to save the heritage. This requires realistic funding and an appropriate export legislation regime.

Safeguarding of collections

All museum collections should have unambiguous legal status, with clearly defined responsibilities for their management.

Caring for collections

Museums should care for their collections to a high standard and should have policies for their management and development.

Autonomy

All museum services should enjoy a high degree of autonomy, enabling rational priorities to be set for scarce finances.

Resources

All types of museums should be underpinned by a system of policy and funding, sufficient at least to maintain or enhance existing standards.

Training

Adequate funding and commitment should be forthcoming from central government and museum governing bodies to ensure training of a progressive and structured nature for all staff and volunteers.

The Museums Charter *was first published by the Museums Association, London, in 1991.*

Part 2
Thinking about museums

3

The museum as a staging ground for symbolic action

Sheldon Annis

There can be little doubt that museums are complex institutions and that there is no simple way of understanding them. In fact, they are better understood as places which give rise to a variety of experiences. The unexpected is the norm, and the best laid plans of curators, education officers and marketing experts can be creatively altered by the imagination and expectations of the museum visitor. Those who visit museums and indeed all those in whose name museum developments take place add a wonderfully subversive element to museums in any society. The joy of museums is their capacity to be places where people explore something of themselves, although this does not necessarily come about in the way the museum itself may intend.

Sheldon Annis has captured these often contradictory aspects of museums and by so doing touches on their extraordinary capacity and potential.

In recent years there has been much scholarly literature written on the concept of the 'symbol'. A host of related terms – sign, signal, semiotic, emblem, icon, *signans*, *signatum* – have spread into disciplines, as diverse as anthropology, art history, linguistics, folklore, geography and literary criticism. The *Concise Oxford Dictionary* defines *symbol* as 'a thing regarded by general consent as naturally typifying or representing or recalling something by possession of analogous qualities or by association in fact or thought'. In other words: something which stands for something else, but ambiguously and with disparate meanings. What a symbol is *not* is an algebraic equation, where S = something else. Rather, symbols are 'multivocal' and 'polyvalent' – that is, they speak with many meanings and in many combinations. They change with backdrop and grow with use. And it is precisely their fluidity, rather than their capacity to represent directly, that makes them central to human thought and action.

A museum is a kind of cultural warehouse. It is a place for things taken out of their natural context to be stored, reclassified and exhibited.

When objects become exhibits, they necessarily take on new meanings: they are transformed. The warehouse, among its other uses, serves as a linking place. The object-symbols twist in meaning between two worlds, the world of their origin and the world of significance created by display.

In presenting them, museums assure visitors that objects are valid and illustrative of larger frames of meaning. Museum curators, after all, are culturally designated to be communicators. By selecting and framing objects, they bestow legitimacy on them. Implicitly, the unseen curator tells the audience: this is the real thing, take this seriously.

Yet just as there is a gap between the world of the object and the world of the museum; so too, there is a gap between the world of the museum and the world of the viewer. Even though the visitor is assured that museum objects are praiseworthy, personal meaning remains *personal*. It is something that exists largely independently of the designer's message. For the visitor, it is something to be found or created.

How does the visitor make his way towards a personalized warehouse of symbols? And what, if anything, does the capacity to associate objects with meaning have to do with the growing popularity and success of museums throughout the world?

The answer to these questions, I believe, lies in the museum's character as an expressive medium. That, in turn, is a function of its physical nature. As a kind of text that projects symbols and is meant to be read, interpreted, or experienced, a museum has its own set of qualities. Unlike a film, a book, or a painting, the museum's symbols are approachable from many directions (literally) and in an almost infinite number of sequences and combinations. The meaning of a visitor's experience depends on choice of movement among stationary symbols.

Compare the museum with a play. In a theatrical performance the audience remains stationary while the symbols on stage move ('act'). The pacing and delivery of the message is in the hands of the theatrical group, subject to the receptivities and sensibilities of the audience. In the museum, the situation is reversed. The 'theatre manager' sets up a sprawling stage with motionless object-symbols, and the audience is responsible for its own 'pacing'. In a fashion, each member writes his own script. The visitor travels in, about, and through a set of symbols, seeking to tie them together with associations and meanings – as if each visitor were author and star in his own play.

A museum designer normally conceives an exhibition as a dramatic whole. Many exhibits – evolution, the story of aluminium, the rise of Etruscan stoneware – are plotted as micro-dramas. However, as anyone who has ever visited a museum knows, one's own thoughts and choreography rarely follow the script suggested by the museum designer. The private script need not preserve the didactic public seriousness, much less the conceptual wholeness. The visitor's script is a more complex affair: disconnected, improvised and usually fun.

In thinking about how visitors distil meaning from the museum's terrain and the symbols in their paths, it is useful to imagine 'scripts', or symbolic engagements occurring simultaneously at more than one level. These levels of object–viewer interaction can be thought of as 'spaces'. Three such spaces – dream space, pragmatic space, and cognitive space – are discussed below.

DREAM SPACE

Dream space is a field of subrational image formation. In the museum, it is the field of interaction between suggesting/affecting objects and the viewer's subrational consciousness.

Consider, for a moment, museum objects detached from their labels and the order that museum design has given them. As such, the museum is transformed into a container for patterns, shapes, colours and sounds. The visitor moves forward, and against this abstract backdrop appears a changing panorama of suggestive things – things stripped of their primary use and natural context but cleverly laid out to suggest other times and places. The viewer's mind and eye subrationally seize upon certain objects that jolt memory or recognition and provoke internal associations of fantasy, desire and anxiety. That subset of objects marked off by the mind and eye delimits dream space.

Dream space is akin to the space created by expressionist painting. Take, for example, the Chagall etching, *The Man and the Sentry*. Here we see objects that are disassociated from real world relationships. Shape and line suggest rather than represent. The disembodied objects become symbols, or at least triggers. A man's face (or a woman's?) perches atop a horse (a smoking horse, a smoking house?) from which marches a sentry (the same man?, guarding what?). A horse, house, and sentry in place of a torso; they rest on pulpy (male?) legs that are seated on a chair.

There is contextual disorder, but it is precisely the disorder that makes the work provocative. The viewer finds a dual pleasure: first, the testing for emotional resonancy with the artist, checking one's own response to suggestion (is there a horse and sentry within me?); and, second, the intellectual process of synthesizing, second-guessing, and interpreting the artist and his symbols (was there a horse and sentry within Chagall?).

The symbols of expressionist painting are flat and frozen. The viewer can only stand before the surface, projecting himself onto it and testing his vision against someone else's dream space vision. The symbolic landscape of the museum, on the other hand, is three- rather than two-dimensional. The visitor can move into, through and past. He can slow down images, speed them up, or hold them steady. The museum is experienced as a flickering of and among symbols. The eyes, the brain, and the feet collaborate to give velocity and direction to the third dimension. In museum dream space there is a flow of images and meanings – highly personal, sometimes lulling, sometimes surprising, more or less conscious: 'I like this', 'I don't like this', 'I don't care about that', 'I know this', etc.

PRAGMATIC SPACE

Pragmatic space is the field of activity in which physical presence rather than objects have meaning. The visitor himself is likely to be the main symbol in pragmatic space. The channels and paths he chooses may have meanings largely independent of the contents of the museum.

Take, for example, the holiday-maker as museum-goer. A trip to the Louvre can be a symbol for a trip to Paris, which in turn has personal significance in light of fifty previous weeks of routine and money management. The museum is experienced more as a conquest than a visit. Having heroically touched the four corners in two hours, the traveller leaves satisfied (if exhausted). The museum hangs like a trophy from his belt – material evidence, purchased in the museum shop, tucked securely under his arm. To have been there is a statement.

The opportunity presented by museum space allows us to indulge our self-imagery: here I am, connoisseur. Here I am, meditating. But most activity in pragmatic space indulges our social natures. An observer who sits at the museum entrance will notice that visitors from out of town are likely to make museum visits in groups of social equals (husbands/wives, friends, tour group members); but locals almost always go in groups of social unequals (parent/child, teacher/learner, guide/guided). Social inequality generates a certain tension. Roles are brought into focus, and then brought to life by talk and movement. As diads and triads of social unequals move through the pragmatic space of the museum, there is a playing to and against each other. For most, nothing is more interesting than acting out and within the social roles of their own lives.

In its physicality the museum is congenial to this kind of social acting – just like a tennis court. But unlike the tennis court (or church or theatre) there are few rules imposed upon the visitor's attention in a museum. Adrift, the visitor finds a speed and direction appropriate to his own roles and expectations. He can seek out quiet/noisy, filled/ empty, child/adult, or serious/frivolous spaces. He may freely ignore curatorial didacticism – or as is frequently the case, a taller, more literate person may interpret and explain for the benefit of a shorter, less literate person. Very simply, museum objects are like living room 'conservation pieces': entry points into realms of more important human concerns.

In pragmatic space, museum-going is usually a happy and social event. Being there in some particular social union is both purpose and product. It does not really matter whether the coins were Roman or Chinese.

COGNITIVE SPACE

Cognitive space is the field that corresponds to rational thought and the designed order. In museums, it is the space defined by a subset of symbols that are manipulated by the viewer in such a way as to lead toward 'cognition' or 'education'.

Curators direct much of their effort to the effective organization of cognitive space. Objects are labelled and displayed to illustrate sets of ideas. When, for example, a visitor sees an exhibit of palaeolithic tools and interprets them as products of a time period, or as functional objects, or as things forming part of an evolutionary sequence, he is interpreting them cognitively.

In cognitive space, unlike dream or pragmatic space, the viewer is often on the same wavelength as the curator. A set of objects has been arranged artfully to communicate an idea; sometimes it is communicated. A gallery of paintings may illustrate the flowering of a Golden Age. A cutaway of a car engine may demonstrate the mechanics of internal combustion. A display case of insects may represent the taxonomic division of insecta – or perhaps at a slightly higher cognitive level, the scientific principle of taxonomy. The ideas are there, waiting to materialize. Physical, visual and mental interaction with the objects regulates understanding.

Museum galleries are almost always designed around cognitive order in the minds of curators. There is an idea – like the evolution of the horse – that the designer writes in physical form across the museum's floor and walls. Objects (and words) are his words. For the most part, lower orders precede higher orders; early periods precede later ones; and primitive precedes modern.

But the ability to elicit meanings depends less on the cognitive *gestalt* of objects than on cognitive *gestalt* in the viewers' minds. Since fully understanding the curatorial message requires patience, some quiet, and no pushing, most museum-goers enter cognitive space selectively. The more casual viewer is less likely to wrestle with sequences and functions and more likely to scan for objects that have personal comparative value. He selects a set of objects for rational consideration on the basis of his interests, background and immediate field of vision.

Cognitive appreciation is often independent of design intentions, because there are many 'valid' ways to view cognitively a museum, an exhibit, or a single specimen. An Australian aboriginal war club, for example, may be thought of as a product of a particular culture, a product of a place, a product of a time, a product of a level of technology, a response to ecological need, a ritual object, a killing object, an art object, a thing made of specific materials, a thing like or unlike something else, a collectable thing, a thing worth money, a photogenic thing. Stripped of the endless cognitive contexts into which it can be placed the artefact itself is dull.

Museums have often been criticized for their ineffectiveness in delivering measurable educational content. Studies affirm that visitors' eyes seldom stay focused on anything for more than a few seconds, and people can rarely answer detailed questions about what they have seen.

That this should be so is neither surprising, nor cause for alarm. Educational tests are verbal, but museums are not. Their power is to expand upon imagery, not to reduce it.

Fortunately for museums, visitors do seem to be enjoying themselves – even if they are not apparently 'paying attention'. The museum business is doing well. Attendance is up; membership is up.

The truth may well be that the public does not really care very much for Cubists and Kwakiutls for their own sakes. Given practical concerns for the welfare of institutions, it is probably just as well that visitors find their own uses and meanings. The magic that makes museums so attractive may lie in the flexibility with which people create their own spaces. Museums are more than the sum of their labels and their designed order. Like the objects in them, museums do not *have* a meaning. Rather, they accept and reflect the meanings that are brought to them.

This paper first appeared in Museum *151 (1987), pp. 168–71.*

ACKNOWLEDGEMENT

The author wishes to thank Professor William D. Pattison of the University of Chicago, who provided stimulation and encouragement for this article.

4

How sweet it is: cultural politics in Barbados

Jeanne Canizzo

Museums are not neutral places, nor do they exist in a state of political independence somehow suspended above the wash of dominant ideology. They embody, directly or indirectly, the distinctive views of those who hold control, those who claim a moral or intellectual right, and those who can afford to make museums happen. Moreover they fit into the socio-political structures of their day. However enabling, democratic and intellectually rigorous museums may aim to be, they cannot be divorced from their own times and circumstances. Sometimes, these processes are easier to detect than others.

Jeanne Canizzo here considers the National Barbados Museum and insightfully discusses the changes which have taken place there.

Museums are symbolic structures which make visible our public myths: the stories we tell ourselves about ourselves are institutionalized and materialized in our museums. They are full of the categories we create and into which we divide the universe, both physical and cultural, in our attempt to understand the world in which we find ourselves. But a museum cannot hold all the artefacts which constitute a people's past, nor display all the objects which make up its artistic heritage. It cannot capture the whole of our material culture and national experience. Rather it presents a particular past and a particular society, what Raymond Williams has called 'the selective tradition' or 'the significant past'.[1]

Museums are thus carefully created, artificially constructed repositories; they are negotiated realities. We need to examine the ideology and cultural assumptions which inform our collection policies, which determine our display formats and influence the interpretations placed upon the objects which we designate as the essence of our cultural and historical identity. In short, museums are amenable to analysis as visual ideologies.

I am not speaking here of ideology in the pejorative sense of political extremism and propaganda. Ideology is a cultural system. You might think of it as a coherent, or at least relatively coherent system of ideas, values, beliefs, etc. which people develop while taking part in their normal political and economic lives, but also in their normal religious or moral, philosophical and aesthetic lives. So ideology is concerned not only with politics, but also with symbols and styles, taste and trends.[2]

Ideologies are important in 'defining (or obscuring) social categories; stabilizing (or upsetting) social expectations; maintaining (or undermining) social norms; strengthening (or weakening) social consensus; and relieving (or exacerbating) social tensions'.[3]

Ideologies are a kind of 'schematic image of the social order' in which we find ourselves.[4]

THE NATIONAL BARBADOS MUSEUM

Most Canadians probably know Barbados as a holiday island whose people, sometimes called the 'Black Englishmen of the Caribbean', are famous for cricket and sugar cane rum. Interestingly enough, none of the elements of this image have been reflected in one of the island's major tourist attractions, the Barbados Museum and Historical Society. Housed in a wonderful building, originally a military prison built about 1853, the collections represent the history of the slave-owning planters and their families.

This situation, however, is rapidly changing as the Barbadian government implements a 'direct action' plan to modify the museum. In return for funding, the government has demanded major changes in the administration, staffing and collections policies of the museum in an attempt to have it function as 'an instrument of national identity' and 'an institution in the service of national development'.[5]

In late 1980, in a letter creating a select committee to make recommendations on the museum's development, the Permanent Secretary wrote: 'My Minister is most concerned about the fact that the Barbados Museum is not really representative of the various aspects of Barbadian life.'[6] More particularly, under the section of the report labelled 'Deficiencies in the Content of the Collection', we read: 'While the collection tells the visitor a great deal about Barbadian merchants and planters, their lifestyle and their adoption of European material culture, it says little or nothing about slaves, plantation labourers, peasant farmers, and fishermen; African cultural survivals and folk culture; vernacular architecture and chattel house furniture and cooking utensils; traditional crafts and means of transportation. The collection focuses attention mainly on *one* segment of society and culture and therefore does not present a coherent or complete story of Barbados in history.'[7]

With noted understatement, the committee's report suggested that 'the museum authorities have possessed a limited view of what was worthy of collection, preservation and display'.[8]

The 'museum authorities' chastized here are the members of the Barbados Museum and Historical Society founded in 1933 by self-described 'public-spirited ladies and gentlemen interested in the history of the island'. As of 1984, all members, except honorary ones, had to be nominated in writing by an existing member and then elected to membership. This could have functioned, certainly in the past, as a social barrier, but I imagine a much more effective screen is that imposed by annual dues: life members $400; annual individual $30, husband and wife $40, junior (under 18) $5. Outside of elite circles, such fees act as both a racial and class barrier even if not consciously designed to do so.

The membership of the Barbados Museum and Historical Society has been overwhelmingly white and wealthy. Obviously it is their history, in the form of eighteenth- and nineteenth-century furniture, glass and china (nearly all of foreign manufacture), that the displays have embodied.

When I first saw the Barbados Museum in January 1985 the contrast between the museum manifestations of European and Afro-Caribbean cultures was probably most pronounced. The displays from the plantocracy were in refurbished period rooms and were quite lovely while those representing the black heritage had not yet changed. For example, arranged alongside a splendid interior courtyard complete with flowering and scented gardens were exhibition rooms created from the jail cells of the former military prison. The most spectacular to my eye was a plantation dining room. It is hard to convey the beauty and sensuality of this room with its beautifully kept and displayed furniture, china, crystal and silver. Cool shadows and soft natural light added to the seductive powers of great luxury.

There was a real contrast with the exhibition labelled *People, Places and Events in Barbados*. Housed in an interior room rather than a cell, it was a selection of local histories and a few photographs of political leaders and civic dignitaries. Here too were a few of the Afro-Caribbean objects, e.g. an old cook stove and a warri board (an African game brought to Barbados with the slaves). No real context was presented and the whole display lacked vitality; it was rather amateurish in style.

The primary black or Afro-Caribbean presence in the museum at that time was actually outside the main building, in an interior courtyard, where a performance of *1627 and All That* took place. The title is a takeoff on a fanciful British history book *1066 and All That*; 1627 is the date on which the first British settlers disembarked. The production is a private, profit-making one and a self-described 'historical celebration of Barbadian culture'. It is performed twice a week so that visitors and tourists can 'enjoy the old-world atmosphere of the Barbados Museum and its fascinating exhibits'. The $60 ticket, according to advertisements, includes government tax, transportation to and from the museum, a tour of the museum, a two-hour dance show, a Bajan (Barbadian) buffet dinner and complimentary drinks all night. It claims to be the 'best value for money in Barbados' and I heard very few complaints from my fellow tourists.

But what of the content of *1627*? The first part, called 'Barbados Then', includes songs of the fieldhands, traditional children's games, European nineteenth-century folk dances, a choreographed flirtation and duel with cane sticks. After a break for a traditional dinner (flying fish, peas and rice, sweet potatoes, pumpkin, etc.), the second act, 'Barbados Now', begins. It features a dance hall scene where young people do the 'ruk a tuk' (a local dance) and calypso, and then a 'Crop-Over' (or carnival) scene with what were described as traditional folk characters including masked dancers and stilt-walkers. The programme notes remind us that 'Both presentations are punctuated by rhythmic African drumming, an integral part of Barbadian culture.'

If we consider the museum and the dance show-cum-historical drama together as a cultural production,[9] we can infer that things representing plantation or white society are inside the building while the performance, the labour or action, representing the slave or black culture is outside, although contained by the museum walls. The message expressed here is obvious. But, and this might explain why the Barbados government is so interested in changing the message, this cultural production – the museum and the performance taken together – is not just or *only* expressive or reflective. It is also instrumental. For as Mark Leone reminds us in *Museum News*, 'reading, writing, telling, presenting and performing history are *active* and *form* modern opinion, modern nationality, modern identity, class interests and social position.'[10] Geertz puts it another way: 'whatever else ideologies may be – projections of unacknowledged fears, disguises for ulterior motives, phatic expressions of group solidarity – they are, most distinctively, maps of problematic social reality and matrices for the creation of collective conscience.'[11]

Museums and their displays, then, are often active agents in shaping all kinds of identity. Although he was writing of art galleries, Terry Smith's thoughts are appropriate to the analysis of the Barbados Museum. He writes that 'culture has been expropriated. High, official, elite culture is used by the ruling classes as tickets of self-definition, by majority exclusion.'[12] In the old Barbados Museum, the products of plantation society are those celebrated. And indeed why would we expect that segment of Barbadian society to celebrate the past of the peoples whose labour they exploited? By not displaying the cultural heritage of the majority of the population, the museum has taken from them, by implication, their role as history makers, as active participants in their own past.[13]

How was this imbalance to be corrected? How were black Barbadians to be 'enfranchised culturally'? The select committee made several very explicit suggestions: the curator should be a Barbadian and not an expatriate; and the new museum Council would include five persons instead of the original one member, named by the appropriate minister of the government.

Besides these structural or organizational changes, a number of recommendations about the collections and their display were made. A real storyline was to be developed: 'The exhibits should feature a sequence of themes which tell a connected story of man in Barbados from earliest times to present day.'[14] It would stretch from the migration routes of the Amerindians to educational policy in the last twenty years. Although lucrative, *1627 and All That* was to cease as it presented preservation and security problems. The period plantation rooms were to be joined by a fabricated and furnished slave hut or chattel house.

Furthermore, public mobile exhibits, radio talks and school tours were all suggested as ways to get the new message to the non museum-going public.

What has happened; what changes have been made? A new director has been appointed, a young Barbadian woman trained in museology at the University of Leicester, England, and the council composition has changed. But what of the museum itself?

When I returned to Barbados in February 1986, the museum had had a facelift to mark the visit of the Queen in 1985, but it was inside that the most startling changes had taken place. The new storyline does indeed now begin with the Amerindians, who had been represented in 1985 by a couple of poor, very small and old dioramas. We are now confronted with a new textual marker, the first in a series of what might be considered huge labels. Since its tone and themes carry on elsewhere in the museum, it is worth considering the message:

> Few traces remain of our island's first people. Their possessions, now unearthed, are spellbinding gifts from a previous world. These rare objects link us to an Amer-indian legacy in some of our region's foods and folkcrafts, words we use, and even in the physical appearance of some Caribbean people. . . . Amerindian exploration and settlement of the Eastern Caribbean islands depended on especially high levels of basic skills and nurtured elaborate forms of artistic and spiritual experience.

Barbados has, in this introduction, become a plural society, with a present growing out of its past. There are no unchanging, pristine 'primitives' here. Indians actively explored and settled, as did the Europeans.

A life-size reconstruction of part of an Indian village, with hammock, pots and baskets, sits on top of a crosscut of an archaeological excavation showing artefacts in situ. More standard displays of decorative items in cases appear; then we move on to the next period, that of the European settlement and the introduction of African slaves and the plantation system. Again a long textual marker introduces the displays:

What do we really know about the history of Barbados after 1627? Documents, objects, and legends provide different, often conflicting views of the past. By looking at these we try to understand history as it relates to today.

History is presented as a living thing, not divorced from experience. The many sources of information about the past, including folk models or constructions, are acknowledged as is the idea that history is not just about dates but about meaning; that it is an interpretive art and not just a question of artefact identification.

It is impossible to discuss the large number of objects, photographs and documents which embody this new vision of Barbadian history. However, mention must be made of the display about 'A Slave Born in Africa', which uses archaeological material from a grave site, and reminders of the horrors of the Middle Passage and the slaves' terrible suffering on their journey to the New World. We learn not just about the pleasures and joys of life but of the financial chaos, epidemics, droughts and riots which affected black and white alike.

A small exhibition on the development of health care in Barbados should also be highlighted. Side by side in the same case are displays on the history of a modern hospital and the herbal medicines and teas used by elderly Barbadian women. Photographs, and a simple basket and hoe convey the ethos of the peasant farmer's life. Throughout the museum, black culture is shown as worthy of serious museological investigation and display.

The storyline, as requested by the government, comes very close to the present. The development of tourism is outlined; the success of Barbadian cricket teams in international competition is celebrated.

The next large project is the chattel house, the Afro-Caribbean counterpart of the plantation period rooms. Eventually the director would like to have the chattel house illustrating not only a typical black household and garden, but functioning as a living history museum, with costumed staff playing music, doing crafts, and so on. But all this remains in the future.

We are witnessing an attempt to say that culture, in its material forms, doesn't come only from the past, from across the sea; that history isn't made only by the wealthy and the powerful. In the presentation and displays in the old museum, the artefacts themselves suggested that the ruling class ruled by virtue of its own natural superiority. Its ability to commission, purchase, order, use and preserve its own objects was just a symptom of its general authority. The absence of their cultural heritage seemed to suggest that the black population had produced nothing of sufficient quality or interest to be enshrined alongside that of their white countrymen.[15]

Thus the Museum Development Plan can be seen as a kind of cultural offensive.[16] However, a number of questions can be raised regarding how successful, ultimately, such a plan might be.

On a very practical level, the museum faces the very real problem of unearthing objects to represent this other cultural tradition. Slaves were literally less materialistic than their owners, poor peasant farmers and share-croppers less than landowners. The general paucity of objects is aggravated by preservational bias; wooden spoons are less likely to be with us after 150 years than Georgian silverware. And it is difficult to capture the performing or verbal arts in the museum context without denuding them of their vitality and artistic integrity.

Assuming, however, that a sufficient number of objects are eventually collected, will the new constituency, the consumers of this bicultural world, come to the museum?

Museum-going is still a minority taste, related to education, income and leisure time.[17] And if they do come, will they 'see' what the government wants them to see?

Tom Adams, Prime Minister until his recent death in office, was unusually attuned to cultural politics. In the late 1970s, ministerial control of the Crop-Over Festival was transferred from Tourism (i.e. an externally oriented ministry) to that of Culture, a move which highlighted national identity and internal or indigenous culture.[18] This attempt backfired when the associated calypso contest, started in 1980, became one of the main forums for political opposition to the Adams government; indeed some of the more critical calypso songs have since been banned.

It can also be questioned if, in the end, the museum will be able to portray history as a process? Or will the chattel house and the plantation just be entombed side by side in some sort of static, ahistorical nether world? Will the displays be able to show how the past and the present are linked; can the objects illustrate relationships between races, classes and cultures?

All of these questions remain unanswered. They shouldn't, however, seem to be totally removed from the Canadian experience, for there is some congruence, not necessarily in terms of solutions but in terms of the issues raised, between the situation in Barbados and that in Canada.

The first stems from the plural nature of Canadian society. How are the indigenous peoples of Canada presented and represented in museums? The Metis? Immigrants? The same questions might be asked in reference to class and gender as well as ethnicity.

The other area is more directly in the realm of government policy in the cultural arena. While we may disagree with such an interventionist policy, particularly one in which popular sentiments could be manipulated in the interest of electoral gains, it is easy to feel some sympathy for this attempt to rectify a historical injustice and present a truer picture of island history. Such cases of government intervention may be seen as a kind of cultural affirmative action, often associated with the will of a repressed people or a minority group to assert its cultural independence, or restore its collective heritage.

We must not offer a blanket condemnation of government intervention in cultural policy without considering the particular historical events and social context within which it occurs. What we must recognize is the inherent ideology lodged in any collection and exhibition and condemn any world view which attempts to exclude or dehumanize any segment of the population.

This paper first appeared in Muse *(Winter) (1987), pp. 22–7.*

NOTES

1 Williams (1973: 9).
2 Hadjinicolaou (1978).
3 Geertz (1973: 203).
4 ibid.
5 Ministry of Information, Barbados (1982: 2).
6 ibid.: 1.
7 ibid.: 6.
8 ibid.: 7.
9 MacCannell (1976).
10 Leone (1983: 41).
11 Geertz (1973: 220).

12 Smith (1976: 134).
13 See Trigger (1984) (1981).
14 Ministry of Information (1982: 14).
15 See also Trigger (1984).
16 See also Wallace (1981).
17 Bourdieu (1973).
18 Manning (1984).

REFERENCES

Barbados, Ministry of Information (1982) *Final Report of the Museum Development Plan Committee.*
Barbados Museum and Historical Society (1973) *Guide to the Barbados Museum*; (1984) By-Laws. Newsletter no. 10.
Bourdieu, Pierre (1973) 'Cultural reproduction and social reproduction', in Richard Brown (ed.) *Knowledge. Education and Social Change*, London: Tavistock.
Campbell. P. F. (1973) *An Outline of Barbados History*, Bridgetown, Barbados.
Devenish, David (1986) 'The Barbados museum', *Museum* 149, xxxviii (1): 15–19.
Geertz, Clifford (1973) 'Ideology as a cultural system' in *The Interpretation of Cultures*, New York: Basic Books.
Hadjinicolaou, N. (1978) *Art History and Class Struggle*, New York: Pluto Press.
Leone, Mark (1983) 'Methods as message: interpreting the past with the public', *Museum News* 62 (1): 35–41.
MacCannell, Dean (1976) *The Tourist: A New Theory of the Leisure Class* New York: Schocken Books.
Manning, Frank (1984) 'Calypso and politics in Barbados', *The Carribbean and West Indies Chronicle* April/May: 14–15.
Meltzer, David (1981) 'Ideology and material culture', in Richard Gould and Michael Schiffer (eds) *Modern Material Culture: The Archaeology of US*, New York: Academic Press.
Smith, Terry (1976) 'Without revolutionary theory', *Studio International* 191: 131–7.
Trigger, Bruce (1984) 'Alternative archaeology: nationalist, colonialist, imperialist', *Man* 19: 335–70.
Wallace, Michael (1981), 'Visiting the past: history museums in the US, *Radical History Review* 25: 63–96.
Williams, Raymond (1973) 'Base and superstructure', *New Left Review* 82: 3–16.
Williams, Raymond (1981) *Culture*, New York: Fontana.

5

A sense of purpose: rethinking museum values and strategies

Stuart Davies

The processes involved with keeping a museum functioning, especially those of collection management, demand some form of continuity. Museums have long-term purposes: what they hold must be passed on, in good order, to future generations. The work must therefore be pursued with meticulous care. This is usually time-consuming, expensive and hidden from public view. Yet, particularly in the last twenty-five years, pressures on museums to be more responsive to the public have prompted the reassessment of the agenda. For some museums, the agenda has been rewritten completely. The ability to change or, better still, to modify museum activities to ensure the meeting of both long- and short-term aims has been an important element of museum survival.

In this paper, Stuart Davies measures the weight of museum 'tradition' and asks whether museum values should be rethought and, if so, how.

INTRODUCTION

This paper attempts to present the case for reassessing the values which underpin museum professionalism and which mould how curators perceive the role of museums and how others perceive museums. It will look briefly at how the introduction of new management methodologies has challenged existing assumptions and put pressure on museums to change. But any strategic or goal-oriented changes will only be superficial if values are not also reassessed. The existing value system (and its Victorian origins) are briefly examined before an alternative set of core values (guardianship, access and social purpose) are offered for discussion as part of what should be a live debate about the future of museums in this country.

MANAGERIAL GOALS AND STRATEGIES

When the history of museums of the late twentieth century is written, one important feature to emerge will be the growth of 'management'. Its rapid ascent as a recognized discipline during this century in all walks of life has been quite remarkable and its encroachment into the intrinsically conservative (and perhaps even dilettantish) world of museums was inevitable. Its growing prominence, particularly from the 1970s, was partly the result of a new generation bringing in fresh ideas, but also a reflection of the increasing complexity and size of at least the major institutions in the UK. 'Management' may be necessary however small the organization, but it can be argued that a rigorous discipline of management only becomes really vital when that organization reaches the point where it cannot be run either in a completely authoritarian way or by genuine consensus (Cossons 1970).

The influence of management in the public sector accelerated rapidly after 1979 with the introduction of a much more strident 'business managerialism' into all areas of subsidized public services. This new view of the world was one in which the individual, the entrepreneur even, soared above a redundant society and therefore seriously challenged, if not displaced, the traditional values of doing or producing something for the common or public good. Independent museums were praised but hardly encouraged and public museums, already accustomed to inadequate resources, faced a particularly hard time.

The messages of business managerialism were specifically (although relatively gently) conveyed to local authority museums in the Audit Commission's 1991 report, *The Road to Wigan Pier?*. This posed a key question to local authorities: did they know *why* and for *whom* they were operating or supporting museums? It also made a key recommendation: that all local authorities should have a policy for their museums. And from this policy would flow all the necessary managerial practices to ensure that museums were economical, efficient and effective. By this time, of course, the language of strategic management, business planning, performance indicators and marketing (to name but a few) had become familiar to curators and managers throughout the museums sector.

The adoption of these processes and methodologies had been encouraged (not unreasonably) by an increasing insistence by funding agencies and especially the Department of National Heritage (DNH), the Museums and Galleries Commission (MGC) and the Area Museums Councils (AMCs) that museums should be able to *demonstrate* good management practice (at least at a strategic level) as a prerequisite for funding in the future. The MGC's national Registration Scheme, for example, requires the production of basic policy documents and indications that their responsibilities are being taken seriously by governing bodies. Most AMCs are now insisting that museums produce a 'Forward Plan' if they wish to be eligible for grant-aid. Indeed, there has been increasing pressure from stakeholders at all levels to be assured that any public subsidy (or private sponsorship) is seen to be 'money well spent'.

The consequence of all this has been the production of numerous impressive-looking forward plans or strategies; widespread interest in and use of performance indicators; a scatter of marketing plans (and even marketing officers); curators have metamorphosed into retail managers; numerous visitor (and some non-visitor) surveys decorate office shelves; and so on. 'Management' has become an identifiable force, and has established itself in the everyday life of at least the middle-sized and large museums.

Much of this has of course been imposed (or at least strongly encouraged) by external agencies or pressures and some of it has only been accepted reluctantly. A recent survey of managerial attitudes found that the great majority of curator–managers recognized the value to museums of introducing modern management methods. More than two-thirds believed that these had been beneficial to museums and had helped to make them more efficient and effective. On the whole the local authority respondents were slightly more positive than those from the nationals and independents. The only serious difference of opinion appeared to be over whether or not the new management methods had increased the credibility of museums. The local authority curators were enthusiastic in their agreement but the others were distinctly lukewarm. Between one-third and one-half of all curators believed that modern management practices were responsible for making museums over-bureaucratic and a significant minority also felt that these practices represented the imposition of an alien culture upon museums (Davies 1993a).

Here can be discerned a dilemma. The environmental pressures facing modern museums, most notably the declining public subsidy, the greater emphasis on accountability and the apparent end of the heritage boom, encourage the utilization of modern management practices. But significant numbers of the profession feel uncomfortable with this trend. Managerial goals and professional values are not completely in harmony. Modern management methods have been (at least partially) embraced by museum curators and managers and considerable attention has been given to various 'output' features of the operational aspects of museums: customer care; marketing; performance indicators; contracting out; collections management and so on. Attention is also slowly being given to strategic issues, principally through the development of forward plans. But, meanwhile, museum values, the cultural underpinning of all that museums do, have been relatively neglected.

The significance of this is simple. Strategies and operational practice can only be truly effective if they reflect the value system of the organization. Only when synergy is achieved between values, strategies and practice can effectiveness be maximized. In a public museum, its policy should include a statement about its core values (perhaps embodied in a mission statement which can only be developed out of clear values) and will explain *why* they should receive financial support from taxpayers. The value system is usually revealed in what may be termed 'professionalism'. Values are ideas and beliefs which individuals hold about what is right and wrong. Values refer not so much to what people do or think or feel in a given situation; instead they relate to the broader principles which lie behind these responses. Although it is very difficult to articulate values of the individual which influence their behaviour, it is possible to talk reasonably about a profession, for example, having a recognizable value system.

This paper will explore the proposition that, assuming the necessity of modern management practices in response to environmental factors outside the control of museums, a serious reappraisal of the profession's value system is needed.

THE VALUE SYSTEM

Why should the profession rethink its values? It may be argued that they have served it very well for over a century. Furthermore they have provided the stability which museums have needed when faced with a nearly continuous stream of external threats and environmental changes. They have been a very necessary focus and, indeed, a strength. How can they become a weakness? The problem is that the changes may be getting so radical or violent that stability becomes dangerous inflexibility, and *might* eventually lead to spectacular collapse. It is rather like the bridge apparently well designed to cope with storms which one day begins to crack. If cracks are beginning to appear, what needs to be done?

Many of the traditional museum values have their origins in the Victorian period of growth in public museums. It has been suggested that, before 1850, Great Britain possessed 59 museums, but between 1850 and 1914 a further 295 were added (Wittlin 1949). This enormous growth accounts for the influence of Victorian values.

The purpose of museums was expressed in municipal museum legislation which talked of museums being 'for the instruction and recreation of the people', and in commentators who spoke of them being 'necessary for the mental and moral health of the citizens', and as 'an advanced school of self-instruction'. The Mappin Art Gallery in Sheffield was founded on the understanding that the corporation would ensure that it was 'to be open to the public in perpetuity and without any charge' (Lewis 1989; Hudson 1975; Brears and Davies 1989).

From the earliest days the curators themselves also began to clarify what museums were about: 'it is our business to accumulate material, preserve it, and render it accessible to everyone who wishes to study it.' In his presidential address to the Museums Association in 1893, Sir William Henry Flower described the 'first duty of museums' as being 'to preserve the evidence upon which the history of mankind and the knowledge of science is based' but also that the 'value of a museum will be tested not only by its contents, but by the treatment of those contents as means of the advancement of knowledge' (Flower 1898). This purpose for the museum is supported by the value system of their curators, who believe that the understanding and appreciation of objects and works of art is an important part of the cultural and intellectual well-being of the nation. This strong belief in the necessity to maintain museum collections, in perpetuity for the benefit of the present public and for future generations, without direct charge to the beneficiaries, formed the keystone of curatorial values and the development of a professional self-image for museum workers. In summary, the traditional values that have come down from the Victorian founding period were culture, knowledge, mass education, philanthropy, civic pride, recreation, preservation of and access to collections. How far have these survived into the 1990s?

Today's museum professionalism and values were moulded and, more importantly, codified during the 1970s principally through the influence of the Museum Studies Department at Leicester University, the Museum Professionals Group (and some of the other 'specialist' groups which were founded at this time) and the Museums Association. In what ways is modern professionalism formally expressed?

By the 1980s the Museums Association found that it needed to define exactly what a museum is. After consultation with its membership, it came up with:

> A museum is an institution which collects, documents, preserves, exhibits and interprets material evidence and associated information for the public benefit.

What values does the definition convey? It says that museums are about preserving objects and interpreting them 'for the public benefit'. Interestingly enough the words 'and associated information' were only included after heated debate. In effect this is a mission statement for the museums profession. In a recent investigation, three-quarters of a sample of museum staff from the whole sector agreed that this accurately reflected what today's museums were trying to achieve. The only serious dissent came from among the local authority curator–managers, 20 per cent of whom could not agree that this was so. Most of these considered the definition to be too narrow, introspective and giving insufficient weight to either the customers or wider social benefits. They were, in other words, concerned that the mission statement did not adequately reflect the needs of all the stakeholders. Their interests might be represented by the phrase 'for the public benefit' but this is not explicit enough for many pragmatic museum managers (Davies 1993b).

A second method of teasing out professional values is to look at the *Code of Conduct for Museum Professionals.* At the very beginning of the Code it is stated that 'all persons employed in a museum in a professional capacity have a duty of care to the collections and to the provision of services to the public'. No explanation is given as to what may be meant by 'a duty of care' or, indeed, 'the public' (although a definition is offered in the *Code for Museum Authorities*). Elsewhere in the Code, in a 'guideline', we are told that 'the collections are the very core of a museum's role and existence', and a key rule is 'that there is always a strong presumption against the disposal of objects to which a museum has assumed formal title'. Collections and preservation again. 'Museum professionals must uphold the fundamental principle of museums that the collections are maintained for the public benefit, and the implication of non-discriminatory public access which this carries.' Access again.

A third evaluation technique is to ask a range of curator–managers which objectives they would include in a forward plan. Their choice may indicate the underlying values which influence their ranking of priorities for action. There appears to be general agreement among about three-quarters of respondents on two objectives: museums should 'maintain, develop and conserve collections held in trust for future generations' and they should 'educate and entertain all visitors'. Thereafter there is less agreement. Local authority curators placed a high priority on providing a service 'which is customer-orientated, accessible and available to everyone'. The national museum curators, as might be expected, ranked research highly, while the local authority and independent curator–managers gave high priority to 'managing services efficiently and effectively'. Once again, then, a measure of commonality of values can be identified where collection care and education are involved.

From the evidence presented here, the major values existing within museums today are (still) the preservation and accessibility of collections. Is this really much different from the values in vogue a century ago? If not, does it matter? If it does, then what are we going to do about it?

CORE VALUES FOR THE FUTURE

The first thing is to tackle the most difficult issue. Most museum professionals would say that museums are about collections, and their preservation for present and future generations. But some of the most exciting developments in recent years have actually not been exclusively about the preservation of collections. The development of educational services for all sectors of society has revealed not simply the educational potential of collections *per se*, but, arguably more importantly, the potential of museums as buildings and sites to act as a medium for new approaches to (and experimentation in) informal education. We have seen how museums have become venues for arts activities of all kinds, and not primarily for the white middle-class audiences which fill theatres and orchestral concert halls, but for local community groups, the disadvantaged and the disabled. Museum workers have broadened their responsibilities to include all aspects of our heritage. They have broken out of the museum compound to link up with local authority planners and other heritage agencies to make a real contribution to the interpretation of the nation's past. The barriers between supposedly distinct 'spheres of influence' (which professionalism desperately tries to maintain) have everywhere been broken down. To take but one example, the similarities between museums, English Heritage and the National Trust seem greater than the differences.

Regardless of what their professionalism says they are doing, museum workers have actually long since left collections behind as their sole *raison d'être*. They have adopted a true guardianship role which extends far beyond the defensive protection and preservation of collections which have in many instances little to recommend them in terms of cohesion, academic importance or just plain usefulness. Even the presumption against disposals is now being openly challenged as stifling, inflexible and philosophically flawed. So **guardianship** should be a core value of museums in the next century, provided that it embraces far more than the simple preservation of collections. It recognizes that society's understanding of 'heritage' has grown very much more sophisticated in recent years and that while museum practice has actually followed that development, its professional thinking has remained stuck somewhere in the 1970s.

The 'permanent collection' is perhaps an outdated idea. It may now be more pragmatic to develop a new concept of *core collections* with satellite collections of different status. From this it would be logical to evolve different levels of 'preservation status' for individual objects or classified groups. Most museums already operate an unofficial, and often ad hoc, ranking system anyway. The issues which curators need to get to grips with is of course deciding if they are going to try and preserve everything or only that which is *significant for the future*. This implies that museums know enough about what they've got and that they are prepared to closely *define the purpose* of holding the collections that they do.

From that point it would follow that 'purpose' must include some consideration of 'worth' and 'use'. Indeed, in this definition of **guardianship**, the concept must include a *developmental element,* incorporating collecting, care and interpretation. In most respects the argument in favour of the 'sanctity' of the 'permanent collection' has been won. But now we need something more sophisticated or 'presentation' (as an ethos) will drive out common sense. To help this process along we need a much better idea about which collections are *really* important and that probably means more external assessments. Curators still say that knowledge of collections, built over many years, is vital to the running of the museum. This belief is embodied in the *Code of Practice* where curators are warned not to delegate collection management to unprofessionals. But is curatorial knowledge *really* that important for the functioning of museums as repositories and services? I am not convinced that this is so. Collection expertise is not the sole domain of museum professionals and the expertise of others can always be contracted in if necessary. The sanctity of curators and collections may not be as secure or important as many curators seem to believe.

Access is put forward as the second core value. There is a very simple reason for doing so. Any organization or group of workers who claim to subscribe to guardianship as a value must accept that this brings with it a responsibility to those on whose behalf guardianship is being exercised: society. The perception of the curator as a barrier to access, sitting in 'his or her collection' with proprietorial jealousy, is surely now an antiquated cliché. Access also implies excellence of communication, which itself encompasses 'education' and more besides as a medium for multiple messages about the past and the environment.

The third core value is that of **social purpose**. The concept of 'public benefit' has failed to withstand the test of the 1980s. Questions of 'which public' and 'for whose benefit' have seriously diminished its attractiveness. It implies that something has a right to exist because, in the opinion of an influential group of arbiters, it is good or 'worthy'. In the post-Thatcher world of diminished resources and uncertainty, museums do need to demonstrate that they have a social purpose. To some extent this is already reflected in the concern of many museum curators to be seen to have a community role and perhaps also a social conscience. Social historians, and particularly those working in Labour-controlled local authorities, have increasingly stressed the importance of museums being people-orientated, class conscious and issue-based. This may reflect their concern to see museums as part of the 'caring society'; on the other hand a less kind interpretation would be that this is a manifestation of the collective guilt of Thatcher's generation.

Measuring social purpose is of course difficult. The importance of heritage and the arts to society is not necessarily best measured by the number of people who actually visit or get themselves in some way involved in museums. There is, for example, a future cost-benefit of museums and CIPFA'S recent definitions of the concept of a 'community asset' is helpful. While measuring the benefits offered by museums may be very difficult, there does appear to be a real human need to have evidence of the past preserved. (This, however, is not the same 'right' as is occasionally claimed by the profession.) The 'sense of need' is demonstrated by the sheer level of use of and interest in museums (for example, when an attempt is made to close one); and visitor survey evidence which consistently gives museums a high satisfaction rating among users, and even non-users, seems broadly in favour of their continuing existence.

However, usage of museums is not, on its own, an adequate justification of social purpose. The value of social purpose is really about museum workers seeking social purpose for all that they do, putting the needs (as well as the wants) of society uppermost in their objectives even if this may mean recognizing that traditional curatorial professional values may have to be put aside in the interest of wider social objectives.

CONCLUSION

Ultimately the importance of dealing with these issues is that arriving at a new understanding of the value systems is important if mission statements with any meaning are to be drawn up to guide a new generation of museum workers and museum users. From the mission springs the strategies, objectives, targets and the monitoring of it all. This may be unwelcome jargon to some but, in essence, it does provide a structure or framework necessary to deal with an environment over which museums have little control but within which they are very vulnerable.

This paper has questioned whether the values which have been handed down from the Victorian and Edwardian period of growth in public museums have withstood the challenge of business managerialism. Are they adequate for the post-Thatcher world of decreasing public subsidies and an emphasis on self-help rather than state support?

If a case for state support as a right is to be made, then the values which determine the strategies and actions of museums have to appeal to those who have got, or have taken, a legitimate interest in museums: the stakeholders. If one looks again at some of the statements from Victorian founders and curators at the beginning of this paper one can discern the beginning of a trend in museum values which may explain a lot about the crisis in which museums now find themselves.

The Victorian founders understood about social purpose. They had no professional axes to grind. They wanted to create something of worth to society. As the professionalization of curatorship proceeded, the curators used the preservation of collections and the primacy of the object to justify their own existence. Self-justification led to self-importance and ultimately, in some instances, self-indulgence. Business managerialism challenges that and exposes it as the unacceptable face of professionalism. A reappraisal of our core values is now essential to return museums to a state of grace with society.

This paper first appeared in the pamphlet Debating the Future of Museums *by Stuart Davies and Cathy Gee, University of Leeds, 1993.*

ACKNOWLEDGEMENTS

A number of colleagues have, over the years, unwittingly or otherwise, contributed to the evolution of my thinking on these issues. Most of them probably would not wish to be implicated! I would, however, like to thank Kathy Gee for initiating the discussions which led to this paper and to Rosemary Ewles for her contribution to the ideas contained within it.

REFERENCES

Brears, P. and Davies, S. (1989) *Treasures for the People*, Leeds: Yorkshire and Humberside Museums Council.

Cossons, N. (1970) 'McKinsey and the museum', *Museums Journal* 70 (3).

Davies, S. (1993a) 'Strategic management in the public museums sector', unpublished MBA thesis, University of Bradford.

Davies, S. (1993b) 'Victorian values in Victorian buildings? The museums profession in crisis', unpublished conference paper.

Flower, W. H. (1898) *Essays on Museums*, New York: Books for Libraries Press.

Hudson, K. (1975) *A Social History of Museums*, London: Macmillan.

Lewis, G. (1989) *For Instruction and Recreation: A Centenary History of the Museums Association*, London: Quiller Press.

Wittlin, A. S. (1949) *The Museum: Its History and its Tasks in Education*, London: Routledge & Kegan Paul.

6

The principles of museum administration

G. Brown Goode

One of the products of going back to primary sources in the study of the history of museums is that one realizes that many of the philosophical issues with which museums now struggle are by no means new. The language may have changed or the emphasis shifted, but there are still some issues or processes that remain very familiar.

This is an extract from a lengthy paper given by G. Brown Goode, Assistant Secretary of the Smithsonian Institution, Washington, to the Museums Association's conference in 1895. Only a part can be given here. The total was received with awe by the assembled profession. The values that Stuart Davies questioned can be read in this paper of 1895 and in many others before or since.

INTRODUCTION

In an article on 'The use and abuse of Museums' written nearly fifteen years ago by Professor William Stanley Jevons, it was stated that there was not at that time in the English language a treatise analysing the purposes and kinds of Museums, and discussing the general principles of their management and economy. It is somewhat surprising that the lack then made so evident has not since been supplied and that there is not at the present day such a treatise in the English or any other language. Many important papers have in the interval been printed in regard to particular classes of Museums and special branches of Museum work. Notable among these have been the addresses by Sir William H. Flower on the uses and conduct of Natural History Museums. Among the especially significant general papers which had previously been printed were Edward Forbes's suggestive essay on 'The Educational Uses of Museums', dated 1853, and the still earlier one by Edward Edwards on 'The Maintenance and Management of Public Galleries and Museums', printed in 1840.

No one, however, has as yet attempted, even in a preliminary way, to formulate a general theory of administration applicable to Museum work in all its branches, except Professor Jevons, who in the paper already referred to presented in an exceedingly suggestive manner the ideas which should underlie such a theory.

It is still true, however, as it was when Professor Jevons wrote in 1881, that there is not in existence 'a treatise analysing the purposes and kinds of Museums and discussing the general principles of their management and economy'. With this fact in mind, I have ventured to attempt the preparation of such a treatise, and to bring together in one systematic sequence the principles which I believe to underlie the policy of the wisest and most experienced of modern Museum administrators.

My ideas are presented in a somewhat dogmatic manner, often in the form of aphorisms, and possibly many of them may sound like truisms to the experienced Museum administrator.

I have no doubt that my purpose in preparing this paper will be at once understood by the members of the Museums Association.

I have had two objects in view.

It has been my desire, in the first place, to begin the codification of the accepted principles of Museum administration, hoping that the outline which is here presented may serve as the foundation for a complete statement of those principles, such as can only be prepared by the co-operation of many minds. With this in view, it is hoped that the paper may be the cause of much critical discussion.

My other purpose has been to set forth the aims and ambitions of modern Museum practice, in such a manner that they shall be intelligible to the persons who are responsible for the establishment of Museums, and the conduct of other public institutions founded for similar purposes, in order to evoke more fully their sympathy and co-operation.

Museums of art and history, as well as those of science, are discussed in this paper, since the same general principles appear to be applicable to all.

The theses proposed are as follows:

I. THE MUSEUM AND ITS RELATIONSHIPS

A. The museum defined

1   A Museum is an institution for the preservation of those objects which best illustrate the phenomena of nature and the works of man, and the utilization of these for the increase of knowledge and for the culture and enlightenment of the people.

B. The relation of the museum to other institutions of learning

1   The Museum in its effort for the increase and diffusion of knowledge aids, and is aided by the university and college, the learned society and the public library.

2   The special function of the Museum is to preserve and utilize objects of nature and works of art and industry: that of the library to guard the records of human thought and activity: that of the learned society to discuss facts and theories: that of the school to educate the individual: – while all meet together on common ground in the custodianship of learning, and in extending the boundaries of knowledge.

3   The care and utilization of material objects being the peculiar duty of the Museum, it should not enter the field of other institutions of learning, except to such a degree as may be found absolutely necessary in connection with its own work.

> For example, its library should contain only such books as are necessary for use within its own walls. Its publications should be solely those which are (directly or indirectly) the outgrowth of its own activities. Its teaching work should be such as cannot be performed by other institutions.

> On the other hand, schools may advantageously limit their cabinets in accordance with the needs of their lecture-rooms and laboratories, and the library and the

learned society should not enter the field of the museum, except in localities where Museum agencies are not provided.

C. The relation of the museum to the Exposition

1 The Museum differs from the Exposition or Fair both in aims and in method.

2 The Exposition or Exhibition and Fair are primarily for the promotion of industry and commerce; the Museum for the advancement of learning.

3 Of the former, the principal object is to make known the names of the exhibitors for their own professional or financial advantage; in the latter the name of the exhibitor is incidental, the thing chiefly in mind being the lesson taught by the exhibit.

4 Into the work of the former enters the element of competition coupled with a system of awards by diplomas or medals; in the latter, the element of competition does not appear.

5 The educational results of Expositions, though undeniably important, are chiefly incidental, and not at all proportionate to the prodigal expenditure of energy and money which are inseparable from every great Exposition.

D. Museum features adopted in Expositions

1 Museum methods have been in part adopted by many Expositions, in some instances to attract visitors, in others because it has been desired to utilize the occasion to give Museum lessons to multitudes to whom Museums are not accessible.

2 Those Expositions which have been most successful from an educational standpoint have been the ones which have most fully availed themselves of Museum methods – notably the London Exhibition of 1851 and the Paris Exposition of 1889.

3 Special or limited Exhibitions have a relatively greater educational value, owing to the fact that it is possible in these to apply more fully the methods of the Museum. The four Expositions held in London in the last decade – Fisheries, Health, Inventions, and Colonial – are good illustrations.

4 The annual exhibitions of the academies of art are allied to the Exposition rather than to the Museum.

5 Many so-called 'Museums' are really 'permanent exhibitions', and many a great collection of pictures can only be suitably designated by the name 'picture-gallery'.

E. Temporary museums

1 There are many exhibitions which are administered in accordance with Museum principles, and which are really temporary Museums. To this class belong the best of the loan exhibitions, and also special exhibits made by public institutions, like the Luther 'Memorial Exhibition' of 1894, the material for which was derived chiefly from the Library of the British Museum, and similar exhibitions subsequently held under the same auspices.

F. Museum methods in other institutions – 'museum extension'

1 The Zoological Park, the Botanical garden and the Aquarium, are essentially Museums, and the principles of Museum administration are entirely applicable to them.

2 An Herbarium in its usual form corresponds to the study-series in a Museum, and is capable of expansion to the full scope of the general Museum.

3 Certain churches and ecclesiastical edifices as well as antiquities in place, when they have been pronounced 'public monuments', are subject to the principles of Museum administration.

4 Many cities, like Rome, Naples, Milan and Florence, by reason of the number of buildings, architectural features, sculpture and other objects in the streets and squares, together with the historical houses duly labelled by tablets, have become practically great Museums and these various objects are administered much in the manner of Museums. Indeed the number of 'public monuments' in Italy is so great that the whole country might properly be described as a Museum of art and history. A government commission for the preservation of the monuments of history and art regulates the contents of every church, monastery, and public edifice, the architectural features of private buildings, and even private collections, to the extent of requiring that nothing shall be removed from the country without governmental sanction. Each Italian town is thus made a Museum, and in Rome, the site of the Forum and the adjacent structures has been set aside as an outdoor Museum under the name of the *Passegiata Archaeologica*. Similar government control of public monuments and works of art exists in Greece, and Egypt, and in a lesser degree in the Ottoman Empire; and for more than half a century there has been a Commission of Historic Monuments in France, which has not only efficiently protected the national antiquities, but has published an exceedingly important series of descriptive monographs concerning them.

II. THE RESPONSIBILITIES AND REQUIREMENTS OF MUSEUMS

A. The relation of the museum to the community

1 The Museum supplies a need which is felt by every intelligent community and which cannot be supplied by any other agency. The Museum does not exist except among highly enlightened peoples, and attains its highest development only in great centres of civilization.

2 The Museum is more closely in touch with the masses than the university and learned society, and quite as much so as the public library, while even more than the last, it is a recent outgrowth of modern tendencies of thought. Therefore

3 *The Public Museum is a necessity in every highly civilized community.*

B. The mutual responsibilities of the community and the museum

1 The Museums in the midst of a community perform certain functions which are essential to its welfare, and hence arise mutual responsibilities between the community and the Museum administrator.

2 The Museum administrator must maintain his work with the highest possible degree of efficiency in order to retain the confidence of the community.

3 The community should provide adequate means for the support of the Museum.

4 A failure on the part of one leads inevitably to a failure on the part of the other.

C. The specific responsibilities of the museum

1   The Museum should be held responsible for special services, chiefly as follows:

a) For the advancement of learning

To aid learned men in the work of extending the boundaries of knowledge, by affording them the use of material for investigation, laboratories and appliances.

To stimulate original research in connection with its own collections, and to promote the publications of the results.

b) For record

To preserve for future comparative and critical study the material upon which studies have been made in the past, or which may confirm, correct, or modify the results of such studies. Such materials serve to perpetuate the names and identifications used by investigators in their publications, and thus authenticated, are useful as a basis for future investigation in connection with new material. Specimens which thus vouch for the work of investigators are called Types. Besides Types, Museums retain for purposes of record many specimens which, though not having been used in investigation, are landmarks for past stages in the history of man and nature.

c) As an adjunct to the classroom and the lecture-room

To aid the teacher either of elementary, secondary, technological, or higher knowledge in expounding to his pupils the principles of Art, Nature, and History, and to be used by advanced or professional students in practical laboratory or studio work.

To furnish to the advanced or professional student, materials and opportunity for laboratory training.

d) To impart special information

To aid the occasional enquirer, be he a labouring-man, schoolboy, journalist, public speaker, or savant, to obtain, without cost, exact information upon any subject related to the specialties of the institution; serving thus as a 'Bureau of Information'.

e) For the culture of the public

To serve the needs of the general public, through the display of attractive exhibition series, well planned, complete and thoroughly labelled; and thus to stimulate and broaden the mind of those who are not engaged in scholarly research, and to draw them to the public library and the lecture room. In this respect the effect of the Museum is somewhat analogous to that of travel in distant regions.

2   A Museum to be useful and reputable, must be constantly engaged in aggressive work, either in education or investigation, or in both.

3   A Museum which is not aggressive in policy and constantly improving, cannot retain in its service a competent staff, and will surely fall into decay.

4   A *Finished Museum is a dead Museum, and a dead Museum is a useless Museum.*

5   Many so-called 'Museums' are little more than storehouses filled with the materials of which Museums are made.

D. The responsibility of museums to each other

1   There can be no occasion for envious rivalry between Museums even when they are in the same city. Every good Museum strengthens its neighbours, and the success of the one tends to the popularity and public support of the others.

2   A system of co-operation between Museums is seemingly possible by means of which much duplication of work and much expenditure of money may be avoided.

3   The first and most important field for mutual understanding is in regard to specialization of plan. If Museums in the same town, province, or nation, would divide the field of work so that each should be recognized as having the first rights in one or more specialities, rivalry would be converted into friendly association, and the interests of science and education better served.

4   An important outcome of such a system of co-operation might be the transfer of entire groups of specimens from one Museum to another. This would greatly facilitate the work of specialization referred to, and at the same time relieve each Museum of the responsibility of maintaining collections which are not germane to its real purpose. Such transfers have occasionally been made in the past and there are few Museums which might not benefit individually, in a large degree, by a sweeping application of this principle. If its effect on the attractiveness and interest of any local or national group of Museums be taken into account, as no one can doubt that the result would be exceedingly beneficial.

5   Another field for co-operation is in joint expenditure of effort and money upon labels and catalogues, and in the economical purchase of supplies and material.

> In the United States, for instance, the iron moulds for specimen jars used for terra cotta mounting tablets, and the dies used in rolling the metal guiding strips for supporting the drawers in specimen cabinets, which have been made at considerable expense for the National Museum, are placed without cost at the disposition of other Museums; drawings and specifications for the construction of cases, and many other results of experiment in this Museum, are placed at the service of all others.

6   Still another would lie in the co-operative employment of expert curators and preparators, it being thus practicable to pay larger salaries and secure better men.

> The curator of Graphic Arts in the United States National Museum is the custodian of the collection of engravings in the Boston Museum of Fine Arts, giving part of his time to each institution – an arrangement advantageous to both.

III. THE SIX CARDINAL NECESSITIES IN MUSEUM ADMINISTRATION

A Museum cannot be established and creditably maintained without adequate provision in six directions:

A.   A stable organization and adequate means of support.
B.   A definite plan, wisely framed in accordance with the opportunities of the institution and the needs of the community for whose benefit it is to be maintained.
C.   Material to work upon – good collections or facilities for creating them.
D.   Men to do the work – a staff of competent curators.
E.   A place to work in – a suitable building.
F.   Appliances to work with – proper accessories, installation materials, tools, and mechanical assistance.

This paper first appeared in Museums Association Conference Proceedings *(1895), London: Museums Association, pp. 69–70.*

7

Museums for the year 2000: a case for continuous revolution

J. Patrick Greene

*It is relatively easy to challenge museum traditions and current practices, but rather diffi-
cult to suggest viable and useful ways forward. The pessimism of the thought can easily be
allowed to blot out the optimism of the action. In this, it is crucially important that stock
is taken of how far museums have come and that both realism and idealism are carefully
balanced in the planning of their future. While no one can deny that efficient and competent work practices are essential, it also has to be remembered that nothing worthwhile
has ever really been gained in museums without belief and at least a little imagination.*

*In 1988 Patrick Greene gave a paper at the first set of Christmas lectures organized by
the Department of Museum Studies, University of Leicester. The theme of the lectures
was the future of the museum. Dr Greene rightly centres the people working in the
museum as the key element in the development of museums and in the achievement of
creative change.*

In eleven years' time we will be on the threshold of the third millennium. What a
prospective gold-mine for museums! Anniversaries are such useful pegs on which to
hang special exhibitions and events. Throughout 1989 we will be celebrating Museums
Year which is based upon the founding of the Museums Association 100 years ago. The
Year is clearly going to be a great success. But in the year 2000 we will, I suspect, be
all immersed in one vast retrospective.

We will – if we and our museums are still in existence. In fact museums do seem to have
remarkable powers of survival even in the hardest of times, so I have little doubt that
there will be plenty of participants in the Museums' Millennium Festival. But what sort
of shape will they be in? I can't answer that question – I don't intend entering the field
of futurology because the past records of experts in prognosis make even the work of
economists look good by comparison. But I can make one confident prediction – that
museums, and the world of which they form part, will be very different in 2000 from
their states in 1988. The next twelve years will see a pace of change that is as fast as, and
in all probability even faster than, that of the last twelve years. Just think of what changes
have occurred since 1976 to get a feel of how different things can be after the passage of
a dozen more years. The museums sector with which I have been most closely involved,
independent museums, is a good example.

The first moves to establish an Association of Independent Museums were under way in
1976, but the term 'independent museum' was unknown – now AIM has a membership of
well over 600 museums, and independent museums are a valued constituent of the museums world. The May 1976 issue of the *Museums Bulletin* reported that 'the Government,

through the Manpower Services Commission, had established a scheme designed to provide jobs for the unemployed. The scheme ends on 31 March 1977, though there is always a possibility that it will be extended beyond that date.' In the event the various job creation schemes have been the most significant source of new resources that museums have attracted. Correspondence in the 1977 *Bulletin* recognized the emergence of shops in museums and a Museums Shops Group was being proposed. A group of Designers in Museums was established. The IRGMA format for museum information records was completed and a variety of specimen cards with instructions was available. A computer program, GOS, was being written. By December, the Museums Documentation Association had been established.

The year 1976 can therefore be regarded as one which ushered in a period of rapid change – the emergence and growing influence of independent museums, the recognition that trading was a valid and valuable activity, a strengthening of the role of designers, the beginnings of collections management based on computer systems, and job creation schemes as a new resource for museums.

There is no doubt that some of the current developments in museums, and outside influences upon them, will have a profound effect upon the way in which they will operate in the year 2000. I can point to a number – the Education Reform Act and the National Curriculum, the acknowledgement of the economic importance of the arts that follows from John Myerscough's PSI study, the introduction of compulsory competitive tendering and other privatization measures affecting local government and the acceptance of marketing as a mainstream museum activity, new museum training initiatives, the ever growing availability of computer-based technology (for example interactive video and interactive compact discs) and shifts in the age structure of society.

There can be no doubt therefore that we as individuals, and the museums and kindred organizations for which we work, are going to continue to experience change – probably at a quickening pace – sometimes manifesting itself in dramatic, overnight forms, sometimes in the form of slow but inexorable trends and pressures. To come to terms with this situation – and indeed to turn it to best advantage – will require an adoption of policies that I will characterize as Continuous Revolution.

What do I mean by Continuous Revolution? In short, it is an approach which combats the tendency in all organizations towards the bureaucratic state – in other words departmentalization, ossification, unresponsiveness to change and, most notably, a desire for a quiet life.

I am advocating an approach in which the people working in the museum, led by management, keep looking at what they do, how they do it, and how effectively they are meeting the changing demands of their publics. It is a culture in which there is a predisposition to regard any organizational structure or operation that has remained unchanged in any way for more than three years as inherently suspect. If the rest of the world is changing and we are not, there is every likelihood that we will get left behind, until ultimately someone else decides we need to change and does it for us. By accepting the inevitability of change and equipping ourselves to respond to it, and to initiate it, we remain in control of our own destinies.

So in which areas of the work of museums should the principle of Continuous Revolution apply? I believe that there is no area which should be immune. There is not space in this paper to examine every application, however, so I'll stick to one important area – people. The people who work in a museum are a valuable resource, embodying knowledge, skill and creativity. They are also, usually, by far the largest component of the budget, accounting for at least 60 per cent of expenditure in most museums (and in cases where the balance of spending between staff costs and operational expenses has been allowed to slip, an even greater percentage). It follows therefore that the ways in which the qualities and capabilities of the employees are utilized is of fundamental importance to the successful operation of the museum.

Continuous Revolution means that individuals' roles and performance should be regularly reviewed, and staffing structures modified to meet changing demands. That requires flexibility in, for example, the way that job descriptions are drawn up, departmental boundaries are defined, and staffing structures are developed.

There is no reason why, for individual employees, working in an environment of Continuous Revolution should be any more stressful or traumatic than one in which there is no discernible change. Indeed, I would argue that the reverse is true. Provided that members of staff have the opportunity to participate in the process of change, and are able to voice their ideas and concerns, there is the prospect of enrichment of individuals' roles that can lead to greater job satisfaction.

The really stressful situation for museum workers at all levels is found in organizations that are incapable of change, that do not respond to ideas, that do not delegate responsibility downwards, and that avoid difficult decisions. These are usually the museums in which the culture of the organization includes an apathetic or even hostile attitude to training.

Training and retraining are the vital lubricants to facilitate change – if a museum expects its employees to take on new roles, to modify existing ones, and to reach their full potential in terms of personal development, it has to invest in training. That sounds rather obvious – but it is worth stating and restating, for in the budgets of the great majority of museums such financial investment is paltry. When training is made available across the whole range of staff on a planned and methodical basis the pay-off is enormous.

It also follows that rewards in terms of salaries or other benefits should be made available to recognize the changing and growing contributions of individual members of staff.

There is another side to the coin, however. In the face of Continuous Revolution it will be discovered that some individuals are not suited to the roles in which they find themselves. A performance which was adequate five years ago may be totally inadequate today. Counselling, training, job assessment – all can help to minimize the problem. But where job performance is still far from the required standard, action has to be taken, however unpleasant it may be, to grasp the nettle. Even fairly large museums are, in organizational terms, small in terms of opportunities to find new roles for individuals, because so many roles are specialized in their nature. The only solutions may be redundancy or early retirement – and if so, the hard and distasteful task of using these measures has to be taken. If the problem is not faced, it will not go away – and frequently it is other colleagues who will suffer from the poor performance of the individual in question and who in frustration or despair are the ones to leave for other jobs.

On a different note is the question of recruitment – the opportunity to acquire the best possible employees to carry out the work of the museum and to achieve its objectives. Current procedures are, in my opinion, gravely flawed and could with advantage be subject to revolutionary change. I would point to two pieces of evidence.

The September 1988 issue of the *Museums Journal* investigated the role of women in management positions in museums and revealed a dismal picture. The second piece of evidence is the tiny proportion of black employees in so-called 'professional' roles in museums. If our museum staffing does not reflect, in broad terms, the composition of the population as a whole and the community in particular in terms of sex and colour, to my mind it is highly doubtful if the service we give reflects the needs that exist either. It also means that the museum is failing to find talented people.

What can be done? Again, training is a key issue. Thank goodness the objective of purely graduate entry to training for museums work has now been abandoned. I believe that the modular, distance learning approach now being adopted for in-service training does provide better prospects for groups that are at present disadvantaged in museums to progress – while not denying the important role of academic training provided at places such as Leicester University as well. It is a broadening of training, not a substitution, that is needed. The other positive factor that has occurred is the route of recruitment through various job creation schemes that has brought people to work in our museums who may have different backgrounds and possibly broader outlooks than conventional recruitment allowed. Above all, however, is the need for Continuous Revolution in the attitudes of those responsible for interviewing and selecting staff, with an awareness of the dangers inherent in appointing 'clones', and the advantages that can accrue in terms of a teamwork approach through the appointment of a variety of personality types.

I have concentrated on people because it is their skills and expertise that make Continuous Revolution possible in all the other areas of a museum's activities. Get the people right and there is every chance that creative change will be introduced to areas of work such as collections management, visitor services, financial and commercial operations, marketing and sponsorship, research and scholarly publication, exhibitions and events.

I recognize that for many local authority or national museums, the opportunity to introduce change on a revolutionary scale may be severely limited. However, the advantage of a conference of the type organized by Eilean Hooper-Greenhill is that it enables one to think without constraints.

This paper first appeared in Museums Journal 88(4) (1989), pp. 179–80.

8

Museum futures

Peter Jenkinson

One of the ways in which dreamers about museum practice are brought down to earth is to be reminded of the hard realities of museum funding and governmental control.

It is a fact of life that museums are insufficiently funded and subject to restrictions and conditions which are not helpful: it has always been so. The most exciting and useful museum work goes on where people of talent, energy and vision make things happen, often by moving heaven and earth to get either the circumstances or the funding right (and it is usually both). Even so, the work will take place within a context which somehow modifies what can be achieved.

Peter Jenkinson argues that the ideological environment in the UK is having a dampening effect on museums through the re-erection of economic, social and intellectual barriers. However, he remains optimistic about what can be achieved and celebrates the work being done in many museums to build new relationships with diverse audiences.

Any discussion of potential future directions for museums has to start with the hard realities. In the UK these are primarily political: the ideological imperatives of a government that is said to have wrought significant changes in the nation's priorities and values. The museum democratization project that has been gaining momentum over the last half century, particularly at local and regional levels, has now run into trouble in the face of a regime that believes that its responsible citizens should be avid consumers of culture, but not necessarily active participants in the creation and transformation of culture.

There is widespread anxiety about what the future holds and widespread frustration that we now appear to be going in reverse, having worked so hard to begin to open up museums to diverse audiences, to forward policies of cultural equity, to break down barriers, to experiment with new methods of presentation, interpretation and education, to encourage a critical curatorship and a spirit of enquiry, and to support living artists, not just dead ones. We appear to be moving away from the ideal of access for all, to a new environment where access to museums and galleries is dependent upon the ability to pay; where the establishment of programmes is based either on cynical, spurious or snobbish assumptions about what would be popular, or on the sponsorship that might be available; where only quantity counts and not quality; where publicly subsidized museums that do not attract large audiences are seen as an unacceptable and unaffordable self-indulgence; and where notions of democratization are considered distinctly quaint. We are witnessing the re-erection of the economic, social and intellectual barriers that so many of us have struggled to clear away and, potentially, a relocation of the ownership of museums, returning them to the influence of the rich and powerful who have always controlled 'Culture'. In the government's projected future, local museums will be freed from the control of local authorities to be managed by boards drawn from prominent local figures, particularly businessmen, as in the newly liberated health and education services.

After a long twentieth century we appear to be re-entering the nineteenth rather than embracing the uncertain promises of the next millennium.

The direct influence of Margaret Thatcher, who began this ideological shift, has waned. But the main strands of Thatcherism – the dismantling of the apparatus of the state, the break-up of local government and the privatization of state assets – continue apace and their effects are felt throughout the museums and arts community.

On top of this, but as a natural conclusion to the Thatcherite focus on the rights of individuals, the current prime minister has introduced the Citizen's Charter for all aspects of public service. His intention is to 'give a better say to people who use our public services. . . . We all pay for our public services through our taxes. We therefore have a right to expect that they will do what their name suggests – serve the public.'

MARKET DEMOCRACY

So is this democratization? Far from it: in fact, central bureaucratic scrutiny increases as museums and galleries, particularly those funded at local level, are to be held to ever greater accountability to the government, supposedly acting on behalf of its citizens. And as the population becomes a citizenry of consumers, the language of arts organizations is infiltrated by terms usually associated with the business world: value for money, customer, profit and loss, investment, competition, delivery standards, total quality management, asset stripping. The future we face is one where business values will be used to judge the utility of our museums and where performance measures such as the numbers of visitors and the spend per head will be used by central government to make decisions on the allocation of funding.

While I would be the first to agree that our museums and galleries could undoubtedly benefit from a greater understanding of the planning, financial and resource management techniques used in the commercial sector, the new enforced market orientation raises questions not just of how we will survive economically, crucial through that is, but also of how we will reinvent our museums and the ways in which we as 'professionals', experts' and 'connoisseurs' will reinvent ourselves.

Simply aiming for the maximum number of visitors does little to increase genuine access to culture. Witness the block-buster exhibition: we offer visitors the opportunity to stand in queues for hours, in heat or cold, to shuffle reverently past artworks, seeing each for perhaps five or ten seconds over the shoulders of people in front, before bolting to the shop to purchase the tasteful merchandise that has been so thoughtfully provided. The three-minute culture has come to museums.

Are we really satisfied that this is what the audience wants? Are we happy with the quality of experience that this provides? It is disgraceful that in many places the very idea of considering the needs, feelings and desires of the public is anathema. Do museums always have to be so brazen in their pursuit of maximum numbers getting a minimal experience?

EXCITING PROSPECTS

Despite the profoundly depressing ideological environment in which museums in the UK are now located, I feel excited at what the future holds. My excitement stems from the work that, despite the difficulties, is being done to bring people into closer and more productive participation in the development of culture – its representation, expression, criticism and reformulation – through the agency of museums. Across Britain, week by week, committed museum staff are working for new cultural visions and experimenting with new ways to build new relationships with diverse audiences. Thus work can be developed much further.

If we accept culture as a dynamic and living thing which is a part of everyone's lives, rather than restricting ourselves to seeing culture as the academy, the canon, the fixed catalogue of dead 'masters' and 'masterpieces' to be revered and showcased in block-buster specials, then a new range of possibilities presents itself.

CULTURAL CONSTRUCTION

Museums have to become more conscious of their role, not just in presenting and repre-senting culture, but in constructing it. Rather than marginal and profoundly demoral-ized sites within the intellectually and politically challenged and imploding hegemonic order, we should see museums as key sites where rapid and extensive transformations and redefinitions of the cultural sphere can be played out. They should be spaces where ideas, values and desires converge and are contested, enabling the collisions, syntheses and fusions that are necessary within and between cultures to create what might one day become a post-ethnocentric order.

A museum has a role not only as a place that contributes, through its direct employ-ment and purchase of services, to the well-being of the local economy, or as an attrac-tor of currency-bearing visitors from far and wide, or as a quality-of-life incentive for companies considering relocating to the area, or as a place that contributes to a sense of belonging, of local identity, and of civic pride, but also – and most importantly – as a place that is working to provide a lively and unintimidating, and at times challenging and contentious, context in which contemporary and historical cultural expressions can be created, represented, explored and criticized by increasingly diverse publics that engage with this process in a broad range of ways from pure spectatorship to direct participation.

The enormous challenges facing the UK museum community should not be used as excuses to abandon the essential project of democratization, of breaking open the idea of culture as a fixed entity, nor as excuses to retreat into a polite, cleansed, and non-contentious practice, where pleasing the majority takes precedence.

We have to regard people not just as consumers and spectators, who tramp past the turnstiles for their subliminal swish past a fixed culture, but as critics and creators. We should welcome partnership and collaboration as the sources of new energy, new ideas and new museum meanings.

We have to respect cultural pluralism and cultural diversity as cornerstones of the long-term goal of a cultural equity in which there is free exchange of information and values beyond the hierarchical, canonically disciplined structures of the past. We should work hard to break down notions of high and low, pop and posh.

As museum staff, we have to be prepared to confront our own cultural authority and move away from our historical role as the gatekeepers and legitimizers of culture. And at every opportunity we have to argue publicly and forcefully that we cannot allow museums to be subject to the inevitable fluctuations of market forces. Access to culture and participation in the creation and representation of culture is a democratic right, not a matter of commercial choice.

Access, quality and cultural diversity are the key issues as we move towards the next century. We must allow neither the excuses of funding nor the sneering of some museum colleagues to stop this critically important work.

This paper first appeared in Museums Journal *(July 1993), pp. 22–30.*

9

Pierro della Francesca and the trainspotters
Mark O'Neill

Objects are central to museums. But curatorial perceptions of them, the methods of study and the questions which underpin their display vary and can give rise to heated debate. Museums operate through categories of material, which relate to discipline boundaries recognized both inside and outside the museum. For example, the fields of fine art, social history and natural science are recognized as much in the system of higher education as they are in museums. These discipline boundaries in museums, however, are not always satisfactory and can give rise to a very restricted view. Such restriction can not only blight the development of innovative interpretation, but also offer a view of the world which is, to say the least, partial.

Mark O'Neill discusses the extent to which curators are conscious of the forces at play within their own work and challenges the views of life offered by industrial and technology museums in their interpretation of collections.

The way many museums collect and display objects, especially industrial objects, bears little or no relation to history as a discipline dedicated to explaining what happened in the past. This is so because of a lack of awareness of the cultural forces which have produced and shaped curatorship, of the traditions within museums, and of the kind of people who are attracted to working within them. To be effective communicators in the service of the public, curators have a professional obligation to become conscious of the cultural and psychological forces which influence us in our work. The alternative – of acting unselfconsciously, without exploring the rationalized explanations of our behaviour – makes us less able to direct our efforts in ways which are both personally satisfying and meet the needs of our audience.

Many cultures have traditions of displaying significant objects, whether these be fragments of the Holy Cross, the heads of criminals on city walls, images of gods, symbols of kingly power and wealth, the spoils of war, or the fruits of the harvest. In modern westernized societies, the role of displaying significant objects is the allocated task of shopkeepers. However, there is a small number of objects which fall outside the great ritual of exchange and consumption. Their exclusion is usually due to their rarity and their value to the community, and they are displayed by museum curators. The boundaries of shopkeeping and curating are increasingly blurred as shopping becomes more and more one of the key modes of participating in society. This is reflected in museums, not just in the increased scale of our retail outlets, but in the displays themselves.

Because we are post-Enlightenment people, we add layers of rationalization to the strange and ritualistic activity of gathering objects and showing them to people. These layers include the application of the principles of bureaucracy, the academic and scientific methods, and the principles of democratization and secularization.

Bureaucracy is the application of the principle of rationality to organizations, based on appointment on merit, and a uniformity of rules for processing the allocated tasks, with the desk or 'bureau' (rather than throne) being the key object. Whatever the explicit purposes they are set up for, bureaucracies naturally acquire other aims, chiefly their own survival and the arrangement of things for the convenience of staff. Museums have until very recently been bureaucratic havens, where the interests of the public were far less important than those of the people who worked there.

The academic method is not a universal phenomenon, but a very specific cultural invention, basically German in origin, reaching its apotheosis in the PhD. Perfected in the nineteenth century, it has had a profound influence on the aspirations of museums and on their thoroughness and comprehensiveness. That this aspiration may actually be a reflection of insecurity rather than confidence is perhaps indicated by the very low levels of contact between museums and universities.

At the same time as bureaucracies and the academic method were burgeoning, great advances were being made in the natural sciences. The initial task of naming and classifying was given added significance by the great explanatory power of Darwin's theory of evolution. Now everything could be classified and placed in an evolutionary hierarchy. The influence on curators led to species and genuses as if they were flora and fauna. The way objects in art, anthropology, folk life and industrial museums are collected and displayed all clearly reflect this tendency.

To the extent that society has become more democratic and secular in the past two hundred years, the task of displaying significant objects has passed from the aristocracy and the churches to the state, national and municipal. The altar and the Big House have, in many cases, literally given way to the display case and the museum. For the state's bureaucrats to justify taking over these bizarre functions, a rationale has had to be created. The idea that viewing the objects on display is good for people is inconvenient, as it does not actually involve any change in curators' arrangements. And in so far as being good for people is interpreted in any way more specific than some quasi-religious civilizing influence, teachers are employed rather than disturbing curators in their real work.

Thus Keepers of the Sacred Objects are no longer priests, temple eunuchs, chamberlains, bards or shamans. We are, rather, academically trained bureaucrats, employed by state agencies to enact a peculiar ritual which has a vaguely educational gloss. This is not to deny the value of any of these layers – the acquisition of sound knowledge, the efficient organization and the enlightenment of the public are valid and worthy aims. I have a persistent feeling, however, that the underlying ritual is much more important and that we need to understand it, if our museums are to survive and develop.

The superficiality of the academic rationale for museums is clearly revealed if they are looked at as history. Most museum disciplines are historical, and the word history is at least implicit in their titles. However, this conference clearly shows that industrial historians have far less in common with social historians that one would expect from what seem like branches of the same family.

History aims to offer explanations of human behaviour in the past, whether these explanations be in the form of narratives or analyses, through words, images or objects. Many museums fail to offer real explanations about the past, showing little more than the appearance of particular bits of it often at unrepresentative stages of their life-cycle. This happens largely because the rational, academic method is applied only within the ritual; after the objects have been collected. Hexter says this leads to what has been called Tunnel History, which 'splits the past into a series of tunnels, each continuous from the remote past to the present, but practically self-contained at every point and sealed off from contact with or contamination by anything that was going on in any of the other tunnels. At their entrances, these tunnels bore signs saying diplomatic history, political history, institutional history, ecclesiastical history, military history. ... At first glance one might think that these kinds of history came into being as a consequence of a rational attempt at an exhaustive classification of what is knowable about the past, and that history continues to be written under these headings because the classifications represent the best way to deal with the past.' Nothing could be further from the truth. What mainly determined the way historians split up history during the past century was 'a ridiculously adventitious set of circumstances: the way in which public authorities and private persons tended to order the documents which it suited their purposes to preserve.'[1]

These remarks are easily tranferable to museums, the 'ridiculously adventitious' circumstances which created our collections being the interests of collectors and curators.

Specialization is essential, but unless the questions about the past are open-ended, and the answers in our displays draw upon evidence outside the traditional genuses and species of museum collections, the answers about cause and effect will be so limited as to be meaningless. Unless the causes which led to technological change or a certain mode of production can be explored using evidence other than the object itself, the museum display offers a fallacious explanation which is so incorrect as to be simply untrue. This is best illustrated by reference to one of the underlying assumptions of tunnel history, which is that the causes of an event – or of an object – are of the same type as the consequences. Fischer calls this Genetic Fallacy, and in museum terms the assumption is that the most significant influence on technology is other technology, that on fine art is other fine art, that on decorative art is other decorative art, and so on.[2] Adrian Forty argues against this in his book *Objects of Desire*, using terms very similar to Fischer: 'The design of manufactured goods is determined not by some internal genetic structure but by the people and the industries that make them and the relationship of those people and industries to the society in which the products are to be sold.'[3]

Thus a collection of industrial machinery or vehicles which includes only objects in that category ignores the financial pressures, the technical training, the change in the market, the innovations in techniques or materials which gave rise to each object in the sequence. It may be impossible to display some aspects of history using objects, but this is often not the case, rather a reflection of a narrow definition of which objects are appropriate. A little imagination and lateral thinking can produce objects which can represent even the most abstract of economic or social forces. Only by exploring and presenting a wider range of evidence from the past than is traditional can museums offer anything approaching an historical explanation.

The prevalance of tunnel history in museums means that they are susceptible to the Whig interpretation of history, which Butterfield has described as the 'tendency in many historians to write on the side of Protestants and Whigs, to praise revolutions provided they have been successful, to emphasise certain principles of progress in the past and to produce a story which is the ratification if not the glorification of the present.'[4] Many industrial history museums show 'progress' in this way, with long lines of cars and steam locomotives or typewriters or whatever. Decorative and fine art museums fall into only a slightly different version of the same rut, showing simple linear and uncomplicated patterns of change.

What do you expect from a social historian?

Cultural forces are not the only unconscious or non-rational forces influencing how we collect and display objects. We have all experienced the disorienting effect of discussing an object with colleagues and wondering if we were looking at the same thing. However, these differences are often dismissed unexamined with an 'Oh well archaeologists are like that' or 'What do you expect from a social historian?' There is considerable evidence in psychology, however, that there are great differences between individuals and how they perceive the physical world. Just as one example, the psychometric tests devised by Myers-Briggs, have some suggestive categories. Based on Jung's theory of personality types, the tests concentrate on how people focus their attention and how they like to take in information – subjects of great interest to museum communicators. It is based on four pairs of opposites. Both aspects of each pair are present in everyone, but always with one dominant. Two of the pairs are as follows:

> *Extroversion* – a preference for focusing on the outer world of people and things.
> *Introversion* – a preference for focusing on the inner world of thoughts, feelings or impressions.
> *Sensing* – a preference for focusing on the present reality and on the information brought to us by our senses.
> *Intuition* – a preference for focusing on possibilities and relationships and looking towards the future.

It is interesting to speculate on which personality types dominate in museums – sensing introverts until recently, I would have thought, whereas theatres, say, are run by intuitive extroverts. No research has been done to match particular musuem disciplines to personality types, however, and the point here is not the particular validity of this test or of tests in general, though they are widely used in career counselling. It simply makes the point that there are major differences in how individuals see the world, and how they take in information about it, apart altogether from their cultural background and academic or professional training.

The mutually reinforcing interaction of psychological and cultural forces leads to such conflicts as that between the 'objects speak from themselves' and 'everything must be interpreted' schools of curatorship. Usually they fail to communicate at all, as happened earlier at this conference. After a presentation making the case for a social history/interpretive approach to industry, one technology curator asked, simply and without elaboration: 'So what?' The communication gap was so complete that it seemed to me to reflect differences more fundamental than simple intellectual disagreement.

Whether history is seen as an open-ended rational exploration of the past or a series of separate tunnels worked by blinkered enthusiasts, clearly has a major impact on how objects are displayed. In the Museum of Transport in Glasgow, for example, the objects are collected in displays in very separate tunnels – trams, locomotives, horse drawn vehicles, bicycles, etc., each displayed in chronological sequence. There is no variety in the display by method or by period, so that the bicycles, car and trams which were used at the same time are widely dispersed, as are vehicles which were used for related purposes such as the post coach, car and bicycle. Furthermore, the policy is to display the objects in the condition they would have left the factory: if it is not in that condition when collected, then it is restored to it. The process of making the object or its use subsequent to purchase are not portrayed anywhere in the museum. As the only place you get objects in this pristine condition is in shops, it seems perfectly natural to display the motor car collection in a showroom. This seems to me to view the object simply as a commodity, as a member of the lay public would. It is a pure ritual with no discernible rational purpose. There is certainly no history or educational interpretation in the displays.

In ironic contrast to a museum aspiring to the condition of a shop, when Patrick, the motor dealer, set up a motor car museum, he set out to make it look like a museum. The objects are displayed in the context of their use, whether for sport, business or family leisure.

The opposite error to the taxonomic sequence of ever improving objects is the total reconstruction. When asked to put their objects in context, curators often decide to re-create the entire context, which is equally impenetrable and equally uninterpreted. Even if it achieves its somewhat morbid aim of creating a perfect image of a bit of the past, it then only creates another problem of interpretation. The street in York, a pernicious influence on museums in Britain, bears no relation to the dynamic of street life, the hustle and the bustle, the whole interaction of people and processes, from the sewers underneath to the overhead wires, to the innumerable people going about innumerable tasks. Exactly the same problem is encountered with the 'authentic' interior in Country Houses, with their static and uncommunicative view of the past. The Patrick Motor Museum, like the Museum of London, uses partial reconstructions which do not pretend to be total: merely allusions to a context or change in the past influenced by the development of the motor car.

Whether it is a street, a workshop, or a period room, it seems to me that the more complete the reconstruction, the less history is conveyed, and the more difficult the interpretation. Such interpretation is possible, with modern technology, but most reconstructions are unselfconscious in their purpose, genuinely ritualistic, and therefore convey their message only to initiates who do not require mediation. So what should museums be doing to combine the power of the object with access for non-initiates? How can real history and explanations be incorporated into our displays, without them becoming books on the wall?

Piero della Francesca

One of the best examples of how looking at objects can be related to real history is Michael Baxandall's book *Painting and Experience in Fifteenth Century Italy*.[5] He aims to describe what he calls 'the period eye' by building up a picture of the visual skills the patrons of the arts would have acquired from their work, religious and leisure activities. Many of the patrons were merchants who had great skills in gauging three-dimensional objects. Before the standardization of barrels, each one had to be measured and gauged individually. Piero della Francesca himself was not only a painter, but the author of a mathematical treatise for merchants, showing how such barrels could be gauged. Baxandall also looks at preaching manuals, with their ritual gestures to evoke emotions and to enact scriptural texts; and dancing manuals, with the ideal of elegant motion. It is thus more possible to imagine what the paintings looked like at the time. Furthermore, 'if we observe that Piero della Francesca tends to be a gauged sort of painting, Fra Angelico a preached sort of painting, and Botticelli a danced sort of painting, we are observing something not only about them but about their society.'[6] Perhaps if we looked at our collections from a detached viewpoint we could identify the skills in society which have led people to appreciate such objects. We could thus turn the adventitious circumstances of their collection into opportunities for displays which genuinely meet our stated rational purposes, without diminishing the ritual power of the objects. Let us attempt to suggest some of the forces in our society which have created the period eye of the late twentieth century.

Trainspotters

The engineering culture which dominated Britain for the 150 years up to about 1960 has had a profound affect on how people see things. We live in a culture where the appreciation of 'engineered objects' is a valuable commercial and social skill. The psychological preparation of boys to work with and dominate these machines is a powerful element in their socialization. The trainspotter, therefore, is just one manifestation of the period eye of the industrial age.

Gender

The existence of the trainspotter also clearly shows that skills for appreciating objects are distributed differently according to gender, something often joked about in museum circles, but rarely taken into account when planning collections or displays. Taken seriously, an awareness of how our experience of objects is gendered could transform industrial collections and make them more suitable for family visits.

Television

By the age of eighteen, most people have spent two years of their lives watching television. Its influence on our visual culture is profound. The division in museums is often between the generations who have and have not accepted the fact that the majority of people now get most of their information about the world from television rather than from books. This makes real things more, not less, important, but also drastically changes the way the information needs of the audience are met.

Shopping and design

The importance of consumerism as an economic, social and cultural force cannot be underestimated, and has had a profound effect on the way people look at and read objects. In an age of mass production, individuation becomes more and more important; hence the designer label and what the marketing people call 'brand awareness'. The skills of appreciating clothing, home furnishings and other fashions are cultivated differently by different social groups, but very few people fail to have ideals and an appropriate set of makers' names which reflect their aspirations, whether they involve B & Q or Paul Smith.

Class

Class is an extremely important factor in determining not just our life chances but our environment and leisure preferences, and therefore our visual culture. In the grim housing schemes around Glasgow, the deserts with windows, the whole experience of looking is different from that of children brought up in leafy suburbs.

So what?

Curators are under a moral and professional obligation to provide displays which are meaningful to as wide a range of visitors as possible. To do this, we must be aware of how personality influences perceptions, and that we live in a society where objects are engineered, gendered, shopped, designed, classed, and where information about our own and other cultures is televisual rather than written. Without this awareness, the curator is acting like a private collector, pursuing personal interests, shared by people like him or her, but not necessarily many others.

This paper first appeared in A New Head of Steam. Industrial History in the Museum *(1992), conference papers published by the Scottish Museums Council.*

NOTES

1 Quoted in David Hackett Fischer (1970) *Historians' Fallacies: Towards a Logic of Historical Thought*, New York: Routledge: 142.
2 ibid.: 155.
3 Quoted in Adrian Forty (1986) *Objects of Desire*, London: Thames & Hudson: 8.
4 ibid.: 137.
5 Michael Baxandall (1972) *Painting and Experience in Fifteenth Century Italy*, Oxford: Clarendon Press.
6 ibid.: 152.

10

Making up is hard to do

Susan M. Pearce

The authority and originality with which museums approach their collections help build their integrity as public institutions. We are learning all the time about the different approaches which might be adopted and the new questions which might be asked. The field of material culture within museum studies is alerting us to theoretical propositions that stand to enliven and reinvigorate museum practice, and in turn offer something to the public which has considerable depth of interest.

A leading figure in this has been Professor Susan Pearce, Director of the Department of Museum Studies at the University of Leicester. In this paper, she discusses the continuing validity of museum collections and how museums need to reconcile different ways of understanding the world.

Collections are the heart and soul of any museum. Holding and interpreting the human and natural heritage is what museums are all about; and it is the job of those who work in them to do this to the best of their abilities. But the content of museum collections, their character and their organization – and therefore the interpretations that they offer – all belong to a particular cultural tradition: roughly that of western 'high culture' since around 1500, when the first museum-style collecting began to be made and catalogues began to be written. Most collection-based work in museums maintains this tradition, which is vital to their purpose and commands the allegiance of many – perhaps most – museum staff.

Now, the centuries-old consensus about what constitutes culture is breaking down. Equal opportunities is one of the over-arching issues of our generation, with implications that touch many areas of our lives – some less obvious than others. At one level, equal opportunities mean broader and deeper access to museums and to their collections; hence the development of community participation schemes and outreach programmes. At another level it means improving access to museum management structures and policy creation for those perceived as excluded. At a deeper level still, equal opportunities implies a profound cultural change. The hierarchy of intellectual and aesthetic values that make up the tradition of western high culture is being challenged by a kind of 'cultural relativism' in which all things are seen as equal and no firm footing of value or understanding can be established.

Museums face a conflict between traditional values perceived as true beyond argument and relative values in which anything goes. Exhibitions of kitsch or popular culture are part of this broad debate, and so is the involvement of first, or native, peoples in museums throughout the world; for example, there are discussions about reorganizing collections in the National Museum of New Zealand according to traditional Maori principles, rather than western scientific ones. The debate is an exceedingly difficult one for museums and it will not, and should not, go away.

MAKING HISTORY

Until a decade or so ago, an archaeology curator studied, let us say, Roman pottery. He or she assembled all the material in the museum's collection, arranged it into groups based on the archaeological consensus about approaches to understanding the Roman past, and then drew conclusions about the nature of Roman society locally – treating the collection as evidence for perhaps a number of early forts, a particular villa and so forth. All of this work would then be displayed under the heading 'Life in Roman Britain' – a very familiar sight. Geology curators and social history curators worked, discipline by discipline, in a similar way.

However, whether museum curators like it or not, it is clear that this approach is not a transparent unravelling of 'history' or of 'nature' seen as a fixed terrain that can be explored and mapped by anyone equipped with the correct techniques. Each academic discipline has built up a way of understanding its material that involves a series of questions and answers designed to put each piece in its place in a classification system. But the questions that are asked derive from the system itself. The way we set about understanding something has an enormous influence on the kind of knowledge that emerges. Knowledge in museums, as elsewhere, is not a fixed commodity; rather there is a sense in which it is made up, with each museum worker adding his or her mite to the overall construction.

Making up has at least two meanings in the English language. It means both to devise a story, and to put paint on the face. Both meanings are involved here: the meanings given to museum material are first created and then they are continuously touched up with the fresh paint of new ideas. The material from classical antiquity in museums has been touched up and worked over more than most. This is a result of its perceived cultural importance stemming from the cradle of European civilization. But why should museums continue to accord this material its traditional, revered place in the scheme of things? Why should one art style be elevated over all the other art styles in the world? And what about the relationship of this to the financial values of the art market? Equally to the point, what are the mechanisms through which a museum worker decides how to choose material for display, and what ideas to select for presentation?

These issues were the subject of *The Curator's Egg*, a 1992 exhibition at the Ashmolean Museum (see *Museums Journal* December 1992: 20). One case in the exhibition focused on value – a subject museums normally fight shy of, but one that undoutedly interests the public. The case included two vases, one Athenian and attributed to a well-known vase painter and valued at £100,000, the other a provincial piece, with a £250 price tag round its neck. To most observers there was little to choose between the two. Elsewhere, cut-out heads of classical characters like Pompey the Great intermingled with Frankie Howerd cast as Lurcio in the film *Up Pompeii*. This tempted visitors to ask questions about appropriate ways to tell the story of the classical past – or any other past. Throughout the exhibition signs shouted 'Display is about value', 'Display is about secrets', or 'Display is about sincerity' and demanded 'What aren't they showing you?' Most telling of all, a new plastic garden centre Venus was placed beside a genuine, but very battered, classical marble female figure. The exhibition invited visitors to say why they thought one was

63

more important than the other, thereby drawing attention to all sorts of thorny issues about how people respond to old things, how they privilege hand-made rarities over mass produced items, and why they think they know what is beautiful.

All curatorial decisions are formed in the light of inherited social traditions, including study and research. These traditions affect even the most basic levels of resource expenditure. Those pieces from a museum collection that have already responded well to conventional, classificatory information-gathering are likely to get the larger share of future research work. The chosen pieces will be those that are displayed, published and used in posters. Other pieces will remain neglected because little is known about them, as a result of either chance or earlier lack of interest (itself, of course, a product of the system). Decisions about which pieces get conservation priority or a place in top-class storage are made in relation to their perceived value in the museological scheme of things; that is, in terms of their intellectual meaning, their aesthetic quality and their potential for public interpretation.

Collection policies and their operation are therefore not neutral or passive instruments of policy. They play a significant part in constructing museum meanings. They are part of a process that includes both the nature and history of collections before and after they have entered a museum and also the inherited mind-set of museum workers, itself in part created by the existence of the collections among which they will work.

It is clear that there must be research into collections in order to understand what museums are doing and why they are doing it, and what effect this has on the meanings that they create. But that is only half of the research story. It is equally important to understand how and why a collection came to be made in the first place. There is a need to research the psychological and social motives that a collection represents, and how these have helped to shape the ways in which the collection influences the understanding of the past. If we know why people collected what they did, we shall have a hope of understanding the biases, gaps and individual narratives embodied in museum collections; biases and gaps that influence the stories that museums tell.

To develop the theme, consider the example of female collectors. It is often said, indeed it is a commonplace in older literature, that, with very few exceptions, women are not collectors. A glance at any museum accession register suggests that, on the whole, this proposition appears to be true. However, it is flatly contradicted by recent research into collecting in North America and Europe, where female collectors loom at least as large as male. Is this because women's economic and social circumstances are changing, or is this only part of a wider explanation?

Consider William Roscoe, a typical early nineteenth-century male collector. He was active in establishing the Liverpool Botanic Garden and the attached herbarium, which opened in 1802. He collected plant specimens and was in touch with the major botanists of his day, including Sir Joseph Banks, president of the Royal Society, and Sir James Smith, founder of the Linnean Society of London. The material in the Liverpool herbarium was organized in accordance with Linnean principles, which still determine how museums describe and differentiate the flora and fauna of the world. The herbarium played its part in working out some of the detail of this notion, and as such it contributed to a peculiarly modern European understanding of the world. The herbarium continued to be added to by collectors like Roscoe; it came to the then Liverpool City Museum in 1909 and now has a place in the history and philosophy of science.

Meanwhile, where are the female collectors? During the craze for blue-and-white china – part of the aesthetic movement of the 1870s and 1880s – the major collectors were women. In Liverpool an important shop, Bunney's had an oriental emporium which sold such wares and several pieces in Liverpool Museum still carry its label (see *Museum Piece*, the newsletter of Liverpool Museums, November 1971). But the collections of blue-and-white china no longer exist and so cannot contribute to the understanding of the social relationships of the period. The kind of experience, the particular vision of reality, that they would have offered, is no longer there.

The reason for the failure of women's collections to survive is not merely that women collectors have usually worked within a web of personal relationships, as much evidence suggests, or that male collectors have tended to collect within, and in encouragement of, a tradition perceived as intellectual, although this is probably true. It is also that the style of the collection is quite different. Men's collections are typically buttressed by an apparatus of special equipment, cabinets, and ultimately museum buildings. Women's collections, on the other hand, often (although not always) tend to look much more like the room in the Fitzwilliam Museum's Edouard Vuillard painting of a woman seated in a sitting room furnished with ornaments and pictures. The woman herself probably could not have told you if her things were a collection, or furnishings, or simply souvenirs of people and places.

What becomes clear is that the definition of what constitutes a collection is shaped by notions of 'proper' content and arrangement. Formal and systematic knowledge of the natural world, or similar knowledge of human history in archaeological or classical collections is valued above material which carried an emotional and personal complex of meanings. Since women often have collected – and do still collect – in the second style, rather than the first, naturally there are few female collectors, since their kinds of collecting do not count and do not survive.

Recent research shows that class differences seem to make remarkably little difference to who collects what. There are, of course, the different values of collections in what we may call sale-room terms, but collections of certain kinds of glass and ceramics, or early computers, or early radios can be found anywhere across society. And this seems to have been true for quite a long time. It matches the finding that in contemporary Britain something like 30 per cent of the population see themselves as collectors. All this I take to be a very optimistic thing for museums as a whole.

I have here just touched the tip of the iceberg of how collections are constituted. The Liverpool collections alone offer striking examples of, for example, how the particular world view of the Christian missionaries led them to construct collections in Africa that reflected their own image of the people they had come among, not just in general ways but in ways that represent victories over another culture. Labour history collections give us another but similar range of references.

What emerges from all this, loud and clear, is that research into the nature of our museum material opens up a different world of understanding, and one that has clear and obvious links with the drive towards equal opportunities in the broadest sense. But a growing understanding of the diversity of value should not wholly outweigh the traditional sense of the virtues of things: of what the aesthetic and intellectual tradition has to offer. How then can museums find any way of bringing these divergent attitudes together?

Museum workers make a selection from the material to hand, both tangible and intangible, which will include elements of what Karl Popper has called objective knowledge, imbued although this is with social practice. The museum narratives that they produce will be judged by those who come to it. Museum workers are therefore taking part in a rhetorical project of persuasion, as part of a participating community. Ensuring the continuing validity of collections and the values that they represent will involve endeavouring to persuade others to share their belief that the cultural code represented by museum material is worth learning, for the sake of the insights and pleasure that its forms and styles can give, and for the bracing, self-reliant attitude that its views about evidence and understanding can foster. This requires a critically reflexive approach to museums and what they do, and a struggle towards honesty in thought and expression which admits to problems and tries to strip the mystery away from solutions. It involves the effort to take on board a genuine dialogue between theories of meaning, data and museum practice. This means that there needs to be more work about the history and nature of museums and collections, more work on the material from a range of standpoints, and more research into how people see museums and respond to them.

When we look at the glass of the showcase, we see both a transparent vision and a reflection of our own painted faces. But making up also has a third meaning; if we can help to reconcile the mutually suspicious ways of understanding the world then we will have done something towards making this image as liberating and as enriching as possible.

This paper first appeared in Museums Journal *(December 1993), pp. 25–7.*

11

Museum as dialogue

Neil Postman

The majority of the papers that appear in this reader are written by museum profes-sionals. They represent the insider's view, albeit highly informed and searching. It is important, however, to have an outsider's view, and to look at museums through the eyes of others. The next two papers, by Neil Postman and Michael Wallace, do just that.

Neil Postman, Professor of Communications at New York University, questions what are the distinguishing characteristics of a 'good museum'.

George Bernard Shaw once remarked that all professions are conspiracies against the laity. He meant that those of us who belong to anointed trades – for example, physicians, lawyers, teachers, and museologists – fortify our elite status by creating vocabularies and procedures that are incomprehensible to the general public. This process prevents outsiders from understanding what the profession is doing and why – and, of course, protects insiders from scrutiny and informed criticism. Professions, in other words, build forbidding walls of mumbo jumbo over which the prying and alien eye cannot see.

Unlike George Bernard Shaw, I raise no complaint against this, for I consider myself a professional teacher and appreciate mumbo jumbo as much as anyone. But I do not object if occasionally someone who does not know the secrets of my trade is allowed entry to the inner halls to express an untutored point of view. Such a person may sometimes give a refreshing opinion or, even better, see something in a way that the professionals have overlooked.

Let me assert, then, what I as an outsider think a museum is. As I see it, a museum is an answer to a fundamental question: what does it mean to be a human being?

No museum I know of, not even the British Museum, gives a complete answer to this question, and none can be expected to. Every museum, even an unpretentious one, gives only a partial answer. Each museum seems to make an assertion about the nature of humanity – sometimes supporting and enriching each other's claims but just as often contradicting each other.

There is a great museum in Munich that is filled with old automobiles, trains and aero-planes, all of which are meant to signify (in my mind) that human beings are pre-eminently tool-makers and are at their best when solving practical problems. The Guggenheim Museum in New York City rejects that claim; there is nothing displayed in the Guggen-heim that is, or ever was, of any practical value. The museum seems to argue that what makes us human is our need to express our feelings in symbolic forms. We are human precisely because so many of our creations are impractical. To this, the Imperial War

Museum in London says, 'Nonsense. You are both wrong. We are at our most human when devising ways to kill each other.' To which Yad Va Shem in Jerusalem adds with inconsolable sadness, 'That is true. But we are not merely killers like sharks and tigers; we are cruel, pointless, and systematic killers. Remember this above all.'

Go to any museum in the world, even one that serves only as an archive, and ask, 'What is this museum's definition of humanity?' You will be rewarded with some kind of an answer. In some cases, the answer will be timid and even confused; in others, bold and unmistakable. Of course, it is folly to say which museums convey the right answers. All of them are correct: we *are* tool-makers and symbol-makers and war-makers. We are sublime and ridiculous, beautiful and ugly, profound and trivial, spiritual and practical. So it is not possible to have too many museums, because the more we have, the more detailed and comprehensive will be the portrait of humanity.

But in saying that every museum gives us part of the picture, I am not saying that every museum is equally useful. To paraphrase George Orwell, all museums tell the truth, but some tell more important a truth than others. And how important a truth is depends on the time and place of its telling. For at different times, cultures need to know, remember, contemplate, and revere different ideas in the interest of survival and sanity. A museum that was useful fifty years ago might be quite pointless today. Naturally, I would never recommend that such a museum be closed, for some day, in changed circumstances, its usefulness may be restored (and in any case, the dialectic of museums requires that its voice always be counted). None the less, for a specific time and place, the truths conveyed by such a museum can be irrelevant and even harmful. Scores of museums – some of them new – celebrate ideas that are not needed.

To help clarify my point, imagine that the year is 1933, that you have been given unlimited funds to create a museum in Berlin, and that it has not occurred to you that you might be shot or otherwise punished for anything you will do. What kind of museum would you create? What ideas would you sanctify? What part of the human past, present, or imagined future would you wish to emphasize, and what part would you wish to ignore? In brief, what would you want your German visitors to the museum to contemplate?

In asking these questions, I mean to suggest that a museum is, in a fundamental sense, a political institution. For its answer to the question 'What does it mean to be a human being?' must be given within the context of a specific moment in history and must inevitably be addressed to living people who, as always, are struggling with the problems of moral, psychological and social survival. I am not urging that museums be used as instruments of cheap and blatant propaganda; I am saying that a museum is an instrument of survival and sanity. A museum, after all, tells a story. And like the oral and written literature of any culture, its story may serve to awaken the better angels of our nature or to stimulate what is fiendish. A museum can serve to clarify our situation or obfuscate it, to tell us what we need to know or what is useless.

In the US, we have a society that most certainly can be improved by museums. What kinds of museums does it need? Consider the Experimental Prototype Community of Tomorrow, popularly known as EPCOT Center in Orlando, Florida. (I should not have to justify calling it a museum, because like Colonial Williamsburg in Virginia, EPCOT is an attempt to create a living portrait of what it means to be human in a particular time and place; it is the world's largest animated diorama.)

Unlike Disney World, which is located adjacent to it, EPCOT is not intended to be merely an amusement park. Like all great museums of the world, EPCOT wants to fascinate and enthral, but it clearly has an educational agenda and has had one from its beginning. It wants to tell part of the story of human intelligence and creativity and wishes its visitors to leave feeling inspired and instructed.

A few years ago, I was one of thirty consultants brought to Orlando by EPCOT's directors, who wanted us to make recommendations to enhance EPCOT's educational functions. Indeed, it is worth remarking that the consultants were told many times that it was never Walt Disney's intention to create in EPCOT one more amusement park; instead, EPCOT was to be his greatest monument – a museum celebrating the possibilities of humanity's future. The fact that EPCOT had strayed from that intention is why the consultants had been summoned.

But from my point of view, the task was hopeless. The problem is not that EPCOT has become more amusement park than museum; the problem is that EPCOT is providing a mistimed truth to a people in desperate need of moral and civic guidance. It is like trying to enlighten a miser by putting forward the idea that a penny saved is a penny earned. The miser already knows this, indeed lives by that philosophy. He will learn nothing from hearing it restated. What the miser needs to consider is something along the lines of the Robert Herrick poem that begins, 'Gather ye rosebuds while ye may'. To quote André Gide, 'That education is best which goes counter to you.' He meant we learn by contrast and comparison, not by redundancy and confirmation.

The unstated theme of EPCOT is *Technology über alles*. In every exhibit, in every conceivable way, EPCOT proclaims that paradise is to be achieved through technological progress, and only through technological progress. The message includes the idea that new is better than slow, that simple is better than complex – and if they are not, we must change our definition of 'better'. To the question, 'What will it mean to be a human being in the future?', EPCOT answers, 'You will find fulfilment in loving your machines.' People who flock to EPCOT warm to this message, as a miser will warm to being told that a penny saved is a penny earned. But these people will learn nothing from it.

To be sure, there certainly are places in the world where the advice to seek salvation in technology may be useful. I have visited a few such places in my travels and have thought that a large dose of EPCOT's philosophy would go a long way towards eliminating some unnecessary inconvenience and misery. In the US, this philosophy was inspiring and useful in the nineteenth and early twentieth centuries; it helped us build a new colossus; it gave us confidence and wealth and vitality and power.

But for a society that has now totally committed itself to the idea that technology is divine, there couldn't be a more mistimed vision of the future. What can EPCOT teach Americans, or inspire us to think? We have already organized our society to accommodate every possible technological innovation. We have deliriously, willingly, mindlessly ignored all the consequences of our actions and have, because technology seemed to require it, turned our backs on religion, family, children, history and education. As a result, American civilization is collapsing. Everyone knows this but seems powerless in the face of it.

You would never guess from a visit to EPCOT that the technologies celebrated there have played a central part in our deepening cultural crisis. In the case of illiteracy, and the toxic environment, and increasing violence, and indifference to politics, a direct connection can be drawn to the society's obsession with the sanctification of technology. In other cases, the connection is indirect but unmistakable. And, I might say, inevitable. For when a society invests most of its material and psychic resources in the development of machines, when it begins to believe that the only possible avenue to the fulfilment of its humanity is through technological ingenuity, when it redefines its aspirations and values to fit the requirements of its technology, it is likely to find it has paid for its mechanical marvels at a culturally ruinous price. But there are no such warnings over the gates at EPCOT, no price tags metaphorically attached to its delightful displays.

Of what use, then, is EPCOT Center to such a society? It does not help us to remember anything of importance. And because it celebrates precisely what already pre-empts the attention of the entire culture, it prevents its visitors from contemplating alternative visions.

In those words – alternative visions – you have in condensed form what I believe is the essence of a useful museum. For as I see it, that museum is best that helps to free a society from the tyranny of a redundant and conventional vision – that is to say, from the tyranny of the present. Museums should be thermostats of culture, for it is essential to the survival of any culture that it maintain a dynamic balance in its symbolic environments. And to achieve that, its educational institutions must provide what its economic, political and social institutions are failing to provide.

The most vital function of museums is to balance, to regulate what we might call the symbolic ecology of cultures, by putting forward alternative views and thus keeping choice and critical dialogue alive. Without such alternatives, societies inevitably find to their despair that whatever paradise they single-mindedly pursued has turned into some or another wasteland. And nobody needs a museum in a wasteland – except, perhaps as a cemetery.

In the US, we do not now need museums that dazzle us with modern electronic equipment (our culture already dazzles us with electronic equipment to the point that we are all but blind), and we do not need museums that celebrate that fact. In a word, we do not need museums that say, 'This is what you are. Come and applaud yourself' – especially not if what we applaud is our own ruin.

What we require are museums that tell us what we once were, and what is wrong with what we are, and what new directions are possible. At the very least, we need museums that provide some vision of humanity different from the vision put forward by every advertising agency and political speech. That is why I have eagerly participated in plans to create a Museum of Childhood in Los Angeles. This is a museum that would remind people of where the idea of childhood came from, what that idea has contributed to world civilization, and why it is important to preserve it. In a culture that has allowed the idea of childhood to decay, this museum will be useful. So is the Museum of Immigration on Ellis Island. America once was (and still is) a land of immigrants, and Ellis Island is where thirty million of Europe's wretched refuse first entered America, bringing with them energies, hopes, traditions and values that are now being obliterated by a furious technological materialism. Ellis Island can offer a forceful counter-argument to the prevailing idea of the citizen as homogenized consumer – of people as a massive and undifferentiated mouth for the products of technology.

A museum, then, must be an argument with its society. And more than that, it must be a *timely* argument. A good museum always will direct attention to what is difficult and even painful to contemplate. Therefore, those who strive to create such museums must proceed without assurances that what they do will be appreciated.

In addressing the purpose of theatre, George Bernard Shaw provided an answer that tells us precisely why museums are necessary – and why a museum of the kind I have been describing is necessary. He said, 'It is an elucidator of social consciousness, a historian of the future, an armoury against darkness and despair, and a temple in the ascent of man.'

This paper first appeared in Museum News 69(5) (1990), pp. 55–8.

12

The future of history museums
Michael Wallace

Although art galleries may have the greater funding and the stronger position within political consciousness, museums devoted to history are now more numerous and attract a much broader cross-section of museum visitors. Each has a very specific set of functions to perform. The history museum has on its agenda cultural empowerment and the recovery of human experience. Both are worthy aims, but the processes involved are by no means easy or straightforward.

Michael Wallace, Professor of History at John Jay College, City University of New York, questions the future of history museums within popular awareness of what constitutes history.

A few years ago I started teaching a course on the history of the 1960s. (I have to tell you it was a sobering moment – my generation was *history* now.) I thought I'd begin by asking my students what they remembered about the period, to see what personal experiences we had to work with. Turned out virtually none of them had been *alive* during the 1960s.

The media information in their heads consisted of a collection of moving images – video clips – culled from endless replays on television. Kennedy getting his head blown off in the Zapruder clip. Astronauts taking one small step onto the moon. A bound and captured Vietcong getting his brains blown out at close range. King dreaming on the steps of the Lincoln Memorial. The Beatles visiting Ed Sullivan. Police dogs savaging southern demonstrators. Crowds listening to Jimi Hendrix at Woodstock. And on and on. A virtual film library. They didn't know quite what to *do* with these images. They had little or no sense of how they connected one to the other. But the raw footage constituted a good part of their mental historical capital.

Such images jostled together in their minds with others recalled from Hollywood and TV movies. Images more narrative in nature and arranged to tell a story – a history. My students' mental film banks were well stocked. On Vietnam alone they could access *Rambo, Apocalypse Now, Deer Hunter, Platoon, Full Metal Jacket*, and a host of made-for-TV documentaries, docudramas and sitcoms. These narratives were strong components of the students' historical realities.

The youngsters also had a whole second division of 1960s information available to them: memories. Not their own, but those of relatives, neighbours, teachers, older friends. These were stories, too – histories – they'd heard from soldiers, anti-war activists, civil rights marchers, police, feminists. Sometimes these memories took the form of vignettes. In other cases, the memories were constituent parts of a larger narrative, an interpretation of the meaning of the period provided by the recollector. Now memories are tricky things, remarkably pliable, amazingly selective. But these second-hand accounts had, to my students, a ring of authenticity about them. The students were convinced these memories were grounded in some directly perceived experience.

It was not easy for them to put the two kinds of information together, since the accounts of memory often clashed with the media narratives. This left some students confused, others cynical. But in the classroom, the dissonance also provided an opening for critical thinking. My students had a purchase point from which they could assess – agree with, dissent from – the narratives purveyed on the silver screen or their living room tube.

As I pondered the question of the future of history museums, I kept coming back to this classroom experience. It got me thinking about the relations between memory and history. My students, it seemed to me, were at an interesting time-spot in relation to the particular past we were considering, near enough to have some personal linkage, and thus some quasi-independence from the media images with which they were bombarded. But as time passes, the personal links will become more and more attenuated. *Their* children will have fewer, more diluted memories, of the 1960s. They will become more reliant on – more at the mercy of – mass produced images for their understanding of the experiences of that generation (our generation) . . .

That's what the passage of time is all about . . . this is a normal process. Indeed, a key delineator of a culture's character is the way it handles this passing of the baton from memory to culture.

How does American culture stack up in this regard? What happens here when memory dies? The record, I submit, is contradictory. On the one hand, we live in a culture that doesn't much believe in the relevance of history. We turn to it for entertainment, escape, identity, a listing (like *The Guinness Book of Records*) of past achievements waiting to be surpassed. We're future oriented. Today, we like to think, is the first day of the rest of our lives. The past seems dead, properly relegated to the dustbin of history. After all, what's the ultimate dismissal of somebody: 'He's history!'

This is not simply an American phenomenon, of course, but an aspect of what gets called 'modernity'. It seems probable that these days memory wanes (and culture waxes) faster than it once did. In traditional societies where the lore of the past was vitally important for a command of the present, perhaps more attention was paid to nourishing and sustaining old information (though it often, in the process, became flattened out into myth). In cultures where people stayed in one spot over generations, it was also easier to pass memories down through time, like heirlooms.

But even among modern societies, America seems to stand out as being a particularly ahistorical culture. We are convinced that the past is at best irrelevant, at worst an encumbrance. This conviction, ironically, is itself a product of our history. It's rooted in our experiences of immigration, our capitalist political economy, our tremendous mobility which severs generations in time and space. And it is sustained by what I have called a historicidal culture that promotes a twenty-four hour (or at most, a seven-day) attention span and undercuts our ability to situate ourselves in time.

There's an attractive quality to this refusal to be bound by tradition's chains. It has led to innovation and experiment, but also to a fair degree of foolishness that stems from not realizing that the past is far from dead; that it continues to shape today; that it has bequeathed us the matrix of constraints and possibilities within which we must act in the present; that to the extent we understand the contours of time, we are more effectively equipped to deal with reality. Pretending the past isn't there doesn't make it go away.

Yet having stressed the degree to which we are marooned in the present, it is now necessary to notice the tremendous attention even go-ahead Americans pay to the past. To do this, let's look quickly at three different cultural arenas in which Americans grapple with questions of memory and history: the worlds of mass media, educational system and – (finally!) – history museums.

For all our unconcern with history, a quite extraordinary amount of recent political discourse has involved a struggle to define the meaning and relevance of the past. By way of example, consider the strenuous efforts of the Reagan administration to reshape popular memories of the Indochina War and, thus, to dismantle a 'Vietnam syndrome' seen as a stumbling block impeding adventures in Central America . . .

Through national debates on such issues, we began to approach the levels of deadly seriousness with which historical matters normally are taken in other political cultures. Consider only the current profound reexamination of Russian history inspired by Gorbachevian *glasnost*. . . . In the world of big league politics, situating the present in a temporal context is not an antiquarian enterprise but an affair of state. History counts!

Certainly the *mass media* devote enormous attention to history. Hardly a week goes by without a major TV mini-series or docudrama being aired . . . Vidal's *Lincoln*, Puzo's *Fortunate Pilgrim*, *Shaka Zulu* . . .; new versions of *Inherit the Wind* and *The Diary of Anne Frank*, the Hearst and Davies Affair . . .; and the biotreatments of il Duce, Hemingway, Onassis and Beryl Markham (to say nothing of such reruns of not-so-ancient classics as *Upstairs, Downstairs* or *The Adams Chronicles*).

We might be tempted to dismiss all of this as costume-drama fluff, soap-opera spectacle, or nostalgic myth-making, but that – as Richard Nixon used to say – would be wrong. Quite apart from the fact that some of these semi-fictions are of a very high quality indeed, consider that alongside them we must set the recent awesome output of documentary film-makers which has included both multi-part series like *Eyes on the Prize* (arguably one of the most brilliant historical works ever produced for the screen), *World at War, Bill Moyer's Walk through the Twentieth Century, The Golden Years of TV* . . . along with a seemingly endless number of single-evening specials . . . and a cornucopia of biographies that have treated . . . Margaret Sanger, Andy Warhol, Stephen Biko . . . John Lennon, Martin Luther King, Rommel, Wallis Simpson . . . and Marilyn Monroe. This highly truncated listing, moreover, completely ignores the series devoted to history (like *Our Century* or *Remember When*), the hordes of current feature films set in historical contexts, and the vast numbers of history flicks rerun on late night network TV, all day on cable, or readily available in video stores.

This media-history world is enormous and complex and highly variegated. It changes over time, reflecting the world around it. And it has its own history. There's quite a distance between *Gone with the Wind* and *Roots*, between the treatments of General Custer in the 1940s and those of the 1960s. Indeed, there is such a bewildering array of different interpretations available that it's conceivable this plethora of media narratives has fostered a peculiarly malleable sense of the past. Where once the critical iconic images were graven in stone on church walls, now they are subject to instant revision as we flip from channel to channel. Or – (a question for the historians of our historical sensibilities in the media age) – do some images/narratives gain an indelible primacy of place? Will Wallace Beery forever be Pancho Villa despite Telly Savalas's best efforts? Will the encircled wagon train revolve forever in our cinematic brain, protecting the women and children as their menfolk fend off the howling redskins while awaiting the Seventh Cavalry, despite the valiant revisionism of Arthur Penn and others?

Whatever the nature of their impact, it's clear that the mass media are unquestionably major players in the history biz – arguably the single most critical source from which most people get their sense of the past. For many, because cinematic modes of perception seem so real, 'movie past' *is* 'the past'. Perhaps it's not surprising that when curators at the Alamo erected a mural depicting their site's historic events, they decided to substitute the faces of Hollywood actors in a 1960 movie for the original heroes: Davy Crockett *was* John Wayne. Or that for Ronald Reagan, who himself portrayed Custer in *The Santa Fe Trail*, the line between movie America and historical reality notoriously was blurred.

Turning to the *Academy*, we find a debate in progress over the ability of professional historians to influence popular historical consciousness. By some indications, notably recent tests of Americans' familiarity with significant names and dates, we're doing fairly miserably. There's a good deal of truth to the charge that we have forfeited public acceptance by hyperspecialization and writing in incomprehensibilese. Yet I'm inclined to agree with Neil Harris's reflections in the pages of *History News* that this critique has been somewhat overstated. There is a steady flow of reasonably well-written monographs; popular syntheses are beginning to appear; textbooks, while exceedingly variable in quality, are superior to those of prior generations in what they include and how they present their information; and academics routinely engage in vigorous debate about the historical context of contemporary issues and attempt to promulgate their findings.

What part do our institutions play in the formation of popular historical consciousness? A booming one, it would appear on the surface. We are beneficiaries of what AASLH director Larry Tise has characterized as an explosion of interest in history, a dramatic expansion of the 'history biz' that has generated over 5000 historical organizations in the last twenty years. Academics, Tise says, have lost the people's ear, but history museums, societies and historic houses have got their full attention.

Well, yes and no. I'm a little less clear than Larry is about exactly what all this activity adds up to. I agree completely about the demand out there. While some dismiss it as a quest for entertainment or escape, I think it bespeaks a deep hunger for historical connectedness – partly, I suspect, a reaction against the historicidal culture of which I spoke earlier. My reservations are not about demand but about supply: what impact have we had collectively on America's historical sensibility?

I guess I'm not convinced that, for all the hoopla, we've made much of a dent in the country's traditional ahistoricism . . . that we've done much toward overcoming our culture's sharp distinction between past and present . . . that we've even tried. Too often we treat the past as an endangered species – partly because we've often had to struggle so hard to preserve it – and visiting the past becomes like going to the zoo: a pleasant experience but essentially irrelevant to 'real-world' concerns. An ironic consequence is that when it comes to connecting past and present, the one institution of those mentioned so far that is explicitly dedicated to presenting history to mass publics is the one, arguably, which is most on the sidelines. Where politicians, movie-makers and academics boldly rush in – the museums hang back. My 1960s students, for example, had heard Reagan, seen *Platoon*, and were taking my course, but they would have been hard pressed to find a history museum that had much, if anything, to say about Vietnam.

I think, however, that this is changing. I think museums are beginning to consider themselves as places that can help visitors develop their historical sensibilities, strengthen their abilities to locate themselves in time, and enhance their capacities as citizens to be historically informed makers of history. The museums are beginning to participate in the debates about the nature and meaning of the past and its implications for the present, even if that means mounting exhibits that can be labelled with the 'C-word', con-tro-ver-sial. And such boldness is being rewarded: audiences are responding positively to provocative new approaches.

I think these splendid developments suggest the direction history museums should go in the future. (I don't mean to say that this is *all* they should do; it's just that I believe this function has been under-represented in their presentations.) The connections between past and present are being illuminated in a variety of ways around the country. The most direct approaches provide historical perspective on a contemporary issue, even if that means adopting a particular point of view.

Consider, for first example, the exhibit *Tropical Rainforests: A Disappearing Treasure* organized by the Smithsonian's Traveling Exhibition Service. Visitors first see a brilliant slide presentation that introduces the dappled reality of a rainforest and its denizens. The show then describes how the forests have been decimated over the past century, not hesitating to ascribe responsibility to specific agents – developers, loggers, ranchers, agribusiness, international banks and even (via a clever mock-up of a suburban living room) American consumers of rainforest commodities. The connection between past and future is made clear by demonstrating how human decision-making in the past affected forest ecology and insisting that its future also depends on human action. The exhibit lays out the cultural, ecological, economic and demographic costs of continuing the environmental holocaust and then, most remarkably of all, explains how visitors inclined to help can actually *do* something.

It accomplishes these ends with a superb array of techniques – some state-of-the-art, others quite simple – and manages scrupulously to present a variety of perspectives of the subject without ever losing its own. Intriguingly, the design was the product of a collaboration between a politically committed academic – a tropical ornithologist and conservationist – and professional curators.

Another show that breaks sharply with conventional practice is the National Park Service's Constitutional bicentennial exhibit at Philadelphia. *The Promise of Permanency* shuns fusty filiopietism and instead explains how the Constitution's development has been shaped by citizen action as well as by judges over the centuries. It also promotes reflection on the document's applicability to contemporary issues. Utilizing clever touch-screen and video techniques, the show tackles the hottest of topics (aid to parochial schools, birth control, compulsory flag salutes, gay rights in the classroom) by presenting exponents of both sides and allowing visitors to vote for the arguments they find compelling. By jettisoning the conventional omniscient narrator stance, the exhibit teaches that historical perspectives – like court cases and current politics – are open to various interpretations.

Richmond's Valentine Museum has launched several pathbreaking shows and is planning others. The exhibit *Race Relations in Richmond, 1945–85*, broke a taboo on public analysis of a most sensitive issue and inaugurated a series of shows devoted to exploring the role of race in the city's past, present and future. Another presentation boldly took up the issue of cigarette advertising – in Virginia, mind you – while a projected one called *Progressive for Whom?* will initiate a debate on the value of the city manager form of government, a legacy of the early twentieth-century reform movement. While the battery of C-word shows has indeed received flack from some conservative Richmond papers, visitation jumped 140 per cent in two years, and the overwhelming response of the community and the trustees has been highly laudatory.

A More Perfect Union at the Smithsonian Institution took similar risks and has been similarly rewarded for its courage. Here the institution tackled a pending political issue – Congressional restitution to the West Coast Japanese who had been interned during WWII – and produced a Constitution bicentennial display that dared to deal with a less than glorious moment in our history. A combination of hi-tech and traditional display techniques vividly re-created the 1940s experience and drew some 1980s lessons, again managing to illuminate contrasting perspectives while never relinquishing a strong position of its own. While the presentation elicited some howls of protest, they were drowned out by the roar of plaudits from visitors, press, and funders alike.

These are but a few shows that 'come current' – refuse to restrict their attention to safely distant time periods – taken from a longer list . . . I take these to be heartening signs, but it is worth emphasizing that these efforts barely scratch the surface of the possible.

Why not have exhibits treating what gets called 'deindustrialization'? The last decades have seen a flourishing of museums devoted to the history of industry. Often these institutions are a community's response to the collapse of its manufacturing base: defunct plants are transformed into marketable historical commodities. But even though these museums boldly tackle the once controversial question, like the history of labour relations, they still tend to avoid the key questions of why the factories left town. They thus miss an opportunity to inform visitors about great historical processes that have drastically affected their lives. Why not have a show that deals with the nature of capital flight, that explains how and why factories have been packed off to cheap labour markets around the world, and that facilitates a debate on how best to respond to such a phenomenon?

Or how about . . . some of the living history farms take on the question of the transition from family farming to agribusiness? Most agricultural museums – which seem to halt their stories in the 1870s – concentrate more on the processes of sowing and reaping than they do on those developments – the rise of tenantry, migrant labour, foreclosures, world markets, commodity exchanges, and agrarian movements – that might explain how the old farms, whose values they celebrate, succumbed to the corporate agribusinesses that today dominate the area of American agriculture.

Or consider the wide range of gender-related issues that history museums might treat? There have been some recent shows – like *Impact: Technology in the Kitchen* – that considered the household as a workplace in a way that breaks with the nostalgia that seems so often a part of historic house museums with their emphasis on butter churns and their provision of home-baked cookies to visitors. But as Barbara Melosh notes in her essay in the recent Rosenzweig/Leon book (*History Museums in the United States: A Critical Assessment*, University of Illinois) curators, unlike scholars in women's history, have shied away from subjects that involve sexuality or male/female conflict in history – topics like divorce, prostitution, birth control, domestic violence, or class and racial conflict among women – to say nothing (literally) of the history of homosexuality.

Or how about an exhibit that takes on not just the social historical aspects of our automobile culture, but its political and economic aspects, such as the pitched battles fought between proponents of mass transit and the auto-based system, or concerns about environmental pollution? Or a show dealing with the history of the energy industry that discusses issues of public versus private ownership, or delves into the debates on nuclear power? Or a presentation that explores the similarities and differences between Prohibition then and the anti-drug movement now? Or an exhibit that takes on the C-word aspects of our past foreign policy – an analysis of the Vietnam War and the domestic response to it, for example, or an overview of the records of our rocky relations with Central America? Or how about presentations on aspects of the history of housing – such as battles over rent control, public housing, and gentrification?

I'm not saying that every exhibit that makes past/present connections has to be so insistently present-oriented. There is plenty of room for shows that (following Blake's dictum about illuminating the general through attention to 'minute particulars') explain how local situations are illustrative of more general processes or which can profitably be compared to analagous situations in different cultures . . .

Nor do they have to be expensive extravaganzas. The rainforest show was not cheap – it cost $1.3 million – but at the other end there is the Smithsonian's *Science, Power, and Conflict,* really more of a 'cabinet of curiosity' than an exhibit. Its remarkable economy encourages visitors to ponder the impact of pesticides and intelligence testing.

The key factor in embarking on such an approach is not resources but willpower. . . . But let's then consider all the reasons why we cannot or should not do any of these things.

First, there are undoubtedly at least some people who disagreed on principle – or perhaps I should say definitional – grounds. This kind of thing is *not* what museums do! They never have, and they shouldn't start now. That's *politics,* not *history.*

My response to this objection is that history, and history museums, are inescapably political, and they always have been. In the old days, in fact, they were a good deal more explicit about it. The museological giants and house museum forebearers all presented narratives that linked the past with present concerns and future prescriptions . . .

Museums routinely set the present in a continuum in such a way as to ratify present arrangements. More often than not they were handmaidens of power, an unsurprising fact given who produced and controlled them. But the Deweyite and Foxite progressives who contested them in the name of a people's history were similarly straightforward about the need for public education. They wanted citizens to grasp where they'd been so they could better figure out where they might go. Indeed, only relatively recently have museums and scholars professed to be 'objective', or apolitical. . . . Failing to present the role of servants, slaves, or women in sustaining a grand old plantation manor underwrote the side of the privileged . . . implying that the past was none the less a superior place to be – presenting a de facto rebuke to the contemporary world.

Second, there are those whose objections to past-present shows are more pragmatic in nature. They point out that the people who pay the piper might well not like some of these tunes. Sponsors or boards are frightened by the C-word, be they cities, unions, corporations, or just the local townsfolk who have saved a building from demolition and want to use it to glorify the town's past. They favour an uplifting optimism or a blandly judicious balance. Something fit for prime time, family viewing. Former AASLH director Gerald George was right on target here with his wonderful little parable about the would-be reforming curator Eddie Gibbon who tried to turn the Hickory City Historical Society upside down. Dismissing the museum's filiopietistic inspirational approach, young Gibbon scrapped the Hall of Pioneers, the Victorian Period Gallery, and the Civil War cannon, and sold off George Washington's wig at Sothebys in order to fund social history exhibits on Chinese restaurant operators, baseball games, Baptist conventions, slavic miners, and analyses of urbanization and industrialization. For his pains he got himself blown away by a pioneer rifle in the hands of the society's outraged president.

An apt parable, but perhaps too intimidating a one. Sometimes, I think, we do too much self-censoring, too soon. We adhere to an unwritten understanding that there are limits on what can be said, even if they have not been explicitly laid down. Often our prudence is justified, but sometimes we are wrong. Certainly recent experience suggests that determined pushing can be rewarded. If the Mississippi State Museum can interpret the Ku Klux Klan, it is at least conceivable that your own money people – properly cultivated – can be pushed farther than you might expect.

George's slaughtered curator was acting on his own. There are now signs that a critical professional community is emerging, one that includes academics as well, which can be mobilized to provide support to beleaguered colleagues. Early in this century, university trustees routinely interfered in staffing and curricular matters, but the professionalization of the discipline and the concept of academic freedom helped forestall much of this intervention, and perhaps there's a lesson there for the museum world.

Collaboration can also take the form of joint funding efforts; an alliance with academics to increase the amount of government funding available for public education might provide additional revenue. If the sources of funding can be more diversified, the influence of individual donors can be reduced.

Finally, it is important to identify new sources of support, groups who might be interested in critical presentations – labour unions, socially responsible businesses, women's clubs and groups, and environmentalists should not be ignored as resources.

A third objection to presentist exhibitions centres on possible adverse audience reaction. Who wants to be lectured, upset, or offended? Who wants to hear about violence, conflict? People don't want to think; they want to have fun. This is the *marketplace*! As Jerry George concluded, 'There are no captive audiences off-campus.' And even if there were, this notion of tackling big issues would never fly given that the average visitor spends 1.07 seconds at each exhibit case, has 2.34 kids whining for hamburgers, and has one eye on the lookout for a chair or a bathroom.

A veritable *barrage* of strong arguments here – based on lots of hard-won practical experience. But nevertheless, perhaps a little too quickly dismissive of actual and potential audiences. Perhaps museum-goers are disinterested in controversy. But if, in fact, people are drawn to our enterprises by a nostalgic urge to escape the present, doesn't that suggest they are less than crazy about their contemporary situation? If so, might they not be receptive to presentations that explain how the glorious past (which, alas, was probably not quite so wonderful on close inspection) evolved into the wretched present (which, in fact, might turn out to have some redeeming qualities)?

Certainly, we should not overestimate what museums do. As to the audiences' presumed disinterest in controversy: perhaps. But there's a contradiction lurking in this assesment of audiences. Reasonably modest goals are surely attainable. Raising issues and perspectives for people's consideration so that the next time they confront the topic they have the gist of the presentation in mind (along with the experience of the exhibit). Enhancing visitor's *skills* of historical analysis – probably of more lasting value than any specific information we can impart about a particular issue. Nor does the exhibit have to be the last stop; it can be supplemented with takehome videos or publications that allow for more leisurely, seated, and child-free reflections.

Still, there's a bedrock core of truth in the audience-objection that all my whittling away won't remove. But there's another way to come at the issue. If traditional audiences *won't* support you, why not roll yourself some new ones? Recent experience suggests that adopting bolder themes about new subjects can attract new audiences and increase revenues. The Smithsonian's *A More Perfect Union* brought in over 5000 Japanese Americans in the first week, some of whom came from the West Coast, and it has since dramatically increased that group's ongoing attendance. The Valentine Museum was at the point of going under in the early 1980s, but its shows have reached out to new audiences, tripled overall attendance, and, specifically, brought black walking attendance from less than 1 per cent to more than 15 per cent (which in turn helped garner funding from the black city council and the black mayor). In Ohio, the Wilberforce Museum's treatment of black history has been made possible by the involvement of African Methodist Episcopalian bishops and black Ohio legislators. Furthermore, its *From Victory to Freedom* exhibit has generated new involvement in the black community. . . . People, it seems, are willing to become museum-goers if institutions speak to their experiences . . .

There are, of course, dangers in targeting new audiences, dangers of provincialism and of particularism and even of ghettoization (as has happened in some cases in the academy). We might fall prey to the kind of fragmentation we see at the magazine racks, where there is a speciality journal for every conceivable taste and interest, and readers can immerse themselves in their own chosen world to the exclusion of others. But this is not inherent in the process of generating new audiences. Nor should relevance be defined only in ethnic/racial, but rather in terms of issues that touch people's every-day experience.

Let's assume that I have made at least a plausible first case for history museums partici-pating more assertively in national discussions on the meaning and relevance of the past. How might our presentations relate to those of other major cultural institutions that I have suggested routinely link the past and the present – the media and the academy (I will leave aside politicians as their interventions are more sporadic in nature)?

If, grossly speaking, media is the domain of the artifact, what might an ideal division of labour be between them? I will suggest – very quickly and schematically – that (a) I think there is a natural alliance between history museums and academics, that linkages are already well established, and that this collaboration should be fostered; and (b) that though relations between museums and the media world are a bit more problematic, there is much to be gained by our institutions borrowing some of their techniques while maintaining an independent and even critical stance toward their productions.

About the museum/academic alliance, I need not say much, for its value, despite a bumpy history, seems self-evident. They have been shaped by similar social forces in the last generation, and they have much to gain by continued interaction, including the pooling of resources and methodologies. At the heart of the alliance lies the fruitful tension between text and artefact. Museums have shifted away from focusing taxo-nomically on explicating or enshrining objects towards using objects to explain social relations; academics are finally beginning to appreciate the value of artefacts as evidence now that they have started studying aspects of social life for which there is abundant material culture documentation . . .

Conversely, as academics are brought more directly into the exhibit planning process and as curators immerse themselves more and more in the ongoing work of the schol-arly disciplines, there will be concern that exhibits not get too wordy, too much like books-on-walls, thus submerging the distinctive design skills that allow museums to reach out to mass publics. These are real tensions, but as long as the participants in the dialogue maintain mutual respect and good communications they will be sources of creative energy.

The museum/media relationship is less well-established and requires greater reflection. . . . I think we must accept that the 'media generation' is a fact. Partly this is a matter of the much decried (if somewhat overstated) shorter attention spans and lessened willingness to read text. But partly, it's a matter of a new kind of expertise: young people, our future visitors, are now tremendously familiar with the new technology and its particular ways of purveying information. Touch screens, data banks, and interactive videos are no longer toys or gadgets, they're commonplaces of the electronic culture. Even more importantly, as I suggested in discussing my 1960s class, visitors are arriving in our institutions with their mental data banks filled with historical information gleaned from the organs of mass communication. If there is to be a future for history museums, I think we must enter as fully into this new world as our visitors will have done.

If an encounter with the media world offers us real possibilities it also threatens us with real perils. It can provide us with tremendously exciting ways of going beyond object myopia. It could also undercut our efforts to develop historical skills by encouraging the kind of passive receptivity of spectacles the media world too often engenders. . . . The media uses that have made the biggest inroads so far are those which work with the grain of traditional practice by increasing our power to explain our artifacts.

The Smithsonian's *Engines of Change* brings machine tools back to working life; *A More Perfect Union* allows soldiers to explain how they used the tools of war; the Statue of Liberty Museum has a video showing craftspeople rebuilding the Lady's toes, vividly illustrating nineteenth-century craft techniques; and the Hugh Moore Canal Park Museum, by obtaining the film archives of Bethlehem Steel, has positioned itself to interpret the workings of gigantic factory artefacts (the promise of which is hinted at by the clips from the Ford plant in the Smithsonian's *From Field to Factory*). On the flashy (if trivial) front, the new Museum of the Moving Image in Astoria, New York, allows visitors electronically to try on Hollywood costumes. The possibilities of this bring-emback-to-life approach are endless. Think how many museums have static period rooms (or entire houses), displays which could easily and vividly be brought to life by a video.

A second, even more revolutionary use of media, allows museums to deploy memory itself as an artefact. *A More Perfect Union* has some dazzling examples. In one, a mockup of a Japanese internee room is enhanced by a full-sized video projection of a survivor – glimpsed as if through a door, with a sage-strewn mountain scene in the background – explaining the site to his daughter. Even more powerfully, in a nearby touch screen cubicle visitors can 'ask questions' of five internees; the moving and powerful testimonies of Mary Sukamoto and her peers brilliantly complement the show's assemblage of the era's more 'material' artefacts. What is particularly exciting about this technology is its availability to even the smallest of institutions. . ..

But museums, I think, should do more than borrow techniques from Mediaworld; they should consider turning media itself into artefact. Why not begin to mount shows that deconstruct for visitors the kinds of historical messages embedded in Hollywood movies or TV docudramas? . . . that use snippets of film along with other objects to raise questions about the narratives people carry around in their heads. . . . The rainforest exhibit has a nice example of what's possible in its Reel Jungle video. By presenting clips that display the way Hollywood has portrayed, and distorted, the jungle – excerpts from Tarzan movies, scenes of drunken natives cooking missionaries, safari expeditions hunting King Solomon's mines – the exhibit confronts our clichés and lays bare their sources.

We could do this even more dramatically by directly pitting memory-as-artefact against media-as-artefact. To return to my 1960s discussion, we might develop an exhibit that contrasted clips from *Rambo* and *Platoon* with filmed interviews with veterans and anti-war activists. The thrust would be to strengthen historical skills by raising consciousness about how people learn about the past. More generally still, we could develop exhibits about the concern with which I began – the ways in which cultural productions replace memory over time.

In the ongoing struggle to overcome America's ahistorical bent, museums have their own distinctive contributions to make. We have made tremendous and exciting advances in the last decades. Granted that many of us are impoverished. Granted we need alliances with educators, mediamoguls, and politicians. But if we press on in the directions we have been going, I think we can make major contributions to the future of the past.

This paper first appeared in History News *(July/August 1989), pp. 5–33.*

13

The proper business of the museum: ideas or things?

Stephen Weil

Stephen Weil, Smithsonian Institution, Washington, reminds us that it is not what museums claim to do that is important, rather it is what they achieve that matters. His image of the National Toothpick Museum is an excellent one and will be recognized by everyone who has questioned museums and their effectiveness.

To begin, let me ask you to imagine a new museum – heavily endowed, well situated in a prime downtown area, installed in its own large, modern and climate-controlled building, and devoted wholly and exclusively to the collection, preservation, study, interpretation and display of toothpicks.

The National Toothpick Museum – or the NTM as it's more commonly known – is multi-disciplinary. In the Hall of Oral Hygiene, for example, elementary schoolchildren learn about the toothpick's role as a humble foot soldier in the never-ending struggle against tooth decay and gum disease. In the Hall of History, visitors can see *Pick the Winner*, an exhibition of toothpicks used by successful politicians and other high achievers. Elsewhere are toothpicks associated with great historic events – those chewed by Roosevelt, Churchill and Stalin at Yalta, for example, or by Reagan and Gorbachev at their summit in Moscow. Nearby are the first three toothpicks sent into space and also a selection of toothpicks used by movie stars. The Rudolph Valentino specimen has proved to be a particular favourite.

Beyond this, the NTM also maintains a full programme of changing exhibitions, regularly offers symposia and lectures, and publishes a quarterly journal, *History's Splendid Splinter*, which carries scholarly articles about the toothpick's role in social history, patterns of forestry and the evolving technology of toothpick manufacture.

Virtually nobody ever visits the NTM, nor does the press frequently write about it. This, however, does not disturb its director. As he commented with some hauteur during a recent interview: 'Here at the NTM we stick pretty close to our mission statement. Our collections are in splendid shape, our records are complete and up-to-date and our scholarship is considered impeccable. We're attempting to run a first-rate, responsible museum – not trying to win a popularity contest.'

What are we to think of this toothpick museum? Shall we permit it to be perpetuated? Ought we, directly or indirectly, to give it our public support? Shall we admit it to our museum associations? Will we welcome its curators as our colleagues?

Our common sense tells us that this is a ridiculous endeavour, a venture that might be acceptable enough as a hobby but which becomes grotesque and preposterous when inflated to the level of a large-scale museum.

Curiously enough, however, if we approach the NTM not in this common sense way but through the conventional wisdom of the museum field, then it can begin to assume a certain, plausible legitimacy. That this should be so is the outcome of three separate but none the less connected developments that we have seen occurring in many museums over the past two decades.

These are: first, a tendency to consider museums in the light of their functional definition rather than in terms of their purposes; second, the assertion that it is the collection and care of objects that lies at the heart of the museum enterprise; and third, the extraordinary technical proficiency that we have developed in the care of objects and in their display, whether as parts of our permanent collections or within the context of special exhibitions.

That museums should be commonly defined in functional rather than purposive terms is not surprising. The very utility of a definition is to clarify what is different and distinctive about the subject it defines. What is different and distinctive about museums, of course, is that they collect and display objects. That they do so for a larger and publicly beneficial purpose – a purpose that they may to a degree share with a community's schools, hospitals, churches, symphony orchestras and day-care facilities – is neither different nor distinctive. Ergo, that museums at bottom *do* have a larger and a publicly beneficial purpose is not a characteristic that often appears in their definition.

One turns to the common dictionary definition of a museum as 'a room, building or locale where a collection of objects is put on exhibition' and the NTM appears well enough qualified. Nor does it fare much worse when one looks, at least superficially, at the definition used for accreditation purposes by the American Association of Museums (AAM):

> an organized and permanent non-profit institution, essentially educational or esthetic in purpose, with professional staff, which owns and utilizes tangible objects, cares for them and exhibits them to the public on some regular schedule.

Not only does the NTM seem just fine – assuming it employs a curator, a conservator or at least an educator, it even seems accreditable.

Turning to a Canadian definition of museums – my source is the 1981 statement prepared by the National Museums of Canada for the Federal Cultural Policy Review Committee – one finds this:

> Museums collect, they preserve and study what they collect and they share both the collections and the knowledge derived therefrom for the instruction and self-enlightenment of an audience.

Again, we can perhaps welcome the NTM to our ranks.

Even if one turns to that most socially oriented of all museum definitions, the one which the International Council of Museums adopted in 1974, the NTM still seems to retain its legitimacy:

> A museum is a non-profitmaking, permanent institution in the service of society and of its development, and open to the public, which acquires, conserves, researches, communicates and exhibits, for purposes of study, education and enjoyment, material evidence of man and his environment.

While some might question to what degree a toothpick museum may be in the service of society and its development, certainly nobody – or at least nobody who ever had a kernel of corn stuck in his teeth – would ever argue that the celebration of this humble but useful implement was a *disservice* to society and its development. From a functional perspective, the NTM still seems to be a museum.

There are, I think, at least two reasons why this functional perspective has taken so strong a grip. For one thing, it has proved comfortable. To focus museum rhetoric on the socially beneficial aspects of a museum would ultimately be to invite discussion on a wide range of political and moral issues that could well pit trustees against staff members and staff members against one another. By contrast, to focus on function – on the good, seemingly value-free work of collecting, preserving and displaying – projects a sense of ideological neutrality (albeit, I suspect, a grossly deceptive sense) in which people of diverse social views are able to work more amiably together.

Beyond that, this functional perspective connects with our aspirations towards professionalism. Among the key elements needed to establish museum work – or any other occupation – as a separate and distinct profession is the ability to identify some aspect of that work as being unique. This process is, in a way, parallel to the way definitions are constructed. We tend to build these around what is most distinctive, not necessarily what is most important. Motive, impulse and purpose are sheared away leaving us simply to function as professional collectors, preservers and exhibitors.

Not surprisingly, a similar reductive tendency is reflected, and even reinforced, by our larger professional museum associations. These derive their strength from what is common among their membership, not what is diverse. What's most common, of course, is how their members – diverse as they may be in discipline – all function as custodians, scholars and public interpreters. Frequently, then, these are aspects of museum work to which our associations give the most stress. There is no harm in this if we understand the context and the limited nature of such an emphasis. There may, however, be great harm when we lose sight of this context and begin to mistake what we do – that is collecting, preserving and displaying – for our *raison d'être*. That's when something as silly as a museum wholly devoted to toothpicks can begin to seem plausible and legitimate.

When we turn to the assertion that objects and their care – whether these be works of art, historic artefacts or natural history specimens – lie at the heart of the museum enterprise, we encounter a similar group of considerations. This is, for one thing, a comfortable assertion. It tends to finesse the philosophic and ideological controversies with which we might otherwise have to contend if we recognized that concepts and relationships, and not things alone, lie equally at the heart of museum work. For another, it offers a further basis on which to build our larger professional associations. The assumption that we are all doing fundamentally the same thing – i.e. dealing with objects – not only serves as the glue to hold these together but also acts to support a growing literature and even a burgeoning array of museum studies programmes.

Again, though, we must be careful. Intertwined with this assertion is the belief – by no means universal, but held broadly enough to be significant – that objects have (and the pun here is deliberate) some 'objective' reality – that a museum object can, with only the most minimal help, in some way speak for itself. Allied with this is a notion of the museum as a sort of neutral and transparent medium – a clear, clean and undistorting lens – throught which the public ought be able to come face-to-face with an object, pure and fresh.

At best, this seems a wilful naivety. The world, as William James has taught us, is not something that we can grasp perceptually. Taken as a whole, it is – in his grand phrase – 'a big blooming, buzzing confusion'. It is only through selective attention and the formulation of concepts that we are able to reduce this blooming confusion to some comprehensible form. These are matters of the mind, the consequences of thought. For us, objects do not exist alone. We perceive them in a mesh of experience. Whether in a museum or otherwise, objects only have meaning for us through the framework of the concepts and assumptions with which we approach them. We see things, as the anthropologist David Pilbeam has observed, not as they are but 'as we are'.

If this is so, then we must never forget that ideas – and not just things alone – also lie at the heart of the museum entreprise. Reality is neither objects alone nor simply ideas about objects but, rather, the two taken together. Of percepts and concepts, James wrote: 'We need them both, as we need both our legs to walk with.'

Too often, though, this thought component remains unarticulated; it remains in the realm of the taken-for-granted. If museums were nothing more than custodial agents, this might not matter. Nor might it matter if museums were simply centres for scholarship. But if museums are to serve some greater beneficial purpose – if museums are to have some real and powerful impact on the lives of those who use them – then it matters a great deal. Unless we can understand the intellectual framework through which we perceive an object, and unless we more fully understand the various intellectual frameworks through which the members of our public might themselves in turn perceive that same object, how can we ever truly hope to be in communication?

In the case of the NTM, our toothpick museum, the third of these three recent developments in museums – the enormous growth in our technical proficiency – seems particularly germane. The issue is one of technology.

Until the twentieth century, the term 'technology' was generally used only with respect to the practical or industrial applications of scientific principles. It referred, for the most part, to the use of tools and machinery. In our own time, though, it has taken on a broader meaning. We use it today to cover all of the systematic means and processes by which we accomplish our various tasks. In his 1954 book *La Technique*, Jacques Ellul referred to these as 'the ensemble of practices by which one uses available resources in order to achieve certain valued ends'.

Viewed in that light, museum work can be considered a technology, of which we who work in museums have indeed become the very skilled masters and mistresses. Along with that bright recognition, however, there must come another and a darker one: that technology is not merely a neutral or inert means by which we are able to pursue our traditional goals. It can also have an insidious side-effect. This is a condition – the phrase was most recently used by Garry Wills, but the possibility was long ago recognized by Ellul – that might be called 'technological determinancy'.

Put in everyday terms, 'technological determinancy' means that we may find ourselves doing things simply because we know how to do them, regardless of whether they truly satisfy any real desire. Put in museum-relevant terms, it means that the 'ensemble of practices' that we have developed permits us to sometimes perform the most dazzling museological feats simply because we can, and not because the outcome necessarily fulfils any legitimate purpose or meets any genuine need. As museum people, we have become so technically proficient, so ingenious in what we do, that we are capable of developing a perfectly plausible museological programme to meet virtually any challenge – even devising and maintaining a museum to glorify the toothpick.

How might this be different? How might we conceive of museums in such a way that the NTM would be a palpable absurdity from its very inception? To begin with, we must resist the siren song of technology. Also, we must better understand that the museum is a place for both objects and ideas. Above all, though, we must begin to shift our focus –

and the focuses of those who supervise and support us – from function to purpose. We must start with the proposition that the museum's *raison d'être* is to provide an important public benefit, to have an important impact on the lives of others – not merely to provide a custodial or a scholarly service – and we must then proceed to enquire into what the nature of that benefit and that impact might be.

Throughout, through, we must also pause from time to time to reflect upon the caution of William Blake: 'To Generalize is to be an Idiot. To Particularize is the Alone Distinction of Merit.' The public benefit and impact that a museum can provide will never be the same in any two institutions. The real guts and glory of every museum is in its particularity, not in what it does in common with others. As museums vary enormously by discipline, collections, scale, facilities, context, location, funding and history, so too must the mix of benefits they can provide be varied from institution to institution. What we can generalize about, though, are some of the elements that might be included in that mix – some of the different ways in which museums might contribute to the better lives of those who use them.

As traditionally conceived, of course, museums may serve as important providers of information. In the rhetoric of the museum as educational institution, this role has generally been given a principal stress. While museums have always been informative, is the museum still an important medium for the dissemination of information? Less so, I suspect, than might once have been the case. Such media as radio, broadcast television and the video-cassette recorder may have come to serve at least as effectively as exhibits to disseminate information about certain subjects that once were the exclusive province of museums.

There is, though, a further difficulty. Common both to museums and to these more recently evolved media is a troubling question about the information that they disseminate. Is this information as objective as we once believed it to be? To an extent not hitherto suspected, we must face the possibility that, despite all our goodwill, the assumptions and biases that colour our larger social and political views may also colour our simplest and most basis acts of identification and classification. As the University of Chicago's Neil Harris pointed out when he addressed the AAM's Midwest Museum Conference in September 1986, 'classification has come to be seen as an act of domination as well as analysis.' As for the traditional authority of museums, he said: 'The museum's voice is no longer seen as transcendent. Rather it is implicated in the distribution of wealth, power, knowledge, and taste shaped by the larger social order.'

Suffice it to say that however we elect to respond to that charge, it will have to be in terms of ideas, not of objects.

What if, instead, we looked not at information but at values? The notion of the museum as a disseminator of values is a complex one. In the mix of what museums provide to the public, this has long been one of their most significant, and at the same time most controversial roles. On the one hand, we are urged to maintain the art museum as the last bastion of aesthetic standards in a world of rising visual mediocrity. On the other, we are cautioned about how easily the history museum can be used – the phrase comes from Felipe Lacouture of the National Museum of History of Mexico – as 'an ideological tool of the State'. Particularly tricky is the fact that what may seem wholly objective to one observer may seem just the opposite to another. Those of us at the Smithsonian Institution who naively believed that our own National Museum of Natural History was a value-neutral institution were certainly astonished several years ago when a group of religious creationists brought a legal action in an effort – unsuccessful as it turned out – to redress what they considered a value-driven and not scientifically based exhibit about human evolution.

If what we take to be factual information is, as Neil Harris said, 'shaped by the larger social order,' is this not even more so in the case of our values? Can we even distinguish what we ourselves believe from the spirit of our time as it finds individual expression through each of us?

Discussing nineteeth-century British municipal museums, the American historian David Lowenthal has most succinctly described them as 'aimed to instil moral thinking and behavior: built in the image of classical temples and Gothic churches (they) served the masses as intimidating reminders of ruling class power and their own ignorance.'

Did the men who built those museums intend them that way? If not, might they none the less have been proud of what they succeeded in projecting? Do we really know what values our own museums project? Or will a century's distance be needed to make that clear?

The issue, certainly, is not one of having value-free museums. Few of us would want this; many of us who work in museums do so with a certain missionary zeal. We do so with a passionate belief in the importance of our subject matter and, not infrequently, with a profound commitment to what we believe to be the underlying values of that subject matter.

The real issue is not how to purge the museum of values, in all likelihood an impossible task, but how to make those values manifest, how to bring them up to consciousness for both ourselves and our visitors. We delude ourselves when we think of the museum as a clear and transparent medium through which only our objects transmit messages. We transmit messages too – as a medium we are also a message – and it seems to me vital that we understand better just what those messages are.

An alternate approach would be to consider the museum primarily as a medium by which to provide visitors with an extraordinary experience – a place in which they might directly encounter rare and/or costly objects not generally a part of their everyday lives. As one proponent of this view – Father M. A. Couturier, the young Dominican who once persuaded Henri Matisse to decorate the chapel in Venice – phrased it, 'A museum should be a place where we lose our head – to be enlightened, dazzled and transformed by the epiphany of art.'

Here, though, another caution might be in order. We ought not to claim too much. While most of us at one time or another have experienced the dazzle, enlightenment and transformation of encountering a great object, the fact is that there are by no means nearly enough epiphanous works of art or wonders of nature to fill the thousands upon thousands of museums that stand on this continent alone.

It seems to me a serious disservice to the public to raise an expectation that museum-going may provide a transcendent experience in those situations when none is reasonably to be expected. What happens when we show less than the best works of art, for example, as if these were masterworks? At best, a visitor may fault us for our inadequacy. At worst, he may fault himself for having failed to respond. The better way, of course, is to be candid. That, again, suggests that we must bring thought into some closer parity with things and make a discussion of ideas – not just a display of objects – an integral part of the visitor's museum-going experience.

Beyond information, values, and experience, what else of social utility might museums provide to their public? Let me suggest two: stimulation and empowerment. Here we approach the museum visit not as an end in itself but as the starting point, rather, for a process intended to continue long after the visitor has left the museum's premises.

In the United States, the roots of this approach can be traced back to John Cotton Dana, the early twentieth-century Yankee iconoclast who bitterly dismissed most of the country's then newly palatial museums as 'awesome to a few, tiresome to many, and helpful to almost none.' In his 1917 book *The New Museum*, Dana urged that the museums of the future make a special effort to attract the young and to interest them in making collections of their own – collections that they might ultimately share with the public. This development of the collecting habit, he wrote:

> with its accompanying education of powers of observation, its training in handwork, its tendency to arouse interests theretofore unsuspected even by those who possess them, its continuous suggestions toward good taste and refinement which lie in the process of installing even the most modest of collections, and its leanings toward sound civic interest through doing for one's community a helpful thing – this work of securing the co-operation of boys and girls, making them useful while they are gaining their own pleasure and carrying on their own education, is one of the coming museum's most promising fields.

In recent years, perhaps nobody has put the argument for the museum as a source of stimulation more powerfully than did Nelson Goodman of Harvard when the CMA and the AAM met jointly in Boston in 1980. Speaking initially of works of art, he said:

> The museum has to function as an institution for the prevention of blindness in order to make works work. And making works work is the museum's major mission.
> Works work when, by stimulating inquisitive looking, sharpening perception, raising visual intelligence, widening perspectives, bringing out new connections and contrasts, and marking off neglected significant kinds, they participate in the organization and reorganization of experience, in the making and remaking of our worlds.

Carrying his observation beyond works of art, Goodman continued:

> Clearly, works of science work in this sense, too, and so also do the collections of science museums, historical museums, and botanical and zoological gardens. . . . Museums of different kinds indeed have some different problems, but their common end is improvement in the comprehension and creation of the worlds we live in.

To the extent that we want such stimulation to be in the mix of what a museum provides, how might it affect what we choose to display and how we choose to display it? What criterion should guide such a decision: the inherent quality of an object or its utility as a stimulus? Or are these the same thing? Here, again, we are beyond any functional view of the museum. However we choose to answer such questions, we will have to begin in the realm of thought, and not collections management.

Closely related to this view of the museum as stimulus is the vision of the museum as an instrument of empowerment. Its goal as such would be to provide the members of its public with a knowledge of the methods, processes, and techniques through which they, in turn, could make better informed judgements about their own past and more insightful choices about their future. The museum would not presume to teach a subject but would provide the means by which its clients could learn the subject for themselves. Rather than holding itself forth as the authoritative or exclusive source of historical interpretation or aesthetic judgement, the museum would hope to enlist the visitor as a collaborator who might, in turn, develop his own sense of heritage, causality, connectedness, and taste – his own links to both an individual and a communal past.

This two-way approach, of course, is chiefly characteristic of the eco-museum movement and has most recently been embraced within the programme of the Committee for a New

Museology. As summarized at the October 1987 International Workshop on New Museology held in Aragon, Spain, it proposes a museology that:

> must be defined according to changing social realities rather than to a theory forced upon populations; methodologies should be based on specific social realities and should aim for the liberation, development and transformation of society through the awareness and participation of the population.

What the New Museology will be able to accomplish remains to be seen. Whatever it is, though, it should certainly be something more significant than that imaginary accomplishment of the old museology – a toothpick museum.

Those, then, are some of the possibilities open to us if we are to envision our museums as fundamentally driven-by-purpose rather than devoted-to-objects. For each of us, the best mix of those possibilities will be different. Common to all, however, should be the notion that the primary and central relationship of museology is between the museum and its visitors and other clients – not between the museum and its collection. Common as well should be the sense that it is ideas, viewpoint, and insight that finally powers the museum – not the care of collections. Good collections management is essential, but it can no more make a museum excellent than good book-keeping can make a business flourish.

The question we must ultimately ask ourselves is this: do our museums make a real difference in, and do they have a positive impact on, the lives of other people? If not, if in the end we are only the servants of our collections and not of our fellow humans, then we might just as well be off somewhere plying our trades at some imaginary Temple of Thumbtacks, Paper Clip Palace, or even the NTM. But if so, if the life of the community is richer for the work we do, if we make an important and positive difference in the lives of others, then the zeal we bring to our daily work will have been well rewarded, and our own working lives well spent.

This paper first appeared in S. Weil (1990) Rethinking the Museum and other Meditations, *Washington, D. C.: Smithsonian Institution, pp. 43–56.*

14

Visiting and evaluating museums
Gaynor Kavanagh

A constructively critical approach to looking at museums must depend upon a range of questions. Visiting and evaluating museums is an effective and indispensable means of learning about them. The following 'checklist' has been developed at the Department of Museum Studies, University of Leicester, and is used by postgraduate students on their museum visits.

A visit to a museum should enable you to compare theory and practice. It should be an occasion when you focus your understanding of museums and construct a critical appraisal of what you are seeing. Throughout your visit, a whole range of questions should be running through your mind and you should actively seek answers. Here are some questions to begin with. As time goes on, add your own or develop your own system.

LOCATION

Where is the museum? Is it easy to find? Are there sign posts? Are there car/coach parking facilities?

Are there other attractions/facilities in the area?

What is the immediate vicinity of the museum like? What implications does it have for the museum and its work?

THE BUILDING

What tells you that this is a museum? Would you know from the outside what was going on inside?

How old is the building? Why does it look the way it does? What impression does the exterior give you? Is it 'purpose built'? Or is it an adapted building, e.g. a former mill or ice-rink?

Is it a suitable building for a museum? What are its strengths and weaknesses? How easy would it be to burgle or burn down?

ENTRANCE

How welcoming/inviting is the entrance? Can you find the entrance?

Are there restrictions on access? How would you gain access in a wheelchair? How would you get in with a double buggy?

Do you feel welcome? Has anyone noticed you? Do they want money?

How are admission charges announced and collected?

What are the staff wearing? What is their attitude? Would it be the same if you were different in some way: a mum with three toddlers; a different skin colour; without English as a first language; or fifteen years old with a gang of friends?

Are there security checks? Why? What do you do with your bag, coat, umbrella?

Where are the loos, first aid points, changing room facilities for parents with babies, museum-provided wheelchairs, pushchairs and carry packs? Can you sit anywhere in the reception area, for example, to wait for friends?

Where are the museum shop, museum cafe (or coffee pot if a very small museum)? Are there maps or signposts? Is there an introduction to the museum telling you what's on offer, where to go?

Are the facilities and information positioned in such a way as to help your visit, encourage casual, but regular use? Do they set you off in a good frame of mind? How would you rate their standards?

How does this museum make money? Does it care?

ORGANIZATION

Who is the director? What is his/her background or specialist interests? How does he/she perceive the role of director and the role of the museum?

How many people work here? How are their jobs defined? What is the staff structure? How does this relate to the aims and purposes of the museum? Has it changed? Is it about to change? Are there obvious gaps in expertise?

What is the atmosphere like? Do the staff display a positive attitude towards the museum and its services? Do the staff speak freely and with enthusiasm? Where does the museum get its energy and ideas from? Does it have energy and ideas? If not, why not?

What is the museum's attitude towards training and professional development? Does the museum ever hold its own staff training sessions, study visits to other museums or staff discussions on the aim and purpose of their work?

Has the museum got a plan, a system of evaluating where it's going and where it's been? How does it know whether it is succeeding or failing?

Is this museum registered? What does that mean?

Has it got a corporate plan, a business plan, an action plan, a policy towards training and development . . . anything lucid/useful?

GOVERNING BODY

How is this museum constituted? How is it governed? Who are its trustees/councillors? What implications does the constitutional form and governance of this museum have for the sort of museum it is, or could become?

What is happening at the moment in their specific sector of the political economy – charities, national bodies, local authorities, etc.? What effect is this having?

COLLECTIONS

What does this museum collect? Why does it collect? When did collecting begin? How do they decide what to collect? How meaningful/relevant is their collecting policy? How even and useful a span of collections does this museum hold? Do they know what to collect next?

Is there evidence of inspiration, innovation and awareness in their collecting? How do you rate their collections?

Do the staff conduct research, enquiries or fieldwork? If not, why not? How do they update their academic and professional skills?

How are the collections housed and organized? How much of the collection is catalogued? If there is a shortfall, why has this occurred and what are they going to do about it?

What documentation system do they use? What are its merits and flaws? Do they use computers? What is the backlog of records not on computer?

What are the storage facilities like? Do they adequately provide for the security of the collections? How do storage facilities relate to the galleries and to conservation? What are the handling procedures?

How does the museum provide for the environmental needs of its collection? Are there conservation facilities? What are the museum's policies on conservation?

What provision is there for visiting researchers? Is there a library? Is it any good?

PUBLIC AREAS

What impressions do the public areas of the museum give you? Is there evidence that the museum cares about its visitors? Does it think about the intellectual, educational, physical and social needs of visitors?

How difficult would it be to evacuate the museum if there was a major emergency?

Is the museum 'policed', 'attended', 'wardened' or monitored by gallery 'enablers'? What would they do in the event of fire or theft? Can they answer your questions about the collections and displays?

DISPLAYS AND EXHIBITIONS

What are this museum's main displays and exhibitions? Why have they chosen these themes? Does the content of the exhibition match the claim of its title?

What are the messages of these exhibitions? Are they intentional or unintentional?

What is included and what is excluded? Does the interpretation seem fair and balanced?

Have you seen it all before or is this a fresh approach?

How helpful are the labels? For whom are they written? Do they answer your questions? Do they help you look at the material on show? How big/long are they? Are they well written? Is the writer speaking to you or to him/herself? Do you need special lenses to read the text? Are there extra interpretative aids, such as audio-visual areas, audio-guides, published handbooks, etc.?

How old are the displays? How secure are they? Could you burgle a case here?

What provision is made for the control of light, heat and humidity in the gallery areas. Is it enough? What special care do these objects need? Are they getting it?

Are there facilities for temporary exhibitions? Is there a temporary exhibitions programme? How is it devised?

Does the display and exhibition work of the museum cater for different sections of its audience? How would you enjoy the exhibitions if you were six years old, deaf and in your eighties, or accompanied by your sixteen-year-old twin brothers?

How does this museum know that its displays and exhibitions work? Has it carried out any form of evaluation? Does it rest its case on the number of people who visit it? Can it be sure that this number wouldn't double if the exhibitions and displays were different?

Who comes to this museum? Why? Who doesn't come to this museum? Why?

EDUCATION

Is there an education service? Is this made clear to you at the entrance or in the galleries? What roles do the education staff play in this museum? To what extent is the museum aware of the National Curriculum? What kind of response has it made?

What do they provide for pre-school children, primary school groups and secondary schoolchildren? Does the museum have a museum club or activities for children outside school hours? Is provision made for adult education? What form does it take? Is this museum working with the elderly, outlying communities or local groups?

Is there a loans service? Who uses it? Is there an education room? Is it well equipped? Is there a proper lecture theatre? How often is it in use?

How does this museum liaise with teachers and local education advisors? Does it provide any training for teachers? Does it have any links with local work experience schemes or local teacher training courses?

How is education provision monitored and evaluated?

VISITOR SERVICES

Does the museum encourage enquiries? How many does it get in a week? Can it cope with them?

What does it publish? Does it have postcards of objects in the collection?

Is this a comfortable place to be? Can you take your time, choose what you want to see, and have a good sit down when you need to? Are there enough loos around? Can you interrupt your visit for a cup of tea?

Do you want to be here? Would you return? Would you bring a friend? Would you bring someone who never goes to museums?

EVALUATE

What can be learned from this museum?

What are its merits?

What are its flaws?

This paper first appeared in the Department of Museum Studies, University of Leicester (1993) Handbook 1993–94, *Leicester: Leicester University Press.*

Part 3
Museums UK

15

The museum scene
Museums and Galleries Commission

Museums in the UK are distinctive for two particular reasons. The first is their disciplinarity and often their multidisciplinarity. The second is the very different forms of funding and organization that underpin them.

The first paper in this section is from the Museums and Galleries Commission (MGC). It summarizes the museum situation in the UK as they saw it in 1992. It makes the point that accurate statistics in some areas are very difficult to come by, a situation which will change when the Museums and Galleries Commission's Directory of Museum Statistics (DOMUS) is published.

Museum statistics are always complicated by the diversity of the museums themselves. Not only do museums come in all shapes and sizes and with different types of collection, but they are funded and organized in quite different ways. This means that statistics are assembled differently and are inconsistent. There are well over 2,000 places calling themselves 'museums' in the UK. If the definition is widened there may be as many as 2,500. Nobody knows exactly at present, but when the MGC's national Registration Scheme is complete we shall be able to say how many there are whose claims to fulfil the minimum standards expected are justified. This is not a function of size, because a respectable museum that meets these standards can be of the age and size and repute of the British Museum, or the smallest and newest village museum run by volunteers and open only at weekends.

THE GOVERNMENT

There is no declared general government policy on museums. Nor is there legislation applying to all museums, although some are covered by specific legislation.

The main responsibility for funding museums is shared between five government departments: the new Department of National Heritage (DNH) which took over the functions of the old Office of Art and Libraries in April 1992, the Ministry of Defence, and the Scottish, Welsh and Northern Ireland Offices. The DNH is the designated lead department, but several other departments have some regular involvement with museums, including notably the Department for Education which indirectly supports university museums, and the Department of the Environment in its dealings with local authorities.

NATIONAL MUSEUMS

There is no statutory definition of a national museum, but the nineteen institutions generally recognized as such have four characteristics in common: their collections are of national importance in terms of the United Kingdom or a part of it; they are vested in trustees on the nation's behalf; they are wholly or mainly funded directly by government; and the governement is able to call on their staff from time to time for such expert advice in their field as it may require.

Thirteen of the nationals are based in London, two in Edinburgh, one in Cardiff and two in Belfast. The British Museum (founded in 1753) is the oldest and largest. It heads the 'big six' London nationals, the others being the Victoria and Albert Museum, the National Gallery, the Tate Gallery, the Science Museum and the Natural History Museum. The National Museums and Galleries on Merseyside, a grouping of seven museums around Liverpool, were classed as a national museum only in 1986 following the abolition of the Merseyside County Council. Most of the national museums have branches outside the capital cities or operate from several sites. The National Museum of Wales, for example, has eleven branches. And the Science Museum, as the National Museum of Science and Industry, operates also the National Railway Museum in York and the National Museum of Photography, Film and Television in Bradford. Between them the national museums have some fifty branch museums or outstations, attract 25 million visitors a year and employ over 6,000 staff – nearly one-third of all paid staff working in UK museums. In 1991–2 they received some £232 million in grants-in-aid from central government, of which some 62 per cent was for running costs, 33 per cent for building and maintenance, and 5 per cent for acquisitions. Together the national museums generate some £52 million each year from fundraising and sponsorship, trading and admission charges and donations.

Every one of the national museums has all or most of its trustees (or equivalents) appointed by the government, which provides them with an annual grant-in-aid and expects them to be responsible for the well-being of their collections and the buildings which house them. This is commonly spoken of as the 'arm's length' principle. The length of the arm can vary. The freedom of the trustees and their quasi-independence from government doubtless have their advantages, but these are inherently difficult to reconcile with factors such as the trustees not having effective control over their salary bills (pay awards are determined between the government and the civil service unions), not being provided with enough money to pay their staff salaries or discharge their responsibilities of collection care properly, and not being able to borrow money. The system works reasonably well up to a point, but it rests on too uneasy a balance of power and responsibility to be really satisfactory, and some trustees feel that they have insufficient information to make important decisions.

A number of other museums receive all or most of their funding direct from the government. These include the Sir John Soane's Museum and the Horniman and Geffrye Museums in London (DNH), and the Ulster American Folk Park (Department of Education for Northern Ireland). The DNH also funds the Museum of Science and Industry in Manchester and (jointly with the City of London) the Museum of London, and (through the MGC) part of the costs of the Tyne and Wear Museum Service.

UNIVERSITY MUSEUMS

The first museum to be opened to the public (nearly seventy years before the British Museum) was the Ashmolean Museum in Oxford, the oldest of some 300 university museums and collections throughout the UK. They are mainly funded from government money which universities receive from the Education Departments through the Universities Funding Council (UFC), and they range from large and famous institutions open to the public to small departmental collections used only for teaching purposes or not at all. A few of these museums receive help from or have been taken over by local authorities. Museums in this sector probably face greater problems than any others, as the funding for universities is under growing pressure, and is likely to be further reviewed from 1993. The UFC grants to fifteen universities currently include an element of 'special factor' funding in respect of twenty-five of the more important museums or collections. This system should be refined and extended, but there are fears that it may be stopped.

ARMED SERVICES MUSEUMS

A third category of museums, also mainly or partly funded by central government, is that of the 200 or so museums of the armed services. Those directly or indirectly under the aegis of the Ministry of Defence range from the national museums of the Army and the Royal Air Force, and those of the Royal Navy, to well over 100 smaller regimental and corps museums and collections, many of them based in regimental headquarters, and many operating on a bare minimum of part-time or voluntary staff. These too are under increasing pressure resulting from defence cuts and the fact that the MOD (although it is currently reviewing its policy) does not see museums as central to the role of the armed services.

LOCAL AUTHORITY MUSEUMS

If the national museums form the hub of the UK museum system, local authority museums are the spokes of the wheel. Most district and many county councils operate some form of museum service. Many were founded in the nineteenth century and a high proportion are based in listed buildings. The total number has increased in recent years and, including branch museums, is now around 800. Expenditure by local authorities was around £128 million in 1991–2, of which around £100 million was covered by the government's block grant. Some 25 million visitors are attracted annually.

Local authority museums vary greatly in size, quality and importance. Glasgow City Museums Service, which includes the Burrell Collection and Kelvingrove Museum as well as eight other sites, has an annual budget of £13.3 million, employs 423 staff and receives some 2.5 million visitors. These figures are unrivalled except by a handful of the largest national museums, and many other local authorities spend in excess of £1 million annually. Collections like those of the Bowes Museum, now funded by Durham County Council, rival those of many national museums. At the other end of the scale, some local authority museums comprise no more than one room in a library run by a part-time member of staff. Many play an important role as interpreters of local history, and as biological, geological and archaeological record centres. What they all maintain in common is a long-standing commitment to local education and community service.

Generally local authority museums are run as part of a larger department. In the past this was usually education or libraries, but today museums are more likely to come under the wing of leisure services, or tourism, or even economic development. Although some local authority museums still deserve the unfortunate epithet of 'worthy but dull', and they generally have a traditional feeling and appearance, great improvements have been made in management and presentation in recent years. Some of the most striking recent developments have taken place in Northern Ireland at places like Derry and Downpatrick and often with the help of capital funding from outside agencies. But standards and practice do vary widely. Much depends on the calibre and interest of those involved at officer and elected member level, and on how the local authority concerned has been affected by the recent changes in legislation and local government finance. The government block grants to local authorities take no account of their museum responsibilities, which are often regional or national rather than purely local, and many museums face further threats with the possible disappearance of county councils and continued moves towards contracting out management of local authority services to the private sector.

INDEPENDENT MUSEUMS

The most numerous are the independent museums, which number upwards of 1,100. Nearly all are set up as charitable trusts, and most receive no regular funding from central or local government. The best are characterized by innovation, by creative flair and energy, and by awareness of the needs of their visitors, on whom nearly all depend financially for survival. Frequently this is supplemented by a significant voluntary input, for such museums tend to be started by enthusiastic individuals or groups. Not surprisingly, this has been the fastest-growing sector, but it is now the most vulnerable to changes in the national economy, and at risk from competition from other types of visitor attraction. Fewer new ones are being created, while an increasing number each year languish and are forced to close. So far this has mainly affected privately owned institutions run for profit and thus outside the scope of this essay, but the trend is unmistakable.

SUPPORT FOR MUSEUMS

The government's main direct input is through its sponsorship of the nineteen nationals. It also funds the *Museums and Galleries Commission* (MGC), which is the government's official advisory body for museums of all types throughout the UK and has direct contacts with each of the departments concerned. The MGC is also in regular contact with museums and has published or commissioned reports on each of the museum sectors outlined above, as well as on particular parts of the UK and on specific subjects such as training. However, the usual channel of support for non-national museums and galleries is at a regional level through the *Area Museum Councils* (AMCs). These were set up by and are run by museum interests on a membership basis. They employ professional staff to advise museums, and some provide specialist services, such as conservation or travelling exhibitions. They also make small grants for 'one-off' projects, help co-ordinate the provision of training, and provide an essential first port of call for anyone wishing to start a new museum or redevelop an existing one. The MGC funds the seven English AMCs, the Scottish Office Education Department funds the Scottish Museums Council, and the Welsh Office the Council of Museums in Wales. The Department of Education for Northern Ireland helps to fund the Northern Ireland Museums Advisory Committee – from which, it is hoped, an AMC for Northern Ireland will emerge.

The work of the AMCs is co-ordinated by the Committee of AMCs (CAMC), and by means of regular meetings between AMC chairmen and directors with the MGC and its staff. Although the AMCs are independently run, in practice they work very closely with us, particularly on the museum Registration Scheme and in assessing grant applications. The system works well, though far more money is needed. The nine AMCs receive less than £4 million in total, a figure that should be at least doubled if they are fully to exploit their potential in assisting and improving museums and museum services.

The museum profession is a small one and fragmented. There is relatively little movement between different types of museum, and this is exacerbated by different pay and grading scales. Many small museums and some larger ones rely very heavily on volunteers. About one-third of the total workforce of 25,000 is in this category. Salary levels outside the nationals are generally low. Those working in independent museums are often in their second career while others, especially in university and armed service museums, find themselves combining museum duties with other roles. Only the larger museums are able to employ specialists in such areas as administration, marketing or design. A high proportion of all staff are engaged in warding and security. Curators – people trained to understand and look after collections – are frequently in the minority and often find themselves having to undertake many other tasks as well. Only in the national museums and in others which have more specialized collections are curators likely to be able to concentrate on their special subjects.

The *Museum Training Institute* was established in 1989 as a direct result of the MGC's report on training and career structure, and in response to government legislation intended to produce a trained workforce by the year 2000. It is now funded by the DNH, and has the support of the Department of Employment and the National Council for Vocational Qualifications in its important task of overseeing and co-ordinating the provision of training for those who work in museums, of developing standards of competence in each functional area, and of maximizing the involvement of museum staff and their employers in training initiatives.

The other support organization mainly funded by the government (through the MGC) is the *Museum Documentation Association*. This works to raise standards of documentation in museums and to encourage and help them to document their collections more comprehensively and consistently, especially with the use of computers.

The main professional organization of museums and their staff is the *Museums Association*, the first such body to be set up in the world and now into its second century. Although its fortunes have fluctuated through the years, it has done pioneering work on in-service training and offers a widely recognized professional qualification, an annual conference and the monthly *Museums Journal*. Most of its members come from the local authority sector, but its *Museums Yearbook* contains codes of practice, policy statements and guidelines for the whole museum community. Each region has a *Federation of Museums and Art Galleries* run on a voluntary basis and affiliated to the Association, and there is also a bewilderingly large number of *Specialist Groups and Societies*, covering different subjects or specific areas of activity. With a membership of 800 institutions, the *Association of Independent Museums* (AIM) is particularly influential. It produces the AIM bulletin every other month and an excellent series of guidelines on aspects of museum management, and also organizes training seminars.

Well over 200 museums have their own organization of *Friends* of the museum; some 150,000 people are involved, many of whom work as volunteers or help with fundraising. Their umbrella organization is the *British Association of Friends of Museums* (BAFM).

The main *international organization* is the International Council of Museums (ICOM), with headquarters in Paris. UK museum staff are active in its work and in that of its specialist committees, such as conservation, training and security. The UK also contributes (through the MGC and others) to the International Centre for the Study of the Preservation and Restoration of Cultural Property (ICCROM), with headquarters in Rome. Until recently there was no established museums forum within Europe but one is now being set up.

The main *charities supporting museums* include the National Art Collections Fund (NACF), which makes grants to museums totalling some £1.5 million a year to help them with specific purchases. It publishes an *Art Quarterly* and an *Annual Review*, and runs an annual awards scheme. The Contemporary Arts Society, also a membership body, buys new works from artists and presents them to museums. The main pressure group and lobby, the National Campaign for the Arts, publishes occasional leaflets in support of museums, but is mainly concerned with the performing arts organizations and their funding. On a more limited scale National Heritage has given support to museums over the years and runs the prestigious 'Museum of the Year Award' scheme.

A number of charitable trusts including those associated with the names of Carnegie, Wolfson, Leverhulme and Pilgrim have been generous over many years in giving grants to museums for particular projects.

Finally, mention should be made of the *National Heritage Memorial Fund*, set up in 1980 under trustees and funded by the government. It has a good record of helping museums, national and non-national, to acquire and conserve works for which their own purchase grants were insufficient, but its terms of reference also include the built and the natural environment.

This paper first appeared in Museums and Galleries Commission (1992) Museum Matter, *London: HMSO, pp. 13–21.*

16

The National Audit Office report on museums: Britain's museums 'deliver the product'

Laura Suffield

The national museums and galleries in the UK account for one-third of the visits and one-third of the staffing involved in museums. They are substantially funded by central government and therefore carefully monitored. Yet the measure of any museum's performance is a difficult affair as it involves both quantitative and qualitative judgements. However, there are some fairly straightforward approaches to looking at museums, of which the counting and profiling of museum visitors is one. This form of research is dependent on questionnaire survey, which is not without its shortcomings. Nevertheless, useful data can be generated.

In the summer of 1993, the National Audit Office conducted research into the visitors to the national museums and galleries. The findings were published in a report: National Audit Office (1993) Department of National Heritage, National Museums and Galleries: Quality of Service to the Public, London: HMSO. The Art Newspaper reported and commented on the findings.

The results of a detailed survey of five of Britain's top museums and galleries have shown that 98 per cent of visitors are satisfied or very satisfied with what is on offer. An analysis of the survey was published by the independent control body, the National Audit Office (NAO) this summer.

The NAO's role is to certify the accounts of all government departments and other public sector bodies including national museums. The NAO's head is obliged to report to Parliament on the economy and efficiency with which these bodies use their resources. It is paid by the government for each report and is therefore keen to obtain such projects. While it is not suggested that the findings of such reports are in any way affected by this relationship, it is certainly the case that their approach and language closely reflect current government thinking: 'It's within the spirit of the Citizen's Charter', was one comment.

Inevitably, in post-Thatcherite Britain, the report is couched in terms of the market: thus the consultants employed to assess the British Museum, the Natural History Museum, the National Gallery, the National Museum of Science and Industry and the National Portrait Gallery looked at 'standard of marketing, of customer orientation, of presentation and of delivery of the product'.

In order to back up the findings of the report an independent visitor survey was carried out by a market research company in May 1992 to provide comparative visitor opinions and statistics.

Table 16.1 Most visited museums and galleries in the UK

	Ranking	1991 visits
1	British Museum, London	5,061,000
2	National Gallery, London	4,280,000
3	Tate Gallery, London	1,816,000
4	Natural History Museum, London	1,500,000
5	Science Museum, London	1,328,000
6	Victoria and Albert Museum, London	1,066,000
7	Glasgow Art Gallery and Museum	893,000
8	Royal Academy, London	808,000
9	Jorvik Viking Centre, York	791,000
10	Birmingham Museum and Art Gallery	754,000
11	National Museum of Photography, Film and Television, Bradford	711,000
12	Castle Museum, Nottingham	695,000
13	Tate Gallery, Liverpool	597,000
14	National Portrait Gallery, London	590,000
15	National Maritime Museum, London	588,000

Table 16.2 Profile of adult visitors

Percentage of visitors	Total	British Museum	National Gallery	National Portrait Gallery	Natural History Museum	Science Museum
First time visitors	61	61	55	55	65	70
UK residents	46	33	48	62	63	54
North American residents	24	36	23	19	11	13
One visitor in party	37	34	48	52	25	31
Two visitors in party	40	41	40	41	46	37
Visitors accompanied by children	14	9	4	1	42	32
Social class						
AB Professional, Manager	45	49	42	53	34	44
C1 Office Workers Junior Professions	41	35	46	36	50	38
C2 Skilled Manual	8	9	5	7	10	12
DE Unskilled, Retired	6	7	7	4	6	6
Aged under 35	44	38	46	41	54	48
Aged 35–54	37	40	32	30	36	38
Aged 55 and over	19	22	22	29	10	14
Male	52	52	46	45	51	65
Female	48	48	54	55	49	35

Inevitably the nature of the questions dictated the outcome of the survey, and thus its presentation of the current role of Britain's museums. Among the worrying aspects of the report is the lack of any reference to the research role of museums or to the use of funds for the care (rather than display) of collections. While the importance of revenue generated by museum publications was noted (£2 million per year at the British Museum) no mention was made of how this is or could be used.

The report highlights five major museums and galleries, of which three, the National Gallery, National Portrait Gallery and the British Museum, operate a free entry policy, while the remaining two, the Science and Natural History Museums charge visitors. It is notable that the survey did not yield any results to suggest that those places which charge entry fees offer higher quality of service. Highest visitor satisfaction was in fact found at the National Gallery where 83 per cent were 'very satisfied'. That institution also saw the highest rise in visitor number – up 15 percent – during the period surveyed. Competing within the marketplace is clearly required of the modern museum. Paragraph twelve of the reports introduction recommends that institutions 'undertake further comparisons, particularly with other major visitor attractions, when planning services'. This is particularly pertinent to independent museums which have to assess their appeal in relation to other tourist attractions. One commentator noted that the Ironbridge Gorge Museum (devoted to Britain's industrial history) recently assessed that it could charge no more than half the entry fee of Alton Towers, the nearby Disney-type amusement park.

The report focuses determinedly on generalist visitors, of whom less than 5 per cent participated in specialist seminars, guided tours and lectures. There was little emphasis on those using the collections for research: there was no reference, for example, to the National Gallery's computer facilities. The report also attaches high importance to numbers of visitors, as this is the most obvious performance indicator.

No survey can report on what is not offered, or no longer offered. The number of visitors no longer consulting a particular expert or department whose services have been cut back over recent years, cannot be calculated, but it is nonetheless part of the overall picture. The shift in the balance of power out of the hands of curators and into management which has radically affected a number of Britain's institutions in the last ten years, is specifically referred to in paragraph nine of the report's conclusion which states that: 'Some institutions considered that, in former years, curatorial dominance of planning decisions had not always resulted in priority being given to service to the public. Changes were such that institutions no longer consider this an impediment to improvements in service'. This rather chilling statement at the very least begs the question of whether 'curatorial dominance' is desirable or not (clearly not in the opinion of the NAO) as well as implying that it is a thing of the past. Overall, the report yields a wealth of interesting and valuable data. The museum with the highest budget for education is the Natural History Museum which has £767,000 to spend, although the greatest number of school-age visitors is seen at the Science Museum. Only one in eight visitors picks up a programme of events and only one in twelve buys a guide book. Despite this, revenue from publications can be a major source of income for the bigger museums. Average spending per visitor ranges from 92p at the Natural History Museum shop to 56p at the National Portrait Gallery, with £1 recommended as a reasonable target by the present report.

Of the visitors questioned for the report, three out of five were first-time visitors. Just under half were resident in the UK and a quarter were from North America. About 94 per cent were from the ABC social classes which compares with 68 per cent of the population as a whole. Overall, 43 per cent of visits were to see a specific object or part of the collection. Some 10 per cent of visitors were prompted to attend by advertising and publicity – a high take-up rate in advertising terms.

A number of museums have looked abroad to institute new approaches. Thus the Science Museum has studied alternative approaches to warding at the Louvre while staff at the Natural History Museum have been sent on 'customer care' training courses at the Disney Corporation.

A survey of 172 museums, commissioned by the Museums Association, has revealed that more than half those surveyed consider that their education services are under serious threat. As more schools in the UK take over the running of their own budgets, a number may decide they cannot afford museum services.

This paper first appeared in The Art Newspaper *(October 1993). Copyright* The Art Newspaper, *1993.*

17

Public palaces or private places?

Barbara Woroncow

In the UK, the best overviews of museum provision often come from those who have first hand experience, yet can also stand back and take a view. This is particularly true of this paper, written by Barbara Woroncow, Director of Humberside and Yorkshire Museums Council. Given at the Museums Association's conference in 1992, it discusses the realities of local authority museum provision and the uncertain futures such museums face. The paper is essentially positive, practical and realistic – with sound advice on strategies for survival.

Museums have been deeply affected by recent changes in the local authority environment, most of which have been the result of central government intervention or legislation. These changes are largely outside the control of museums, but they must adapt to the new environment if they are to survive. Since 1979 the government has espoused the cause of freedom and choice for *individuals*, but it has sought to centralize and formalize the control of all kinds of *organizations*.

A NEW ENVIRONMENT

How far have museums been affected by key changes in local authority working practices?

Nearly all museums are familiar with *limits on expenditure* as a result of restrictive Standard Spending Assessments, however enigmatically they may be calculated (see *Museums Journal* June 1991: 37; May 1992: 10; September 1992: 17). However, tough as these cuts may be for individual museum services, museums are not usually singled out for unduly harsh treatment. Special pleading simply will not work in the face of unavoidable cuts and in such circumstances professional intransigence can lead to irreparable harm.

To defend and justify their budgets, museum staff must be ready to quantify the social, educational and economic benefits that museums bring. They must also be sensitive to changes in political philosophy. Throughout the 1980s museums played a leading role in tourism development, but now local communities are concentrating more on services for local communities. The range of benefits which museums provide can be highlighted in turn to support changing requirements.

Local authorities are changing *from providers to enablers*. Their role is now to identify the needs of their local poll or council tax payers, specify the services that are required and then ensure that the services are delivered to standard. The result of this separation between 'client' and 'contractor' roles is that many services which used to be provided in-house are being put out to tender. Taken to an extreme conclusion, a local authority could meet only once a year to award contracts for services for the following year.

Such an extreme scenario is unlikely, and in practice there would have to be at least a core of staff to monitor service delivery, but some authorities, such as Southampton, have already begun to introduce internal client contractor splits, with the museum service working within 'service level agreements' or to specific targets that are closely monitored. Local authorities are not yet under any legal compulsion to tender their museum services competitively (compulsory competitive tendering – CCT) but, if they wish to do so, they are able to put virtually all their services, including museums, out to tender. Poole is one of the few authorities that has chosen to do this.

It is useful for museums to prepare a detailed specification of their services as an internal management tool. Quantifying the services provided, the standards to which they are delivered and the resources required can provide an objective method of self-appraisal. It also provides the basis for establishing appropriate targets for service delivery.

There is a risk that local authorities may take things to extremes and try to abnegate their duty to care for their museum collections by attempting to hand responsibility for them to other organizations without providing adequate revenue funding. There are elements of this in recent restructures in Kent (see *Museums Journal* July 1992: 10) and it highlights the need for clarification of the law relating to collections that local authorities 'own', or hold in trust for the public.

On a more positive note, the *increased emphasis on customer care* (or customer orientation) is an area where museum and local authority interests coincide. Museums have always sought to provide accessible, user-friendly services. However, curators' perceptions of the user-friendliness of the service may differ significantly from those of the wider public! Far more effort has to be put into training front-of-house staff and all museums, even those on very tight budgets, must carry out regular market research. Market research is not just a frill, it is an essential component of a public service. Not least, it is only by obtaining regular feedback that museums will be able to demonstrate the level of appreciation and support for their activities.

Local authorities increasingly require *tighter control of resources*. In this area museums often fall down by ignoring their most expensive input: staffing. The real cost of services can only be established through regular time-logging by all staff, from director to part-time attendant. I still hear that old chestnut, 'we mounted the exhibition for only £500', a claim that ignores the fact that inefficient use of labour probably added another £25,000. It is simply not economic for high-salaried staff to Letraset labels for days on end. It is absolutely essential to ensure that staffing costs are balanced with a suitable working budget, even if that equation leads to some harsh decisions. Posts may have to be lost in order to provide enough money for those that remain to carry out their duties; otherwise the museum will go into a spiral of decline as inadequate funds lead to poor quality services, leading again to further budget cuts.

Corporate planning is often seen by museums as a threat, but it can enable museum services to take greater control of their own destinies, rather than being victims of circumstance. If there is a clear plan of what needs to be done, in what order and at what cost, it is far easier to argue for resources both within the local authority and externally. Museum services should also see whether they can contribute to furthering the local authority's overall objectives (see *Museums Journal* September 1992: 20).

In many ways *performance measurement* is an extension of things museums have done for years. Numbers of visitors, school parties, enquiries and exhibitions are all performance measures of long standing. However, the government's over-riding concern with value for money means that the cost-effectiveness of these services will now have to be measured. To do this, museums must argue for appropriate performance measures, which include collection management standards, rather than ones like those proposed recently by the Audit Commission (see *Museums Journal* October 1992: 9).

Greater management flexibility is a development that museums should welcome. It allows more flexible approaches to the employment and reward of staff. Museum staff will have to be increasingly multiskilled to cope with changing demands. In particular, entrepreneurial skills are now positively welcomed in most local authorities. Few other local authority services have the capacity to generate such positive media coverage and authorities will welcome newspaper stories about new museum successes as a refreshing contrast to the usual diet of reports about unfilled holes in the road.

However, some new management practices threaten museum services in other ways. In larger services, budgets and responsibilities may be totally devolved to site managers. But if this is done without strong leadership then there may be duplication and fragmentation of the service, and there may be inadequate resources to instigate strategic or service-wide projects. In the words of one curator with totally devolved management: 'Devolved management is only helpful if a service is flush with money. Where resources are tight, all the sites will operate on a two-shillings-and-sixpence Blu-tack standard.'

The final key development in local authority practice is the growth of *partnership arrangements*. These are very much a political flavour of the month and it is important that they are carried out within an overall framework of a museum policy. Arguably, there are already too many museums competing for the available collections, resources and visitors; yet we still receive about one proposal per week for a new museum somewhere in Yorkshire and Humberside alone. Too many of these proposals involve ill-conceived 'heritage' projects at the expense of existing museums and their contents.

Many local authorities appreciate the important role played by independent museums, both large and small, in their areas; some have established curatorial posts on a district- or county-wide basis to advise and support volunteer-run museums. Some local authorities assist independent museums by releasing staff to act as curatorial advisers for registration. (Indeed, registration has been the most important single benefit of the last decade for local authority museums themselves.) Conversely, the voluntary sector may have an increasing role to play in the management of some carefully selected aspects of local authority museum services, as recently shown by new arrangements at the transport museum in Bournemouth.

However, partnerships between local authorities and other bodies, including voluntary ones, will come under much more careful scrutiny, if not actual contractual arrangements, so independent museums will need to develop their own forward plans as a basis for future support.

SURVIVAL STRATEGIES

The above eight points summarize key recent changes in the local authority environment. Other changes loom, such as the review of local government (see p. 111). Indeed, we should not assume that local authorities will retain responsibility for all their current functions. Already colleges of further and higher education have gone, and schools now have the chance to opt out. For museums, some have suggested independent trust status as a possibility. But trust status is a non-starter for most local authority museum services unless there is guaranteed revenue funding for core functions. Museums are not simply today's services, they are also tomorrow's heritage. If, like schools, museums could opt out, would there also be 'hit squads' brought in by government to sort out bad management?

Sadly, while uncertainty about the future structure of local government continues, many museum services suffer a type of planning blight. Local authorities are reluctant to take decisions, even on schemes that have been long planned. Some projects will be set back by up to five years, if they are ever started at all.

In difficult times, museum staff must maintain a clear vision of their core values. But to be able to defend these values museums must first put their own houses in order. A recent survey of industrial and social history collections in Yorkshire and Humberside has shown that many of the problems faced by museums were caused by poor curatorial practice, not necessarily by a lack of resources (see *Museums Journal* July 1992: 19).

In practice the success of a museum service depends on the personal charisma, advocacy skills and management ability of the senior member of museum staff.

If museums are to survive in the new flexible contract culture then they will need the best possible quality of leadership. It is therefore alarming to note the repeated waves of restructures that have taken place within local authorities, many of which have led to a downgrading of senior museum posts. Museum directorships have disappeared recently in Lincolnshire, Brighton and Portsmouth, to name but three of many. The over-riding factor in most restructures is to save money, but in many cases there can be no net benefit because of lost opportunities, unrealized potential for income generation and, most importantly, lower quality of public service.

To summarize, in this rapidly changing environment, there are several strategies that museums should adopt:

- Get to grips with the new contract-culture jargon.
- Justify benefits clearly – you are not a special case.
- Quantify what your service actually does and the resources needed to maintain specified standards.
- Carry out regular market research – and act on the findings.
- Cost activities properly (including staff time) and ensure that a working budget is maintained.
- Develop a clear, costed forward plan and ensure that it fits into the authority's over-all objectives.
- Take the initiative in establishing appropriate performance measures.
- Capitalize on entrepreneurial skills and media contacts.
- Encourage the authority to adopt a policy that takes account of all museum provision in the area.
- Improve advocacy and management skills.
- Establish essential core values for the museum service.

I would not go so far as to say that museums are endangered species, but they will have to adopt a chameleon strategy in order to survive. They will have to learn to blend in with the current demands of their working environment by means of efficient surface camouflage, while maintaining the same core values under the skin. Like the chameleon they will have to learn to seize swiftly the passing insects of opportunity in order to sustain their growth. Only by adopting such an approach will we be able to ensure that our museums continue to remain public palaces of pleasure, and do not become private places of profit.

MUSEUMS AND THE LOCAL GOVERNMENT REVIEW

The underlying purpose of the review of local government in England, Scotland and Wales is, to quote the Department of the Environment's (DoE's) Policy Guidance to the Local Government Commission for England, 'to secure effective and convenient local government . . . having regard to the need to reflect the identities and interests of local communities'.

Factors relevant to community identity are specifically defined as including history, topography and cultural affiliations. Of all local authority services, museums are uniquely placed to reflect such aspirations.

The museum community can also take comfort that, unlike previous reorganizations of 1974 and 1986 (when the Greater London Council and the metropolitan counties were abolished), museum collections are at least mentioned in the policy guidance for *England*. This guidance specifically states that 'some functions such as archives and museums may require the development of small teams of experts for the maintenance of specialist assets such as collections and the commission should consider arrangements for their maintenance and management.' It is also reassuring to note that the Local Government Commission is required formally to consult the Museums and Galleries Commission.

I suspect that the review will result in a plethora of different arrangements with various sized unitary authorities in some areas and the continuation of two-tier systems in others. There will be a variety of district, county and joint services in a complex web of museum management. Much will depend on local circumstances, but many joint networks will probably be needed to maintain specialist skills, and joint committees may be recommended by the Local Government Commission in some areas.

In *Wales* the review process is much further advanced than in England. There is no equivalent of the Local Government Commission for England and there was little public consultation in the early stages. Draft proposals for about twenty-three unitary authorities have been put forward before any detailed consideration of service delivery has taken place. Principality-wide working groups representing counties, districts and the Welsh Office are now looking at this in more detail – one covering leisure, culture and the arts includes museum services in its remit.

The review process in *Scotland* mirrors that in Wales with a lack of public consultation during the early stages. In Scotland there are already three equivalents to unitary authorities – for the Western Isles, Orkney and Shetland. These demonstrate the potential variability of future administrative arrangements: in one case museums come under education, in another planning. In the third they have just been transferred from education to planning. The single-tier metropolitan districts in England also demonstrate enormous structural variety.

In the process of reorganization the key concern must be for the care and integrity of museum collections. It is vital that irreplaceable material held by local authorities on behalf of the public should be properly safeguarded and the Museums Association will be doing all it can to ensure that its needs are considered properly. (For more details of the local government review see *Museums Journal* November 1992: 8, 10.)

This paper first appeared in Museums Journal *(December 1992), pp. 27–9.*

18

Purpose of museums and special characteristics of independents

V. T. C. Middleton

Those museums which constitute the independent sector are known for their competitiveness and their high public profiles. In many respects, they have led the change to a form of provision which is more visitor orientated. Many independent museums were founded in the 1970s, when the need for some form of record of the changing industrial landscape was keenly felt and much encouraged. As the majority of these museums move into their second and third generation, the circumstances that fostered them no longer exist and their strength of purpose and direction is being well tested.

It is increasingly apparent that there is only an uneasy consensus on the underlying purpose of museums. There is certainly no agreement on how and by whom they should be financed, or on the most appropriate form of management, or the balance to be struck between caring for collections and caring for the public.

Although defining purpose appears simple, semantics assume an absurd importance and there is rich scope for academic dispute on the meaning of bland statements such as 'service to society and its development', and 'open to the public' (does open mean free?). But there is international agreement that museums are institutions which exist to collect, conserve, exhibit and interpret material evidence, and to do so for the public benefit. The interpretation of 'public benefit' may as easily incorporate enjoyment and entertainment, as study and education.

NO PURPOSE WITHOUT COMMUNICATION

The purpose of museums generally and independents in particular is not synonymous with education, knowledge, leisure or entertainment; it is a combination of these elements in which a common aim is selective communication of information and experiences to targeted groups of users who visit by choice, mainly at their leisure. Definitions of purpose not leading to survival have no meaning for independent museums and rising visitor numbers and revenue, especially through repeat visitors, is a key measure of achievement.

'Independent museums have learned that satisfaction in value-for-money terms is achieved by attracting a visitor's attention, stimulating interest, conveying information and thereby creating an experience. Another word for this . . . is communication. Indeed . . . without effective communication [in the language of the audience] museums have no purpose. . . . Therefore independent museums are fundamentally visitor orientated.'

BALANCING NEEDS OF VISITORS AND OTHER USERS WITH THE NEEDS OF COLLECTIONS

Neither the international definition of museums nor its present British variation offer any clues as to the appropriate *balance* to be struck between the traditional dominance of curatorial functions of collecting, conserving and research on the one hand; and newer visitor orientated functions of display and interpretation to give satisfaction and value for time and money, on the other. Defining and achieving a better balance will remain a key issue for museums over the next decade, accepting that there are minimum levels of curatorial care below which any compromises would put the essential purposes of museums at risk.

MISSION STATEMENT FOR INDEPENDENT MUSEUMS

This study is concerned with how independent museums can best respond to the forces of change influencing them over the next decade. Response means management decisions and action, on a stand alone basis and in collaboration with others. It is however clearly understood that the core purpose of museums is not management but the care and conservation of collections and objects. Accordingly the working party agreed the following mission statement for independent museums.

The mission

Based on conservation of collections and exercise of curatorial expertise and scholarship:

> To communicate and stimulate curiosity and fascination at the scope of human endeavour, culture and the natural environment, through an understanding of the evidence and significance of the past, in ways which relate to individuals' current aspirations for themselves

through creating enjoyable and satisfying access to and interactions with collections, by means of existing and new techniques of display and interpretation; to do so at times and in ways which simultaneously meet the changing needs and expectations of the public and other users, while ensuring the integrity of the artefacts for posterity.

The intended outcome

To enhance the attraction, value and frequency of museum usage in the lives of more people, whose choices and continued willingness to pay for their experiences (directly and indirectly) are the only means through which museums can survive and develop.

To enhance the role of museums in the life of the communities of their location.

THE NUMBER AND TYPE OF INDEPENDENT MUSEUMS IN THE UK

Recognizing that 'it seems to be impossible to arrive at an accurate and up to date figure for the number of local authority museums in the UK', it is not surprising that the exact number of independents is still an unknown quantity in 1990.

Drawing on the Museums Association Data-Base Project, the MGC refer to some 1,300 independents in a recent annual report. There is no firm validation for this figure, however, and it is known to be based on the widest possible trawl of addresses of institutions which might have been museums in 1985, and estimates based on postal questionnaires.

AIM has 750 members on its records at the end of 1989, although as PSI noted in a 1989 study, some of these are not museums but individuals and companies offering services. Having distributed a questionnaire to all members through AIM, PSI achieved 280 usable responses from active museums, which AIM subsequently estimated to account for around three-quarters of all the visitor numbers and revenue achieved in the sector.

Pending the production of better data, which is expected to emerge in 1992/3 through the current museums Registration Scheme, the working estimates below are provided to establish the approximate size and characteristics of independent museums in the UK. Table 18.1 notes that there are between 760 and 930 active independent museums in 1990. The range is consistent with the verified data from the Data-Base Project and the information for the UK collected annually by the five UK tourist boards. The total is less than current estimates indicate. In Table 18.1, the 45 steam railways operating in GB, are excluded.

Table 18.1 The estimated size and characteristics of independent museums in the UK

Estimated number of museums	%	Typical size in visits p.a.	Typical annual income p.a.	Typical staffing (full and part time)	Typical admission charge (1989 prices)
15–18	2	200,000+	£350,000+	16+	£2.50+
15–18	2	100,000–200,000	£200–300,000	10–15	£1.50–£2.50
55–70	7–8	30,000–100,000	£ 50–150,000	5–10	£0.75–£1.50
225–75	30	5,000– 30,000	£ 10–50,000	Under 5	Mostly under £0.75
450–550	60	Under 5,000	Under £7,500	Mostly volunteers	Mostly under £0.75 or free
760–931	100	16–18 million			

Source: PSI; BTA, *Visits to Tourist Attractions*; AIM; and author's estimates

The number of museums achieving over 30,000 visits per annum (85 to 106 establishments) is judged to be broadly accurate as is the larger number achieving 5,000 to 30,000 visits. It is the hundreds of smaller museums receiving less than 3000 visitors a year (8 a day on average) which are the unknown quantity. If there are more than 550, they are very small indeed and many would be unlikely to meet the requirements of the MGC Registration Scheme. Their capability and wish to organize themselves to respond to perceived change is likely to be very low.

THE CHARACTER OF INDEPENDENT MUSEUMS

AIM was founded in 1977 through the mutual recognition of needs and interests by a group of curators and directors, most of whom were involved in the formative years of museums opened since the 1960s. The origins and growth of the Association and its members are rooted in economic and social growth. Independents always were and still are a broad church. They are not bound by precise definitions or bureaucratic organization procedures; the spontaneity of the Association and its vigour owe much more to a spirit of community of interest than to the professional niceties of their vocation.

Diverse as they are by size and type, AIM members represent a distinctive group of institutions, typically owing their survival and growth to the determination of founder trustees, the first curators, and numerous friends and volunteers. Independent museums which overcame their initial difficulties were led by self-reliant pioneers, entrepreneurs, innovators of necessity, typically close to their roots. Many of the techniques they initiated for display and interpretation have since been adopted in the public sector.

Independents are typically alive to the needs of visitors as their principal means of survival and growth. Some are visitor responsive more by necessity than choice, but a user orientation gives important validity to their innovations. In the important objectives of collection policies, conservation and documentation, and overall commitment to exhibit for the benefit of the public, independents are increasingly indistinguishable from public sector museums of similar size. Most independent museums fit as easily into the current criteria drawn up by MGC for registration as public sector institutions.

The other main characteristic the independents have in common is that they are owned and administered by trusts or private owners, not by central or local government. The forms of charitable trust adopted by most independent museums have provided vital conduits for plural funding, and organization models increasingly being used in the public sector. Independents are not subordinate to administrative and political committees over which they have little influence. They often have severe financial problems but they are not at the mercy of unpredictable, restrictive public sector requirements, rigid accounting procedures, and the arbitrary spending limits which affected so many public sector museums in the last decade.

Although their resources are seldom adequate, independent museums are free to undertake all tasks within their broadly drawn objectives which they can finance through their own efforts. In the event of difficulty they may seek aid but cannot depend on the lifeline of public sector grants. On average, independents currently draw around a fifth of their annual revenue from national and local government and from statutory agencies and enjoy other support in kind, but this does not remove their essential independence of action.

At their best, independent museums are a splendidly British blend of opportunistic, creative flair and energy; they combine voluntary contributions and often determinedly amateur approaches with their professional skills. Inevitably with hundreds of very small museums, there are also many organizational weaknesses.

This paper first appeared in V. T. C. Middleton (1990) New Visions for Independent Museums in the UK, *Chichester, W. Sussex: The Association for Independent Museums.*

19

Higher concerns
Alan Warhurst *et al.*

The museum scene appears to be dominated by national, local authority and indepen-
dent museums. However, the universities in the UK hold both collections and museums
of international importance. The Fitzwilliam in Cambridge, the Ashmolean in Oxford,
the Manchester Museum and the Hunterian Museum in Glasgow spring easily to mind.
The university museums hold incomparable collections, yet since the early 1980s have
been required to find new senses of identity and purpose. This has not been easy, as the
parent universities have themselves been facing a series of severe financial difficulties.
Nevertheless, many university museums have survived these times remarkably well.

In this article, Alan Warhurst, the former Director of the Manchester Museum, considers
the progress made by university museums and the possibilities the future holds. His
themes are picked up by Rosemary Ewles, Penny Thomas and Charles Hunt.

In 1986, at the Museums Association annual conference in Aberdeen, the profession was
alerted to a state of crisis in university museums and collections in the United Kingdom
(see *Museums Journal* December 1986: p. 137). Part of that crisis, the insecurity of
university collections, had been highlighted by Newcastle University's sale of the greater
part of the George Brown collection of Pacific ethnography to the National Museum of
Ethnology in Osaka, Japan, in the same year. Newcastle was thought to be a secure home
but the university perceived that the collection had no further teaching or research purpose and disposed of it accordingly (see *Museums Journal* March 1990: p. 32). At about
the same time, several publications on university museums and collections were launched,
including pioneer surveys of university collections in London and the south-east of
England. Additionally, new thinking led to the formation of a University Museums Group
in 1987 and the introduction of 'special factor' funding by the University Grants Committee for certain university museums (see p. 121). Added to concern at the sale of collections
was the realization that universities were not recognizing their true importance. More
worrying still, it had become apparent that not enough was known about the existence,
content and whereabouts of university collections. These problems were further
compounded by government constraints on university finance during the 1980s.

The range of university museums and collections is considerable; all have a part to play
in preserving the nation's heritage. First, there are the major university museums in
Oxford, Cambridge, Manchester and Glasgow, which have centuries of museological
pedigree behind them. Second, there are the museums and collections which were
embraced by universities in the halcyon days of the 1950s and 1960s. Many of these were
private society collections or those of individuals. For these, universities – seemingly

wealthy, altruistic and stable educational institutions – looked set to provide a secure financial future. Such museums have nationally important collections of science, archaeology and the arts. And last, but not least, are the much larger number of departmental collections. At best these may still be curated to minimal standards but at worst they may have been long forgotten, once the person responsible for their aggregation has left the scene.

In the 1980s, proper concern was expressed at the lack of information about university owned collections which were not in recognized institutional museums. The George Brown collection is an obvious example. But how much more insecure are the sorts of collections which form the source material for research projects? When a postgraduate student or member of staff has left, there may be no curatorial input or resource support. And what of material which has been benefacted to a university by well-meaning alumni? In 1984, the Area Museum Service for south-eastern England led the way with its *Survey of University Museums in South Eastern England*. This was followed by its more detailed publication, *A Survey of Museums and Collections Administered by the University of London*. The baton was taken up by Scottish university curators and the Scottish Museums Council which, with support from the Museums and Galleries Commission (MGC), charitable trusts and Scottish University Principals, published the survey, *A World of Learning: University Collections in Scotland* (HMSO 1990: 29). In the same year the University Museums Group and the three area museum councils of northern England, supported by the MGC, the Universities Funding Council (UFC) and the Committee of Vice-Chancellors and Principals (CVCP), commissioned a survey of museums and collections in the eleven universities of northern England. Publication is due shortly. So far, all the surveys reveal greater numbers of collections of museum material than had previously been suspected. This is real progress and it is now possible to begin to talk realistically of a national audit of university collections. Much still remains to be done by extending the survey to the midlands, southern England and Wales, not to mention implementing the published surveys' recommendations. But the museum community, the public and the universities themselves are now aware of the large corpus of material held in this way. The surveys which remain to be carried out need new impetus and funding but another three or four years could see the national audit completed. If the future disposition of any of these surveyed collections is called into question, there is now a reference point for informed and rational consideration of what should happen.

AVOIDING DISPOSAL

Although universities have charitable status they are not registered charities. For the most part (but not in all cases), they own their museum collections and their buildings, and employ any staff connected with them. This indicates a presumptive right for the governing body of a university to dispose of any collection which it holds for what it perceives to be the benefit of the university.

There are two main, if imperfect, safeguards against the possible disposal of museum material by universities. One is knowledge of the existence of collections and informed public and academic opinion about them, something the surveys are achieving. The other is registration under the MGC Registration Scheme which implies that a university governing body accepts the commission's criteria and guidelines. While a handful of larger university institutions have been registered, the vast majority of such collections have problems meeting even the most basic standards of the present scheme. Public access, constitutional and financial security, documentation, among others, present difficulties (see pp. 120–1). The published surveys consistently recommend that universities accept responsibility for all collections on campus by providing arrangements for curation, an administrative framework and committee structure. The MGC clearly cannot register a collection in a university department where standards of curation fail to meet the required minimum. But where a university intends to subscribe to minimum standards and provides some administrative and resource framework for this to happen, then there is a case for at least provisional registration of such a 'university museum service'. The MGC registration committee needs to look more closely at this problem as soon as possible. Area museum councils need to extend sympathetic advice to universities in their areas to enable such development to take place.

As long as university museums or collections remain unregistered they are not only vulnerable to disposal, but may well remain ineligible for grants from the Museums and Galleries Commission, area museum councils, the Museums and Galleries Improvement Fund and perhaps, in due course, even from the National Lottery.

FINDING FUNDING

Both the methods and the extent of the funding of university museums and collections continue to provide problems. Even when large amounts of money were invested in the 1960s and 1970s, university museums were not well financed. During the 1980s funding for British universities was curtailed and in such circumstances no university museum is likely to receive better treatment than other university departments. Indeed the museum will be hard-pressed to hold its own in its claim to a share of the block grant received by a university from the UFC (see p. 121). University museums have more than their fair share of frozen posts, deteriorating buildings and collections and reduced or non-existent purchase grants.

Currently, the UFC notes the financial requirements of twenty-two museums or collections in fifteen universities. Finance for these is indicated as 'special factor' funding in the financial letter sent by the UFC to the university. This amount, although now identified, is not earmarked and the university is at liberty to pursue its own fiscal policy with regard to its museum. The amount of such special factor funding is based upon the university's Form 3 return of expenditure for the last year but one, indexed up to present-day values. In theory a museum listed in this way should be protected and level funding maintained. Most of the large university museums were among the first sixteen institutions in eleven universities so indicated as special factors in 1986 as a result of a joint initiative by the UGC and the MGC. In addition, six other collections were awarded special funds although these were only added to the special factor list in 1990 (see p. 121). Following recent legislation a new Higher Education Funding Council England (HEFC) will supplant the UFC from April 1993. Now is the time for a further exercise between the MGC and the new funding council to extend the list of university and departmental collections which may be financially assisted as special factors.

Natural science and science collections, which are under-represented in the present lists, should be given priority. The surveys will provide the information to extend this process further. Special factor funding means that universities shouldering the responsibility of holding part of the national heritage are not financially worse off for so doing. It is vital that such funding should be continued and extended. If the University of Newcastle's financial contribution to the Hancock Museum had been recognized for special factor funding (although the collections and the building admittedly do not belong to the university) then the university might not have needed to shed some of its financial responsibilities for that museum (see *Museums Journal* May 1992; 54).

University collections or museums, other than those listed for special factor funding, may well receive no special funds. Such collections are dependent upon whatever the university, or the department holding the collection, is prepared to do. Their plight is often desperate with little or no funds, no opportunity to become registered and no hope of attracting grants to improve their lot. With current university funding based upon research and teaching profiles, there can be little hope of ameliorating their condition without some new consideration of the situation of the UFC/HEFC and the MGC.

In the present financial climate it is unlikely that taking university museums and collections out of the university system will be of any help, unless accompanied by some massive injection of finance to bring such museums into line with national institutions. Additional funding from local authorities, which may well be struggling to maintain their own institutions, is largely unrealistic. Commercial sponsorship is fine for exhibitions or special features but is unlikely to be of help in funding core functions of a university museum or assisting a collection with little or no public appeal.

At least, to remain within the system may have some benefits. Many universities are now running large scale appeal schemes and university museums and collections ought to have a call on these. Museums with research-active and teaching staff may lay claim to a share of the university budget in respect of such activities if mechanisms can be established for this to happen. There are also some indirect advantages accruing to a museum which is part of a university: a scholarly environment, access to libraries and equipment, ready consultation with academic colleagues and students and the possibility of maintaining premises, frequently listed and historic buildings.

Amid these difficulties, two welcome developments may be noted. Following the 1988 review of earth sciences, the UFC has recently injected substantial funds for one-off and recurrent expenditure, amounting to £1.662 million and £305,000 respectively, at five Earth Science Collection Centres based in museums or university departments at Glasgow, Manchester, Birmingham, Oxford and Cambridge.

New storage, equipment and staff will enable these to develop as centres of excellence and become the gathering point for other university geological collections in five regions of Britain. Some members of the geological community feel this rationalization might have been handled differently. But a comprehensive exercise involving geological collections in the United Kingdom was clearly beyond the writ of the UFC. Each of the five centres has improved staff, storage and equipment resources and the safety net is now in place to house any university's geological collection whose owners do not feel able to sustain it. This is to the good.

Second, the Museums and Galleries Improvement Fund provided by the (then) Office of Arts and Libraries (OAL), the Department of Education and Science (DES) and the Wolfson Foundation and Family Trust contains a very large element to assist university museums and galleries. Providing the required matching funds by universities for such incentive grants may present serious problems, but several institutions have already benefited and it is hoped that the present scale of such grant-aid will continue (see *Museums Journal* June 1992: 10).

Addressing the annual general meeting of the University Museums Group in April this year, Graham Greene, chair of the Museums and Galleries Commission, called for an enquiry into the problems of university museums and collections. He rightly pointed out that the reluctance of the (then) OAL to become involved in what it saw as the affairs of universities and a similar reluctance on the part of the DES to become involved with museums was a major obstacle to improvement. Let us hope that the new Department of National Heritage, with its wider remit, will feel no such inhibitions and that the new government can break the log-jam. No solution can even be considered unless representatives of the two ministries are prepared to sit down and discuss the matter together.

The recent Museums Association initiative in establishing a working party on higher education and museums is also welcome. The working party is charged with producing a policy statement for the Museums Association and much of this will be concerned with university museums and collections. Of equal importance will be the working party's views on research and scholarship in museums which may remind us that amid current pressures on museums to become popular, competent research and sound scholarship form the basis for all our interpretive work.

The profile of university museums and collections has never been higher. We need to encourage and maintain the high level of debate in government, the Higher Education Funding Council, the Museums and Galleries Commission, the Museums Association and among all those concerned with museums, research and scholarship.

REGISTERING UNIVERSITY MUSEUMS AND COLLECTIONS
Rosemary Ewles

By April 1992 there were fifty-four university entries on the Museums and Galleries Commission (MGC) register. Some of these museums and art galleries, like the Fitzwilliam, the Ashmolean or the Hunterian Museums, are established museum institutions within a university. For these, with their own formally constituted governing bodies, registration has not posed any unusual difficulties.

On the other hand, bringing collections not held within formal museums into the ambit of the scheme has proved more problematic. Each university presents individual problems and different potential solutions, but commonly a university submits a pan-university application for the university as a whole. This enables the MGC to consider registering the university as a museum authority as long, of course, that it meets minimum standards in respect of named collections.

This assumes that the university can satisfy the MGC registration committee of the following:

- That arrangements for the curatorial care of and public access to each individual collection have been made.
- That the university has adopted an institutional museum policy (which includes an acceptable disposal policy).
- That there is some appropriate form of collections management committee to oversee museum policy and advise the university's governing body on museum matters.

In a number of cases registration has stimulated the initiation of such a framework. It has also been instrumental in linking 'orphan' collections with existing museums to provide curatorial care.

However, this approach leaves room for a number of concerns. In the eyes of the Museums Association a museum is an 'institution which collects, documents, preserves, exhibits and interprets material evidence and associated information for the public benefit'. So how far can a group of departmental collections, some of which might have no display or other interpretive facilities, be considered to meet this definition? A university may have a responsible attitude towards preserving and curating its research collections, but does this necessarily mean that it has any positive policies for encouraging public use? Will pastoral care mechanisms and university collection committees place undue burdens on the few existing university curatorial staff without the likelihood of additional funding to support this area of university activity? Many of these questions remain unanswered.

Since departmental collections outside a museum rarely fulfil registration criteria individually, the committee welcomes moves towards a university-wide collection policy and management framework. Indeed this is vital if only to prevent hundreds of collections in UK universities slipping beyond the reach of registration. However, as a corollary, a university must convince the committee that positive intentions towards its collections are more than just token. University initiatives must contribute towards creating a working museum policy, one which will build a 'museum purpose' into an amorphous organization whose primary aim is not care of collections. Each university governing body is asked to adopt the disposal policy outlined in the registration guidelines on the understanding that this will apply to all collections named in the application. In relation to one class of material which has been the subject of concern recently, it should be noted that no university has yet included its library collections in an application for museum registration.

Although a *modus vivendi* has been established for university museums and collections, the first phase of the Registration Scheme will be completed with the majority of university collections still outside the registration framework. Added to this number is the as yet unknown number of collections held by polytechnics which, following the abolition of the distinction between university and polytechnic, will now be assimilated into the university system. And the problem remains. How will these 300 or so collections be preserved and interpreted without, for the most part, any formal funding structure? Only twenty-two museums or collections in fifteen universities are recognized as constituting special factors in grants made to their parent universities by the University Funding Council. Until this wider matter is resolved and other changes in higher education funding assimilated, some of the useful developments initiated by registration are unlikely to progress.

UNIVERSITY FUNDING COUNCIL
Penny Thomas

In October 1985 a circular letter was sent to all universities inviting them to inform the University Grants Committee (UGC) of what special factors they wished to be considered for funding.

Special factors were defined as 'commitments which the institution concerned cannot shed, or which the UGC would not wish it to shed, but which do not fit easily into those parts of the funding model that cover teaching and research'. Museums, galleries and observatories were included as one heading in the section covering facilities provided partly for national or regional use or for use by the local community. However, universities were warned that they would not receive an allowance unless these commitments were 'exceptional'.

In January 1986 Andrew Martindale, professor of visual arts at the University of East Anglia, wrote a background paper for the UGC on university galleries, museums and collections. He advised the chief executive to consult the Museums and Galleries Commission for information, advice and comment. The commission was able to supply a list of those collections which it felt were of 'undoubted national distinction'. On the shortlist were 76 out of the 148 known collections.

The main committee of the UGC accepted that twenty-two of these collections should be funded – sixteen via special factor funding, six via individual departments. This meant that fifteen universities received financial support for their collections starting in the 1986/7 academic year. In 1988 there was a review of earth sciences which included looking at the geographically disparate nature of collections. The review recommended rationalizing the collections in five major centres. The UGC funded moving and rehousing costs and then added these five to the special factor list from 1991.

A year earlier, the six collections which since 1986 had been specially funded through individual departments were added to the special factor list. This was necessary because money for teaching was now openly calculated on a number of students multiplied by a set-price basis. This made it impossible to account for collection funding except by showing it in the list of special factors. No additional funding was involved. Until 1990, the University Funding Council, as it was then called, had chosen not to publicize full details of its special funding to university collections, but in 1990 this policy was changed and the full list of the twenty-two collections was made public.

In April 1989 the UGC was separated from the Department of Education and Science and changed its name to the Universities Funding Council (UFC). Although the funding methodology was changed, special factor funding for museums and galleries was to continue.

Special factor funding originally covered the total expenditure of the museum excluding the cost of premises. Initially, the exact value of the grant was based on information received from the universities for 1984/5, increased by a small percentage each year. Now, however, the latest available returns of expenditure are used as the basis for UFC calculations.

Sir Peter Swinnerton-Dyer, former chief executive of the UFC, articulated the organization's views in a letter to a university museum director in 1986. 'It is not the job of the UGC [as it was then] to adopt a general responsibility for development of museums.' In fact UGC never informed universities exactly how much money was allocated for specific special factors. They were just given a total. Since the academic notification of funds for 1991/2 universities have been told how much money has been awarded to them for museums and collections on the list. However, the UFC does not interfere with universities' internal distribution of money.

Although the UGC can have no general responsibility towards university museums, it does recognize the contribution that they make to higher education in particular and also to the nation. Hence, this was one of the special factors which the UFC continued with after its inception in 1989.

The Further and Higher Education Act 1992 will affect future funding agreements. A new Higher Education Funding Council England will come into existence in April 1993. This will fund all the universities, polytechnics and higher education colleges in England, leaving Scottish and Welsh institutions to be funded by separate councils (for details of Scotland see p. 123). Since the university and polytechnic sectors are allocated money in different ways, creating a new council involves reviewing all former funding arrangements. This is a lengthy process involving consultation with all interested parties and no decisions have yet been made. The new council will be responsible for higher education funding from the start of the 1993 academic year.

In 1986, the UFC began to support the following museums, galleries and collections:

• University of Bath: Holburne Museum and Crafts Study Centre.

- University of Birmingham: Barber Institute of Fine Arts.
- University of Cambridge: Fitzwilliam Museum, Museum of Archaeology and Anthropology.
- University of Durham: Durham University Oriental Museum.
- University of East Anglia: Sainsbury Centre for Visual Arts.
- University of Hull: Hull University Art Collection*
- University of Kent: Centre for Study of Cartoons and Caricature.*
- University of London: Courtauld Institute Galleries, Petrie Museum of Egyptian Archaeology, Percival David Foundation.
- University of Manchester: Manchester Museum, Whitworth Art Gallery.
- University of Newcastle upon Tyne: Greek Museum*
- University of Oxford: Ashmolean Museum of Art and Archaeology, Pitt Rivers Museum, Bate Collection of Historical Instruments*
- University of Reading: Institute of Agricultural History and Museum of English Rural Life, Ure Museum of Greek Archaeology*
- Aberdeen University: Marischal Museum.
- Edinburgh University: Russell Collection of Early Keyboard Instruments*
- University of Glasgow: Hunterian Museum and Art Gallery.

* These collections had been receiving extra funding since 1986, but they had not appeared on the special factor list because funding was allocated via individual departments. Due to changes in funding arrangements, these collections appeared on the special factor list from 1990.

In addition to the above, special factor funding was accorded to the following universities museums for their Earth Science Collections Centres, from 1991:

- University of Birmingham: Department of Geology.
- University of Cambridge: Sedgwick Museum of Geology.
- University of Manchester: Manchester Museum.
- University of Oxford: University Museum.
- Glasgow University: Hunterian Museum and Art Gallery.

UNIVERSITY MUSEUMS IN SCOTLAND
Charles Hunt

After more than a decade of enforced change and reduced funding, Scottish universities face continued instability. New higher education legislation is set to abolish the distinction between universities and other institutions of higher education which will add four more to the eight existing universities. A new single funding council will be responsible for all Scottish higher education and the increased number of universities will be fishing in the same funding pool. They will be given less money to teach more students with fewer staff.

All this would seem to augur ill for university museums and departmental collections, especially where collections are no longer directly related to teaching or research but are still of historic value. That said, it is perhaps too easy to be pessimistic about the situation. Surprisingly, evidence from the past five years shows hard-pressed Scottish universities actively supporting their collections and showing little inclination to put them in cold storage or make panic disposals.

Any improvements to the situation facing university collections in Scotland are due largely to the commitment of Frank Willet, former Director of the Hunterian Museum and Art Gallery. Without his energy and inspiration, the threats of the early 1980s might well have turned into the grim reality of sale and closure. Since his 1986 article (*Museums Journal* December 1986: 141), there has been slow but substantial progress. This has culminated in two events which, in concert, have clarified the agenda for managing this important part of Scottish material culture. In 1990 the Scottish Universities Collections Research project published *A World of Learning*. Researched and written by Laura Drysdale with financial, practical and moral support from the Scottish University Principals, the Scottish Museums Council and other interested organizations, the report provides a template for managing university collections and measuring progress. Also, its recommendations largely anticipate and reinforce the model of good practice implicit in the Museums and Galleries Commission's museum registration process (see p. 120). Both the report and the registration scheme alerted individual universities to the value of their collections and the need to reveal the anomalous machinery by which they are administered.

Now all eight universities have established committees or groups to oversee the welfare of collections and determine policy towards them. Six of the eight have designated posts, full-time or part-time, responsible for implementing collection policy and reporting through committee to the university court. (In Scottish universities the court is responsible for the structure of the university, while the senate governs the academic aspect of the institution. This means the court is the ultimate governing body.) All of them have been given, or are seeking, registered status. The University Museums in Scotland group, whose membership comprises all staff responsible for collections, provides some solidarity and enables museum staff to articulate common museum concerns to university authorities.

In short, the Scottish situation reflects the virtues of a small country where close-knit ties exist between colleagues within universities and between universities and the wider museum world. But the financial situation remains critical. Edinburgh provides a salutary reminder of the continuing fragility of the status of our collections. Here the university is facing pressure to relieve a massive financial deficit by selling precious items from its collections (see *Museums Journal* May 1992: 14). The arguments against such disposals are worn smooth with repetition.

This paper first appeared in Museums Journal *(July 1992), pp. 27–31.*

Part 4
The museums profession

20

Curatorial identity

Gaynor Kavanagh *et al.*

The museum workforce is constituted by a range of specialists in both subject and service fields. However, curators still have the key role. With so many different types of museums, museum collections and audience expectations, uniformity within the profession can be found more in a jointly held, but broad philosophy about the value of museums than in specific sets of skills and tasks. The museums profession is an 'open' one: it does not have controlled entry as do medicine and the law. It attracts to it people with a very wide variety of qualifications, talents and backgrounds. Moreover, it is in a continuous and possibly very healthy state of expansion and development.

In this first set of papers, published in the Museums Journal *in October 1992, a variety of perspectives and experiences of modern day museum practice are brought together. They encompass both the worries and the new approaches to be found in museums today.*

Defining 'curatorship' can be as unprofitable as defining the 'museum'. Definitions certainly help clear the mind, but are by their very nature reductionist and lead to often tedious lists of functions, lacking any reference to the spirit, scale or standards of the task. Yes, a curator is someone who is central to the museum and who, on the public's behalf, studies a collection, adds to it, documents it, interprets it and enlarges a body of knowledge for a wide audience with very different needs. But there are issues of effectiveness, appropriateness and comprehensiveness; titles and definitions are not sufficient in themselves. Ultimately, it is achievement (in intellectual, educational and resource terms) that counts.

Perhaps, given all that museums went through in the 1980s, the fact that the term 'curator' is still being used at all is to be wondered at. That is not to say that the tasks that make up curatorship, as the term is traditionally understood, are no longer essential: far from it. But museums are, and always have been, highly complex organizations calling on many different forms of 'museum professionalism'. Strictly defined curatorial work is pivotal, but not necessarily exclusive. The museum profession now includes people with a tremendous range of discipline and service specialisms. A museum world without education officers, conservators, registrars and audience advocates would be as unthinkable as one without archaeologists, geologists and costume experts.

Further, museums are in themselves very diverse; different agendas exist and give rise to distinctly different orientations. Curatorial identity is embedded in this and as soon as identity emerges, clashes of personality are sure to follow.

The lack of unity was recognized as far back as 1894 when James Paton declared at the Museums Association's conference that there were two types of curator: 'the specialist who belongs to the great public and national museums, and the provincial curator who has to do everything in his own much embracing institution'.

Nearly 100 years on, such differences still exist. For example, those engaged in independent museums may accentuate the value of their commercial contract with the public; the community museum person may be more concerned with cultural empowerment through the museum; while curators in larger public museums may be more concerned with the ethical responsibilities for collections. This is not to say that these values and the identities they produce cannot be shared: they often are; but most museum people will find themselves having to declare a priority.

Conflicting, even directly opposing, views about more or less the same type of museum work are nothing new. In 1919, E. E. Lowe and Martin Conway, on behalf of the Museums Association, were arguing vehemently to a dumbfounded permanent secretary at the Board of Education that museums were 'not fundamentally educational institutions' and that acquisitions were not made 'to educate some person or persons unknown'. In contrast, six years later, H. L. Madison laid before the Museums Association the code of conduct developed for the American Association of Museums with the imperative that the value of museums was in 'direct proportion to the service they render the emotional and intellectual life of the people'.

Effective provision hinges on the successful combination of different specialist skills, built upon a deeply held, common understanding of the roles and potential of museums in society. To underestimate this imperils both museums and professionalism alike. With their largely monopolistic responsibility for collections, museums are dependent, to a substantial degree, on the human capital which is their workforce. In turn, the workforce is dependent upon the quality of debate, the extent of knowledge and the training on which it can draw.

Postgraduate training has been developed to emphasize the common ground of museum activity – collection management, communication and management – while still giving people the proper opportunity for subject- or service-specialist development. The effects of this are gently becoming apparent: a workforce that sees itself as a profession constituted of interdependent skills with an over-arching sense of social and educational purpose.

Such a workforce should have little truck with the kinds of divisions and rivalries that have beleaguered museums, crippling them before they can even begin their task, let alone complete it successfully. Many museum professionals are now looking for open dialogue and for museum development based on consensus and mutual respect for a full range of skills and ideas.

The museum profession is changing from within as much as from without. The basic tenets of faith in collections are still intact and strongly held, not just by curators but by the body of the museum workforce. In a profession naturally given to at least a little discord, what is becoming more evident than ever before is a shared identity of museum professionalism. If this is where more effective, stimulating and worthwhile museums are to be found, then it is a path more people ought to take.

THE COUNTY TEAM
Stephen Locke

There are fashions in management as in much else. This is rarely admitted by management gurus because it would undermine their credibility if they admitted there is no holy grail of ideal management practice. Two poles between which management theory hovers are, on one side, an emphasis on structures and, on the other, a jolly free-for-all, driven by enthusiasm and motivation.

Probably the most common management structure is the staff structure. 'There's nowt so queer as folk', and the appeal of a structure to help deal with them is obvious. Consistency, rigour, discipline and order reinforce the director's status. It is very comforting for a director to survey his or her grand design, and still more satisfying to reproduce it at seminars, embellished with some radical new job titles, to increase the anxiety of less advanced colleagues.

Staff structures are becoming increasingly diverse and complex in response to new approaches to delivering services. Great energy is expended on staff structure, yet in itself it is a very feeble tool for achieving results. Indeed, the ability of staff to produce results within a variety of structures says more about the resilience of the human spirit than it does about the efficacy of one structure or another.

What do we need to do our job properly? A good idea of what the job is, motivation to do it, and the resources to do it. Each of these baldly stated requirements embraces more complex factors, of course. For example, 'the resources to do it' may mean the ability to find resources, or the imagination to redesign the task to fit available resources. Most people would probably agree that something like these three requirements are the crucial ones. What they are unlikely to say (if they are not directors) is that they need a good staff structure.

As an established director, I am not about to give up all my vested concern with staff structures, but I am prepared to explore their limitations. The (potential) benefits of a (good) staff structure are: a reflection, in the type of staff employed and the way they are organized, of the priorities and the purpose of the museum; a support for good communication; and a method of presenting staffing issues to senior managers. However, I do not think that staff structures are often much help with: creating the right jobs; recruiting and motivating the best people; paying them properly; achieving good team work; managing projects; or indeed achieving any results which matter to anybody outside the organization. Yet these are all important outcomes which staff structures are commonly designed to address.

It is a crucially important characteristic of good museum work that it relies on teamwork. There are few decisions of any importance concerning collections or museum services which do not require the contribution of several elements of skill and knowledge. Our collections and the people we serve (so we say) come first, second and third. So any operational decision based on staff structure and job title is misconceived. We should not say 'curators curate objects', 'conservators conserve objects' and 'designers display objects'. Rather we should ask what the object or person wants – a question which usually requires several points of view even to be properly put. Then we should try and do what we can.

In practice, museum workers join shifting teams of colleagues in countless different interactions as they pursue what they see as 'their work'. Individuals operate along a spectrum from (rightful) total control of a task to a useful contribution to a discussion. Their contributions to a project should move rapidly and frequently up and down this spectrum as they assert the value of their expertise and acknowledge that of others.

All staff need to understand the purpose of the museum, and their role in relation to the care and use of collections, and to have an accurate awareness of the scope of their knowledge and skill. There must also be a system of management which correctly assesses priorities and ensures that the best possible expertise is focused upon them.

Achieving this is the crucial management responsibility. People appreciate the benefits of working within a well-managed organization (by which they usually mean one in which other people are doing their jobs as well as they do theirs). The really hard part is focusing individual personal endeavour and expertise to tasks which mostly require a combination of skills in non-routine situations. Museum staff have to cultivate assiduously an approach to work which rigorously places the collections or public service at the centre of a shared pool of knowledge and experience. This approach is a prerequisite to effective training, because it encourages the appraisal of existing skills against the needs of the job, and motivates people to supply and accept training which will lead directly to improved performance.

What staff structures facilitate this? What arrangement which puts conservators, curators, designers, educationalists and so on in any particular line-management relationship to colleagues, helps the assertion and harmonization of special expertise? I certainly have no particular model to offer. I rate quality of decision-making, planning, communication, project management and training as more important. Any staff structure which facilitates these is a good one. A staff structure which concentrates on the arrangement of personal responsibilities and territory, described either by outdated and prejudicial – or meaningless and new – job titles is a poor one. The staff structure may well be the least important element of management (while being thought the most important) and changing it without compelling evidence that practical achievement will result is most likely to absorb, rather than radiate, energy.

DISCOVERING NEW IDENTITIES
Richard Ormond

The traditional role of the curator and other specialist staff has been called into question as a result of the policies being pursued in many museums. The title 'curator' itself needs redefining, since it is far from clear what areas curatorship now embraces, and those which properly lie outside. Managing and developing collections calls for many skills apart from those of knowledge and research. They may be combined in a single person, or be exercised by different specialists. There can be no question that national museums need scholarly research and a high level of expertise. The question is how best it can be organized, and how it relates to other areas of museum activity.

Museums face formidable challenges on a number of fronts. Many national museums and galleries have inherited buildings that have been poorly maintained in the past, and require major refurbishment. Successive ministers for the arts (and national heritage) have emphasized their commitment to putting our buildings in order by the year 2000.

- National museums and galleries are now required to be better managed, more accountable and more enterprising. The annual corporate plan is not only a bid to government for funds, but an integrated strategy document and action plan that defines the way forward.
- Front of house operations in museums have not received the attention they deserve. The public has come to expect a much higher standard of interpretation and presentation. They want more stimulation, more information, and an altogether higher quality of service.

- Those of us with large multidisciplinary collections face huge problems in getting our collections in order, in documenting and conserving them, and in improving access to them. Our predecessors were the great acquisitioners, we are the more mundane housekeeping generation, putting in the required systems and sorting everything out.
- Finally, no museum will achieve anything unless it has a well-trained and flexible workforce and a modern organization capable of carrying through complex projects. Managing change, transforming attitudes and motivating people is not the least of the challenges we face.

The National Maritime Museum has recently launched its 'Masterplan', a vision of a revitalized and refurbished museum that lies at the heart of our forward thinking. A new entrance and huge concourse area on the site of the present Neptune Hall will open up the museum, transform circulation, and enable us to present and interpret the collections in exciting new ways. Even more ambitious is the plan to put all our reserve collections (over two million items) in a two-storey 10,000 square metre structure under the front lawns. In this coming year we shall be spending over £1 million on the refurbishment of the Old Royal Observatory, and installing our first properly designed office accommodation in the top floor of the East Wing. Implementing the Masterplan, with all the disruption involved, will test our resources to the limit and necessitate tough decisions on priorities.

Meanwhile we have to ensure that we keep the business going. Placed as we are away from the centre of London, and with poor transport links, we rely on well-presented and well-marketed exhibitions to maintain visitor numbers at around 600,000 per annum. The *Henry VIII* exhibition last year and *Pirates* this have proved popular successes that also meet exacting standards of quality and scholarship. The money that we earn at the door (some £1.7 million in 1991/2) enables us to make good the shortfall in government funding and provides the investment for the Masterplan (an estimated £4 million over the next five years). We are also investing in new galleries, like 'twentieth-Century Seapower' which opened this July.

The museum is organized in three divisions. The *Development Division* covers site management, visitor services, education, exhibitions, marketing, sponsorship and commercial operations. Finance personnel, management services and buildings are the province of the *Support Service Division*. Everything relating to the care and upkeep of the collections comes under the *Collections Divisions*.

Within the Collections Division, the recent establishment of the Maritime Information Centre (MIC) has led to dramatic improvements in the service offered to more specialized users. Previously, access to the library and collections, and the answering of enquiries (some 30,000 a year), was done on a departmental basis. The new MIC is able to provide a reliable level of service for the first time, and through its systems work it is opening up the collections to public use as never before. In its final home it will be adjacent to both the galleries and the reserve collections, providing access to information and knowledge at a multiplicity of levels.

The Collections Division is organized along functional lines. Responsibility for managing the collections, including documentation, is vested in the registrar's section. By 1994 we will have generated records for a million items, using six teams of cataloguers, a production rate inconceivable under earlier regimes. MIC is responsible for access to the collections and the museum's extensive databases. The specialist curators, organized in three groups – maritime history, ship technology and navigational sciences – take responsibility for collections policy, acquisition and loan decisions, and research and scholarly publications; they also contribute to displays and exhibitions. Finally the conservation group looks after the physical welfare and condition of the collection.

There will be individuals who have or wish to develop a specialism, and whose knowledge is of paramount importance to the institution. National museum status requires a high level of scholarship, and in certain technical fields we are going to have to foster that ourselves. There is no natural constituency for recruiting curators with specialist maritime knowledge. Our existing experts often need time rather than training to pursue their particular work. We have instituted a series of sabbaticals for our senior staff, to give them the time for research, and we also offer a number of fellowships to scholars outside. That is very healthy for the intellectual life of the institution which should be renewed by people coming in from outside.

Some of our ablest curators are currently deployed on major development and works schemes, particularly those concerned with the Masterplan. The two staff currently managing the Old Royal Observatory project are former curators of ship technology and paintings respectively. The project manager for the Neptune Hall project is a navigational expert, and another ship technologist is leading the gallery team. Senior staff are learning new skills in handling multimillion pound projects. Without their talents and commitment, the Masterplan will never be achieved.

Exhibitions and major gallery developments are the responsibility of Development Division, but they draw heavily on the expertise and practical skills of curators and conservators. Development Division is the money-making end of the museum operation, concerned with shops, catering, marketing, sponsorship, revenue from admissions and visitor services. In attempting to satisfy the demands of our customers we have developed a system of site management for our three attractions, the National Maritime Museum, Queen's House and Old Royal Observatory. Instead of the old system in which everyone and no one was responsible for running sites, we now have dedicated managers controlling all front-of-house operations. Many junior staff have moved between documentation teams, curatorial departments, exhibition and display projects and the Maritime Information Centre. This enables them to get a good grounding in museum work, and to become well-rounded museum professionals. The new structure has opened up career opportunities for staff, who often move within and between divisions on a project-by-project basis and are learning to adapt to changing jobs and roles. They must be given the skills and tools they need, which is why we have invested heavily in training. None of the great plans and visions of the future will be achieved without people. And more than ever we need a well-trained and highly skilled workforce. We used to spend less than £10,000 per year on training. We now spend £100,000 – and that is probably too little.

Of the museum's fifteen most senior staff none is in the same job they were in two years ago; they are likely to be doing something different again in two years' time. They are the people turning our vision of a new National Maritime Museum into reality. The challenge of doing new things has released fresh energies and skills which very often staff did not know they possessed. Some of them will go back from time to time into more traditional spheres of activity, younger staff will emerge to run projects and become planners and the cycle will continue. I for one find it an exciting prospect.

THE RESTRUCTURE OF OXFORDSHIRE'S MUSEUM SERVICE
Martyn Brown

Oxfordshire Country Council's department of leisure and arts was created in 1988/9 when the traditional library, museums, archives, countryside and arts services were combined into a new conglomerate under a single chief officer. About the same time a new chief executive began to lead a new corporate quality programme.

For some time the department of leisure and arts continued to operate under the old professional management structure with assistant directors leading the library, museums and archives, and arts and recreation services. Ideas were sought on how to integrate all support services, leaving the direct public services – such as individual museums – as individual cost centres managed by museum professionals and reporting on traditional lines. However, it was felt that did not go far enough.

The debate hotted up and eventually a structure was submitted to the Museums, Arts, Libraries and Leisure Committee in September 1991. Approval came in December and implementation followed fast with two new second-tier officers appointed in early January 1992 and a complex sequence of internal interviews leading to appointments and relocations in order to launch the structure by the start of the new financial year (April 1992).

Under the new structure, management of all services is integrated in area divisions which follow district council boundaries, and are managed by area directors. In each area a client services manager leads the provision of all services to the community and identifies and monitors client needs. Museum officers and librarians provide professional services to the area and the community – not to specific sites or buildings. Each building or 'service point' is managed by a site manager who is responsible for the day-to-day operation of the site and for the local staff.

Each area director, client services manager, museum officer or librarian also carries a countywide professional responsibility. This gives a 'matrix structure' in which professional disciplines cross line management. For example: my role as area director for South Oxfordshire is combined with county museums officer, the lead professional for museum services throughout the county; the client services manager also leads provision of all countywide services to young people (as a special client group).

Three of the five areas also contain, by virtue of their location, countywide services. The South area, for example, includes libraries, collections management, the countryside service, 'Resource Plus' (integrated library and museum loans and services to schools), recreation (sport), and transport. Museum collections management remains a centralized function within the West Oxfordshire area, where a site has been purchased for the construction of a new £2 million purpose-built store to house collections, conservation and documentation. Similarly Cogges Manor Farm Museum is being managed by the Cogges development officer as a countywide service.

The operation and delivery of museum services throughout the county is managed in two ways. First, area management teams concentrate on the needs and requirements of their local services and customers. Led by area directors it is here that all services will be integrated. Second, there is a museums and archives professional services team. Led by the county museums officer, this team is a guardian of professional values and standards of service. Through this team all museum officers have agreed proportions of their time to be spent on countywide work – this might be the documentation of collections or planning a museum education inset programme.

The restructuring should strengthen a number of elements in Oxfordshire museum services:

- Provision of museum service in areas where no museum base exists.
- Defined standards of museum service binding on all area managers.
- Separation of professional and administrative work, releasing professional staff to carry out professional work.
- Closer management and support for museum staff working in each area.
- Creation of a professionally managed museums collections management team including documentation, conservation and storage.
- Appointment of a senior museum professional to lead the development of Cogges Manor Farm Museum.
- Appointment of a documentation officer to establish and maintain standards of documentation countywide.
- Closer working arrangements with colleagues in related professions – archives, local studies, libraries.

As county museums officer I am challenged to lead the museum services without direct line management. My control is exercised through the setting and monitoring of standards, by my support and advice to each museum officer and by advocacy of museum issues on the departmental management team.

What the museum profession in general and the Museums and Galleries Commission Registration Scheme committee in particular make of this remains to be seen. They will, without doubt, judge the success, or otherwise, on the results.

HERITAGE SERVICES IN LINCOLNSHIRE
Ray Taylor

When Lincolnshire County Council underwent a structural reorganization in the early 1980s it was at the cutting edge of the 'Thatcherite Revolution': cut the number of committees; reduce the number of chief officers; create trading units.

In this atmosphere a new recreational services department emerged with one of the most comprehensive leisure portfolios of any county council. It was organized into three divisions dealing quite conventionally with the then logical groupings of libraries and archives; museums and archaeology; and countryside and tourism. A fourth division – administration – was created, in the words of a contemporary job description 'to free "professionals" from the burden of administration and allow them to be creative and innovative managers'. It seems ironic, only nine years on, that 'professionals' were to be shielded from administration in order that they could get on and manage!

Since then the philosophy and culture of local government has changed again and once more Lincolnshire is at the forefront. The pressures for change have been both external and internal: the shift towards the 'enabling authority'; statutory competition and Lincolnshire's own competition policy (which goes much further); the delegation of responsibility; the integration of functions to cut costs and (more importantly) to improve the efficiency and effectiveness of service delivery.

The latest restructure of the recreational services department is based on three principles: to group like functions; to delegate responsibility as close as possible to the point of service delivery; and to align management responsibility as close as possible to the point of service delivery; and to align management responsibility and financial responsibility.

This has created a structure with three particularly notable features. There are two operational divisions: *Community Services* is market-led and comprises libraries, arts development and community grant-aid; *Heritage Services* is resource-management led and comprises ten management units. Each unit has a manager responsible for financial, staffing and other resources and for delivering pre-arranged targets. The resulting structure is very flat, with unit managers occupying the third tier in the departmental hierarchy. The extensive and diverse range of facilities within the Heritage Services Division could not be managed by conventional pyramid command. Delegation through service plans, target setting and performance review is essential.

Management of this structure also required simplification and standardization of systems. Perhaps surprisingly all unit managers (with the exception of the countryside manager) work to the same job description. Management accounting has been simplified with each management unit becoming a cost centre with standardized areas of spending. The heritage of a county is not just contained in glass-cased museums. Archaeology and historic buildings, paper history contained in archives, and natural history in field and foreshore: are all worthy of protection and promotion. Why keep stuffed birds when nature reserves are to hand? Why not encourage people to join archaeological digs or to warden ancient green lanes rather than just look at excavated objects?

This broad approach brings together the ten management units including the Usher Art Gallery, the Museum of Lincolnshire Life (and its associated Church Farm Museum and three working windmills), the City and County Museum in Lincoln, and Stamford and Grantham Museums. Perhaps the widest ranging unit of all is the council's work on rights of way, tree planting, conservation and recreation land management and field archaeology (including the sites and monuments record).

The delegation of responsibility to unit managers risks the fragmentation of the service and the loss of economies of scale. This is overcome by the creation of a small advisory team reporting to the assistant director. In the first instance this team provides skills in marketing, publicity, design and publications, museum services (such as conservation, security and documentation) and performance review. Other skills (such as education) may be added as resources allow. In addition to offering advice to unit managers this team will co-ordinate countywide policies, maintain links with outside bodies (such as the area museum service and regional tourist board) and keep a benevolent eye on local groups such as tourist associations and independent museums (essential if they are to achieve registration).

When the new structure was first proposed, comments were anticipated such as: 'If the present system ain't broke, why mend it?' and: 'I came here to be a curator, not push paper.' However, reality has proved quite different. The will and enthusiasm of staff are now self-evident; new energy has been released. Managers have the incentive to manipulate opening times and admission prices and to maximize grant-aid and trading profits. The highly regarded 'Museum Roadshows' have been expanded to include the countryside and archives, researching family histories and arranging village footpath walks, for example.

On hearing of the new structure for the department many fellow professionals asked to see the 'family tree'. The variety and flatness of this innovative structure led to the response that there was no family tree: just a collection of ground-cover shrubs. As with any gardening, only time will tell whether the seeds sown in 1992 will yield rich harvests in years to come.

RESTRUCTURING AT THE V&A
Charles Saumarez Smith

During the last two decades it has become increasingly difficult for members of Victoria and Albert Museum staff to secure the necessary dedicated research time to undertake and, more especially, to complete major projects, particularly publications, but also galleries and exhibitions. The way that curatorial work is structured within the museum means that members of staff can gain exceptional knowledge and expertise about particular areas of the museum's holdings, accumulated during the transaction of a multiplicity of duties surrounding the management of the collections. But the very multiplicity of these duties has sometimes militated against the freedom which is required to keep up with a rapidly expanding secondary literature, to visit archives, libraries and other museums, and to develop knowledge and ideas into articles and books. As E. P. Alexander wrote in his book *Museums in Motion: An Introduction to the History and Function of Museums* (Nashville 1979: 163): 'A museum must realise that an effective research and publication program demands that curators be given time for defined research projects on prescribed schedules and with high priorities. Not much will be accomplished if a curator is expected to do research on his [sic] time off or during occasional moments taken from regular responsibilities: nor should other duties be permitted to interrupt his research schedule.' The establishment of a research department at the V&A in 1989 was an attempt to manage the opportunities for research more efficiently. Staff working on major research projects can be seconded into the department. The organization of the new 'Gallery of European Ornament' was supervised by Michael Snodin working full-time as a member of the research department, with curatorial assistance from Clare Graham, and additional support from Maurice Howard, a lecturer in history of art at the University of Sussex on the Sussex Exchange Programme (see *Museums Journal* July 1992: 22). The quality of ideas within the gallery, the range of objects represented, and the amount of thought which went into the accompanying didactic material was a result of the time and freedom which could be devoted to the project.

For lesser projects, particularly associated with academic publications, it is possible for members of museum staff (not only curatorial, but also education, conservation and library staff) to apply to the museum's research fund which consists of £30,000 a year, allocated from the income from donations, and administered by the museum's research and publications committee. The fund is used principally in order to facilitate major periods of research leave (between four months and a year) for work towards a major research project, normally a publication. In 1990, for example, it was used to enable Craig Clunas to take up a visiting research fellowship at Dumbarton Oaks, Washington DC, and to provide part-funding for a research project by the National Art Library for listing, sorting and researching previous V&A publications.

I hope that this summary of current policies shows that the proposals for reorganization of the museum's administration were not intended to demolish the research standing and traditions of the museum, but were a genuine attempt to come to terms with the changing nature of the subject area represented by its collections, and the increasing difficulty of maintaining its research profile to the highest standards.

SCOPE FOR EVERYTHING
Peter Lassey

In proposing a curatorial identity the Museum Training Institute (MTI) would simply expand upon what it has been told by the museum community. It is clear from its work that there is no simple definition of a 'curator'. The museum sector is extremely diverse and the role of a curator is as much dependent on the nature and size of the employing institution as it is on some commonly held understanding of curatorship.

Instead of trying to define the indefinable it is probably more useful to describe the main areas from which a curatorial identity would spring. These areas would be scope, competence, knowledge, professionalism and development.

Scope would describe the breadth or area of responsibility in which curators should legitimately function. These should include the management, preservation and interpretation of the collection and other organizational responsibilities such as personnel and resource management. The levels at which individual curators engage in these different functions would obviously be determined by the employing institution.

To give curators the responsibility to perform the functions outlined above would be meaningless unless they could perform these functions adequately; in other words they should be competent. The standards of competence developed by MTI and the museum community should define accurately exactly how well each function should be performed and the knowledge required in order for them to be deemed competent. A standard of competence expresses the minimum requirement for that particular function.

Curators are professionals and as such are responsible to the profession as well as to their employers. As professionals they are responsible for shaping the profession and conducting their functions as curators in a manner acceptable to themselves, their colleagues and the profession.

Finally, curators should be forward-looking, committed to developing themselves, their institution and the profession.

ENDANGERED SPECIMENS
Steven Miller

Over the past few years there have been disquieting attempts in some United States museums to change dramatically the traditional role of the curator. Apparently this is also occurring in several British museums.

These actions are unwise. Museums that monkey around with curatorial positions seriously compromise fundamental responsibilities to acquire, care for and explain art, historical artefacts and scientific specimens. These are the essential activities that define museums. Curators are assigned to carry them out. Other jobs may support curatorial work but none are substitutes for a post that demands a unique blend of talents, interests and abilities.

Museums are measured by their collections. Great museums have great collections. Not surprisingly they usually have great curators.

These people learn their craft by working directly with objects, day in and day out. It takes a long time to become a good curator. The skills are acquired, of necessity, on the job. The best curators learn their trade as apprentices, working directly with collections and usually under the tutelage of another curator. Their studies involve looking, reading, conversing, analysing, comparing, thinking and compiling. These are activities often pursued quietly and alone, or through contact with a very small circle of individuals. (Could this be why some are so suspicious of the job?) Academic credentials, personal connections, social position, political contacts and a predilection for opportunism are

137

of little long-term help in curatorial performance. What is required is a love of objects and the meanings they hold for society.

Curators of any worth are really quite visceral. This characteristic is legitimized every time they quantify information, offer insights and provide knowledge. The results of their work enlighten us all.

The enemy within

The most astonishing aspect of the assault on curatorial positions is that it emanates from within the museum community. The public has no problem with the traditional role of a curator. The havoc is wrought by museum administrators who are apparently either ignorant of what curators do or are jealous of their esteem. In counterproductive efforts to be managerially efficient (or personally vengeful) curatorial posts are eliminated, redefined, truncated or repositioned in operational hierarchies.

Those who attack curatorial positions are usually political appointees, lapsed academics, so-called museum educators, professional managers, or rank-and-file bureaucrats. All seem to be only marginally committed to museums as repositories of a shared cultural and scientific patrimony. Once on the job these people can be inept, insecure, defensive and egotistical. Staff who appear to have power, such as curators, may be threatening. Staff whose work is not easily quantified are viewed as simply wasteful.

The dismantling of curatorial authority plays out in predictable ways. Positions are eliminated, or the scope of responsibility is reduced. Job titles are diluted by expanding them to include museum work previously separated from curatorial duties: we encounter curators of education, interpretation, design or history. These are disingenuous appellations used by administrators to achieve job parity. They insult curators, educators, designers and academics alike.

Another trick employed to reduce curatorial responsibilities includes relying on acquisition committees to determine collecting programmes. The futility of this measure is clear, as participants normally defer to an appropriate curator's judgement. But the annoyance factor can be high, as meetings waste time and occasionally hinder collecting activity.

To further neutralize curatorial authority, museums have become more energetic in seeking people outside their staff to organize exhibitions. They hire guest curators or a team of contributors. This idea is predicated on a firm tradition but as applied today it can prove fruitless. The freelance curators are completely unfamiliar with the collections with which they are to work and (if it becomes the norm for an institution) the permanent staff often find the approach offensive.

Finally, as more and more academic transients decide to work in museums, the idea of the curator as scholar is being questioned. This further erodes the status of the position. Teachers, researchers and students who base their work solely on the written and spoken word are perplexed by people who see objects as documents of information, inspiration and edification. The idea that mere things can be as important as words baffles them.

Respecting collections

Perhaps the fear of the demise of the curator is premature. While serious attacks have been mounted, their folly eventually becomes obvious. A museum with which I was once associated has suffered severe setbacks in its curatorial departments. Positions have been eliminated and staff turnover is high. The pace and quality of acquisition activities has consequently suffered. Research upon collections has completely ceased in some areas. Supervision of conservation is minimal. These developments have been blamed on a faltering regional economy – yet administrators flourish. Their salaries are high, their offices have been redecorated and the museum even purchased a fine executive residence. Social events continue apace and public relations edicts flow ceaselessly.

The situation was predictable. The director responsible for this institution thinks very little of curators. These minions must toe the line. Heaven forbid they should feel any affection for their work, the public they serve or the collections for which they are responsible. The attitude from the top was obvious when the director pronounced at a meeting of the institution's curators: 'I'm tired of hearing curators talk about *their* collections. They don't own the collections. The collections belong to the museum.' Of course collections belong to the museum. But, frankly, I wouldn't trust curators who didn't have deep proprietorial sentiments about the materials for which they are responsible.

The problems faced by this museum are obvious and will, in time, probably be corrected. Eventually the institution's governing authority will realize changes are due.

Collections need to receive the attention they deserve and, as a result, curatorial positions will be accorded the respect they deserve. This is the clear and obvious answer for any museum that has decided traditional curators are passé.

Museums must know about what they own and want to collect. Committees can't do this. Administrators can't do this. Educators can't do this. Registrars can't do this. These people have neither the time nor the full authority to do so.

It is the work of curators.

UNNATURAL SELECTION
This article was written by a specialist curator, who wishes to remain anonymous.

The forced resignation of nine senior specialist curators from the V&A in 1989 was given widespread publicity. Things have settled down there now (see *Museums Journal* January 1990: p. 26 and March 1992: p. 18), but the affair gave the green light for many smaller museums to replace their expert curators with arts administrators. Those responsible for museum recruitment have not thought through the implications of such appointments, but alarm bells should now be ringing: in removing specialists from museums, the collections themselves are being put at risk.

Specialists are experts on their subject, usually as a result of their publications in scholarly journals, catalogues and reference books. At the time of the 1989 controversy, several of the V&A experts were described as 'walking encyclopaedias'. The daily work of the specialist curator in a small museum is extraordinarily varied. In the course of a normal day the curator must monitor the display conditions for current exhibitions and plan new ones; arrange for items to be photographed; answer queries from all round the world; arrange loans; see visitors; catalogue new additions to the collection; and discuss future purchases. Curators must keep abreast of advances in display, lighting and security techniques while, at the same time, constantly researching items in the collection and publishing the results. Above all, they must be completely familiar with the material in their care – to such a degree that they would instantly recognize any illicit replacement that had been made or damage done.

Specialist curators in large national museums and galleries usually enter the profession with a doctorate in a relevant specialist discipline such as art history, an oriental language or zoology. Very few of these specialist curators have passed through courses of the type now considered a prerequisite to entry in smaller museums. In contrast, the non-specialist 'new' professionals are not required to hold qualifications in specialized disciplines, but rather join the museum service following a one-year course in arts administration or 'museology'. Many of these graduates have first degrees as diverse as politics, economics, sociology or business administration. Once inside the museum environment, curators from this background find it difficult to understand the needs and problems of the specialist scholar–curator.

Differing perceptions

Each type of curator inevitably has a different perception of the role of the museum itself and of their place in it. On the one hand, many specialist curators believe that their duty is less to do with the everyday administration of the museum and more in advancing knowledge of their collection with its potential for public education. On the other hand, 'new' professionals often have little interest in scholarship, yet feel that they, and they alone, are the ones with the right training to tackle the enormous challenges facing museums in the 1990s. Here we have a root cause of the conflict within the museum profession. There is, of course, a place – and a very important place – for the non-specialist in the museum world today. Many museums employ personnel whose job it is to fundraise, carry out public relations, publicity and marketing, promote sponsorship, and assist in the activities of the friends organization; but to place non-specialists in charge of museum collections can be a recipe for disaster.

The general public would be aghast to realize how little scholarly research has actually been published on a huge range of museum artefacts, and how difficult it is for many non-specialist curators to identify objects. When someone arrives at the curator's door asking for identification of anything from an Indian brass vase to what might be a Rembrandt drawing, that person is acting on the expectation that every museum curator is a fund of knowledge not available elsewhere. In large museums the enquirer can normally be directed towards the relevant 'walking encyclopaedia'. However, the non-specialist curator in a smaller museum is often at a complete loss.

Access to museum collections becomes more difficult every year; a large part of the blame for this situation must be directed towards those museum administrators who regard visiting scholars as nuisances at best and security risks at worst. Without easy access to the collection, scholars simply cannot undertake the sort of original research that allows material to be accurately catalogued. Any museum collection that is not fully and accurately catalogued is, inevitably, extremely vulnerable to the potential thief.

Specialist benefits

Specialist curators have other, and perhaps less obvious, roles to play in museums of the 1990s. It is very often through those 'walking encyclopaedias' that wealthy patrons prefer to make donations. It is not always the governors and directors of museums who are most successful in attracting sponsorship. Rather, it is the curator–experts, with numerous publications to their credit, who are most successful in persuading benefactors to contribute artefacts to collections and cash to the museum. Donors feel that their gifts will be in safe hands, with their true worth properly recognized, appreciated and valued.

At a time when it is recognized that accountants are not the best people to run machine-tool factories, and administrators are not necessarily the wisest choice to organize hospitals, why should museums be expected to succeed in their goals by staffing their institutions with non-specialist administrators rather than experts?

We risk moving towards a future when exhibition catalogues are no more than hand lists, exhibitions are increasingly arranged for the effect on the eye rather than on the brain, and old and rare objects are kept permanently in storage because they do not look attractive. Even now, reproductions are sometimes preferred to the real thing because they present no difficulties with lighting and security.

Nevertheless, many curators who are superb scholars are hopeless administrators. The solution to this problem lies in recruitment policy and training. All museums should require their new young specialist curators to undertake training in administration, conservation, marketing and museum practice, among other essentials. Potential members of the profession must be most carefully selected from candidates who show evidence of administrative ability in addition to the highest standards of scholarship. Their museum training should be done shortly after they enter the profession. Surely it is obvious that it is both quicker and easier for a one-year training course to be made mandatory for post-doctoral entrants rather than to require all those museum curators without a research degree to write a relevant doctoral thesis? It is also necessary to arrange for long-serving specialist curators to be allowed time away from their museums both for further training courses and for museum exchanges.

It is imperative that the museum service as a whole recognizes what will happen if the present trend is allowed to continue. If we believe that our museums should advance knowledge of material culture, then specialist curators must not be threatened, as they now are, with replacement by arts administrators – especially those who do not realize that without scholarly research our museums will swiftly degenerate into arid Disneylands where one can go and look but not learn, except at a most superficial level.

This paper first appeared in Museums Journal *(October 1993), pp. 27–33.*

21

Defining curation

John Murdoch

In this article, John Murdoch from the Victoria and Albert Museum questions the approach being proposed for the future training of museum staff. He discusses the fundamentals of museum practice and the organization of museum work.

The historical process of the division and specialization of labour, described by Adam Smith, has affected museums as it has affected all other sectors of industry. Intellectually, the encyclopedic responsibilities of the early curators have been divided into subject areas corresponding to the academic disciplines in which contemporary curators have generally had their training and carried out research. And since the Second World War, or more particularly since the 1960s, the responsibility of the curator to carry out every aspect of managing the museum has been broken down in larger institutions by the growth of new specialisms, such as conservation, design, education and management.

As more and more of what had once constituted the job has been split off, the question 'what is a curator?' has become a question of power. Who decides, for example, whether to lend an object? The curator or the conservator? Who decides what goes into a gallery: the curator, the designer or the head of public affairs? What sort of person is the director? Should museum managements have any grasp of any of the main subject areas of the organization? And are numbers through the door more important than the quality and educational value of the experience?

As a case study of this debate, which was taking place throughout the 1980s in Europe and the United States, the events at the Victoria and Albert Museum (V&A) leading up to and following the restructuring of February 1989 are probably still fairly clear in people's memories.

The immediate cause of conflict was the proposition that the 'knowledge' function of curatorship should be separated from the day-to-day operations of collection management. Some commentators understood the proposition to be that curatorship was to be a form of store-keeping requiring organizational efficiency, accurate records of movements and good security, but no curiosity as to the nature or use of the objects being kept and no role in their display or interpretation. What were seen as the higher intellectual activities of the curator were to be divided off into a new museum specialism with its own departmental structure called 'Research'.

Well, history ran its course and the process of discussion and negotiation which was intended to follow the initial proposals produced outcomes which do, I think, clarify the nature of curatorship in our time. First, we recognized that the pressures of administering the national collections were now very much greater than they had been before and just after the war and that, for the present generation of museum scholars, collection management had therefore to a great extent crowded out publication. There had been a very noticeable drop in the number of serious monographs and *catalogues raisonnés* produced by the museum's senior scholars. A number of staff had reached retirement age and left, taking with them the fruits of a lifetime's study of their subject, with very little even in the records, let alone in print.

The solution to this problem of space and time in the curator's career seemed to be to provide, as far as possible, more space and time. So, curators with a project nearing maturity, nearing the time when a period of concentrated work is normally required to bring a text to a finished state, would have the possibility of transfer into the research department.

This would have the corresponding benefit of highlighting the fact that the curator's work on the management of the collections was not going to be done in his or her absence. It would at least raise the question of substitution, even if there were no money to provide for a temporary promotion or new blood. There should be no question of pretending there was no cost in terms of collection management when curators undertook major projects of publication or gallery development. It was intended to signal the end of the shabby, genteel pretence that limited resources could be indefinitely extended to cover all demands.

The 1988 National Audit Office report on the national collections and the subsequent hearings by the Public Accounts Committee had highlighted this pretence and the V&A was determined to change. Implicit in what we did for the collections was the assertion that collection management was best done by those who could recognize individual objects, understand the relationships between them, profit deeply from the opportunities for handling and close day-to-day study of objects, and make them enlightening to visitors. There was never any intention that collection managers should not be as expert as possible in the objects they dealt with, but there was a recognition that the job of the curator was, as the term implied, to care for the collections. The job specification of the curators of the collections was accordingly refocused on the management of the collections, and the staff structure in each unit was rebuilt to concentrate curatorial resources on the crucial areas.

These were defined as *documentation* and *care and access*. The first reflected the need not only to develop the core record of objects acquired by the museum and to eliminate backlogs, but also to provide a focus for the increasing use of information technology as a tool of museum record-keeping. It was felt absolutely necessary to locate the application of information technology within the curatorial structure, with experienced curators articulating their own needs and able to enter into dialogue with systems and hardware experts. The idea was that the technology should serve the subject, not that the subject should bend to the technology.

The pairing of care and access was intended to express the essential dilemma of the curatorial profession: whether to provide care at the expense of access, or access at the expense of care. The priority here was to take control once again of the collections. They had in some cases become spread between different off-site stores of extremely dubious quality, or deposited in parts of the South Kensington site which had to be cleared for building works. There were objects out on loan which had not been checked or physically seen for many years. There was, overall, a need to survey the collections in conjunction with conservation to assess their condition and prepare plans of work.

Lest this should seem too unglamorous, curators on the care and access side could remind themselves that they had the prime, though not the exclusive, responsibility for the displays and for developing ideas about improved access to objects in those areas not already served by efficient study rooms. Coming as I do from the print room culture, in which immediate access to works of art is offered in conjunction with relevant secondary literature and expert staff to consult, I have had to avoid the pitfalls of over-ambition in this area, but there are colleagues now in the collections who are thinking actively of how to do it in their field.

In the medium term, that unglamorous task of clearing stores had resulted in a series of developments at our Blythe Road site in which, for example, reserve collections of furniture have now become accessible to visitors by appointment; and even the large flat textiles – very large tapestries, for example – which previously were notoriously difficult to see, can now at least be inspected by the staff.

One of the most important facts about museums, which we should all take every possible opportunity to stress, is that sound collection management, defined on the basis of the two areas of responsibility outlined above, is the key to success. It is this activity, carried out by curators who are scholars but who are also alert to the changing range of skills required to deal with very large numbers of old, fragile and valuable objects, which lies at the heart of our business and constitutes the main challenge for the future.

I often feel that when discussing museums, collections tend to be treated as though they were marginal or merely a resource to be drawn on, or somehow an embarrassment to the totality of the business. I know very well how this happens, how the real need to set large amounts of money free for other projects can squeeze provision for collection management. However, experience has taught that unless the infrastructure is properly maintained, the rest becomes an increasingly fragile and unsupported shell: curators become increasingly demoralized, and are more likely to occupy their time in academic work unrelated to the collections; conservators despair when objects, expensively cleaned or mended, are returned to languish in dirty or damaging environments. To put it no more highly, it is extremely useful to be able to show the minister, or the Arts and Heritage Group of both Houses of Parliament, or a potential sponsor, objects beautifully conserved, in clean orderly environments, palpably ready to go on display, if only the money were available. But show them dirty and broken objects in a dusty store and they will go away with a strong sense of the institution's basic incompetence.

But what are the other elements of the debate about museums that have characterized the last few years? Curators attending the Museums Association annual conference last year (1991) in Newcastle might have contemplated the trade fair alongside the conference rooms with some amazement. It seemed to epitomize the present schizoid state of the profession. On the one hand we had the stalls of companies selling acid-free card, stainless steel rollers, mobile high-density racking and shelving systems – all the equipment, in other words, necessary for the proper care of collections. On the other hand, we had a mock-up of a dungeon in expanded polystyrene, with bloodstains and rusty 'iron' chains; we had stalls selling Roman and medieval shoes; 3D image projection of Constanze Mozart talking English in an echo chamber – in short, everything for the installation of an authentic historical experience in the museum.

Much of it, at least in the cold light of the conference, was obviously tacky and horrid by almost any criterion, and I am not one of those who generally dislikes set dressing and the imaginative re-creation of the past. I like television adaptations of nineteenth century fiction and read historical novels – I wrote my thesis on Walter Scott's imagination – and I like antiquarian confections in architecture; but when I became a museum curator,

I felt that the business I was entering was about a different sort of intellectual and aesthetic activity, one of sufficient importance to mark out for defence. The museum's contribution to history involves precisely the recognition that the past is not available to the present, except by traces and echoes that have a variable and diminishing resemblance to their causes.

Therein lies the inherent sadness of the curatorial project, of history and of time itself; but therein also lies the beauty and the aspiration of our work. For what we do in museums is retain the trace and attempt to explain to the present that this is all there is. There is no reality in the past that we can reach either by imagination or by excavation. History is transmission, and what we can know of it exists in what connects us to the past, through everything that has happened since.

So the museum is important as an almost precise antithesis to the theme park or the living history display. It is not that the museum is dead history, but it is the only palpable means of knowing that history is about things that have gone, and that in going have changed.

I hope this makes clear my view of the curatorial profession as involving both historical knowledge and operational skills. I explicitly dissociate myself from the suggestion in the programme of the 'Staying on Course: Museum Training for the 1990s' that 'unsuitable individuals were recruited to some national museum posts in the 1970s – i.e. those with too many academic qualifications and too high intellectual aspirations for the post to which they were appointed'. This is red-neck rubbish. On the whole the problem in museums is that we have too few people of great intellectual ability and in that I suppose we reflect the state of the nation as a whole, for we are by international standards under-educated.

The problem has to some extent been exacerbated by the virtual ending of fast-stream entry to the profession in some museums, so that entrants now spend long years in junior grades which are very poorly paid, some are put off from applying and some leave. But the great advantage of this is that everyone gains a thorough grounding in basic hands-on object management and learns the skills required to operate automated systems not through courses but through long practice. For this is what is distinctive about the job. A good scholar who is a good teacher may work in a university; a good scholar who is a good collection manager may be a museum curator. A museum curator who does not know how to care for and control objects is simply not doing the whole job. But those of us who say this and who recognize the necessity of acquiring and developing skills for more effective collection management have to be extremely careful not to appear reductive in our attitude to curatorial work and not to marginalize scholarship or the scholar.

It has been the apparent reductiveness of the Museum Training Institute (MTI) draft standards workshop process that has, I would say, most worried participants and has surprised the profession during the consultation phase. I was involved in the collection management workshops and gladly contributed to discussions on the basis that collection management was the characteristic activity of the curator, requiring at its different levels the full range of intellectual and technical skills. However, what paralysed our comprehensive discussions was the fact that the methodology of the workshops provided for parallel and separate discussions of the main elements of collection management and for their separate listing in the draft standards.

The idea of collection management as an integrated activity thus seemed to disappear, or was reluctantly admitted as the rump of doings not included in, for example, conservation, documentation, handling or research. Knowledge, not only as an 'under-pinning' factor in the management of collections, but as a strategic aim in itself, was also excluded from our agenda, despite the impassioned protest of curators in our group, from all types of institution.

The current phase of the MTI process, together with the 'Staying on Course' conference, has been intended to provide us with an opportunity to voice these thoughts once again, and to counteract the simplicities arising from work-study methods that bear more resemblance to Taylorism[1] than to our own experience of the work as an integrated whole. It is this vision of curatorship as an adaptive, expanding profession, well able to accommodate new specialisms and new technologies and assimilate them to its humane purposes, that we must inject into the forthcoming stages of the MTI process.

This paper first appeared in Museums Journal *(March 1992), pp. 18–19.*

NOTE

1 Frederick W. Taylor's 1911 study, *The Principles of Scientific Management* (New York: Harpers and Bros), is associated with the reduction of skilled jobs into small parts that could be done by unskilled and unthinking workers.

This article is edited from a personal statement made at the close of the conference 'Staying on Course: Museum and Gallery Training for the 1990s', held in November 1991 at the National Gallery.

22

Cross-community curatorial competences
Patrick J. Boylan

Museum work is subject to variation throughout Europe, not least in terms of entry qualifications. In this paper, Professor Patrick J. Boylan compares European approaches to the training and organization of the museum workforce at professional level. This paper was written in partial response to the proposals, from the Museum Training Institute, that training in the UK be concentrated more on competence and skills than knowledge and understanding.

The UK is currently out of line with most other European countries in some key aspects of the organization, qualifications and status of its museum personnel. If anything, current UK trends towards competence-based skills – rather than advanced education and research – as the prerequisite for professional museum work will widen rather than narrow the gap between this country and continental Europe. If this happens it will certainly affect the opportunities for UK museum staff within the planned unified professions across the European Community.

ORGANIZATION AND EMPLOYMENT

A study of the structure, organization, qualification requirements and remuneration of the museum profession cannot be divorced from national patterns of museum provision and organization. In comparison with the rest of Europe the UK system of museums is in many ways very untypical. Elsewhere, even in countries with highly developed museum provision overall, one rarely finds the kind of comprehensive multidisciplinary museums and (especially) multibranch museum services of the sort that are found in most cities and larger towns in the UK. In continental Europe a museum is far more likely to cover a single discipline or special collection, of the kind represented in the UK by the major national museums and galleries of London (but not those of Edinburgh, Cardiff or Belfast) and by the various kinds of specialized independent museums.

Although we often complain (justifiably) about chronic understaffing across all kinds of UK museums, staffing in the UK compares favourably to that in the rest of Europe. In France, for example, though the old national laws severely restricting the allocation of qualified curators are at last being relaxed a little, it is still unusual to find more than two curatorial staff in any one provincial museum. Often there is just a single curator (see *Museums Journal* August 1989: 23). Such a philosophy and system (found in several other countries of Europe) means that collections and services tend to be fragmented into separate buildings, each of which can then claim to be a separate museum entitled to its own curator and (if it is lucky) deputy curator.

Even within the eighteen European Community and European Free Trade Area (EFTA) countries there are at least 100 (and possibly as many as 200) different public sector regimes covering museum employment and professional qualifications and recognition. This reflects the different governmental, regional, local or other public structure, law and practice relating to the type, location and ultimate ownership (though still public sector) of any particular museum or group of museums. In particular, the rapid progress of policies of internal decentralization in accordance with the principle of subsidiarity is leading to the widespread transfer of cultural policies and responsibilities from central governments to regional and local government.

In some such cases national qualifications, professional status and even salary are being retained, but in others the new autonomous regional or local governments are adopting their own entry and promotion requirements and examinations. For example, in Spain where most major museums have now been tranferred from the formerly highly centralized national government to the new autonomous regional governments, separate 'oposiciones' (museum-work postgraduate entrance competition examinations) are now set by different regions and may not be recognized by the government of a neighbouring region (see *Museums Journal* June 1992: 31).

Commonly museum staff are central government civil servants. Curatorial staff in French national museums are statutory state functionaries and so too are the professional staff of major local authority museums. In the case of art and history museums these staff are all ministry of culture civil servants, on attachment to the local authority museum. This can make for divided loyalties as they are ultimately answerable to their employer, the Direction des Musées de France in Paris, for all matters of professional practice, standards and procedures, but to the mayor and local authority in operational and public service matters. In a second group of countries the majority of museum professionals are civil servants of devolved autonomous regional governments on much the same basis.

In a third common pattern, museums and their staff are integrated with universities (as with most museums in Norway, other than very local community museums), or the national higher education system. The national natural history museum in Paris (Musée d'Histoire Naturelle) is funded by the higher education ministry as – in effect – a state research council (as indeed was the Natural History Museum in London until its controversial transfer from the Advisory Board for the Research Councils to the Office of Arts and Libraries in the mid-1980s).

A growing number of countries are moving museums out of direct state control into arms-length trustee or similar bodies, along the lines of trustee national museums in the UK. The Netherlands is experimenting with this, calling the process 'privatization' (though in fact the museums concerned remain predominantly state funded – see *Museums Journal* May 1990: 24) while in Sweden the staff of most public museums are now legally employed by trustees.

Last, but by no means least, there is a bewildering variety of different patterns of local government museums, and staff structures within these, across Europe. In marked contrast with recent trends in the UK, continental local authority museums, however small, are almost invariably autonomous units within the range of the local authority's services. The head of the museum is directly responsible for its operations to the city or town's political administration, whether a council, committee, mayor or specialist deputy mayor. In most other European countries the idea of the town museum, even if it has a professional staff of only one, being grouped with 'leisure services', tourism or the like, would be regarded as absurd.

---

1. Ministry of culture civil servant model

Denmark	National museum staff
France	Art and history museums, national and local
Greece	Most national and regional museums: part of the state antiquities department
Italy	National Museums and regional services of the cultural soprintendenza (inspectorate)
Spain	National museums

2. Regionally devolved civil servant model

Germany	Under the constitution the central government has no legal standing at all in the fields of education and culture – entirely a matter for the Länder (states)
Belgium	Almost all culture has now devolved to the two language-based regions (excluding Brussels as capital)
Spain	Museums in autonomous regions – e.g. Catalunya, Pais Vascos (Basque Country, etc.)

3. Museums as part of university higher education research council system
(*Museum staff usually civil servants within higher education system*)

France	Natural history museums (higher education ministry)
	Many workers employed by national research council (Centre National de la Récherche Scientifique – CNRS) are attached to museums of all kinds, e.g. national survey of rural French ethnography
Germany	Some Länder (states)
Greece	Some museums
Italy	Some museums
Norway	Most major museums, even the nationals, are fully integrated parts of the university system
Portugal	Some museums, especially natural history museums

4. Quasi-privatization in terms of management and staffing – e.g. trustee museums

Netherlands	Experiments in progress with what the Dutch government calls 'privatization' – in fact devolved independent management on lines of UK trustee national museums
Spain	Museums of 'pro bono' quasi-public charitable foundations e.g. La Caixa – national insurance organization which must use 50 per cent of its surplus for public works
Sweden	National and some local museums
UK	Most national museums now devolved to autonomous trustee bodies and the museum's own senior management
	Museums of government agencies, e.g. English Heritage
	Publicly financed, 'arms-length' independent museums

5. Local government

France	Though curatorial staff are Ministry of Culture civil servants seconded from ministry
Netherlands	Also county cultural advisers and curators
Denmark	Also county cultural advisers and curators
Germany	In some Länder (states)
Italy	Some museums
Greece	Some more local museums
Norway	Small local museums
UK	800 local authority museums

Fig. 22.1 Examples of the different patterns of museum staff organization and status across Europe

QUALIFICATIONS AND STATUS

A country's perception of the nature and status of museums as reflected in the organization and structure of the museum system has a significant effect on that country's view of what is expected of a museum professional in terms of education and qualifications.

It is hardly surprising that where museums are regarded as an integral part of the country's higher academic and research system, as in Norway or in the French museums of natural history, standard national criteria of academic and research excellence and performance are applied. Thus in one Norwegian museum the minimum entry requirement is a 'full' university degree – that is, one taken full-time over between five and seven years and with a significant research element and so nearer to an English M. Phil. than even a taught M.A. or M.Sc. degree. For promotions to senior museum posts, such as a senior curatorship in charge of a significant collection, standard university promotion criteria for progression to professional level apply, i.e. at least a Ph.D. if not a higher doctorate plus a record of successful research and publication in the relevant field. Similar criteria apply for both entry and promotion within museums in other European countries including the natural history museums in France and many German, Italian and Portuguese museums.

Unusually, Norway carried forward academic practice to the museum director level. Directors of the university-based national museums are not appointed: there is instead a system of rotating heads of museums who are periodically elected by the professional staff of the museum from among the suitably qualified senior curators for a limited term (normally five years and not renewable more than once) before reverting to a curatorial or research position in the museum.

Where museum staff are closely integrated into the national or regional civil services, as in French art and history museums, and many Spanish and Italian museums of all types, candidates for entry to the museum profession have to win a place through a rigorous public competition. Typically, this involves several written examinations covering history, public policy and law, taken over a period of several days and including a searching oral examination.

Although in some cases these competitions may theoretically be 'open' to all citizens (subject to specified age limits), in practice candidates almost invariably need the equivalent of a relevant bachelor's degree and significant postgraduate study, almost invariably to the equivalent of a master's degree, and probably a substantial period of museum work experience, usually as a volunteer or as a museum-based researcher (e.g. by doing a research degree on museum material). Nearly half of the successful students on the entry competition for the first eighteen month pre-entry training programme in the new Ecole Nationale du Patrimoine established in 1990 by the French Ministry of Culture had research degrees. Almost all the rest had some form of advanced postgraduate academic or professional qualification (e.g. the postgraduate diplomas of the Ecole du Louvre or the national archive school). Within five years the school hopes that almost all entrants will have at least master's degrees and preferably doctorates (see *Museums Journal* May 1992: 19).

In Denmark the new national law of museums lays down that in order to receive any grant from public funds (including those equivalent to the UK's area museum council grants) there must be a full-time 'professionally qualified' head of the museum. The Danish Council of Museums is responsible for determining what levels of academic qualification and museum experience constitute 'professionally qualified' in relation to each museum. It is also responsible for verifying and sanctioning the qualifications of museum professionals from other European community countries for the purposes of the 1990 directive on the mutual recognition of professional qualifications. In practice, an MA in a subject relevant to the proposed area of museum work is now the minimum entry qualification for any established professional post in Danish museums. However, a relevant doctorate would normally be expected for promotion to a more senior position, such as head of department or director in a larger, more important, museum.

In Sweden, where virtually all museums are now devolved to quasi-independent boards of trustees who are entitled to choose their own staff, a relevant (five-year) university degree is in practice the minimum requirement, and a relevant doctorate is now expected for appointment or promotion to the directorship of the larger national, regional and local authority museums.

After only the briefest overview of the European situation, it is clear that current UK practices and attitudes are totally out of line and perhaps quite irreconcilable with the approaches of most of the other European countries surveyed. The yawning gulf is one of attitude and not just a matter of 'paper' qualifications, though as in so many other areas of life, the UK appears chronically undereducated and underqualified. Consequently, as the European Community becomes more open to cross-national professional employment in practice as well as theory, inward movement of more highly qualified museum staff from the continent to the UK seems far more likely than movement in the opposite direction, even ignoring the traditional British fear of learning and using languages other than English.

Differences extend beyond the minimum level of relevant academic knowledge and ability to carry out professional museum work successfully. Many continental museum professionals are baffled by the current UK concentration on developing what are basically technical skills and competencies for museum work within the constraints of the National Vocational Qualification system. Such a system, they feel, diverts professionals from developing a philosophical understanding of the nature of museums and their functions as part of advanced studies in museology, and gaining relevant higher degrees to enhance their academic reputations to levels matching those of university staff.

PAY – AND TAXES

Levels of pay for museum professionals across Europe vary widely. This is illustrated in Figures 22.2, 22.3 and 22.4, in which all sums have been converted to annual salaries in UK pounds, using exchange rates prevailing in August 1992. No attempt has been made to adjust these for very widely varying levels of tax and social security deductions across the various countries, nor for the much higher levels of education and qualification demanded by many of the other European countries surveyed. Because of the highly fragmented position in Germany, especially in the former West Germany, where both education and culture have been the exclusive responsibility of the state governments for more than forty years, no German examples have been included in the graphs.

Also, before planning to emigrate, a UK museum professional should be warned that (despite our constant complaints of high taxation) both income tax and (especially) social security/national insurance deductions are far lower in the UK than in almost any other European country. Indeed, after allowing for the generous personal allowances, the UK's total level of deductions from pay for – say – a senior keeper in a major local government museum is probably only half that in most of the more developed community and EFTA countries. Consequently the 'real' (after tax, national insurance and superannuation) pay of most UK jobs is likely to be more attractive in relative terms to colleagues in many other European countries than the bare gross salary figures suggest.

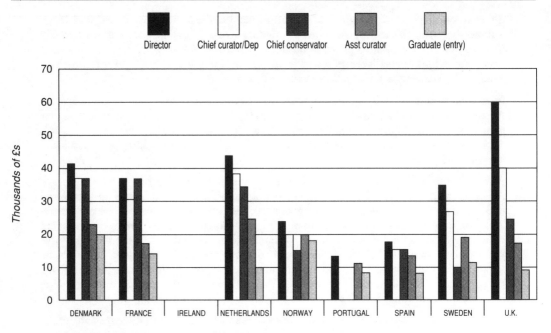

Fig. 22.2 Major national museums: maximum pay

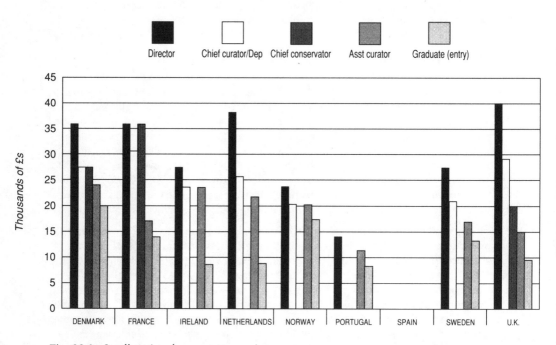

Fig. 22.3 Small national museums: maximum pay

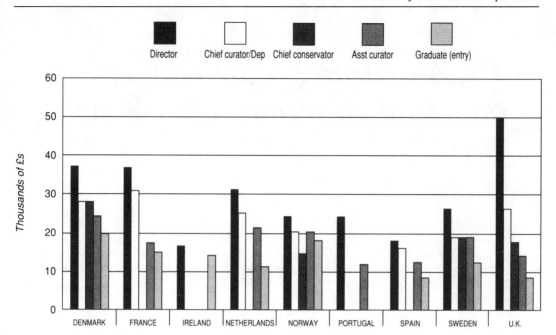

Fig. 22.4 Major regional/local museums: maximum pay

This paper first appeared in Museums Journal *(January 1993), pp. 26–9.*

23

The American art director as professional: results of a survey[1]

Paul DiMaggio

There are very few detailed studies of the museum profession and most tend to be concerned principally with statistics. A very valuable exception is the work undertaken by Paul DiMaggio on directors of American art museums. DiMaggio raised questions about how 'professionalism' is perceived and considered this in relation to the profiles of those who held key positions.

The art museum, as we now know it, came to America in the 1870s, a product of the conflicting impulses of first- and second-generation commercial elites for cultural respectability, popular enlightenment, and the definition and control of a distinctive high culture. The early museums, for the most part modelled after South Kensington, sought to educate the masses and provide moral uplift, and required little in the way of management or sophisticated aesthetic stewardship to do so.

The professional directorate emerged as a consequence of three related developments: the museums' acquisition of enough wealth to aspire towards artistically distinguished collections, the founding of art history departments at Harvard and other American universities, and the growth of collections. With the first of these came a shift from educational and social to aesthetic aims, as museums sought to toss out casts, copies, and 'inferior' works, to improve exhibition quality, and to upgrade collections. Such reforms required the supervision of trained art historians, and the art history departments provided these. The gradual expansion of art museums required full-time administrative personnel capable of integrating the work of the museums' many departments. From the beginning, then, the art museum director has performed both an aesthetic and administrative function.

No sooner had a critical mass of full-time trained staff appeared on the scene, than the notion of the 'museum professional' emerged with great force. By the 1920s, the American Association of Museums was heralding the ascendancy of the professional art museum director, qualified by a background in art historical studies.

The number of art museums in the United States grew throughout the twentieth century, requiring constant vigilance to ensure that gains in professional standards pioneered in the nation's major museums would be preserved in the regions. In the postwar period, economic growth, the rise of mass higher education, and, after 1965, public subsidy, fuelled an expansion of art museums' budgets, publics, and missions. The enlarged scale of museum activity, the proliferation of programmes and departments, and the differentiation of the funding environment to include corporations and government agencies as well as private patrons, increased the complexity of the administrative task exponentially.

The art museum director, long meant to be a scholar, was now expected, in the words of the Director of the Yale Art Gallery, also to be a 'businessman, educator, and lobbyist'.

The question of directorial professionalism became particularly vexed in the wake of the Metropolitan Museum's decision to adopt a dual directorship, shared by an art historian and an administrator, and by suggestions elsewhere that directors should be managers first and scholars second, if at all. The definition of professionalism appeared to be shifting from the aesthetic to the administrative, a development that shocked and threatened many directors. Although the Metropolitan's precedent has not been widely copied, the issue of what, in fact, the museum director is meant to be remains an important and sensitive one in the American art museum community.

In fact, Americans have had very little systematic information about who their art museum directors *are*: how they have been educated, how they evaluate their own training, and what opinions they hold about their profession. In order to address these issues, a survey was undertaken of the directors of the United States' 192 largest art museums. These 192 were identified on the basis of operating budget and attendance data collected by the National Centre for Educational Statistics. Members of the Association of Art Museum Directors not included in this data were added to the survey population. These museums represent about one-third of this country's art museums (617, according to a study sponsored by the National Institute of Museum Services), and account for far more than half of art museum expenditures in the United States. Directors of these museums were mailed a questionnaire in spring 1981. The first form was followed by another, then by a postcard, and finally by a succession of telephone calls, netting responses from 67.2 per cent of the directors surveyed.

PROFESSIONALISM

The term 'professionalism' is often used as a synonym for 'competence' or 'virtue'. Such a working definition is unilluminating, since competence, virtue, and even expertise can be found among the practitioners of any occupation. Nor can 'competence' – which is difficult enough to recognize close up – be assessed with questionnaires. Consequently, when I write of the 'professionalization' of the American art museum director, I refer only to changes in the extent to which the directorship has taken on a set of formal characteristics that distinguish professions from other skilled occupations, and make no evaluation of the performance of current directors or their predecessors.

These formal characteristics of a profession, drawn from decades of research on professionals and professionalizing occupations in other realms, include the following:

1 Advanced training and possession of a standard set of credentials.
2 Orderly careers entailing a lifetime commitment to professional practice.
3 Participation in professional activities outside one's home institution, including professional or quasi-professional associations.
4 Peer control of licensing, peer establishment and enforcement of ethical standards, and adherence to an ethic of responsibility to the profession as a whole.
5 Claims to authority based upon expertise, rather than, for example, status, wealth, or political influence.

Nowhere, of course, are art museum directors 'professionals' in all these senses. In the United States, for example, museum directors are not licensed, ethical standards are promulgated but not centrally enforced, and standard credentials are not required. None the less, occupations can be more or less professionalized according to the extent to which they conform to these five criteria. In the sections that follow, we shall look at the professionalization of the American art museum directorate along each of the dimensions noted above.

TRAINING AND CREDENTIALS

While advanced degrees are not legally required for art museum directors in the United States, more than 95 per cent of those surveyed had pursued their education beyond college. Only 30 per cent, however, possess Ph.D.s in art history, suggesting that the domination of the art museum directorship by professional art historians is less than complete. More than half of the directors majored in either art or art history in college, and another 30 per cent majored in one of the humanities. Almost three-fifths attended prestigious small colleges or universities.

In recent years, however, the Ph.D. in art history has become more prevalent. Of these directors who took their first art museum job before 1963 (approximately one-third of those surveyed), only one in six has a doctorate, as do fewer than one in four of directors who took their first museum job between 1963 and 1968 (roughly another third). By contrast, more than half (55 per cent) of the directors who have entered museum work since 1968 hold Ph.D.s in art history.

The increase in the importance of the Ph.D. has been accompanied by a decline in the social status of the directors' families of origin. Almost twice as many fathers and mothers of the most senior directors were college graduates as those of the post-1968 generation. Twice as many of the former's principal guardians owned or held top manegerial positions in large businesses or were professionals. One in five of the grandparents of the more junior directors were born in eastern Europe, compared to just one in twenty of the grandparents of the pre-1963 cohort. Almost half of the more senior directors attended a private secondary school, compared to just over one in six of the post-1968 generation.

These figures suggest a dramatic professionalization, in educational terms, of the American art museum directorship during the past twenty years. The concomitant relative democratization of the position is consistent with a change in the basis of the directors' claims to authority from social distinction to expertise. (It should be noted, however, that the directors surveyed were more than 80 per cent male and less than 5 per cent non-white.)

CAREERS

There is no single progression of jobs that leads inexorably to the art museum directorship. More than two-fifths of the directors moved directly into museum work at the conclusion of their formal education; another quarter taught at the university level before entering the art museum. (Fewer than one in ten came from business or administration.) Of those entering directly from school, almost half became curators, while almost another fifth worked in research, conservation, or registration. Of those entering museum work from university teaching, more than half became directors immediately, while more than a quarter took curatorial positions. Most directors reached their current position through curatorial work, university teaching, or some combination thereof. During the course of their careers, more than two-fifths of the directors have been curators, almost two-fifths have taught in a university, one-fifth have been assistant directors, and about one in eight have worked in museum education. More than one in five have, at some point in their lives, worked in a business unrelated to the arts.

Like their educational preparation, however, the directors' career experiences appear to be changing. Since 1968, art museum directors have been entering the field later and starting at a higher rank than they did in earlier years. Three-fifths of the pre-1963 generation went from school into museum work, compared to two-fifths of the 1963–8 cohort, and only one-fifth of the post-1968 directors. Almost a third of the latter entered art museum work as directors, compared to just one in seven of the most senior directors.

What is more, almost half of the post-1968 generation taught at university level before entering museum work, compared to just one in twenty of the pre-1963 generation and less than a quarter of the 1963–8 cohort. (Many of the more senior directors have taken part-time university positions after entering museum work, however.) The post-1968 cohort are less likely to have served as associate directors. Strikingly, given the fears of some American directors that the managers are taking over, fewer of the relative newcomers have ever worked in a business unrelated to the arts. And, also strikingly, fewer (just over one-third compared to almost 60 per cent of the pre-1963 cohort) have ever worked as curators. What this suggests is that the art museum directorship is, if anything, becoming less of a career, or rather that art museum work is becoming one branch of a career in art history, rather than a lifetime commitment in itself. Curatorship has been at least partially supplanted by university teaching as preparation for the directorship.

It is possible, of course, that although art museum directors are recruited from university art history faculties, once recruited they do not stray. We asked the directors to estimate on a five-point scale (ranging from 'very unlikely' to 'very likely') the probability that they would, at some point in their careers, hold a number of different kinds of jobs. Two-thirds of the respondents reported that they were 'somewhat' or 'very' likely to take jobs as directors of similar museums, or of larger or more prestigious art museums. Since the total includes a number of older directors who may view their current position as their last, these figures suggest a strong commitment to art museum work. A fifth of the directors thought it likely that they would some day return to curatorships, and another fifth expected to work for public arts agencies. Almost one-third of the directors, however, reported it 'somewhat' or 'very' likely that they would accept a job 'unrelated to museums or the visual arts', a rather high percentage anticipating eventual departure from the field. This latter group included almost half of the post-1968 generation. Its size, however, is less indicative of alienation than of ambivalence, since almost four-fifths of this group also expect to direct a larger or more prestigious art museum.

Another way of defining the contours of a profession is to see it as a class of people who participate in a single labour market. There does appear to be a single market for art museum directors: careers involve moves back and forth between large generalist art museums, university galleries, museums of modern art, and local 'art centres'. There does not, however, seem to be a single museum labour market spanning history and science, as well as art, museums. Only one in ten of the directors have ever worked in a museum that was not an art museum; fewer than one in five (and none of the pre-1963 generation) expect ever to do so.

PROFESSIONAL PARTICIPATION

By any measure, American art museum directors participate actively in a professional community. Almost three-quarters are members of the Association of Art Museum

Directors (the leading professional association); more than half have served on committees of that association, and almost two-thirds have attended one or more of its national conferences during the past five years. Almost half are members of the association of art historians (the College Art Association), and more than half have attended at least one of its national conferences. More than a fifth have served on committees of the American Association of Museums (the leading service organization for the museum field), and nearly two-thirds have attended at least one of its national conferences during the past five years. More than half are members of a state museum association, almost two-thirds of a regional museum association, and about one in six have served as officers or board members of each.

Art museum directors also participate actively as reviewers or panellists for public agencies that provide subsidies to museums. Despite the size and inclusiveness of the group surveyed, almost two-fifths have served on the Museums Panel of the National Endowment of the Arts, and about a quarter have served on other NEA panels. A third of the directors have been panellists or reviewers for the National Endowment for the Humanities (which also supports museum projects). And almost one-quarter have been reviewers for or advisors to the Museum Services Institute, a small federal agency that gives operating support to museums of all kinds. Almost two-fifths of the directors have sat on grant-award panels of state arts agency museum programmes, and more than a quarter have been members of other state–arts–agency review panels.

Although directors of the pre-1963 cohort are more likely than others to be active in the national professional community, activity levels among the post-1968 generation are relatively high as well. Nor are such activities solely the prerogative of directors of the larger art museums, or of directors with doctorates in art history. In short, American art museum directors appear to be active participants in the professional community knit together by a broad array of opportunities for collegial interaction.

ATTITUDES TOWARDS PEER CONTROL

Do art museum directors espouse the typically 'professional' attitudes that professional associations should promulgate and enforce standards of ethics, and control (either directly or through government) the licensing of practitioners? Yes, and no, respectively. Almost all of the directors rated establishing ethical standards as a 'very important' (3 on a 3-point scale) function of museum service organizations. But only one in six rated preventing unqualified persons from working in museum positions as a 'very important' role.

If directors believe that service organizations should promulgate ethical standards, who do they believe should enforce them? Strikingly, about half of the directors said that standards should be enforced by each museum's own board of trustees, a 'non-professional' response in so far as it rejects professional autonomy in sanctioning peers. About one-fifth would vest enforcement with the American Association of Museums, and one-fifth with the art museum directors' professional association, the Association of Art Museum Directors. Ten per cent chose other options, and not a single director would vest enforcement responsibility in government agencies that support museums.

Directors with doctorates in art history were more likely to offer 'professional' responses: Almost 30 per cent considered the 'licensing' role of service organization an important one. Only one-third would leave enforcement of ethical standards to their own trustees, while a third would vest responsibility with the Association of Art Museum Directors.

The American Association of Museums has developed a voluntary programme to accredit American art museums that some see as the first step towards national certification. Given a choice between a statement approving of the accreditation programme and one deploring it, more than 90 per cent of the directors chose the former. Directors were asked to choose between another two statements, one of which asserted that museum directors must act in the interests of their own institution when those interests and those of the museum profession diverge; and a second stating that, given such a conflict, directors are obliged to act in the best interest of the field. The former statement – again, the 'non-professional' response – was chosen by 57.5 per cent of the directors.

The 'museum profession' has never been in a position to restrict entry into museum work nor to enforce its own standards of ethics. These responses indicate substantial, albeit not majority (except among the Ph.D.s), approval for collective enforcement of ethical standards; and broad and strong support for an accreditation programme that may be seen as a tentative step towards formal certification. What is more, a sizeable minority of the growing number of art history doctoral degree holders is prepared to support some version of professional licensing. None the less, there is substantial ambivalence among these directors about the extent to which the profession rather than their own trustees deserve their allegiance. Slightly more than half feel a primary responsibility to their trustees, and half would let trustees enforce ethical standards without outside interference.

ATTITUDES TOWARDS PROFESSIONAL EXPERTISE

The hallmark of any profession is the grounding of claims to authority in some kind of expertise. Since the director is expected to provide both aesthetic and administrative leadership, it is less than obvious, a priori, which form of expertise – in art or in management – will provide this grounding. To explore this question, we asked directors to indicate if they considered each of several factors 'very important', 'somewhat important', or 'unimportant' as qualifications for a directorship like their own. These factors included (but were not limited to) scholarship, connoisseurship, management experience, and formal training in administration.

Almost half of the directors rated scholarship a 'very important' qualification, while fewer than one in twenty called it unimportant. Even more (almost two-thirds) said the same of the connoisseurship. Nearly three-quarters of the directors rated management experience 'very important', but fewer than one in ten attributed great importance to formal training in administration. (Almost one-third called the latter 'unimportant'.) Directors, then, demonstrate concern for both aesthetic and administrative competence, but express little conviction that formal training in the latter is important.

Directors were also asked to assess the importance of several possible roles for 'service organizations' (like the American Association of Museums) in the museum field. Fewer than a third rated providing opportunities for management training a very important function, while fewer than half indicated it 'very important' for service organizations to keep members 'up to date' on current management techniques. (By contrast, administrators of orchestras, theatres, and community arts agencies were far more likely to rate these functions highly.)

Finally, directors were asked to choose between two statements. One read, 'While business sense is useful, it is essential that a museum director have a strong scholarly and curatorial background'; the other stated, 'While a museum director must be sensitive to artistic questions, it is crucial that he or she have a strong background in management.' Three-quarters of the respondents chose the first of these two statements, indicating that, as a group, directors consider aesthetic expertise more vital to their role than administrative. Directors were also asked to indicate how difficult it was for them to make the choice: Almost three-quarters of the directors who chose the first option reported the decision an 'easy' one, compared to only two-fifths of those who opted for the latter.

There is some evidence that more recent entrants to the art museum field place greater stock in administrative skills than do their predecessors. Almost one-quarter of the post-1968 generation, compared to not a single director who entered the field before 1963, consider formal training in administration a very important qualification for directors. Almost all of the pre-1968 cohort (90 per cent) chose the first ('scholarly and curatorial') forced-choice Not surprisingly their responses of the directors who entered the field since 1963.

Not surprisingly, directors who hold doctoral degrees in art history were less likely to emphasize administrative skills in their responses. Just over three-fifths of the Ph.D.-holders, compared to about four-fifths of other directors, considered management experience a 'very important' directorial qualification, and none of the Ph.D.s so rated formal training in administration. Directors with doctoral degrees were less likely than others to rate management training a 'very important' function of museum service organizations. Nearly all (93.55 per cent) of the art history doctoral degree holders opted for aesthetic over managerial qualifications in the forced-choice question, compared to just over two-thirds of the other directors. The fact that directors who have earned their doctorates (a growing proportion of the field) tend to reject a professional self-definition as administrators, while among directors without the Ph.D. the percentage embracing such a self-definition appears to be increasing over time, suggests the possibility that the profession may be in the process of polarizing between advocates of the aesthetic and administrative views.

THE PROBLEM OF TRAINING

Whatever their beliefs about the relative importance of aesthetic and administrative qualification, the art museum directors surveyed tended to agree that they could have benefited from better preparation for the administrative aspects of their work. Asked to rate their preparation at the time they accepted their first directorship for each of seven management functions as 'good', 'fair', or 'poor', a plurality reported 'good preparation' for trustee relations alone. Over half reported that they were poorly prepared for labour relations; more than two-fifths that their preparation for government relations and financial management was poor, and approximately one-quarter that they were poorly prepared for personnel management, planning and development, and marketing and public relations. Nor do preparation levels appear to have improved over time. The self-evaluations of the post-1968 generation were not more positive than those of the pre-1963 cohort.

For each of these functions, directors were more likely to report having learned 'on the job' than through any other means. None the less, significant minorities indicated that they had attended workshops, retained consultants, or even attended university art administration or general management courses to develop their skills in these areas. Curiously (given the post-1968 cohort's greater emphasis on managerial training), it is not the most junior cohort, but rather the generation that entered the field between 1963 and 1968, that is most likely to report formal training in specific management topics. Directors were divided in their overall assessments of all training formats but 'on-the-job learning', about which they were overwhelmingly positive. Those directors who had actually employed each means of learning a specific skill tended to report that workshops and consultants were useful for most kinds of learning while university arts administration and general management courses were less well regarded.

THE PARADOXES OF PROFESSIONALISM

In some respects, American art museum directors are professional and becoming more so; in other respects, their attitudes do not correspond to those typical of practitioners in other, more established professions. Art museum directors have become more educated, particularly more likely to hold doctorates in art history. They participate actively in a professional field. They support efforts to promulgate standards of professional ethics, although only the doctorate holders are very likely to recommend vesting responsibility for enforcement of these standards in a professional association. Overall, support for collegial rather than trustee control of the museum seems limited and ambivalent. Careers do not have the orderly sequential character of those in many other professions. And most directors hold that their first responsibility is to their own institutions rather than to their profession.

This professional ambivalence of art museum directors is attributable to three enduring paradoxes in the demands of directorial work. The first of these is endemic to all 'professional managers'. The second and third are peculiar to the art museum.

Management versus professionalism

Professionalism involves a primary allegiance to standards set autonomously by one's professional peers. Management involves an ethos of responsibility to an organization and its governing board. When the values of the profession and the needs of an organization conflict, the director is bound (unless the conflict is sufficiently acute to warrant resignation) to pursue the interests of the museum entrusted to his or her care. While professionalism may be a useful strategy for administrators who wish to increase their autonomy and power, the 'professional manager' can never realize the collegial idea.

A satellite profession

The conflict between professional and organizational responsibility may be particularly acute for museum directors from academic backgrounds, who see themselves as professional scholars first and administrators second. To the extent that the American museum directorship is becoming a branch or satellite of the art historian profession, the director may find that museums afford less autonomy than universities. (University museums, which often do not have their own boards of trustees, are in some cases an exception to this rule.) A pattern of recruitment of directors from the university also militates against the development of a standard career pattern internal to the art museum itself. Such a pattern, in other professions, serves both to socialize practitioners by subjecting each to a similar succession of roles; and to motivate them by holding out the promise of eventual promotion. To the extent that the museum directorship becomes a satellite profession, we would expect the community of directors to become less well integrated and the attractiveness of curatorships to decline.

Administrators without expertise

Art historians who work as curators can justifiably claim that their expertise informs directly the execution of their professional responsibilities. By contrast, as the directorship becomes more an administrative and less an aesthetic position, directors find their scholarly credentials irrelevant to an increasing portion of their regular duties. For professionals, whose claims to authority are based on a nexus between training and responsibility, such a disjucture may be a threatening one.

One solution, of course, would be to restrict art historians to curatorial positions and let trained administrators run art museums. Most American museum directors, however, would raise at least two objections to this solution. First, the directors must frequently, in an administrative capacity, allocate resources among alternative curatorial goals: making such decisions intelligently, it is argued, requires that the decision-maker have a substantive understanding of the issues at stake. None the less, this argument is not entirely compelling. The experience of American corporations indicates that generalist managers can make technical allocation decisions (e.g. among research and development options) with sufficient specialist advice.

More compelling is the fear of many directors that professional managers would alter the museum's traditional goals, exiling scholarship, conservation, and connoisseurship in favour of entertainment, education, and earned income. Indeed, such fears are borne out, to some extent, in the data we collected. Directors who emphasized the importance of administrative training and experience more than others were also more likely to approve (and less likely to worry about the side effects) of a range of earned income producing schemes and, to a lesser extent, educational and outreach activities. By contrast, the responses of directors with Ph.D.s were more likely than those of others to indicate a concern about the effects of commercial and educational ventures on the art museum's aesthetic mission. It is not necessary to take a stand on the relative importance of aesthetic, commercial and educational values to suggest that changes in the training and recruitment of museum directors could cause a marked shift in the balance of attention devoted to those values in American art museums.

The imperfect professionalism of the American art museum director, then, is a response to tension between, on the one hand, the increasing complexity of museum administration and, on the other, the American art museum's traditional (if not uncontested) aesthetic and scholarly mission. Responses to this tension have ranged from the dual directorship of the Metropolitan Museum, to the addition to museum staffs of numerous specialists in finance and administration, to the efforts of directors to acquire management educations on a continuing basis. The current era, then, is one of flux and experimentation. The paradoxes of professionalism, and the tensions these reflect, are likely to vex American art museum directors and the museum community for some time to come.

This paper first appeared in Bullet *(June 1993), pp. 5–9.*

NOTE

1 The research described herein was supported by a grant from the Research Division of the National Endowment for the Arts, and received financial, moral and institutional support from the Program on Non-Profit Organizations of Yale University. The research assistance of Elizabeth Huntley, Naomi Rutenberg, Caroline Watts, and, above all Frank P. Romo and Kristen Stenberg, is gratefully

REFERENCES

Professor DiMaggio, at the time of writing this paper, was with the Program on Non-profit Organizations, Institution for Social and Policy Studies at Yale. He is currently Professor in the Department of Sociology, Princeton University. Among his other papers the following also have relevance for the European scene:

DiMaggio, P. and Useem, M. (date) 'Cultural democracy in a period of cultural expansion', *Social Problems* 26(2): 179–97.
—— (1978) 'Cultural property and public policy – emerging tensions in government support for the arts', *Social Research* 45(2): 356–89
—— (1978) 'Social class and arts consumption – origins and consequences of class differences in exposure to arts in America', *Theory and Society* 5(1): 141–61.
—— (1980) 'Small-scale policy research in the arts', *Policy Analysis* 6(2): 187–209.
DiMaggio, P. (1982) 'Cultural entrepreneurship in nineteenth-century Boston': (Part I): 'The creation of an organizational base for high culture in America'; (Part II): 'The classification and framing of American art', *Media, Culture and Society* 4: 33–50; 303–22.
—— (1983) 'Can culture survive the marketplace?', *Journal of Arts Management and Law*, special issue on public policy towards the Arts, ed. A. Keller

24

Museum sector workforce survey: an analysis of the workforce in the museum, gallery and heritage sector in the United Kingdom

Mary Klemm and Nicholas Wilson (University of Bradford Management Centre) and Monica Scott (Museum Training Institute)

At the time of preparing this reader, the most up-to-date summary of the museums profession in the UK was that published by the Museum Training Institute (MTI). Based on a questionnaire survey, it provides some indication of the current workforce profile. It should, however, be borne in mind that in this survey MTI purposefully took a wide definition and included figures which related to jobs in historic houses and on heritage sites. Within the museums profession these are seen as complementary to, rather than constituent areas of, museum work.

1 INTRODUCTION AND OBJECTIVES: PURPOSE OF THE STUDY

1.1 This study was commissioned by the Museum Training Institute in December 1991. The primary objective was to obtain accurate statistics on the numbers and characteristics of the workforce in the museums, galleries and heritage sector. Further objectives were to obtain information on training needs, skills shortages and more broadly the approaches to the planning and development of human resources by employers throughout the sector.

1.2 Definition of the sector

1.2.1 The survey is aimed at measuring the size and composition of the workforce, and examining the situation vis-à-vis training across the entire heritage sector, which has not been attempted before. Other studies have been more narrowly focused, but the remit of this study, and the changing environment in which museums are operating, required that the sector be defined in the broadest sense. The approach incorporates traditional national and local authority museums and art galleries with historic houses, gardens and a variety of arts and heritage attractions. This wider view is in keeping with the International Council of Museums definition of a museum as a

> permanent institution in the service of society and of its development, open to the public, which acquires, conserves, researches, communicates and exhibits material evidence of man and his environment for the purposes of study, education and enjoyment.

1.2.2 Consequently, both public and private sectors are included, as are some museums and attractions which are run as a business. The range of organizations and their employees is thus broader than that of previous studies.

1.2.3 The justification for this approach is that in terms of employment and career structures, these organizations are in the same labour market, are served by the same government ministry, the Department of National Heritage, and form a subset of the broader tourism and leisure industry. Clearly there are major differences in the type and level of abilities required by a major national museum and a small voluntary one, but there are also common elements, for example skills in conservation, interpretation and customer care.

1.2.4 For the purposes of this study, the workforce is defined by the functions performed by its members, not the particular type of organization in which an individual is employed. Ideally, where generic skills exist, they should be transferable across the sector. *In view of all the above, the term 'museum' will be used henceforth to represent all the types of institutions mentioned in para. 1.2.1.*

1.3 Executive summary

1.3.1 This study shows that the museums galleries and heritage sector is larger than was previously thought, both in terms of employees and number of organizations.

1.3.2 There are currently around 40,000 people employed in the sector, of whom two-thirds are full time. Around 20 per cent of employees are on various types of temporary contracts.

1.3.3 The number of volunteers is estimated to be between 25,000 and 30,000 people. A considerable number of museums are dependent entirely on volunteers. There is a higher proportion of volunteers in the independent than in the local authority sector.

1.3.4 Two-thirds of employees, the largest group overall, work in security and support roles: guarding and transporting the collections, dealing with the public, performing clerical, retailing, catering and 'DIY' duties. One-third of museum employees are doing curatorial and/or managerial jobs of various kinds: conserving the collections, interpreting them for the public and managing the planning, finance and human resources of the organization.

1.3.5 There are equal numbers of men and women in the museums workforce as a whole. The proportion of women is higher than the national average for all employees. Women hold 51 per cent of all curatorial and managerial posts in the local authority sector and 46 per cent in the nationals and independents.

1.3.6 In terms of age the workforce is reasonably balanced overall. There does not appear to be a succession problem with nearly 70 per cent of curators and managers under 45. The average of security and support staff is somewhat older, with 46 per cent over 45.

1.3.7 The ethnic minorities are under-represented with 2.2 per cent of the total museums workforce nationally, most of whom are concentrated in security and support roles. This compares with 3.9 per cent from the ethnic minorities in the UK workforce as a whole.[1]

1.3.8 Staff turnover is perceived as low in this industry. There is also variability in the level of demand as a result of seasonal and other trend factors. This variability creates special problems for the planning of work and responding to training needs.

1.3.9 The museums and galleries sector is full of highly qualified people in terms of academic qualifications, with over 85 per cent of curators and managers having degrees and higher degrees, including the voluntary sector. Around 8 per cent of security and support staff have university degrees, and over 50 per cent have GCSE level qualifications.

1.3.10 British museums and galleries spend an average of £91 per year per employee on formal training for their staff. This averages out at just over 1 per cent of their total personnel budget, although more is spent by the nationals.

1.3.11 In-service training is perceived as important by all types of museum, although only about half of the workforce had received any in-service training in the past five years. The exception to this were curators and managers in local authority museums, where the percentage was 69 per cent. Major training providers were the Area Museums Councils, the local authorities and the Museums Association. The majority of employers offered incentives to undertake training.

1.3.12 Many small museums, particularly independent ones in the remoter parts of the UK, found it difficult to obtain affordable training. They were especially concerned to obtain the knowledge to conserve their collections. Local authority cutbacks have meant that there is much less professional help and advice available.

1.3.13 Respondents felt that their skill deficiencies could be remedied by training courses, particularly in curatorial and managerial skills, and information technology.

1.3.14 The evidence showed some disappointment with the lack of career routes within organizations for museum employees, particularly for security and support staff for local authorities. Curators and managers complained of lack of status and pay compared to other local authority professionals. Overall low pay and the inability to offer continuity of employment was seen as a barrier to obtaining good quality staff.

1.3.15 On the issue of planning mechanisms the picture is a mixed one. Three-quarters of museums and galleries have a business plan, and nearly half have performance appraisal and performance related pay. However only a small minority had a skills audit, and only a third had a training plan. This suggests that some of this planning may be superficial, as it would be difficult to achieve the targets set out in a business plan without knowing the skills of the workforce and making arrangements to remedy the deficiencies.

1.4. Numbers employed in the industry

1.4.1 As a background to the current survey, it is appropriate to consider the information on the industry workforce which is available from Government Employment statistics.

1.4.2 The tourism and leisure industry has grown in recent years and now employs 1.5 million people in the UK. The majority (70 per cent) of these employees work in hotel, catering and travel, but approximately 20 per cent of employees in the sector work in leisure and related services. Ten per cent are self-employed.[2] The leisure sector, including sport and recreation, employs in the region of 350,000 people and within this total the numbers employed in libraries, museums, art galleries, botanical and zoological gardens was 64,900 in June 1992, having fluctuated between 60,000 and 68,000[3] in the past few years. Breakdowns of these statistics are available from the most recent census of employment in 1989 and are as follows:[4]

Full time < 30 hours per week	40,800
Part time > 30 hours per week	26,500
Total	67,300

1.4.3 It is more difficult to segregate museums and galleries' employees from this total, but it is possible to make an estimate for 1992 as follows:

Total for Standard Industrial Classification (SIC) 977 (libraries, museums and art galleries)	64,900
Less Employees in public libraries[5]	28,600
Total museums galleries paid workforce	36,300

1.4.4 Using the same ratio of full- to part-time workers that existed in 1989 would give the breakdown for 1992 as:

Full-time employees	23,600
Part-time employees	12,700
Total employees	36,300
plus an estimated 10 per cent self-employed (based on Parsons 1986 study)	3,630
Grand total (excluding volunteers)	39,930

1.4.5 Because of the method of calculation this figure can only be an estimate of the total paid workforce in the museums and galleries sector. However, it is considerably greater than the estimated total of 12,000 employees given by the Museums Data-Base study in the mid-1980s.

1.4.6 Recent government reports point to the importance of museums, arts and heritage attractions in providing future economic growth and employment, as well as balance of payments stability. If it is to fulfil its potential in this respect one requirement for the industry is a coherent training strategy, supported and informed by a database which provides information on skills, qualifications, delivery methods and other training-related issues.

1.5 Previous research

1.5.1 Previous studies of the employment and training in this sector include:

- *The Hale Report on Museum Professional Training and Career Structure*, 1987.
- *The Museums Association Data-Base Project*, 1987 and 1989 update.
- *The Macmillan Intek Report*, 1988.
- *The Welsh Joint Education Committee Report on Occupational Mapping*, 1990.
- *The Manton Report on Training for Museums*, 1991.
- *The Road to Wigan Pier: Managing Local Authority Museums*, 1991.
- *Local Authorities and Museums*, Museums and Galleries Commission Working Party, 1991.

- *New Visions for Independent Museums in the UK* by Victor Middleton, for the Association of Independent Museums in the UK, 1990.
- *Museums and Galleries Funding and Finance*: *Cultural Trends* 14, edited by Jeremy Eckstein, Policy Studies Institute, 1992.
- *The Report on the Development of Performance Indicators for National Museums and Galleries*, Office of Arts and Libraries, 1991.

A brief summary of the relevant aspects of these reports follows.

1.5.2 The *Hale Report* was critical of training policies and provision in the sector and recommended the establishment of a new national body to co-ordinate training for staff at all levels. MTI was established with the aim of fulfilling this role.

1.5.3 The *Museums Data-Base Project* was intended to be the most comprehensive survey and analysis of all aspects of museums in the UK. It collected and analysed an impressive amount of data of which information about staffing formed only a small part. The initial research identified 2,131 institutions in the UK which it classed as museums, according to the following precise definition: 'an institution which collects, documents, preserves, exhibits and interprets material evidence and associated information for the public benefit'. The sample was reduced from an original number of 3,537. This total of 2,131 museums was accepted as an underestimate even at the time of the publication of the *Hale Report* which noted that in the south-east (AMSSEE) area there were 58 per cent more museums in existence than were recorded by the survey. On the basis of this survey, the report estimated that the full-time paid workforce in UK museums numbered around 12,000.

1.5.4 *The Macmillan Intek Report* was the result of a study done for the Museums Association in 1988–9 to determine training needs. The main focus of the results was on the training needs of curators – only 13 per cent of the sample referred to training for attendant staff.

1.5.5 The study in *Occupational Mapping* was undertaken for MTI in 1990. Its purpose was to identify first the range of occupations across the museums, galleries and heritage sector and second the extent of qualifications standards. The complexity of the sector, and the huge variety of tasks undertaken by museum staff made the mapping exercise extremely difficult. No nationally accredited standards had been specifically developed for the sector. In terms of other qualifications provision was patchy, with some well-established academic courses but other pockets of specialism for which there was no training, and a plethora of short courses to meet specific needs on an ad hoc basis.

1.5.6 The *Manton Report* looked at expenditure on museum training in a sample of 412 UK museums, and noted a growth in this expenditure between 1988 and 1991, with spending per head highest in Scotland. Elsewhere levels of spending were very variable; neither size nor type of museum were determinants. The author noted the need to distinguish between general and specific training for museum employees.

1.5.7 The Audit Commission report, *The Road to Wigan Pier* was specifically concerned with the management of local authority museums. It was critical of the way that some local authority museums were managed, particularly with respect to the care of collections and the lack of management skills, such as business planning, financial control and market awareness.

1.5.8 The *Middleton Report* on the independent museums sector pointed to the difficult market conditions faced by many independent museums, particularly the traditional type. These museums are facing increasing competition for consumers' time and disposable income from other leisure attractions such as theme parks, new heritage attractions and retailing and leisure centres. Using data on visits from the English Tourist Board, he notes that with an average of twenty new museums opening each year the capacity of museums is growing faster than the level of demand. Only a modest growth in museum visits is predicted for the next decade. To prepare them for this more vigorous commercial environment the report recommends that the independent museums (who are mostly dependent on self-engendered income) undertake more management training, especially marketing and research, business planning, financial and human resource management and information technology.

1.5.9 The *Cultural Trends Report* on museum and gallery funding reviews the complex administrative and funding structure for the different types of museums in the UK structure now united under the purview of the Department of National Heritage. It notes the move towards more commercial awareness by national and local authority museums and the need to provide benchmarks against which to monitor their performance. This implies the development of occupational standards for all aspects of the profession and the provision of training programmes for the curatorial, management and customer care aspects of museum work. This report estimated the total number of museums in the UK to be in the region of 2,000.

1.5.10 The report on the *Development of Performance Indicators* for the National Museums and Galleries emphasized that 'national museums and galleries need to show that they are using the funds provided by private taxpayers as efficiently and effectively as possible'. This indicates a need for strategic and operational planning, and obviously involves the effective deployment of human resources in the museums and galleries.

Conclusion

1.5.11 These reports provide valuable information on aspects of general and human ,resource management in the museums and galleries sector. However, there remained a basic deficiency in respect of basic data on the size and characteristics of the workforce. This was partly due to the highly varied and complex nature of the sector, and the difficulties encountered by previous researchers in attempting to define it.

2 METHODOLOGY FOR THE WORKFORCE SKILLS SURVEY

To conform to the broad definition of the museums sector outlined at the outset of this report, and to take note of the variety of institutions and the patchy nature of existing information, it was decided to conduct a postal survey of as large a number of UK museums, art galleries and heritage attractions as could be achieved within the time and budget allowed. To do this it was necessary to look more widely than the museums registered in the Museums Association *Yearbook* and those registered under the Museums and Galleries Commission DOMUS scheme. The museum definitions used by the MA and the MGC exclude museums which distribute profits and make no mention, as the ICOM definition does, of 'public enjoyment'. The mailing list was compiled from a variety of sources.

2.1 The pilot survey

While the mailing list was being compiled, a pilot questionnaire was sent to fifteen museums, mostly in the Yorkshire area. The returns from this resulted in several modifications:

- The questionnaire was simplified, particularly with respect to staff qualifications.
- Some local authorities had a shared workforce between the museums in their service. To avoid double counting it was decided to send a separate and modified questionnaire to the directors of all UK local authority museums services.
- For the sake of consistency in the resulting data it was decided to send the same questionnaire to all museums on our composite list, despite the wide variation in their size, status and objectives. To elicit a good response from the small establishments a covering note asked for the basic workforce information only.

2.2 The final questionnaires

Two types of questionnaire were sent out:

- One for individual museums which asked the curator or manager of the museum for information on the size and characteristics of the workforce (numbers employed, age, gender, qualifications) and about problems, policies and budgets with respect to training, careers and workforce planning.
- A second questionnaire for all local authority museum services to be completed by the head of the service. The information requested closely mirrored that for the individual museum questionnaire but was to cover all employees and institutions in the service.

2.3 The sample

2.3.1 Because of the changing nature of the sector, and the limited nature of previous surveys, it was decided not to take a sample, but to attempt to reach total population of museums, galleries and heritage organizations which fitted the ICOM definition. Time, budget and the need to obtain the co-operation of several organizations were the main constraints. The mailing lists were drawn up from a variety of sources. For the individual museums the mailing list of 2,556 institutions was selected from:

- The MTI mailing list.
- The 1992 Museums *Yearbook*.
- The membership list of the Historic House Association.
- The National Trust for Scotland *Handbook*.
- The BTA *List of Tourist Attractions*.
- The *Local Government Companion*.
- The Historic Royal Palaces Agency.

2.3.2 Regrettably, neither the English National Trust nor English Heritage consented to take part in the survey on an institutional level, although a few of their members who were on the MTI mailing list did respond positively.

2.3.3 To obtain a figure for the total population of museums, galleries and heritage attractions in Britain, we have added the figure for the total sample of individual museums, which included local authority museums, to the number of visitor sites of English Heritage, and the number of houses owned by the English National Trust.

Sample compiled from above list	2,556
English Heritage	350
English National Trust	300
Total	3,206

2.3.4 This figure is estimated to be close to the total UK population of museums, galleries and heritage attractions. This figure is larger than that recorded by previous studies because of the wider definition explained at the outset of this report, and also because we suspect that some small museums have hitherto been unrecorded. This applies particularly to some voluntary museums, and some privately owned and commercially based heritage attractions which own and manage collections.

2.3.5 The local authority museum services were treated as a separate sample as it was investigating the service rather than individual museums. A mailing list of 198 local authorities was compiled from the *Local Government Companion*. In some cases it was possible to identify the existence of a museums service from the local authorities entry and a named head of the service. In other cases it was not clear that the authority had any museums under their control. Both questionnaires were mailed in July 1992 and a response requested within eight weeks.

2.4 Methodology for evaluating results

It was decided to evaluate the results of the two samples separately since, although some local authority museums were included in Sample 2, the respondent would be different. The two samples meant that the views of both the head of the service and the curators of museums in the service could be canvassed separately. However, in practice there were not many incidences in which the same museum appeared in both result samples – most services had decided to do one or the other. To eliminate double counting the samples were cross-checked and, for the totals count only, the number of employees was reduced by 4.2 per cent.

2.4.1 Response rates

The response to the survey was excellent, giving an overall response rate of around 40 per cent of the total population (see note above) of museums, galleries, etc. in the UK. Of the 2,556 individual museums and historic houses the number of useable responses received and analysed totalled 914 – an actual response rate of 36 per cent. However the real rate was higher because some council museums routed their response via the questionnaire for the whole service. For the local authority services the response rate was 52 per cent.

This paper first appeared in Mary Klemm, Nicholas Wilson and Monica Scott (1993), Museum sector workforce training: an analysis of the workforce in the museum, gallery and heritage sector in the United Kingdom, *introduction and objectives, Museums Training Institute, Unversity of Bradford.*

NOTES

1 Department of Employment (1991) 'Ethnic origins and the labour market', *Employment Gazette* (Feb.), London: HMSO.
2 Source for all numbers quoted: government statistics.
3 Department of Employment (1992) Historical Supplement 3, 100 (6), *Employment Gazette* (June), London: HMSO.
4 Department of Employment (1991) 'Results of 1989 census of employment', *Employment Gazette* (May), London: HMSO.
5 Chartered Institute for Public Finance and Accounting (CIPFA), Public library statistics, 1992.

25

Image and self-image
Marista Leishman *et al.*

The discussion so far in this section has been dominated by interest in curatorial and professional grades. But to leave it at this would be to distort the picture. As museums become more complex, a greater sophistication of ability and understanding at all levels of museum work has, in turn, become essential. The word 'professionalism' means 'with extreme competence' and it follows that professionalism at all grades is a vital ingredient in modern museum provision. This is especially true of those staff who meet and deal with the public.

In this set of articles, the confidence and training of front-of-house staff are discussed.

'In England, where ignorance, vulgarity, or something worse are the characteristics of the lower orders, and where frivolity, affectation, and insolence are the leading traits of a class of lounging persons who haunt most public places, it would be the excess of folly for gentlemen who possess valuable museums to give unlimited access to the public.' In 1806, when this was written for the catalogue of the gallery at Cleveland House, it was also requested that in wet or dirty weather visitors would arrive in carriages. Some fifty years earlier the British Museum opened in Montagu House and one of the trustees noted: 'If public days should be allowed, then it will be necessary for the trustees to have the presence of a committee of themselves attending, with at least two justices of the peace and the constables of the division of Bloomsbury.' The need to guard valuable collections has as long a history as the admittance of visitors, so spare a thought for today's warders and attendants working within a tradition which once allowed ticketed entrance only to 'studious and curious persons'.

All dressed up with nowhere to go, most attendants have about as much to look forward to as an underemployed subpoliceperson. After all, rarely do thieves remove paintings in broad daylight, or vandals spoil precious objects. And it is not that often either that curious hands fondle exhibits, umbrellas jab enthusiastically at canvases or children stick chewing gum onto the noses of statues. But these are the few moments in which the traditional attendant comes into his or her negative own, fulfilling the message of the stern uniform, and mingling assumed authority with the sheer relief of having something to do. Intervention becomes the high point of the day.

Most of the time the job is unspeakably boring and even staying awake becomes a problem. One attendant described his patch as 'a beautiful prison, into which not many people come, not even troublemakers'. Not surprisingly, visitors are put off by this band of melancholy minders who communicate their dejection, subtly suggesting that museums perhaps aren't very interesting after all.

KNOCK-ON EFFECTS

Most larger museums grew up in the nineteenth century, often as assertions of civic triumphalism; the demeanour of the warding staff was consistent with the grand manner of such institutions. But, since the 1960s, many new places have opened. As well as the steady acquisition of properties by the National Trust and the National Trust for Scotland, historic houses in private ownership, heritage centres, visitor centres attached to open-air sites and theme parks began to compete for the public attention. Independently run specialist museums appeared: for the first time there were specific collections for cycles, pencils, lace and lawnmowers. In 1984 English Heritage began work to present some 400 historic properties with push and profile and their Scottish counterpart followed. The royal palaces continued to absorb millions of visitors, the cathedrals even more.

These new 'visitor attractions' (the phrase itself is significant) use new kinds of staff. Historic houses may be staffed by volunteers who take pride in knowing about the history of the house and its inhabitants. At mining or maritime museums staff may be ex-miners or seamen – proud of their pits and their ships, and more concerned with the safety of the visitors than the exhibits. The farmstead at Aden Country Park in Grampian is staffed by farmworkers who explain what they are doing. At Blists Hill Open Air Museum, part of Ironbridge Gorge Museum, demonstrators dressed in character work as locksmiths, iron-workers, candle-makers and so on while at the same time chatting with the visitors. At hands-on science centres like those at Catalyst, Snibston Discovery Park and the Museum of Science and Industry in Manchester, staff are there to explain how things work, to see they don't go wrong and, occasionally, as at Eureka!, to engage the interest of younger visitors. At Amberley Chalk Pits Open Air Museum volunteer staff drive the traction engine and work in the sandwich bar.

In most of these places the staff that visitors meet have responsibilities and objectives different from those of traditional museum attendants. They are there to welcome and to answer questions rather than to exercise a watching brief. This puts pressure on museums with displays of valuable and vulnerable objects to provide the same service to their visitors, and to encourage them to feel at home, but without putting collections at risk. There was no place for traditional warders ('les gardiens-robots') at the Pompidou Centre in Paris when it opened in 1977. Instead, 'hotesses d'accueil' combine the tasks of welcoming and interpreting with responsibility for security. At the 1991 Japan exhibition at the Victoria and Albert Museum separate staff responded to visitors' enquiries in addition to normal warding staff – a solution out of the reach of smaller museums.

Other museums and galleries are reassessing the role and image of the traditional warder. At the Royal Naval Museum in Portsmouth, Melanie McKeown, customer services manager, seeks to relate customer care to security. One of the warders, Ken Shergold, tells how he 'thinks customer' by asking himself how would he like to be treated if he were a visitor. Susan Bourne, curator of Burnley's Towneley Hall Art Gallery and Museum believes that appearance and personal pride are important and that police-style uniforms are now redundant. At the National Museum of Scotland, Alan Young, head of administrative services, looks forward to a service which is rewarding for staff and more welcoming for the public. This calls not for a reduced security role, but for a more discreet one which replaces an aloof presence (with matching uniform and persona) with a more outgoing image (without a peaked cap) but with authority still intact. Windsor Castle, despite, or perhaps because of the blaze, will continue to be near the top of the league table of visitor numbers. In the view of the management the formal dress of the warders makes ever more important their need to relate well to the thousands of visitors.

BUILDING CONFIDENCE

In spite of these changes traces of the old culture persist in some museums. There is still the unmistakable feeling that makes the visitor ill at ease, that forces him or her to experience the museum as solemn and the staff as grim. Too often, visitors keenly seeking information are met with attendants who neither know nor care. For a visitor fresh from an historic house where questions are likely to be encouraged such treatment is unlikely to prompt a return visit.

Recently, in reply to a visitor's very ordinary question, an attendant in a national museum quickly said he had no idea. 'I'm only a menial here,' he explained. Museums may be working on the external image of their attendants but are they looking to improve the self-image of the individual? Christopher Amey, head of security at the National Portrait Gallery, feels that warders must be conversant with the subject of the gallery's exhibitions. To work well and to project a positive image, attendants need support and training. Attendant staff need to be fully integrated. This means keeping them informed of what is happening in the museum, why and when. If attendants are not told about a new development, given an explanation of a new exhibition or the chance to ask questions, they receive the unequivocal message that they are unimportant and that the important matters are going on elsewhere. It also means more than team briefing, feeding information from the top down. Managers must listen to the experience and advice of attendants who regularly witness the reactions of the public. As Sir John Harvey-Jones says: 'We make pathetically inadequate use of the capabilities of our people.'

At Stoke-on-Trent Museum there is a regular exchange of information between front-of-house staff and curators. At Tullie House Museum in Carlisle, director Nick Winter-botham, like management at Marks and Spencer, regularly arranges temporary closures for in-house training. Duties are rotated hourly because boredom is inimical to a happily operating institution and curators as well as front-line staff meet the public. Staff at the National Museum of Wales are considered the public face of the museum, and their training programme involves everybody, at all levels. Training programmes at Ironbridge Gorge Museum include site maintenance workers, curators and telephonists. At the National Maritime Museum the view is that 'we are here for the customers'. Regular team briefing and training are embodied in the museum's corporate plan, according to Stephen Deuchar, development manager.

But training is not so simple. Disappointingly, the *Hale Report on Museum Professional Training and Career Structure* (Museums and Galleries Commission, 1987) does not recommend career structures for attendants. Failing to notice the ways in which the role of the attendant has changed, the report offers little in anticipation of continuing development. Instead it proposes a core syllabus – an inadequate response to an important need.

In addition, training alone is not enough. In the *Industrial Society Magazine* (March 1989), David Turner regrets that training is becoming 'hung up on standards, qualifications, status and accreditation. The real issue is how to move away from standardization in favour of individuality and from conformity to creativity.' He goes on to note that the concept of accumulated competences for training at all levels is sound, 'blending the skills, knowledge, aptitudes, temperament and personal qualities' that are needed by all members of the workforce. But when these competences 'are required to conform to a set of standards defining a performance requirement' and leading to an award, something is missing. A single national set of standardized competences, however diligently prepared, should be understood as a menu and not as a diet. Museums, people and circumstances all vary; museum managers and attendants need to be able to choose from a broad spectrum of training material and approaches.

When training becomes a prescription for action, it shows. The telephonist, lifelessly delivering a formula response ('Good morning, Jones and Baker here, Brian speaking, how can I help you?') voices a contradiction between style and content. At one gallery the double doors are importantly flung open by an attendant on either side at the approach of every visitor. Flattered, a visitor enters, only to catch part of an uninterrupted dialogue on pay and conditions from the other side of the gallery. The mechanics of training are there but the central matter is lost. Managers should encourage human rather than mechanical responses, and give attendant staff the confidence to relate easily to visitors. This will help them to remain interested, alert and welcoming and to convey through their attitude the message that all questions will be dealt with politely, that information or assistance is there if needed and that complaints will be taken seriously.

Museums have come a long way from those early days when they worked to keep the public at bay. Those museums who through their staff are 'engaged in a dialogue with the public', as Val Bott, curator of the Passmore Edwards Museum, put it (*Museums Journal* February 1990: 28) are now getting the results they deserve. By investing in front-of-house staff, museum managers can move attendant staff out of the category of 'the menial' to their proper place at the forefront of the museum experience.

TRAINING FOR ALL
Katie Foster

Staff at Ironbridge Gorge Museum subscribe to the philosophy that taking care of the visitor is as important as taking care of the collection. High standards of service are expected of each and every member of staff.

At the end of 1991, to ensure that museum staff did not become too isolated in their separate departments, the museum instigated a completely different kind of training for all staff, from cleaner to curator, from typist to tourist information officer, sales receptionist to steam-winding operator.

The following March, all 230 members of staff took part in customer care training, which was organized by Insite and part-funded by West Midlands Area Museum Service. Staff responded enthusiastically to the training sessions which took them back to basics, forcing everybody to rethink their roles. Through this process many staff realized that they too were valued because of the role they played, even if they were invisible to the public.

In a typical day, Ironbridge staff will be asked a wide variety of questions often unrelated to their official functions. It is vital that they are able to respond, and want to respond, positively to all demands. The coffee shop manager at the Museum of Iron must be able to tell the enquiring visitor about the Jackfield Tile Museum and vice versa, and recruitment and training must take all this into consideration. At the beginning of the main season all staff attend tours to all the museum sites to familiarize themselves with visitor facilities and with the history of Ironbridge.

The attendant at Ironbridge has never conformed to the stereotype – the barely civil, uninterested philistine clothed in grey uniform and wearing a peaked cap. Ironbridge attendants could be better described as facilitators, particularly those in costume at Blists Hill Open Air Museum. Visitors expect these members of staff to be accessible, to talk to them and to answer their questions. This kind of service can be very demanding and there is intensive training of these staff, mainly at the beginning of the season.

QUIET REVOLUTION
Stewart Coulter

Since 1990 Glasgow Museums staff have seen their duties, career opportunities and the service they provide for the public completely redefined. The first group to have their duties reviewed were those in the front-line, the people on the museum floor, the visitors' first point of contact. Security attendants, cleaners, shop assistants, porters and enquiries staff were amalgamated into a new hybrid museum assistant whose role encompassed all these former duties.

The new scheme has three grades designed to give a clear career path. The basic grade A for new recruits involves training in security, cleaning, portering and customer care/information duties. In the next grade, B, training covers: handling enquiries, museum shops and added security measures in control room duties. The top grade C deals with collection information and involves curatorial staff in training.

Staff progress from one grade to the next through on-the-job training and assessment and through specific courses developed with Glasgow City Council's central personnel department and the Museum Training Institute. Training beyond grade A is voluntary but applications from staff have exceeded expectation. Attaining the necessary skills not only means a higher salary, it also offers job enrichment and personal satisfaction.

The first line managers in the scheme are known as museum officers (MOs) who are on higher graded posts linked to curatorial scales. MOs are themselves trained in administrative and supervisory skills.

The scheme aims to create a highly motivated team dedicated to improving visitor and staff access to collections. The scheme is designed to:

- Help staff develop a knowledge and interest in the collections.
- Teach principles of communication.
- Develop interpersonal skills in order to relate to visitors' expectations.
- Enable staff to evaluate public response to all museum services and to play a part in forward planning.
- Empower staff to take ownership of their role in Glasgow Museums.

Now in its third year of operation, the scheme has not all been plain sailing. Although we are still learning, we are well on the way to creating a team of ambassadors for the museum.

This paper first appeared in Museums Journal *(June 1993), pp. 30–2.*

26

Museum director as manager
Charles Phillips

The changes in attitudes and approaches to museum work that have been witnessed in the past decade are summed up in this profile of a museum director. The passive approach to museums, based on the expectation that they are above all a Good Thing and therefore inviolable, has been overtaken by a pro-active approach, based on a combination of realism and imagination.

'What the hell are you going to collect in the next five years – the same old garbage?' Raymond Pisney asks the group of young AASLH seminarians.

'Do you know what the collections of your institution include?' he asks them. 'Where are their strengths and weaknesses?'

They have come to hear him talk about effective fundraising for historical societies and museums, and Pisney begins where he always begins – with aggressive, no-nonsense management, which for him includes collections policy. Specifically, he is stressing the importance of analysing collections as a necessary step in writing a planning document. It's part of his style, this emphasis on planning. And if what he says about collecting sounds harsh, assaulting, even abrasive . . . well, that too is part of the style, a style that has helped him effect one of the more dramatic financial turn-arounds ever in state and local history.

When Pisney came to St Louis as director of the Missouri Historical Society in December 1978, it was virtually bankrupt. He was determined not to be the caretaker of its demise, and in less than five years he has brought $3.6 million into society coffers that once bare-ly held two to four months' operating funds. He has changed a dull, lustreless publications programme into one that produces a slick, full-colour popular history magazine fast becoming the envy of the field. He has bulldozed his way through antiquated exhibits and thoroughly professionalized the display of the society's collections. And he has turned out all but a handful of the 35-member professional staff in place when he arrived. In all of this, he has acted on a management creed and a vision of the museum profession's future that, like his personal style, is aggressive and challenging.

'It is no achievement of museum administrators to preside over the progressive dis-mantling of the museum's institutional programs they were hired to manage,' the tall, trim conservatively but impeccably dressed Pisney tells seminar groups. 'There are ways out of the dilemmas like the [current] financial one. Mosly what we must do is really to do what we say we have been doing. As professionals we have made a commitment with our trustees or our government employers to manage our institutions. Now that times are hard, we must still manage them, if anything, we must manage them better than we have in the past. . . . The success or failure of all museums can be traced to leadership – this is the key.'

Pisney has been called 'ruthless' in his handling of staff, but he has a reputation for getting things done. In St Louis he has consciously committed himself to 'solving the funding riddle' and to making the Missouri Historical Society a model organization, well managed, financially secure, professionally sound and breaking new ground in services and programmes. He is someone worth watching.

CREATIVE MANAGEMENT

For Pisney a graduate of the University of Delaware's museum management programme, management is more than a buzz word meaning 'control', the monitoring and – in hard times – the cutting of costs, which he calls 'the cost-reduction syndrome'. He is perfectly aware of the need to watch expenditures at a time when 'museums find themselves in a rapidly changing environment that is highly unfavorable to them'. But he worries that the 'back to basics' (collecting, conserving, researching, interpreting, educating and publishing) movement in management prompted by economic pressures might be 'harmful in the long run to our field' because it 'de-emphasizes some of the highly innovative directions which we previously demanded.'

The cost-reduction syndrome and getting back to basics (which Pisney calls 'the retreat into somnolence') fail to confront the major problems of the field. Those problems, according to Pisney, stem from the fact that museums are and have been for a long time 'a growth industry', one that has outgrown its funding bases. The growth is a result of museums attempting to meet the leisure time and cultural needs of a wide variety of publics. To quote, as Pisney often does, John Russell of *The New York Times*: 'American museums are not just a place where works are assembled, protected and displayed to advantage. They've come to double as a fraternity house, a cut-price restaurant, a travel bureau, a movie theatre, a college which does everything but give out degrees, a non-denominational church and a proving ground for aspiring hostesses.'

To support this growth, Pisney says, museums have gone through a number of funding sources. First, money came almost entirely from private donations by individuals. Then added to that was money from trustees and membership dues; to that was added the aid of volunteers, groups of associates and auxiliaries; to that, help from local state and federal government. But the money these sources offer our institutions has proved insufficient to close the expanding gap between income and expense and it had proved so even before government began to cut funds. Slashing expenses will not provide new and needed sources of revenue.

In addition to outgrowing their financial bases, museums suffer some serious image problems, according to Pisney. Surveys indicate, he says, that the American public believes that museums either break even or make money. Highly publicized thefts and half a dozen popular novels and movies have created the image of curators as crooks. The news media often paints a picture of museums as 'extremely wealthy institutions . . . careening wildly from year to year not because of their funding problems but because of the moral bankruptcy of the people who run them'. A retreat into the archives that ignores that we 'live in a new era of accountability, especially financial accountability', and a cutting of public programming will not establish the kinds of community ties museums need to generate support and raise funds.

What finally bothers Pisney most about these responses is their lack of imagination. 'When we see effective leadership in the museum field', he says, 'it is always marked by introspection, imagination, self-assurance and a willingness to take risks.' It is the planning side rather than the control side of management that attracts him, and he is always touting 'the master plan' – the single document that will launch you full speed into the future.

A NEW BREED

Rather than simply cut costs and programmes, Pisney would reorganize the way we work. Using only trained museum professionals and paying them well, he would cut down the size of staff overall. To handle many of the basic tasks in collecting, archiving, researching and cataloguing, he would invest in computer hardware. To maintain, and even increase innovative public programming with smaller staffs, he advocates the 'task force' approach, forcing professional staff out of narrow specialties and making staff members accept responsibility for a wide range of activities. He would judge performance by how an individual benefits the institution as a whole as well as by how he or she exercises validated skills. This, he thinks, is the shape of the future.

'More people is not the answer,' he says. 'Fewer people, better paid, harder working. You use task forces, organized around projects, and borrow people – despite their background – for a particular task. That way you get major chunks of work done – you get better results in a shorter time with 22 people working as a team on one project than one person slogging away in the trenches for 10 years. Instead of 25 professionnals on a staff, you can keep it down to 15 using task forces. Otherwise, we don't have the resources.'

Instead of returning to basics, Pisney says we should be looking for new, more aggressive museum leaders who are willing to experiment and take the necessary risks that will lead to 'multiple sources of funding and multiple methods of building an institution's reputation. ... Merchandising the museum has become as much a part of the survival methodology for a modern museum as it is of the high-class department store down the block.' Pisney thinks that complicating the funding and image problems of the museum profession is 'a widespread feeling ... that long-range planning and financial affairs are functions that museologists should not spend much time doing ... that museum professionals should stick to making ends meet in the operating budget while trustees set policy and then go out and raise the necessary funds.'

He can get worked up about traditions such as this, and has sharp words for those who hold to them: 'We cannot be self-satisfied. It is easy for others, after 20 or 30 years on the job in this field, to say, "We've never done it that way," "We're not ready for that yet," "We're doing all right without it," "We tried it once, and it didn't work," "It costs too much," "That's not our responsibility" or "It won't work". I personally disagree with all of these. They are excuses for – rather than answers to – our problems.'

Pisney also is outspoken about the relationship between trustees and director, which he sees as trapped in a tradition peculiar to historical societies of 'strong volunteers and hands-on trusteeship dictating the goals that the professionals should be formulating'. Though entrenched, the tradition should be abandoned. Directors should work as full partners with trustees, educating them about museum operations and professional standards during the process. Sometimes, he is more flamboyant. At a recent meeting he surprised his fellow panellist when he told the audience bluntly, 'If you have a trustee who isn't bringing in the bucks, get him the hell out of there.'

Part of the Pisney style is to overstate in order to be heard and a lot of what he advocates in management has to do with style. Once again Pisney would allow John Russell to speak for him: 'As for the ideal [museum] director, he is no longer a quiet-spoken scholar, well on in years, who could be trusted in our grandfather's time to dine out once a week with his constituents and not fall under the table. Many new burdens are laid upon him, and he is expected to be a combination of a lobbyist, an escort, a public relations executive, a talk show host, an investment counselor, a tour guide, an unpaid psychoanalyst, a marriage counselor and a probation officer.'

THE MISSOURI HISTORICAL SOCIETY

Was the Ray Pisney talking here the Ray Pisney who showed up at the hoary and encrusted Missouri Historical Society half a decade ago? By all accounts the situation at Missouri when he arrived was less than ideal. Fresh from six years as director of the Woodrow Wilson Birthplace in Staunton, Virginia, he was no novice at running historical organizations. No doubt much of his thinking about management was in place when he took over the society, but many of his points about management and some of the edge to what he says seems to have grown out of his time in St Louis. If nothing else, the society was a tough proving ground for his ideas about management – an excellent test for his personality and his theories.

Formally established in 1886, the privately supported Missouri Historical Society – under the inspired leadership of its early presidents, Elihu Shepard, Edward Bates, Henry Shaw – quickly began to amass a collection of some pretensions, which today includes such significant rarities as Charles Bodmer's prints of his 1833–4 journey up the Mississippi with Maximilian, Prince of Wied, and documents from the Lewis and Clark Expedition. Charged with collecting and preserving 'the authentic history' of St Louis and later of Missouri and the Louisiana Purchase territory, its first archives were housed in the basement of St Louis's Old Courthouse. During its first year, the society purchased the Larkin mansion to maintain its growing collection. In 1904, following St. Louis's Louisiana Purchase Exhibition (organized in part by society members), the Jefferson Memorial was built and donated to the city with the understanding that it would become the society's permanent home. The organization made the final move to the memorial in 1913.

Like many such places, the society was a custodial institution, strong on collecting, weak on exhibiting its materials. Exhibits were expensive, and the society – funded by membership dues and private donations – sometimes ran short of monthly operating capital. Those times, board members usually passed the hat among themselves. If the trustees undertook more elaborate fundraising efforts, they limited them to the people they knew, to friends and friends of friends, or they raised money indirectly through special events and sales.

A recent article in the *St Louis Post-Dispatch* relates an apocryphal story from the 1950s. When a wing of the memorial building needed $4,000 worth of caulking, then-Director Charles Van Ravenswaay suggested to the trustees that, since the society was a valuable part of the community and the repairs extensive, they might consider asking the public directly for the funds. 'Oh, I don't know Charles,' one of them said doubtfully. 'It seems like an awful lot of money to be dunning perfect strangers for.'

For Pisney the story would be as piquant for what it says about the role of the professional staff in managing the museum as for what it says about the genteel fundraising of the trustees. Strong volunteer groups soon began to handle any sustained effort at fundraising and, after 'innumerable fleamarket and fashion-show fundraisers', the society managed – in 1972 – to add a basement wing with 20,000 square feet of gallery and archive space to the memorial building. It was the first time the society was able to house any of its valuable collection in a properly temperature-controlled space. Otherwise, the situation was worsening. Membership steadily declined, and by 1978 the organization was on the edge of bankruptcy.

It was a nineteenth-century institution, founded by antiquarians and talented amateur collectors, floundering its way through a modern world it would rather have ignored. Time's revenge had been to tarnish its class. Its shabby genteel calm was about to be shattered by collision with the administrative fury of its new twentieth-century manager.

HORROR STORY

'When I arrived here,' Ray Pisney says, 'the society had been under an acting director for 14 months. Volunteer groups were pretty well running the show. They are good, our volunteers – the Women's Association and the flea market and the volunteer staff – but they were getting no help from the professionals. No one was assisting the board, helping it to decide what policy should be set. There were no museology goals. No work goals. Membership was declining, just eroding away. The people of St Louis simply were not interested any more.

'I inherited an organization with only enough resources to last for two to four months, with galleries that had not been painted for three decades, with high-density, low-interpretation exhibits that were real "Granny attics" – old-line stuff in place for 20 or 30 years. The collections had not been cataloged or had been badly cataloged. There was no collections management.

'Twelve people from 12 different work areas reported to the director. Some of the departments were over-staffed. One of the previous leaders here had a background in English literature with a minor in music. She was in charge of personnel, so she hired 13 others with exactly the same qualifications she had.

'The society had watched the art museum down the street move forward to a greater attendance, reversing a trend it had set early in the century. I heard a lot of "horror stories" like that from the staff here then when I first arrived. They were always blaming it on the board. The staff had fallen into self-fulfilling negativism. Just a lot of negative-think.

'In fact the board had articulated an extremely clear vision of what the society should become. It was calling for an activist approach in management with clear goals and a highly qualified professional staff. But the real visionaries were the trustees. The trustees said to me when I got here, "You tell us what you want. Give us a master plan. Get to work on making money. Hire a full-time public relations officer. Find yourself a good development officer."

'The place was ripe for something,' Pisney laughs. 'It was ripe for a turn-around.' So was Pisney.

PISNEY'S PURGE

Pisney immediately set about the process of 'rebuilding the society's programs professionally from the inside out'. He went after – and got – a $25,000 self-study grant from the National Endowment for the Humanities, which led to an emphasis on meeting as an institution a wide range of community needs and developing programmes specifically for ethnic and minority groups. He reorganized the twelve previous work areas into four divisions – museum and public programmes; library and archives; administration and operations; and development and public relations. He began to search for the best professionals he could find to head each of these divisions.

As for the staff he inherited, he began to 'judiciously reorganize work assignments' and to call for an active recommitment of the professionals to the institution.

'It was very painful making the transition,' he says. 'But it was a matter of goal setting and goal seeking and measuring staff achievement against that. When someone didn't have the professional training or the personal commitment to meet those clearly defined goals, then . . . it was a matter I personally had to deal with, and you know what that means. It took three-and-a-half years, but we have totally restaffed the organization without adding substantially to the number of positions. In fact we've reduced the staff from 35 "individuals" to 25 professionals. Three-fourths of the staff is all new, with at least master's-level training.'

Another thing that staff, old and new, at the society had to adapt to was Pisney's penchant for 'task-force' work. The notion in part grows out of Pisney's passion for planning, but he also has a theory that it is good for the soul of the employee. 'You get a peer group organizing and evaluating and doing everything rather than one little specialist with blinders on,' he says. 'That may be anathema for these specialists, but they have forgotten that the bottom line is history – state and local history. Oh, people play a lot of games in this profession, and they seem to never really pull things together and to do what we're supposed to do – the humanities. Our professional training will have to change dramatically if we are going to make this thing work. Training programs are going to have to move into the Renaissance mode aimed at producing historians, rather than continuing more of these museology science courses.'

Specially seeking out 'professionals', forcing them to handle work beyond their professional training and then measuring their performance by the latter as well as the former does not necessarily make for a calm work environment. It is probably not very surprising that Pisney at first ran up against some resistance from his curatorial staff when he asked some to take inventory or help catalogue outside their specific 'areas.' But as more and more of the task forces – which can last as long as a year or so – have been developed to organize and catalogue the research and library collection, say, or to work on pictorial history projects, the staff has more and more come to accept, even enjoy, the work. Several who talked to *History News* mentioned the special sense of involvement task-force work offered, and a new employee or two talked with regret about having 'missed' the last such assignment but said they were, happily, 'slated' for the next.

Despite the special demands, and the high staff turnover since his arrival, Pisney seems to have managed to avoid the low morale that has afflicted many historical agencies recently. For one, he has increased salaries substantially. But staff seem also to be generally caught up in the excitement of the change going on at the society. Employees tend to see Pisney as demanding, but good for their own development. Pisney – all-work, constantly on hand, checking, pushing, demanding – evidently tends at the same time carefully to protect his people and liberally to recognize and reward competence and talent.

'I would say he is demanding as a boss,' says April Walgren, the society's new public relations officer. 'He has very high standards, and we know that quality is very important for our organization as a whole, for the staff itself and for the individual work we do.

I was very impressed at my first staff meeting – where I was introduced to the staff – to find that everybody goes, from the director to the maintenance workers.'

GATEWAY HERITAGE

This tendency to involve everyone – Pisney's task-force mentality – evidences itself even in work that seems especially resistant to such an approach – the society's *Gateway Heritage* magazine, for example.

If one has noticed anything happening at all at the Missouri Historical Society in the past few years, it will most likely have been the appearance quarterly of *Gateway Heritage*. It is the pride of the society, a high profile, large format popular history magazine bursting with colour and reeking of money. It has found new members for the society, reaped compliments from around the country and opened a number of doors belonging to potential donors. Yet, according to Pisney, it does not even have a full-time editor. Instead, 'staff serves those functions'.

Pisney himself plays an active role in producing the magazine, choosing the material and spreading out the copy-editing among five staff members. He uses his book-keeper to do proof-reading. And while to the practised eye the magazine has its gaucheries, it does seem admirably to serve the purposes Pisney has in mind for it.

'Before we created *Gateway Heritage*,' he says, 'the society – back in the 1950s, '60s and '70s – was putting out the standard local history publication. It was small, with articles by scholars or pseudo-scholars, conservative, unintelligible, highly footnoted, not illustrated. In our 1979 self-study, our membership survey found that fewer than 10 per cent ever read *anything* in it. "Why go on?" we thought. And we asked the members, "What is it you want?" What they wanted was something highly readable, something that told them of the great resources of the society and something that went beyond the usual in presenting the history of the state. That's what *Gateway Heritage* is designed to do. It is intermediate history, popularly written, compelling, that uses other resources – like illustrations of our collections – than archives and libraries. With it we, literally, do the humanities.

'We also wanted something that would appeal to everybody in the community [membership has doubled in the three years since the magazine began, from 2,200 to 4,500] and a door-opener for institutional advancement – something that would be effective in capturing the imagination of potential givers.'

The society then found a design consultant, who had retired from work on a large circulation farm magazine, to design the magazine and see every issue through production as 'a labour of love', and a paid editorial consultant, whom Pisney admiringly describes as 'one hard-nosed SOB, whose emphasis is totally on good writing'. But one suspects that much of the magazine's obvious success has to do with Pisney himself, with his insistent planning. Each issue has, according to his plan, a mix of articles carefully calculated to serve every potential audience – one story on St Louis itself, one on the history of Missouri, one on the American West and one on the society – its collections, exhibits, activities.

NEW DIMENSIONS

And that plan – serving every potential audience – is in essence Pisney's plan for the society as a whole, which is part of the larger plan to put the society on solid financial ground. In February 1982 Pisney announced his New Dimensions fundraising campaign, aimed at bringing in $4.2 million for his organization. On the day the campaign was launched, 60 per cent of those funds had already been secured. In the three years he had been at the society, Pisney had obviously been at work doing more than solving a few personnel problems and restructuring his organizational chart. Currently, 86 per cent of the $4.2 million rests in society coffers – nearly $2 million of which is from corporate donors, most of them local businesses or area branch offices; almost $1.5 million from individuals; $700,000 from the society's trustees; and the rest from non-corporate foundations.

Seventy-five per cent of the money is for capital purposes, for renovating and refurbishing. A large segment of it will go to a central temperature and climate control system in the old, above-ground part of the memorial building. One large single gift is for roofing over a courtyard in the building for use as a special gallery. But the $4.2 million is only phase one of the New Dimensions plan. The society then plans to go after an additional $3.5 million to establish an endowment.

Ask Pisney's development officer, George Lukac, who came to the society from an academic fundraising and public-relations background, how the society did it, and he will give you a number of answers. 'We made extensive use of *Gateway Heritage* and of the revitalization of the Missouri Historical Society. We became attractive to corporations committed to the renewal and revitalization of the city. We were seen as one of the major institutions involved. They felt comfortable giving to us for the sake of the city, for the sake of the people we employed, for the sake of their own corporate image. They realized that culture goes hand-in-hand with revitalization.

'And in some ways we lucked out. There had been no history [at the society] of a campaign of this type, so we had no working models to fall back on. We put together five individual volunteer divisions of 125 people each. They selected their own prospects and went out and actually made the calls. If not for them, we'd be struggling.'

Lukac's explanations sound almost technical in print, but behind them lay something else, a sense that the society was on the move, that it had not only 'turned around', but that it was going places, that it was something to be proud of. And behind that lay Ray Pisney and his planning.

Pisney has convinced the people of St Louis, and he is convincing many of his colleagues in the field, that he has the answer, the key to state and local history's future. From his notions about the organization of daily work, to his driving professionalism (he wants nothing more desperately right now, for example, than to get the society accredited by the American Association of Museums), to his investigations into the possibilities of computers to meet the field's information needs, he is striving to be a leader And one of the attributes of a leader is the ability to involve others in his visions, to convince them to see with his eyes, to believe as he does.

Listen to a former employee of Pisney's at the society: 'I worked for him for about a year on a special project before I came back here [to my current position]. Yes, he is known for his abrasive personality. He can be very demanding and he goes off in 10 directions at once. He is married to the job, works 24 hours a day. And with these task forces he wants you to do 70 years of work overnight. He likes to delegate authority but still keep his hand in the pie and two weeks later you are in a new ball game. Everything for him is now, now, now. But he is definitely what the society needed – a good swift kick in the pants. And they are going to be the leading cultural institution in St Louis. In another year, he'll make that place nationally famous. He may lose some more people because of his personality, and he *is* hard to work for, but if I could have stayed there I would. And if I didn't have 20 years invested [in this place] I'd be over there today looking for a job.'

IMAGE AND IMAGINATION

'Administration has always been my avocation,' Ray Pisney says. 'I have no desire to be in a secondary position. I don't enjoy life in the trenches.' In his director's report to the membership published in the society's latest annual report he concludes with a quotation from Marcus T. Cicero: 'Criticize by creating, rather than by finding fault.'

Pisney's creative solutions seem to be working in St Louis. When he speaks to public groups about management, planning and fundraising, what he says plays against his background there. At a time when much of our profession is retrenching and looking for new directions, Pisney's voice is bound to become stronger, especially if the Missouri Historical Society develops as he believes it will. Does he have the answers – shrinking staffs, computerization, merchandising, innovative and expansive programmes, hard-driving personnel management? Some of that may depend on how representative we think his experience in Missouri can claim to be. How much of that experience has to do with Pisney being the right man at the right place at the right time; how much has to do with the simple application of a vitally correct theory?

For Ray Pisney and the Missouri Historical Society just now that question, no doubt, seems hardly important. For them this *is* the right place and time. Pisney is *here*. He has answers, and he has them *now*.

This paper first appeared in History News *38(3) (March 1983), pp. 8–15.*

27

The state of pay

Phyllida Shaw

At the end of 1988, a survey was undertaken of the salaries paid to museum and gallery staff in the UK. Regrettably the survey had only a 25 per cent response rate, which inevitably affected the conclusions which could be drawn. However, the broad picture of underpayment and considerable pay disparity is one that museum staff will recognize. This survey is now rather dated, but it is unlikely that the general features it reveals have changed a great deal.

People working in museums are badly paid and, if the rate of response to the Reward Group's 1988 salary survey for the Museums Association is anything to go by, far too busy to fill in questionnaires. Six hundred museums were invited to supply salary information on a range of posts. Only 145 (25 per cent) replied, and although these provided facts about more than 2,400 posts, most were in small and medium sized museums. A more representative sample might have enabled the survey team to draw firmer conclusions about the state of pay in museums. None the less, it did come up with some convincing arguments for an urgent review of the structure of pay in museums.

In comparison with people doing similar jobs in other sectors, museum staff are, on the whole, badly paid, but perhaps the most remarkable finding of the survey is that differences of several thousand pounds a year, in the salaries of employees with broadly similar responsibilities, are commonplace.

THE RESPONSE

Each museum responding to the survey was categorized, according to its main source of funding, as local authority, national, independent, university, regimental or 'other' (for museums with multiple sources of funding). Altogether, information on 2,448 posts was submitted, almost two-thirds of which were in local authority museums; 48 per cent of the posts described were salaried management posts; 19 per cent were salaried clerical; and the remaining 33 per cent were posts paid for on an hourly basis, such as attendants, cleaning staff and canteen assistants.

WHAT'S IN A JOB TITLE?

In the museums world, the same job title has different meanings in different institutions. After consultation with museum authorities, the survey team gave each job a rank, according to its status within the museum, the responsibilities it carried, the size of the museum and the number of staff employed:

Rank *Description*

0 Director with overall responsibility.

1 Senior manager or senior specialist: the heads of major functions reporting to Rank 0. Rank 1 usually involves some responsibility for policy formulation. Also covers the most senior specialists, who may not have a management function e.g. curators and keepers. Curators and keepers also appear under other ranks, according to the level of responsibility and experience required.

2 Senior middle manager: heads of main departments reporting to Rank 1 or, in smaller organizations, to the director. Includes heads of smaller departments, such as education, exhibition officer; specialists whose work relates to an individual or specialist skill rather than to management; and keepers and curators with curatorial or management functions in smaller museums.

3 Junior middle manager: most Rank 3 staff have supervisors or section leaders reporting to them. Includes non-specialists with wide-ranging functions and commercial and marketing managers.

4 Junior manager: lowest level of management, e.g. assistant keeper, assistant curator and heads of small departments, such as design and photography. Includes office managers in larger museums, administrators and personnel officers.

5 Supervisor, senior technician: supervisory staff, e.g. office manager in smaller museums, chief technician, assistant to specialist, senior secretary, graduate trainee.

6 Senior clerical staff, technician: minor supervisory roles such as senior clerk, senior telephonist, security supervisor. Also includes junior trainee managers.

7 Skilled grade: skilled but working under supervision, e.g. craftsperson, salaries and wages clerk, word processor operator, attendant.

8 Semi-skilled grade: e.g. general driver, general clerk, typist.

9 Unskilled grade and juniors: e.g. apprentice, filing clerk, canteen assistant, cleaner.

SALARIES MILES APART

The survey revealed marked variations in the rewards offered to people with equivalent responsibilities in different types of museum. The survey found museum directors (Rank 0) earning less than £11,322 and more than £31,122; assistant directors of museums (Rank 1) on less than £11,940 and more than £20,632; and principal curators (also Rank 1) earning between £9,207 and £20,615. Curators (management) (Rank 2) were earning between £7,917 and £13,655 and curators (curation) between £7,674 and £27,000. At Rank 3, one senior assistant keeper was being paid less than £8,122 while a colleague in another museum was receiving more than £14,750.

Lower down the ranking, the differentials were no less astonishing. Chief electricians (Rank 5) earned below £7,356 and more than £11,000; technicians were receiving anything from £6,398 to £9,549. Lower down still, even the highest paid people within each rank receive very poor rewards. Salaries of assistants to the personnel officer started at less than £5,480, with only the top 10 per cent earning more than £7,376. Telephonists (Rank 6) were earning between £4,713 and £6,903.

Among members of staff paid on an hourly basis, senior attendants earned between £2.66 per hour (including bonus) and £3.82. If we assume a 39-hour week, this amounts to less than £5,400 per year at the lower end of the scale, rising to around £7,750. The comparable figures for an attendant are £4,907 at the lower end rising to the handsome sum of £7,188.

The survey team took all the salary details submitted and found the middle point or *median* salary for each rank. These are shown in Table 27.1. Column A shows the point below which one-quarter of all the salaries of a particualar rank fall and column B shows the point above which one-quarter of all salaries rise.

Table 27.1 Summary of museum salaries by rank

Rank	Sample	A 25% earn below £	Median £	B 25% earn over £
0	50	14,687	18,177	26,201
1	116	12,075	13,928	17,151
2	203	10,536	12,804	14,625
3	180	9,873	11,246	12,729
4	244	8,709	9,873	10,887
5	230	7,674	8,541	9,687
6	261	6,847	7,335	8,150
7	184	6,386	6,957	7,416
8	179	5,400	6,133	6,786

But what accounts for such differentials? There are seven possible factors: the size of a museum's budget; the value of its collection; the size of its collection; the location of the museum; its funding base; the number of staff employed; and the age, experience and qualifications of the staff. The survey examined each of these in turn.

THE SIZE OF THE BUDGET

The size of a museum's budget does have some impact on the pay of some employees, but not all. The median salary for a Rank 1 employee in a museum with a budget of between £20,000 and £50,000 was only £9,339, rising to £17,090 for a comparable post, in a museum with a budget of more than half a million pounds. At Rank 2, there was a differential of more than £5,000 between museums in the £20–£50,000 bracket and those with budgets over £500,000. However, in both Ranks 1 and 2, the median salary in institutions with budgets of less than £20,000 was higher than that in more generously funded institutions. Therefore, no firm conclusion can be drawn. It is true, however, that in Rank 3 and below, there was no discernible relationship between the museum's budget and the size of salary paid.

SIZE AND VALUE OF THE COLLECTION

Salaries are not consistently affected by the *size* of a museum's collection. For example, the Rank 0 employees surveyed, who were in charge of collections of 20–100,000 pieces were paid more than those managing collections five times as large. The *value* of the collection turned out to be a more significant factor. According to the survey, the more valuable the collection, the more the most senior staff were paid. However, the pay of Rank 3 and below was not affected, so the value of specimens is not the most influential factor.

REGIONAL VARIATIONS

It is often the case that pay for similar jobs is better in more prosperous parts of the country, but this appears not to be the case with museums. Pay was examined in each of the nine Area Museum Council regions, but no definite trends were spotted. There were insufficient replies from the north-east and Wales for conclusions to be drawn about pay in those areas, but overall, pay seemed to be more or less consistent, with only £833 separating the median salaries for all jobs in each of the regions. The survey offered no details on London weighting.

AGE, EXPERIENCE, QUALIFICATIONS AND SEX

Most Rank 0 and 1 posts surveyed were held by people aged over 36, who had spent more than 11 years working in museums and who are male. Many also have a Ph.D. or professional qualification. The survey did not look at whether people of equal rank were paid equally, regardless of age, qualifications, sex and experience. However, the samples for Ranks 0, 1, 2, 3 and 4 contained much larger numbers of men than women. In Ranks 5, 6, 7 and 8, the women outnumbered the men, yet in all but Rank 8, where the women's median salary was 2.5 per cent higher than that of the men, men's median earnings exceeded those of the women by between 4 per cent and 11 per cent. The median salary of the seven women directors was £12,240 (well below the overall median of £18,177) while for the men it was £18,587.

WHERE TO FIND BETTER PAY

Undoubtedly the most important influence on salary levels in museums is the way in which a museum is funded and the number of people it employs. The national and university museums, which are funded mainly from central government funds, offer the highest pay across the board. Some of the large local authority museums are not far behind, but on the whole, pay less – a fact which may be related to the restricted funds available to them through the rates and rate support grant. Independent museums, unless associated with a major commercial company, tend to operate on tight budgets and offer smaller financial rewards. Variations in pay for technicians, craftspeople and attendants are less marked, but local authorities usually offer the highest levels. There was insufficient information submitted about Ranks 1 and 0 for them to be included in Table 27.2 below.

Here we can see that the median salary for a Rank 3 post is one and a half times bigger in a university than in an independent museum, and that local authority pay is well below that of the nationals.

Table 27.2 Pay by type of museum

	Median pay by rank				
Type of museum	2	3	4	5	6
	£	£	£	£	£
Independent	10,000	9,992	8,524	6,985	7,302
Local authority	11,925	10,887	9,873	8,271	7,485
National	27,087	14,629	12,024	9,687	6,881
Others	14,625	11,105	no data	8,288	no data
University	15,720	15,435	12,237	10,160	8,372

Salaries increase markedly, at managerial level, according to the number of staff a museum employs. The median salary for a director responsible for up to 50 staff was £15,477 while that for directors in charge of between 101 and 200 employees was £33,819. Rank 1 employees in the smaller museums were paid a median salary of £13,456, compared with £20,739 for colleagues working in organizations of twice the size. Right down to Rank 5, pay increased in accordance with the number of staff employed.

Table 27.3 Pay by number of employees

	Median pay by rank								
Number of employees	0 £	1 £	2 £	3 £	4 £	5 £	6 £	7 £	All £
Up to 50	15,306	13,456	11,322	10,191	9,474	7,833	7,317	6,396	8,979
50–100	25,000	17,029	14,223	12,684	9,292	8,271	7,476	7,122	8,548
101–200	33,819	20,739	14,625	15,581	10,887	9,635	7,335	6,957	8,754

BELOW THE NATIONAL AVERAGE

It will come as no surprise to many museum employees that they are paid considerably less than employees with comparable positions in other sectors. The Reward Group publishes its own assessment of median salaries taken from a survey of 800 different companies. These appear in Table 27.4, alongside the salaries available to museum employees. Rank 0 salaries are 36 per cent behind the national average, Rank 1, 35 per cent behind and Rank 2, 27 per cent behind.

Table 27.4 A comparison of museum salaries and those paid in other sectors

Rank	Median salary in other sectors £	Median salary museums £	% difference %
0	28,500	18,177	36
1	21,614	13,928	35
2	17,490	12,804	27
3	14,375	11,246	22
4	11,726	9,873	16
5	9,556	8,541	11
6	8,052	7,335	9

If it is any consolation, colleagues with similar responsibilities working in theatres, arts centres, orchestras and other arts organizations are also paid badly. The discrepancies, however, are probably not as marked as they are in the museums sector and, above all, it is this question which needs to be addressed.

The Reward Group team concludes with the following thought: 'On assessing the data returned in the survey, it became clear that museums are highly individualistic and that the skills required of the personnel are often so specialised as to be almost unique. Such specialisation would suggest that it would be unwise to impose a hierachy that was too rigid, as an individual with unique qualities could be caught in the system, resulting in unexpectedly low levels of pay. That some form of structure is necessary, however, is all too apparent, in that there are so many different job titles and tremendous variations in the assessment of responsibilities.'

And there, the case rests.

This paper first appeared in Museums Journal *89(4) (1989), pp. 26–8.*

NOTE

The salary survey was carried out in 1988 by The Reward Group, with financial assistance from the Museums and Galleries Commission.

28

Are you sitting comfortably? Are equal opportunities a luxury?

Gaby Porter *et al.*

Greater attention to the understanding of the museum workforce demonstrates the inequalities to be found within it. In many respects, these reflect the inequalities within society as a whole. However, this cannot be a licence for their perpetuation within museum work, especially if the greater democratization of museum provision is a genuine goal. The commitment to change is prompting many museums to reassess thoroughly their policies and approaches. Further, the Museums Association has undertaken research on equal opportunities in museums, from which proposals for change are being made.

In this set of papers, introduced by Gaby Porter's piece, positive approaches to overcoming the barriers to museum work are discussed.

Can we afford equal opportunities? Equal opportunities are seen as a luxury – a crusade of the left, outdated in the current political and financial climate. Race and sex equality initiatives were among the first posts to be axed in Bradford; in Sheffield Museums, the key post of community outreach worker has been frozen.

The contributors whose articles follow demonstrate that equal opportunities lie within the framework of openness and access. Equal opportunities offer the prospect of receptive and consultative museum workers, listening and responding to new voices inside and outside the museum.

In the September 1991 issue of *Museums Journal* in 'Representations of black history', authors addressed the exclusion or segregation of black histories in museums; a future issue of *Museums Journal* will extend these discussions to other aspects of provision. This issue offers case studies and practical guidelines to facilitate access for those groups and individuals who are under-represented, particularly in museum employment.

The need for improved physical access for people with disabilities is not disputed. Yet, as Rosalinda Hardiman points out, few of our museum buildings have been adapted. Her article shows how lack of provision *disables*, rather than *enables* employees and users to participate fully. The problems which follow may be seen to reside with the individual rather than with the institution.

Access in the fullest sense is far more controversial and complex than physical provision. Many institutions which advertise themselves as equal opportunities employers have no programme to substantiate their claim. The contributors stress that equal opportunities begins in building strong links between the museum and its communities, visiting or non-visiting. Local communities are not simply a source of labour but an important resource and partner in the museum's development across the full range of activities. Susan Ollerearnshaw points out that museums may appear unwelcoming, outdated, even irrelevant. Amina Dickerson describes initiatives in Chicago to overcome these barriers, by inviting local groups to contribute to the programmes and services of the museum. Similarly, in Sheffield, local people are consulted and their views fed into the planning process. This is, itself, a collective effort of working parties.

Vivien Lloyd makes the important connection with staff training, and particularly with training in customer care. At the initial stage, this prepares the ground within the museum for new initiatives, by creating a more positive and receptive culture in which visitors and colleagues alike may be respected, and their needs and points of view given due attention.

Equal opportunities programmes are not pious statements on paper. They are new ways of thinking and working, concerned with a fundamental redistribution of power and resources. None of us will be sitting comfortably throughout the process, which demands that we are all, individually and collectively, committed to change.

NOTE

Have you prepared equal opportunities policies and programmes? If so, the Museums Association Equal Opportunities Working Party would like to receive copies or information for redistribution to interested members. Please send to: Equal Opportunities Working Party, c/o Museums Association, 34 Bloomsbury Way, London WC1A 2SF.

REFERENCES

'Women in museums' (various contributors), *Museums Journal* September 1988.
'Representations of black history' (various contributors), *Museums Journal* September 1990.
'Equal Opportunities Joint Advisory Booklet', NJC for Local Authorities' APT&C Staff, 1988.
'Working with Oxfordshire County Council, employees' guide', 1989.
'Does it begin at home?' Interim report of the Museums Association Working Party, *Museums Journal* July 1990.

CAREER BREAKS: A GOOD PRACTICE GUIDE
Prepared by the Equal Opportunities Commission

A career break scheme allows men and women to break off their career for an agreed length of time with the opportunity to return to the same or a similar job.

The leave is unpaid and contact between employee and employer is usually maintained, with a minimum compulsory attendance requirement to update essential skills.

A good career break scheme should be flexible enough to meet the needs of the organization and its staff, but should include the following elements:

- Must be open to men and women.
- Should provide opportunities for contact between employer and employee during the career break, e.g. paid work sessions, 'keeping in touch' schemes, newsletters.
- The employee should be re-employed on terms and conditions no less favourable than at the commencement of the career break.
- The employee should be reinstated with the length of service previously accrued to count towards service-related terms of employment, e.g. holiday entitlements, sick pay, redundancy pay, long service awards.

- An employee should remain a member of the pension scheme while on a career break, although no contributions will be made.
- Flexible working arrangements should be available to ease the return to work.
- There should be a period of retraining and confidence-building after re-entry, as well as opportunities to refresh and update skills.

Further points to consider

- Are full and part-time staff at all levels eligible?
- Is a minimum service requirement necessary?
- Do staff have to satisfy a qualifying reason, e.g. childcare, care of the elderly, adoption, further education, community service?
- Is there a minimum/maximum length of time for the career break, e.g. six months/five years?
- Can more than one break be taken?
- Is it possible to take a part-time career break?
- How much notice must be given of an intention to take or return from a career break?
- Can staff return at any time during the agreed break?
- Must re-employment commence within a specified number of years before retirement?
- Can the employee make up pension contributions?
- Is there a minimum/maximum compulsory attendance requirement?
- Who will be responsible for 'keeping in touch' arrangements?
- Can benefits, such as company cars and loans, be retained while on the career break?

Why career breaks are an advantage to employers

- Helps to keep staff with scarce skills.
- Helps to keep highly trained staff.
- Helps to keep staff with the potential for promotion.
- Helps to attract high calibre recruits.
- Can help reduce time and money spent on recruitment, selection, induction and training of new employees.
- Can provide, by arrangement, a pool of skilled and flexible workers to draw upon for temporary cover or special projects.
- Allows staff to show a commitment to the organization and can assist them in long-term career planning.

JOB SHARING: A GOOD PRACTICE GUIDE
Prepared by the Equal Opportunities Commission

Job-sharing is a form of part-time employment where two people voluntarily share the responsibility of one full-time position. The salary, leave and fringe benefits are divided between them according to the number of hours worked and each person holds a permanent part-time post.

A job-sharing situation can come about in a variety of ways: two people may apply jointly for one full-time post; individual employees may come to an agreement with management which allows them to reduce their working hours and management to appoint an additional part-time employee; or an employer may advertise full-time posts as being suitable for job-sharing.

Although there is no legal right to job-share, a refusal to allow part-time working could lead to a claim of indirect discrimination under the Sex Discrimination Act 1975 (Holmes *v*. the Home Office).

The elements of a good job-share scheme

- Must be open to men and women
- Consideration should be given to all posts being filled on a job-share basis.
- There should be a written contract of employment and job description for each share.
- Pro rata entitlement to the same pay and conditions as full-time employees.
- A minimum 16-hour working week for sharers to safeguard their rights under employment protection legislation, e.g. the right to redundancy pay, maternity pay and maternity leave.
- Non-statutory occupational benefits which are given to full-time staff should be extended to job-sharers, e.g. occupational pension schemes, company sick pay, profit sharing, subsidized mortgages and discounts.
- Equal access to training and promotion.
- The right to return to full-time work after a period of job-sharing.
- If one sharer leaves, the remaining sharer should be offered the post full-time. If this is not acceptable, another sharer should be sought, either internally or externally.

Additional points to consider

- When adopting the work pattern, e.g. one person works every morning and the other every afternoon, or each works 2.5 days per week, consideration should be given to the nature of the job, the wishes of the sharers, and the protection of their employment rights by preserving continuity of employment.
- Does some overlap need to be built into the work pattern, either for communication time or to provide extra cover at peak periods?
- If one sharer is absent, will the other sharer have first refusal, but be under no obligation to cover for the whole post?
- Will there be any contractual limitations on a job-sharer undertaking outside paid employment or another post within the organization?
- How are such matters as overtime, performance targets, job evaluation, allowances and bonuses to apply to job-sharers?
- Is job sharing welcomed within the organization rather than merely permitted? Are staff given training in equal opportunities issues?
- Do recruitment advertisements state that applications from job-sharers are welcome?

The advantages to employers

- Job-sharing can help reduce staff turnover, thus cutting highly expensive recruitment and training costs.
- Efficiency may be increased as a result of greater flexibility of staffing, e.g. the possibility of peak period cover or sharers could attend two meetings at the same time.
- The availability of a wider range of skills than can be provided by one full-timer.
- Job-sharing makes it possible to employ talented people who are not available for full-time work.
- Job-sharing can be a way of easily introducing part-time hours into areas of traditional full-time work.

- Job sharing can aid continuity. If a full-time employee is absent, the whole job usually stops.
- With job-sharing, at least half the job can continue and there is always the possibility of the remaining sharer standing in on a full-time basis.
- Job-sharing may make it easier for women to return to work after maternity leave and so increase the use of maternity leave provisions.

PEOPLE WITH DISABILITIES DESERVE YOUR RESPECT
Mainstream Inc.

Guidelines for those interviewing or working with people with disabilities:

- When interacting with a person who uses a wheelchair, place yourself on the same eye level with him or her; do not grab or push the wheelchair unless asked.
- In an interview with a person who is deaf and who will be lip-reading, enunciate clearly, keeping your mouth free of obstructions, and sit in front of a light source. Use gestures, facial expressions, and note-passing to communicate effectively. Do not shout.
- When interviewing a blind person, use detailed verbal cues: identify yourself and others who are present; cue a handshake verbally or physically; and describe the layout of the office, emphasizing the location of the chair. Keep doors either fully open or fully closed; a half-open door is a hazard to people who cannot see.
- When interviewing a mentally handicapped person, use simple language and be aware that you might have to repeat yourself several times. Also give positive feedback whenever appropriate.
- In any interview with a disabled job applicant, do not ask 'What happened to you?' or 'How will you get to work?' Instead, ask job-related questions, such as 'How would you perform this task? Wait to ask about the kinds of accommodations the applicant will require until you are seriously considering making an employment offer.
- Always make eye contact and offer to shake hands. Offer assistance, but don't expect it necessarily to be accepted.
- Treat the applicant like an adult; do not be patronizing.

GUIDELINES FOR THE USE OF NON-SEXIST LANGUAGE
Helen Coxall

When constructing examples and theories, remember to include those human activities, interests and points of view which traditionally have been associated with women.

Eliminate the generic use of 'he'/'his'/'him'

The key to using non-sexist language lies in the acceptance that half of humanity is female, half male. A writer or speaker should not start out by excluding half the potential audience by referring only to 'he', 'his' and 'him'.

- Use plural nouns and pronouns: e.g. 'the modern television viewer does not have to leave *his* chair to experience life, which comes distorted, violent and glamourized into *his* own living room' *becomes* 'modern television viewers do not have to leave their chairs to experience life which comes distorted, violent and glamourized into their own living rooms'.
- Use 'he/she' or 's/he' instead of 'he'.

196

- Eliminate the pronoun 'he' altogether by using an article ('a' or 'the'): e.g. 'a writer should not start out by eliminating half *his* potential audience' *becomes* the opening sentence above.
- Reword sentences to use 'who' instead of 'he': e.g. if the writer is aware of the implications *he* will not use sexist language' *becomes* 'the writer who is aware of the implications will not use sexist language'.
- Repeat nouns: e.g. repeat 'the writer' in the sentence above.
- Remove pronouns altogether: e.g. 'style means that the author has fused his material and technique' *becomes* 'style is the fusion of material and technique'.
- Use 'you' instead of 'he': e.g. if the purchaser has cause for complaint, *he* can return *his* purchase' *becomes* 'if you have cause for complaint, you may return your purchase'.
- Use 'it' not 'he' when speaking of an animal of unknown sex: e.g. 'look at *his* long tail' *becomes* 'look at its long tail'.
- Use indefinite pronouns ('anyone', 'someone').

Eliminate the generic use of 'man'

Writers who persist in using 'man' in its old, generic sense often slip unconsciously from the general meaning to the limited one.

- For 'man' *use* 'person'/'people'/'individuals'.
- For 'mankind' *use* 'humanity'/'humankind'.
- For 'man-made' *use* 'hand-made'.
- For 'man-power' *use* 'personnel'/'staff'/'labour'.
- For 'man-hours' *use* 'working hours'.
- For 'one-man-show' *use* 'one person-show'.
- For 'man-to-man *use* 'one-to-one'.
- For 'to man' *use* 'to operate'/'work'/'serve in'.
- For 'manhood' *use* 'adulthood'/'maturity'.

Eliminate sexism when addressing people

Call a woman a woman. 'Used as a noun "woman" connotes independence, competence and seriousness of purpose as well as sexual maturity. Because these qualities in women are often found threatening, some people shy away from the very word as though it were taboo, and use alternatives like 'lady' and 'girl' as euphemisms' (Miller and Swift 1989).

- Use 'female' only when the corresponding choice would be 'male'.
- Use 'lady' only when evoking a certain standard of propriety or correct behaviour.
- Use 'Ms' instead of 'Mrs' or 'Miss', even when a woman's marital status is known.
- Use a married woman's first name instead of her husband's: e.g. Margaret Thatcher, not Mrs Denis Thatcher.
- Use the corresponding title ('Dr', 'Prof.') for women whenever a title is appropriate for men.
- Use 'Dear Colleague' or 'Editor' etc. in letters to unknown people (instead of 'Dear Sir' or 'Dear Sirs').

Eliminate sexual stereotyping

In our culture we are not inclined to diminish people's prestige. Nor should we. But that is what labelling someone with an incidental characteristic, like sex or colour or country of origin, does. In real life competence depends upon training, experience, talent, personality.

- Eliminate irrelevancies: e.g. 'lady lawyer' *becomes* 'lawyer'; 'pretty blonde secretary' *becomes* 'secretary'; 'woman doctor' *becomes* 'doctor'.
- Use the *same* term for both men and women: e.g. 'housewives' *becomes* 'homemakers'/'householders', 'chairman' *becomes* 'chair'/'chairperson'; 'forefathers' *becomes* 'ancestors'; 'workmanlike' *becomes* 'efficient', 'skilled', 'skilful'.
- Substitute verbs for nouns; e.g. for 'chairperson' substitute 'chair'.

Do not alter direct quotations

Comment may be made on the use of sexist language, or the quote may be paraphrased, using non-sexist language.

NOTE

Guidelines compiled by Helen Coxall, based on Casey Miller and Kate Swift (1989) *The Handbook of Non-Sexist Writing for Writers, Editors and Speakers*, London: Women's Press.

RECRUITMENT AND SELECTION FREE OF SEX BIAS: THE ESSENTIAL STEPS
Prepared by the Equal Opportunities Commission

Throughout the recruitment/selection process

Do
- Be objective: seek to identify the candidates' abilities and judge them on their individual merits: set the same standards for men and women.
- Train all personnel involved to avoid sex bias.
- Monitor at every stage of the recruitment process to check for possible sex/marriage discrimination.

Do not
- Make generalized assumptions about ability or ambition, based upon applicants' sex and/or marital status, or the fact they work part-time.
- Think of certain jobs or types of employment as 'men's work' or 'women's work'.

2 Application form

Do
- Process application forms from men and women in exactly the same way.
- Include a section to enable candidates to give details of unpaid experience (for example, in the voluntary sector).

Do not
- Include questions about personal circumtances, for example, relating to marital status or family responsibilities.

3 Job description

Do
- Describe accurately the requirements and duties of the job.

- Distinguish between requirements that are necessary and those which are merely convenient.
- Avoid wording which implies that members of one sex are more likely to be able to do the job.

Do not
- Set unnecessary conditions or standards. Use special care if stating age, mobility requirements, length or type of experience.

4 Person specification

Do
- Produce a specification of the essential/desirable aptitudes and characteristics of the person required to carry out the job satisfactorily.
- Assess each individual, man or woman, against that standard.

Do not
- Set standards which are higher than necessary, where physical ability is required (for example, strength).
- Set unnecessarily high education standards.
- Appoint on the basis of assumed 'acceptability' to peers, subordinates or clients.
- Specify hobbies or interests which could lead to the sex stereotyping of recruits.
- Include marriage plans, marital status, numbers and ages of children or any other similar considerations relating to personal circumstances in the person specification.

5 Obtaining candidates

(a) Advertising

Do
- Publicize vacancies, wherever possible.
- Encourage applications from one sex where few or no members of that sex have been employed in your organization in the previous 12 months.

Do not
- Use wording or illustrations which could be taken to indicate a preference for members of one sex.
- Place advertisements only in journals or papers which are intended primarily for men or primarily for women.
- Display vacancy notices where more men (or more women) are likely to see them, when advertising internally.

(b) Other sources of recruitment

Do
- Ensure that both sexes learn of any vacancies when seeking recruits in schools or other educational establishments.
- Inform job centres, private employment agencies and management consultants that you are keen to interview candidates of both sexes.

Do not
- Recruit solely or primarily by word of mouth, especially in a workforce or department predominantly of one sex.

6 Shortlisting

Do
- Use the objective standards of the person specification as the basis for shortlisting.

Do not
- Reject applications on the basis of assumptions about the abilities of men or women in general.

7 Assessment interview

Do
- Train all interviewers in the avoidance of sex bias. Issue written guidelines to the interviewer.
- Relate questions to the requirements of the job. Where it is necessary to assess whether personal circumtances will affect performance of the job, discuss this objectively without detailed questions based on assumptions about marital status, children and domestic obligations.
- Base assessments, wherever possible, upon factual evidence of past performance, behaviour and achievements, since these provide a better guide to intelligence than do answers to interview questions.
- Arrange for candidates to be assessed by a panel rather than by one person alone, wherever possible.
- Record reasons why candidates were or were not appointed.
- Review records of interview for possible sex/marriage discrimination.

Do not
- Make decisions based only on impressions formed during the interview.
- Rely on the facts rather than on generalized hunches.
- Ask any discriminatory questions.

8 Selection test

Do
- Use professionally designed tests.
- Check the suitability of the test for the job under consideration, using a thorough job description, as the basis.
- Validate tests separately for men and women, wherever possible.
- Assess whether the level of skill demanded is essential and, if so, whether it is more economical to train, as well as to seek the fully skilled.
- Check whether a high percentage of one sex fails to be shortlisted or appointed despite high test scores.

Where professional validation is not possible

Do
- Compare the average scores of men with the average scores of women on the same tests.
- Compare the rejection rates, on the test, for men and for women.
- Investigate any marked differences.

9 Assessment centres

Do
- Train assessors in the avoidance of sex bias.
- Use rating scales on specific items or aspects of the candidate's work, in the marking of paper exercises, rather than a general mark for the work as a whole.
- Refer to candidates by a number, where possible, so that assessors are unaware of the sex of candidates when marking papers.

10 Final selection

Do
- Base judgements on facts rather than impressions.
- Match the 'profile' of all the job requirements against the complete 'profile' of the individual.
- Allow each assessor independently to form his/her views, when the decision is to be made by several assessors together, with the most junior of the assessors going first.
- Check the various job requirements and discuss each in turn where there are differences between assessors on overall grading.
- Concentrate on the facts revealed and the assessments made during the procedure.
- Pause and question whether sex bias has influenced the proposal to reject a candidate.
- Check the final decision for potential sex and/or marriage discrimination, where consensus is not possible.

11 Promotion and transfers

Do
- Organize selection for promotion and transfers along the same lines as recruitment.
- Exercise special care where age limits, mobility requirements or seniority lists are in operation.
- Consider, if appropriate, whether the job could be held by two part-timers rather than one full-time worker.
- Publicize all vacancies, to internal as well as external candidates.
- Ensure that procedures for promotion are in writing and made known to all staff.
- State who is designated to approve appointments and to take part in the selection process for posts at the various levels.
- Assess all possible candidates, if promotion is by nomination, to ensure that everyone suitable is considered and that nobody with potential has been overlooked.
- Monitor each stage of the promotion or transfer process.

Do not
- Presume that proven ability at a lower level necessarily implies a good prospect of success at a higher level.

12 Management responsibility

Do
- Implement and publicize equal opportunities policies.
- Train and issue guidelines to all concerned.
- Check that the policies are carried out.

SOME MORE EQUAL THAN OTHERS
Rosalinda Hardiman

I write from two viewpoints: one as a female professional and as a member of the working group set up following the Museums Association's 1989 AGM to develop draft policy statements on equal opportunities.

Every reader of *Museums Journal* should be aware of the insistent statistic that 49 per cent of the Museums Association's membership is made up of women. The Association's Council acknowledges that 'women form a large and committed part of the Association, yet are under-represented on its governing body and in its public profile.'

My second viewpoint is as a disabled museum professional, but here there are no statistics even in that repository of knowledge, the database. No figures are available for what I suspect is an extremely rare breed. There may be under-representation of women at council level but as the MA again acknowledges, there are 'no representatives from disabled groups' or indeed from ethnic minorities. The working group and the Museums Association are anxious to redress the balance, stating that 'future positive measures are required'. In the field of equal opportunities some are indeed more equal than others.

Since the International Year of Disabled People in 1981, arts venues have focused attention on making provision for disabled people. In many cases, museums and art galleries have attempted to make their often intractable buildings accessible to the visitor. However, of the 1,726 venues listed in the *1989–90 Yearbook* as open to the public, only 689 stated that they had access for disabled people. Others admitted to having only partial access. The database does not yet ask for details of access to staff areas but it is unlikely that many of the 689 would qualify.

I welcome this gathering awareness of the problem and the actions taken to provide disabled access to our institutions, but I have to regret that virtually all of these approach the provision of facilities from the one-sided viewpoint of the disabled visitor. That is rightly stressed, but there is a widespread assumption that all museum staff will be able-bodied. The idea of planning for potential disabled members of staff is alien to most employers.

If the thought of provision for possible future employees is absent, the need to provide continuing employment for members of staff who become disabled while employed is rarely confronted. All too often when a member of staff becomes disabled, immediate recourse is made to the medical referee and the person is retired on grounds of ill-health. Many staff, who at present are forced into early retirement through disability of whatever kind, could have continued their careers with more flexible attitudes on the part of the employers. Admittedly, in most cases some financial input will be necessary, but if the corporate will is lacking, then no attempt will be made at all.

Disability covers a wide range of conditions, but it is worth bearing in mind that someone with severe heart problems and emphysema is just as frustrated by a flight of stairs as is a paraplegic, but only the paraplegic is generally regarded as 'disabled'.

Legislation and codes of practice: only theoretical support?

There are three main sets of legislation regarding the employment of disabled people. The Disabled Persons (Employment) Acts 1944 and 1958; the Chronically Sick and Disabled Persons Act 1970 and the Companies (Directors' Report) (Employment of Disabled Persons) Regulations 1980, which is part of the Companies' Acts 1948 to 1983. The first two, for technical reasons, do not apply to government departments (such as the national museums) although the obligations the acts impose fall equally on them. The third does not apply to public sector employers although the obligations which the regulations (1980) impose fall equally on them.

The (in)famous quota, whereby employers with twenty or more workers have a duty to employ a quota of registered disabled people, was introduced in the 1944 Act. The standard quota is 3 per cent of an employer's total workforce. It is not an offence to be below quota, but it is an offence to engage anyone other than a registered disabled person without first obtaining an exemption permit from the local job centre. An employer must not discharge a registered disabled person without reasonable cause if the employer is below quota or would fall below quota as a result. Most local authorities are below the 3 per cent quota but have exemption certificates and in government departments there is an average of just 1.3 per cent compliance.

The 1970 Act has twenty-nine sections, one of which requires physical access to public premises. However, a convenient get-out clause is often used, as compliance is required only 'in so far as it is in the circumstances both practicable and reasonable'. Many authorities find that it is *not* reasonable to make their buildings accessible.

The Companies Act Regulations relate to policies towards the employment of disabled workers generally, and not only, as in the quota scheme, to those who are registered as disabled under the Disabled Persons (Employment) Acts. On registration, it is worth adding a word of personal experience here. Many disabled people choose not to register, so that in employment terms they can cheerfully fill in an application form and put 'no' in the box that asks 'are you registered disabled?', as I did when I applied for my present post. Within two weeks of taking up my post, considerable pressure was placed on me to register, so that my registration would help towards the quota. Newly in post and less militant than I am now, I agreed, although unhappy at the pressure that had been brought to bear upon me.

Both the 1970 Act and the Companies Act Regulations emphasize training, whether for those who become disabled while working for the company in order to permit their continued employment, or for the training and career development of existing disabled employees. Considerable government help can be given in both instances, but it is not always tapped by employers. Through the disablement advisory service attached to job centres, two main schemes operate. The Adaptations to Premises and Equipment scheme (APE) and Special Aids to Employment (SAE) either purchase equipment outright, which is then lent to the disabled employee, or part-fund (up to £6,000) adaptations to buildings.

It is significant that in my own case, although pressured to register by the personnel department in 1980, it is only through my own initiative in finding out these sources that I obtained a special chair, keyboard and footrest in 1990. It is likely that many people are forced to give up work simply because neither they nor their employers know about the advice and funds available.

Many authorities and departments have drawn up codes of practice, not government legislation but morally binding upon the employing authorities. The civil service produced an excellent code of practice for disabled people in 1985 although an earlier statement was in force in 1981. The national museums may be among the smallest government departments but each has its own departmental disabled persons officer. The Arts Council issued its arts and disability plan in 1989 following on from its code of practice on arts and disability which was circulated to all its clients in 1985. The plan is very much a kick in the pants, stating that 'most client organisations have not implemented most aspects of the code of practice. Only one regional arts association had an action plan . . . it was now clear that reliance on the goodwill of clients to implement had resulted in very little progress.' The main thrust in the plan is to make venues accessible, along with encouragement to develop 'employment of disabled people in all areas of the organisations' work'.

In future, clients will have to reach certain access standards in order to qualify for project funding. The Council of Regional Arts Associations has now issued an equal opportunities code of practice in which it is stated that a disabled applicant should not be barred from employment on grounds of 'restricted access and inadequate equipment where both, with reasonable efforts and expenditure, the problems could be resolved.'

Many local government authorities which run most of the museums in Great Britain have declared that they are 'equal opportunity employers', yet as the *Local Government Chronicle* admits: 'Disability is the Cinderella of equal opportunities and comprehensive information on what local authorities are doing is virtually non-existent.' A number have been very active in this area, notably Leeds City, Manchester City, Derbyshire County, Gloucestershire County and the London Boroughs of Lambeth and Hackney. Manchester City Council has pledged £3 million per year to improve access to its buildings and public places and has as its target an employment quota of 9.2 per cent by 1997 – it has currently reached the regulation 3 per cent.

However, according to the *1989–90 Yearbook* Manchester City Art Gallery is noted as having only 'limited access for disabled'. Leeds City Council proudly states in its employment policy that 'inaccessibility of a building is not a reason for refusing a job' (quoted in *Local Government Chronicle*). However, the entries in the *Yearbook* state for Leeds City Art Gallery 'access for disabled difficult', for Leeds City Museum 'no access for disabled'. Although Leeds Industrial Museum and Lotherton Hall are listed as having disabled access, Temple Newsam House is listed as 'access for disabled difficult'.

In my experience most local authorities, whether county, city or district may well be exemplary equal opportunities employers as regards their civic centre or town hall but not when it comes to their other buildings, particularly their museums. I realize that most of this country's museums are in older buildings, many of historic and architectural interest, which pose problems of access, but that is of little consolation if the much vaunted equal opportunities statement does not apply to the one council building you want to work in.

You want to work?

There are few disabled curators. This is partly due to intractable buildings that deny access, partly to segregation of the severely disabled into 'special' schooling with less stress on academic attainment and also to attitudes and prejudice of employers. Regrettably these last two points are commonly encountered and a candidate's disability will be held as an excuse for non-employment, often without legitimate grounds, either through a lack of knowledge or an unwillingness on the part of the interviewer to look at the candidate and recognize ability rather than disability.

Most prospective museum professionals are discouraged even before they reach the interviewing panel. The postgraduate courses at Manchester and Leicester universities rightly demand a serious commitment which can only usually be demonstrated by volunteer experience. To get a volunteer place is difficult, to get a permanent museum job can be a major battle. Keeping that precious job can also be a battle. Small wonder that many disabled people, whether working in a museum or elsewhere, choose to keep their heads down and not make waves.

Increasingly I am abandoning that attitude and becoming militant, but that is not every-one's choice. It is not surprising that few care to rock the boat for most are in a catch-22 situation: if you manage to get and keep a museum job at whatever cost or pain, you will not win special facilities if you are seen to be managing, and for many, if you can-not cope you will be quickly retired on ill-health grounds. Consideration of adaptations, government funding and even more flexible attitudes to work and alternative working methods are very rarely considered.

In conclusion I will say that it is not illegal to discriminate against disabled people, how-ever much it may stink morally, but just consider: what would happen to *your* job tomorrow if you became disabled?

REFERENCES

Museums Association Policy Initiatives Drafts, March 1990.
The Chronically Sick and Disabled Persons Act 1970.
Arts Council, *Arts and Disability Action Plan*, October 1989.
The Council of Regional Arts Associations, *Equal Opportunities Code of Practice*, 1989.
Jackie Wills, 'Cinderella equality issue', *Local Government Chronicle*, 9 February 1990.
Museums Association, *Museums Yearbook 1989–90*.

COLOUR CONSCIOUS
Susan Ollerearnshaw

There are still many professional and technical areas in which Afro-Caribbean, Asian and other ethnic minority groups are under-represented. Employment in professional jobs in museums and art galleries is one of these. When organizations are asked to look at the rea-sons for this, a common answer is: 'We just don't get the applications . . . or the right ones.' Yet research shows there are plenty of graduates and qualified people from ethnic minority communities in the labour market. What, then, is causing the mismatch?

One cause is the gap between the ways in which employers recruit and select and how potential applicants are likely to be reached. Another is image – on both sides of the equation. In addition, no recruiting organization can afford to assume that direct or indirect discrimination is not occurring at any stage in the recruitment and selection process. Between these causes, there will often be many subtle factors which, unless addressed, can produce long-term barriers to equal opportunities.

It is important, therefore, for the museum and gallery profession, as any other, to iden-tify the particular reasons and barriers which might apply, both for potential applicants and those who do come forward, in order to find the right remedies. From this sort of practical analysis, considerable changes can be made. This article focuses particularly on the less well-understood causes of unequal experience.

A recent piece of research, *Ethnic Minorities and the Graduate Labour Market*, funded by the Commission for Racial Equality, shows that Afro-Caribbean, Asian and other ethnic minority students are more likely to study in polytechnics and colleges than in universities, and are unevenly spread across the types of course taken. Employers who traditionally recruit mainly from universities, therefore, will automatically reduce their chances of attracting these groups. Similarly, preference for particular universities and 'traditional' subjects may bias the intake significantly. *Ethnic Minorities and Recruit-ment to the Solicitors' Profession* showed, for example, that reliance on Oxbridge pro-duced fewer ethnic minority candidates.

Another issue is that of the selection criteria, both formal and informal, used in shortlisting and interviewing. Emphasis on particular subjects, or particular experience in previous jobs, can have a disproportionate impact, and there are other more subtle influences which have a major effect. In the Commission's formal investigation of access to chartered accountancy contracts, for example, we found that firms 'tended to recruit to an implicit "model" of a well rounded, able candidate who had to show intellectual ability, social and leadership skills and high motivation. They looked at evidence, such as academic attainments and positions of responsibility at school, holding office in societies and choice of vacation jobs. These indicators may be less appropriate for applicants from minority racial groups . . . Interviewers were often influenced by stereotypes or by subtle, unconscious assumptions and beliefs about applicants from different cultural or racial backgrounds. This could lead them to misinterpret non-verbal "signals" at interview, or to shape their perceptions of an individual according to their own expectations.'

There is another side to this 'image' factor. Employers recruiting across a spectrum of opportunities from youth training schemes to senior management may find that ethnic minority groups have a very different image of them to the one they would want to convey. Organisations and the jobs they offer can be seen as outdated or unwelcoming, for example with an all-white staff and 'culture'. *Ethnic Minorities and the Graduate Labour Market* found that ethnic minority students had lower expectations and higher anxieties about job prospects. When these are linked to perceptions of particular professions which show little evidence of employing ethnic minorities, the gap between an employer's equal opportunity intention and reality is not hard to understand.

There are some very practical remedies, however, which have been tried to good effect. If it is clear that few applicants are from ethnic minority groups, museums and galleries can start by looking at their likely image as employers and at how they can best encourage those from Afro-Caribbean, Asian and other backgrounds, from school age through to university and beyond.

Where there is already a 'multicultural' variety in the objects and arts they display, this can be used to excellent effect in outreach to schools and centres in areas of ethnic minority population. There is likely to be scope for more activity in this respect. People from Afro-Caribbean, Asian and other ethnic minority groups have played a role in this country's local and national history for much longer than is often recognized. This is very relevant to the debate earlier this year (*Museums Journal* February 1990) on the role of museums in relating to the lives and interests of all the communities they serve.

Work to make sure that a museum's image is relevant to 'consumers' from ethnic minority communities may also be used to put over a message to potential staff.

Care needs to be taken, though, to ensure that ethnic minority staff are not just recruited to work on these activities, or to specialize in certain sections of a museum or gallery. For equal opportunity to mean what it says, it should apply across the organization.

Job advertisements can give positive, welcoming messages too. The civil service, for example, ran an advertising campaign in 1987–8 with photographs of Afro-Caribbean and Asian staff describing their jobs at skilled and professional levels. Local authorities have done this for town hall staff – why not for curatorial and professional gallery staff?

Recruitment can target polytechnics and colleges, and should certainly question the need to concentrate on students from particular, traditional subject areas.

The selection process throughout needs to emphasize what is needed for the job in question. Interviewers need training and guidance on avoiding direct and indirect discrimination, including the sort of subjective, stereotyped assessments found in the CRE's chartered accountants' and other investigations. Selection criteria need to be assessed for unjustifiable bias. If they disproportionately reject candidates from particular racial groups and cannot be justified in job-related terms, they are unlawfully discriminatory. And selection decisions should be monitored for possible bias.

An initiative which can help to remedy under-representation is access or development training for skilled and professional jobs. Such approaches are worth exploring, both by employers and colleges offering museum studies. They should not be seen as the only remedy and will not always be the most appropriate.

Where qualified, able applicants are not being reached or selected, the emphasis should be on getting those processes right.

Where positive action is used alongside measures to ensure that recruitment and selection are both free from discrimination and sufficiently flexible to reach and recruit suitable Afro-Caribbean and Asian applicants, as well as white, it can bring early improvements to a profession's equal opportunities profile.

It is important for any profession or employment sector to look closely at the reasons why ethnic minority staff are under-represented, or unevenly spread among the opportunities programme, which includes regular reviews of recruitment and selection and practical action based on these. This is the basis of the CRE's employment code of practice.

Many museums and galleries have 'parent bodies' with equal opportunity programmes in varying stages of development. Examples may well be found there of what has worked (and what has not), and these can often be applied to good effect across specialisms.

NOTE

Further information on equal opportunity programmes and guidance booklets on implementing them are available from the Commission for Racial Equality (Employment Division), Elliot House, 10–12 Allington Street, London SW1E 5EH.

REFERENCES

John Brennan and Philip McGregor (1990) *Ethnic Minorities and the Graduate Labour Market*, CNAA Report, CRE.
Michael King, Mark Israel and Selina Goulborne (1990) *Ethnic Minorities and Recruitment to the Solicitors' Profession*, Law Society Research and Policy Planning Unit.

STRATEGIES FOR INCLUSION
Amina J. Dickerson

At the Chicago Historical Society (CHS) and elsewhere in the United States, a number of strategies are being employed to increase the representation of African Americans and other ethnic groups. In 1989–90, the society hosted a series of evenings entitled 'Meet the CHS', during which specific groups of community representatives – ethnic, educational, racial – were invited for a reception, tour of galleries and introductions to the society's staff and programmes. What followed was a discussion about the communities' perceptions of the society, their ideas for programmes and services and, for the museum, the opportunity to recruit new volunteers.

Working with local schools, the Chicago Historical Society is about to embark on a 'junior docents' programme, which will enable local secondary school students to familiarize themselves with various aspects of museum work, especially in third person interpretation in the CHS's 'Pioneer Life' gallery, which is reserved for live demonstrations of various eighteenth- and nineteenth-century crafts practised on the Illinois prairie. This programme expands on an annual programme which the society conducts each summer in co-operation with the local school system. Called a 'summer sampler', up to thirty students receive an intensive behind-the-scenes exposure to all aspects of museum work, including research and exhibition development, collections management, conservation, interpretation, marketing and public relations. Because the society believes more aggressive recruitment must be conducted to ensure there is a strong cadre of future museum professionals, and especially if the goal is to have greater multicultural representation, the society staff participate in career day programmes at local schools and visit classrooms to talk about museum work and the training required to enter the field.

Efforts to include more minorities on the staff require the society to build strong relations with local community service organizations. For entry level positions requiring limited training – front desk, reception, personnel, visitor aids, and so on – the society will call upon these organizations to recommend possible candidates. Often, these organizations do pre-screening interviews so that the society can see what the community views as its best candidates. Once on staff, CHS and other institutions with similar programmes make every effort to provide in-service training to further familiarize new staff with museum work, as well as to enhance possibilities for their career advancement.

At CHS, plans are being made for an intensive summer fellowship programme geared to graduate level students who have an interest in museum work, or who could be encouraged to consider careers in museums. Working in a collaborative effort, museums devoted to science and industry, art, natural history and history will provide an intensive exposure to museum work on a two-week rotation basis for up to ten fellows.

Financial support to fellows is particularly important for the candidates; without it many could not afford the eight-week programme, since they must earn in order to continue their studies. The programme will be advertised in art, science and history departments in regional universities, as well as with school counsellors. A panel representative of all the institutions will select finalists to participate.

The New York State Council on the Arts is implementing a similar programme which will create fellowships for up to five students each year. Unlike the rotation policy which Chicago hopes to establish, the New York programme will be restricted to history museums and will place one or two fellows in a specific institution for the course of the year.

To augment their experience, the council will conduct a series of seminars, classes, readings and 'mentorships' for the fellows. Operating in the belief that the students need internal support, a co-ordinator/counsellor will maintain weekly contact with students. Institutions which can host more than one fellow will be given preference. For their part, these institutions will receive a full-time person for a one-year appointment, with the salary/stipend paid by the council.

In their recruitment efforts, both New York and Chicago have determined that it is important not to restrict eligibility to current graduate students. Often the best candidates come from complementary fields such as education, public relations or corporate management. They tend to be experienced professionals who wish to make career changes, are highly motivated and often require less training. In considering the goals of multiculturalism, thinking beyond traditional curatorial and education positions can make it easier to fulfil goals, for the number of trained professionals in business, marketing, management and finance far exceeds the number of already trained and experienced minority museum professionals. And such professionals bring with them a range of contacts and supporters that can help efforts to build new audiences and create new opportunities. Their presence is reassuring for younger fellows and those newly entering the profession, providing a useful internal mentoring system for the institution.

ADDRESSING THE ISSUES
Vivien Lloyd

If you, reading this, are white, male, able-bodied, thirtysomething, heterosexual, employed and living in south-east England, you've got nothing to worry about. Right? If you don't fit this definition, then you and people like you constitute a problem to be tackled. Right?

Writing equal opportunities policies and seeing them through the relevant working groups, panels, sub-committees and committees is not easy; but it is simple compared to implementing what has been agreed with staff, governing body and users. Within the last three years, I have prepared two editions of a *Race Equality Policy and Report* and one *Women's Positive Action Report*. I am only too well aware of the gap between pious policies and reality, especially at a time when the resources to reach our sincerely held objectives are dwindling by the day.

Sheffield City Council has units (with full-time, paid officers) to address race equality, women and disability. There is an officer group (council members, officers and community representatives) to consider each of these issues. The race equality panel is chaired by the leader of the council, which indicates the level of importance accorded to these policies. Obviously there are other areas of disadvantage and groups of people needing special help: the elderly, carers, the unemployed, parents with children under the age of five and so on.

Few people would quibble about the introduction of improved physical access to buildings, and the provision of special toilets for people with disabilities. However, overtly or covertly, some continue to resist acknowledgement of the need for programmes to combat racism or sexism.

The first step in the preparation of an equal opportunities policy in Sheffield Museums was to convene a staff working party. SWIM (Sheffield Women in Museums) has been meeting since 1986. All women staff, including manual and clerical, are eligible to attend and the chair is rotated among members. The staff working party on race issues has been harder to keep going. Manual staff were invited to send a representative but have not done so. It has not been easy to reach a consensus.

The units prepared guidelines for the use of departments compiling their mandatory policies and reports. These have been less than helpful. A department might content itself with a formulaic approach, mouthing the right words while avoiding thinking about its own particular circumstances and services. Only arts and museums departments have collecting policies: equal opportunities guidelines (naturally?) omitted mention of these.

Equal opportunities starts even before the recruitment and selection process. It means making the whole workforce, especially young people, aware of museums as a potential employer and museum work as a potential career. Raising museums' profile can be achieved through careers advice, contact with the local careers service, offering priority to, for example, black youngsters for work experience placements and positive action traineeships. All the national and local museum groups, Museums Association, Museums and Galleries Commission and specialist bodies, federations and area councils, as well as individual museum services can play a part in the process.

'An equal opportunity employer' might well be the wording on your job adverts. This does not just mean that you have one or two black attendants. It means career archaeologists as well as section 11 posts or community outreach workers. Without the awareness described above, suitable candidates for the whole range of museum jobs will not apply.

Sheffield City Council has been training its managers in recruitment and selection, including a strong equal opportunities element. Museums was the first department to have its entire management team accredited. Main points of the recruitment procedure include examining aspects of the vacancy, rewriting the job description and person specification to eliminate bias and unnecessary criteria which exclude good candidates; the conduct of a standard interview; the maintenance of records relating to all applicants, including reasons for not offering an interview, or not offering the post. As a result of following these steps, staff have found selection easier, not more difficult. Once employed in the department, all staff need equal access to training, to advancement and promotion. There are special needs relating to personal safety, and to the care of dependants. We are awaiting council-wide guidance on the latter: special service conditions for women with dependants might simply reinforce the fact that women traditionally bear the brunt of caring. Flexible working times, creches, compassionate leave when necessary – need to be available to men and women.

We are responsible for the equal opportunities of our users. A physical access 'audit' was carried out for us at all our sites by members of the Forum of People with Disabilities. They pointed out what obviously needed putting right. For example, the pull cord for the light in the special toilet was too high to reach from a wheelchair. It was often fairly easy to rectify the problems. Members of the forum were sympathetic to the constraints of opening historic buildings not originally designed for public admission, and that these factors can preclude major alterations to fit lifts, widen doorways and flatten out floors.

It is not only physical access that needs to be examined. Non-users who feel the museum is not for them must be consulted and their perceptions fed back into the planning process.

The museum department has six questions in Sheffield City Council's Household Survey, a sample of 1,700 hour-long interviews conducted in people's homes. To non-users' perceptions is added data which does not have the favourable bias known to influence responses taken on the premises. Data related to disadvantaged people will come from this survey. At the moment we have resources to pursue only the Household Survey. Programmes like Priority Search and Focus Groups go into much greater depth with far smaller samples and can be targeted specifically at disadvantaged people.

These soundings of people's perceptions overlap, to a considerable extent, with basic marketing. Obvious equal opportunities measures include the provision of information, promotional as well as on-site, in languages of ethnic minorities and in Braille; signing for the deaf and hearing impaired at talks, demonstrations and events; induction loop systems and creches. Sheffield does not have resources to provide most of these.

Customer care training is essential and needs to reflect these policies. The culture of the service must be developed to create receptiveness to equal opportunities issues. All staff

must undergo it: not only reception and warding staff, but those at all levels in the organization. Front-line staff need support and guidance on how to deal with any negative
responses they encounter: to what extent they can provide an answer, and at what point
they must refer it to management. The sympathetic hearing scheme provided short training sessions for staff, at no charge, and at different sites.

Asian gold and silversmiths have given Sheffield industry a shot in the arm in the way
that the Huguenot refugees once did. The Tyzack family, at Abbeydale, is a case in
point. We are currently showing archaeological material from Pakistan in the city museum shop. It could well be that a local museum's collections no longer reflect the ethnic
composition of the local community. Acquisition policies need to be revised to ensure
that the museum contains material relevant to the city's present population. Disposal
policies must not be anti-disposal policies that are covertly racist. A country's laws and
ethical rights to its original material must be scrupulously respected.

Positive images enable the museum to be pro-active in redressing ancient wrongs. We
have examined our displays, storyline and information for sexist and racist language,
but it takes time to effect the alterations. It is possible to use good, clear language without racist or sexist expressions. If you are using the term Inuit instead of Eskimo,
explaining why will help visitors to perceive that old attitudes and terminology were
racist. Merchandise in museum shops must not perpetuate old stereotypes or leave
unchallenged baseless assumptions about racial groups or gender roles.

Pro-active initiatives are often events: exhibitions, demonstrations, family activities.
In Sheffield, these programmes are now severely limited by budgetary problems. The
exhibitions budget has been cut drastically, and the post of community outreach worker
is frozen.

Equal opportunities must be available by right not by concession. I have not been able
even to start many of the procedures I believe are essential, and this note has done no
more·than outline them. There is still a very long way to go.

This paper first appeared in Museums Journal *(November 1990), pp. 25–30.*

29

Women and museums

David R. Prince

There has been very little empirical research into the number of women in museums, their profiles and experiences. This piece dates from research undertaken in 1985 and as yet has not been updated. Unpublished research at master's degree level has pointed to certain developments since this paper was published. Clearly women are now reaching more senior appointments in the museums profession. But the picture is still one of inequality. A significant proportion of women in senior positions do not have children and have therefore not had to deal with either the career breaks or the role conflicts experienced by others. No museums in the UK, not even the nationals which can have over 1,000 employees, have any form of creche provision and most museums have conditions of service which afford little support for employees who are parents. Gender differences can also be found in certain subject disciplines, for example the majority of curators within the field of technology are male. They can also be found in museum type: most directors of independent museums are male. The services such museums provide tend to bear evidence of this imbalance.

This article looks at the data held on the Museums Data-Base at the Museums Association and compares these with other data held in the public domain within, for example, the Office of Population Censuses and Surveys (OPCS), the Registrar General's Office for Scotland, the Department of Education and Science (DES), the Scottish and Welsh Offices, the Manpower Services Commission (MSC), the University Grants Committee and made available through such publications as the *Social Trends* series, the *General Household Survey* and the various reports of the Equal Opportunities Commission.

The article also explores briefly data held by and about other professional institutions, for example, the British Medical Association, the Institute of Personnel Management and the Law Society, which are compared with grouped profile data held within the Association's own membership files.

It is fair to say that there has been no extensive survey looking specifically at the role and position of women working in museums. This should be given research priority, particularly in the light of the findings of the Data-Base's analysis.

The pamphlet advertising the MA seminar on 'The Position of Women in Museums' opened with the quotation (which is basically a paraphrase of the material in *Museums UK*, although (unlike *Museums UK*) it was not written by the Data-Base Unit) that:

> Women occupy the lower echelons of the museum service and relatively few hold the most senior posts. Why is this? Do women in museums suffer from a lack of opportu-

nity, or lack of ambition? Or is the museum world lagging behind in offering working practices which enable women to achieve fulfilment both at work and at home?

While the last part could equally apply to men, the point here is that the reasons underpinning the relative performance, and position, of women in museums (the first part of the quotation *is* a broadly accurate reflection of the current situation) must be sought from sources far beyond any consideration of the managerial structures and occupational characteristics of museums themselves and into wider, deeply held and, in many senses, entrenched social values and political attitudes towards the role of women in society as a whole – irrespective of the particular profession or working practice under consideration. While these reasons can be assumed to point towards ways to make the overall situation (at least, perhaps, for museums) more equitable, their consideration will be left to others more qualified than me.

I propose to examine previously published statistics in the museums field and from elsewhere that, I hope, provide an accurate and neutral view of the current position of women in museums. To look at this problem realistically, six main areas of data will need to be considered:

1   Base statistics on the composition of the UK workforce as a whole.
2   Spreads of attainment in the formal education system that influence career patterns.
3   The known UK museum population in terms of location, growth and fields of specialization (on which the first two aspects can be assumed to have an influence).
4   The roles performed by women within museums (as far as can be ascertained from a survey not specifically devoted to this issue).
5   The composition of the Association's own membership (individual, associate, fellow and so on).
6   How this known composition compares with other professional bodies.

With these fields examined, it should be possible to provide a summary picture of the position of women not only in museums but also in comparison with other professions.

There are more women (Table 29.1)[1,4] (51 per cent as at 1985) within the total population of Great Britain of 55.1 million than there are men, with equality in population being reached at forty-five years. In terms of working age (say twenty to fifty-nine) the population is broadly fifty–fifty with 14.4 million men and 14.3 million women. At this fundamental level, therefore, no statistical differences can be found.

As soon as patterns of working practice are included in the model, however, differences begin to emerge (Table 29.2).[2] As a base statistic, the total workforce of Great Britain (as in 1985, and excluding the armed forces and those seeking work irrespective of whether they are claiming benefits) accounts for some 26.6 million people of which 15.5 million (or nearly 60 per cent) are men. These figures reflect an increase in the overall working population of 1.3 million in the decade 1975–1985 which is, according to the Equal Opportunities Commission, attributable entirely to the increased number of women in the workforce although, as most of the currently available evidence suggests, these have tended to be in part-time jobs. The Department of Employment is predicting a further increase in the workforce into the early 1990s with the proportion of women expected to rise to about 42 per cent of the total, or some twelve million workers.

These total figures are broadly reflected in the breakdown of the working population by age, but there are clear differences in the type of employment: for example, in 1986 of the 2.6 million self-employed people, 1.95 million (or 75 per cent) were men, while for the jobs classified by the OPCS as temporary, casual or seasonal, over 60 per cent of the workforce were women, many being between the ages of twenty-five and fifty and with dependent children.

Table 29.1 Estimated resident population of Great Britain by age, 1985 (millions)

Age	Male	Female	All
0–9	3.5	3.3	6.8
10–19	4.2	4.0	8.2
20–39	8.2	8.1	16.3
40–59	6.2	6.2	12.4
60–74	3.6	4.3	7.9
≥ 75	1.2	2.4	3.5
Total	26.9	28.3	55.1

See Notes 1 and 4.

Table 29.2 Labour force composition, 1987*

	(%)
All men	58.2
All women	41.8
All persons	100.0

* All those over sixteen with jobs, excluding the armed forces, together with those seeking work, irrespective of whether they claim benefit.
See Note 2.

The rapid increase in unemployment, especially between 1979 and 1984, was felt equally by men and women. However, the ways in which the government has changed the unemployment counting process (by now only including those that register at an Unemployment Benefit Office and declare that they are fit for work), besides making time-comparisons difficult, has, according to the OPCS, had the effect of removing a disproportionate number of women from the register. Even based on this definition, the number of unemployed women has continued to grow (up to latest figures) while that for men has steadied over the same period. A 1985 Labour Force Survey by the OPCS found that while the majority of unemployed men and unemployed single women were seeking full-time work, most married women were seeking part-time employment.

Thus, at this level, differences between the various working populations can be noted. One potentially important contribution to these difference can be presumed to exist within the educational system, especially as it relates to subjects studied and therefore to potential working environments: indeed as the Equal Opportunities Commission notes, 'the subjects studied and examinations passed at secondary school have a considerable influence on girls' and boys' future career opportunities.'[4]

If we look at the O Level pass figures for 1985 (Table 29.3)[5] produced by the DES and the Welsh Joint Education Committee (which are not only representative of previous years but also mirror those for CSE Grade 1, and A Levels) the following points of significance emerge:

Table 29.3 Women as a percentage of GCE O Level passes in selected subjects (summer examinations), England and Wales, 1985

Subject	Women passes %
Technical drawing	6.23
Physics	28.46
Computer studies	26.93
Chemistry	41.29
Geography	43.28
Mathematics	44.13
Economics	39.54
History	50.77
Art/Craft/Design	60.20
Commercial subjects	57.10
Biology	60.22
English language	56.74
English literature	60.81
French	60.96
German	62.70
Sociology	74.99
Cookery	96.94
All subjects	51.51

Source: Department of Education and Science and Welsh Joint Education Committee.
See Note 5.

1   Girls are under-represented in all the science subjects (especially physics and computer science and including economics) to a considerable degree; the only exception to this being biology where over 60 per cent of the successes were achieved by girls.
2   As a balance to this, girls are over-represented in the arts (including sociology here) and in languages.
3   The sex representations in technical drawing and cookery need no additional comment.

With this as the basis, the destination of all school leavers indicates important trends:

• While half (49 per cent) of all leavers are women, only 46 per cent of all those destined to directly enter the labour market are women.
• Women outnumber men on higher education courses (particularly on teacher training courses) save for first degree courses, where of the 55,000 enrolling in 1986, only 41 per cent were women.

Looking at the subjects studied by those school-leavers entering higher and further education (full-time, undergraduate level) (Table 29.4)[4] reinforces, perhaps not surprisingly, the sex differences noted for O Level passes. As the Equal Opportunities Commission notes 'the sex stereotyping evident (at school) determines subject choice to a large extent'.[4] For example, over 90 per cent of those studying engineering and technology are men while for science the figure is 65 per cent. In nearly all the other subjects, women are in the majority with educational studies being the most notable.

Table 29.4 Undergraduate students in full-time education by type of course by sex, 1984–5

Course	Male (000s)	Female (000s)	Female (%)
Education	6.1	23.0	79.0
Medicine/Dentistry	16.6	17.5	51.3
Engineering/Technology	54.9	5.4	9.0
Agriculture/Forestry	3.1	2.0	39.2
Science	58.1	30.0	34.1
Business/Social studies	55.7	48.4	46.5
Architecture/Other professional studies	8.7	7.0	44.6
Languages/Literature	11.5	27.3	70.4
Arts	11.9	14.6	55.1
Music/Drama/Design	12.6	19.3	60.5
Total	239.2	194.5	

Source: Appropriate Education Departments; Equal Opportunities Commission. See Note 4.

This stereotyping also flows through the type of employment school-leavers engage in to a considerable degree whether it be full-time jobs or YTS courses (Table 29.5),[6] 82 per cent of all those on clerical, selling or catering YOPS courses are women, compared with only 8 per cent in manufacturing.

Table 29.5 Occupations undertaken by school-leavers after reaching the minimum school-leaving age

	Males		Females	
	YTS	Jobs	YTS	Jobs
Materials processing	44.0	39.0	7.0	11.0
Transport and operating	3.0	8.0	1.0	1.0
Painting and repetitive assembly	6.0	7.0	1.0	7.0
Construction	11.0	7.0		7.0
Clerical and related	6.0	8.0	32.0	43.0
Catering and cleaning	5.0	5.0	30.0	17.0
Selling	7.0	7.0	20.0	13.0
Total (%) (not 100)	82.0	81.0	91.0	100.0

Occupations classified by condensed KOS based on CODOT (Classification of Occupations and Directory of Titles). See Note 6.

Looking at jobs, irrespective of the age of employees (Table 29.6) (both full- and part-time and as categorized by the New Earnings Survey),[3] reinforces a number of the trends isolated so far:

1 Only 11 per cent of all those employed in general management are women.
2 Three-quarters of those employed in personal services (hairdressing, cleaning and so on) are women.
3 Three-quarters of those employed in clerical and related work are women.
4 Certain employment sectors remain predominantly male environments (mining and construction, transport and storage).

Table 29.6 Percentage distribution of women by occupational grouping, 1986

	Females
General management	11.0
Professional and managerial support	69.0
Professional Education, health	32.0
Literary, artistic and sports	9.0
Professional in science, engineering, etc.	16.0
Managerial (excluding general)	74.0
Clerical and related	57.0
Selling	11.0
Security and protection	76.0
Catering, cleaning and personal	10.0
Farming, fishing and related	24.0
Material processing (not metal)	35.0
Making and repairing (not metal)	5.0
Material processing and repairing (metal)	45.0
Painting and repetitive assembly	0.4
Construction and mining	4.0
Transport and storage	5.0
Miscellaneous	42.0

Source: The New Earnings Survey.
See Note 3.

The 1986 *New Earnings Survey* concluded that only 19 per cent of all working women were in professional jobs (including education, health and welfare), although they were more evenly distributed in the service sector than in any other. As we shall see this does not apply to museums, given that they are also in the service sector.

This, together with the fact that the majority of part-time jobs are occupied by women, has a profound effect on earnings, not withstanding the legislation in this field (Table 29.7).[7] The average gross hourly earnings, excluding overtime, for women are some three-quarters of their male counterparts, although there are considerable differences when types of employment are taken into consideration. The OPCS, summarizing this type of information, concludes that it reflects the fact that 'men tend to be concentrated in the higher paid grades';[7] a fact reinforced by the *Social Trends* data on socio-economic groupings of full-time employees (all jobs) (Table 29.8)[8] where, for example, 90 per cent of the professional and managerial (I) group are men.

Table 29.7 Average gross hourly earnings (excluding overtime) for full-time employees on adult rates, Great Britain, 1986

Occupation	Men	Women	Women's as
	(pence per hour)		percentage of men's
Police (below sergeant)	617.2	566.8	91.8
Nurses, midwives	421.7	381.1	90.4
Bar staff	266.7	238.1	89.3
Library clerks	357.1	317.4	88.9
General clerks	389.7	323.5	83.0
Laboratory technicians	473.0	380.8	80.5
Repetitive assemblers	367.2	280.2	76.3
Footwear workers	358.8	262.7	73.2
Sales supervisors	488.3	317.4	65.0
All occupations	486.6	360.7	74.1

Source: *The New Earnings Survey.*
See Note 7.

Table 29.8 Socio-economic groupings of full-time employees by sex, 1984

Category	Male		Female	
	(%)	(%)	(%)	(%)
Professional and managerial (I)	90	6	10	1
Intermediate (II)	62	23	38	21
Skilled non-manual (III–NM)	38	12	62	40
Skilled manual (III–M)	87	35	13	9
Partly skilled	53	16	47	21
Unskilled	53	5	47	7
Totals		100		100

Source: Social Trends (37) 1984.
See Note 8.

While much of what has so far been noted will be familiar, it is important to consider the basic trends in employment patterns before looking specifically at museums in order to put the Data-Base's findings into a clearer perspective.

Turning to museums, the Data-Base[9] found that although there are no counties in the UK without some form of museum provision, in real terms this spatial distribution is markedly uneven with a strong tendency for concentration within the south of England. The South-East and South-West Area Museum Council regions combined, for example, hold 47 per cent of the total museum institutions. This is even more pronounced in terms of the national and government departmental museum distribution, with nearly 60 per cent concentrated in the south. Of the purely national museums with boards of trustees, nearly 70 per cent are in London.

In relation to the population of the UK taken on a regional/county basis, it is possible to state that the old, heavy industrial areas of, for example, the north-west of England, south Wales and the Strathclyde area of Scotland are currently significantly under-represented in terms of total museum allocation, even in terms of local authority institutions. These observations, however, are based solely upon the recorded numbers of museums, and do not take into account the size and operational capacity of the institutions, the types of collection they hold and so on. All of these can be presumed to have an immediate impact in terms of the perception of the total museum provision (from both the public and professional perspectives) within a stated area.

Nevertheless, the significant concentration of museums in the southern counties of England cannot be denied. Although not differentiating between men and women, it is therefore clear that the greatest employment opportunities within museums are concentrated in the south. There is some evidence in the Data-Base that this may not always be the case; Scotland, for example, has witnessed a growth in museum provision since 1974 that surpasses all the other Area Museum Council (AMC) areas. However, these tend to be the smaller, privately run museums providing limited employment opportunities.

In general terms, three-quarters of the total museum provision (in purely institutional terms) has been established since the Second World War, with nearly half of the total since 1971. Since 1950 the majority have been in the non-public sector, and of these nearly 64 per cent have been founded by voluntary associations or private individuals with, significantly, given the above observation, 48 per cent of these being in the south of England. This trend is even more marked since 1971.

The rise of the non-public, voluntary association museum is reflected strongly in the types of collections upon which the museums were originally founded. Whereas before 1950 most of the foundations were based on the so-called traditional collecting areas of fine arts and archaeology, together with the pure and natural sciences (particularly in the public sector museums), their dominance has been eroded rapidly in recent years (particularly since 1961), and replaced by foundations within the fields of industrial archaeology, social history (particularly rural social history) and technology and transport. The fact that three-quarters of site museums (defined by the Data-Base as those with more than ten acres of open land dedicated as 'exhibition space') have been founded since 1970 supports this view. The periods immediately following the two World Wars, perhaps not surprisingly, saw a significant growth in the foundation of military and service (particularly regimental) museums.

There has thus been a clear shift in the foundation of museums from the public to the non-public sector in recent years, from the large to the small, together with an orientation towards new forms of base collections, with a renewed focus in the south of England. However, it must be remembered that these observations are drawn solely from the number of museums extant at various times in the past, with no account being taken of their perceived or actual impact on the overall museum scheme as determined by their size, collections and operational capacity.

Turning now to staffing, the Data-Base[10] survey examined this aspect in ten main areas: age, sex, salaries, part-and full-time staffing, departmental distribution, educational background, training, and the role performed by volunteers and MSC workers in staff-support operations. The directors of the institutions were given separate consideration by the survey.

While the Museums Association's definition of a museum does not include the employment of qualified staff as a necessary parameter, it should be remembered that its own

Code of Conduct for Museum Authorities (1987 revision)[8] states that one of the minimum requirements is that 'the governing authority has a special obligation to ensure that the museum has staff sufficient in both number and kind to ensure that the museum is able to meet its responsibilities'. This is a modification of its 1977 Code,[12] which stated that 'the staff must comprise at least one full-time properly qualified curator ...'. So both versions imply that museums, to be museums, must be staffed properly.

However, the Data-Base survey produced the important finding that of 1,354 valid responses to this question, no less than 457 museums (a third) did not have any full-time members of staff at all, let alone curatorial staff. Of these non-staffed museums 70 per cent are in the non-public sector and consist primarily of museums founded and operated by voluntary associations and private individuals.

The Data-Base survey looked at the total number of full- and part-time staff employed by museums, and the numbers of volunteers and MSC personnel working within them and found that of the 10,045 full-time staff 43 per cent were employed by the nationals, 37 per cent by local authorities and the remaining 20 per cent by so-called independent museums. The patterns for part-time and MSC workers are broadly similar, although we concluded in *Museums UK* that the non-public sector museums employ one-half of all part-time museum staff and rely very heavily on both MSC workers and, particularly, volunteers.

The departmental distribution of the full-time staff can be assumed to have an impact on employment potential, and the Data-Base examined this in detail. If we look at the results (Table 29.9)[10] a number of trends can be isolated.

Table 29.9 Proportion of total full-time staff employed by activity by type of museum

Activity	National	LA	Other
Management and administration	12.2	12.1	19.8
Administrative support	7.7	7.9	11.1
Conservation	3.6	4.3	3.2
Curatorship	9.9	19.6	11.1
Education	1.8	3.6	2.1
Exhibition and design	3.7	3.9	2.1
Technical support	8.2	7.1	12.8
Advertising and publicity	0.9	0.3	1.1
Fundraising and sponsorship	0.1	0.1	0.7
Security and attendant duties	34.9	32.6	16.4
Research	9.8	1.4	1.2
Retail Sales	2.9	2.6	6.6
Library	2.4	0.5	2.6
Documentation	0.5	1.6	1.3
Unclassified	1.4	2.4	7.9
Total	100.0	100.0	100.0
No. of museums	60	435	438

Source: Museums Data-Base (Original Survey) (1987).
See Note 10.

220

First, less than 5 per cent of the total full-time staff are employed in each of the following discrete activities: conservation, education, exhibition and design, advertising and publicity, fundraising and sponsorship (this area being negligible), documentation, and library work.

Second, by far the largest single category in the public sector museums is security services (including warding) at around one-third of all the full-time staff. This level is halved for museums in the non-public sector.

Third, management, administration and administrative support services (excluding technical support) employ one-fifth of the staff of the public sector museums, and 30 per cent of those in the private sector. Technical support services (including maintenance) average 7.5 per cent in the public sector and 13 per cent in the private.

Fourth, the proportion of full-time research staff is highest in the national museums (at 10 per cent of total staffing), compared with just 1 per cent of the staff in the local authority and private sector museums.

Fifth, the private sector employs 7 per cent of its staff in retail sales (including catering and shop services), whereas the public sector institutions employ less than 3 per cent.

Sixth, while nearly 20 per cent of the staff of local authority museums are involved specifically in curatorial work, the figure is halved for the national museums and those museums of the private sector, although the allocation of staff to the research category by the nationals has probably had an indeterminable effect.

Taking the activities used by the Museums Association to define a museum (conservation, curatorship, education, exhibition, research, library work and documentation) it is clear from these figures that just over one-third of the full-time staff of the public sector museums are employed in them, compared with one-quarter of those of the private sector. The remainder of both sectors are employed in management, support and ancillary services, including security.

Looking now at the directors, senior curators and chief museum officers the survey produced the clear finding that nearly 80 per cent are men, over 90 per cent of the directors of national museums are men, with approximately 80 per cent of the other two main categories of museums also having male directors. However, we did not explore any reasons for this.

The educational background of the directors was examined. The survey looked at whether they held university degrees (or their equivalent) at both first and higher levels, and whether they held the Museums Association's professional qualification (the Associateship, AMA) or its Fellowship (FMA).

As far as first and second degrees are concerned, the majority of the national, and even more of the local authority, directors hold first degrees, with 42 per cent holding higher degrees. Half of the private sector directors hold first degrees and approximately one-quarter higher degrees.

The penetration of the Museums Association's own qualifications appears to be primarily within the local authority sector, where over 40 per cent hold the AMA and over one-quarter the FMA. Less than 10 per cent of the directors of the national and non-public sector museums hold either the qualification or the Fellowship.

The length of service of the directors in their current museum, in museums as a whole, and in other occupations was also considered by the survey which showed that while 52 per cent of the national directors have been at their present museum for less than five years (81 per cent for less than ten years), the corresponding figures for the local authority museums and those of the private sector are 41 and 66 per cent, and 43 and 72 per cent respectively. *Museums UK* concluded, perhaps rather obviously, that the national directors tend to be appointed as directors (rather than progressing through the managerial system within their current museum) to a greater degree than directors in the other sectors and also that they tend to be older on appointment. This may have career-path implications for women in the nationals.

As far as length of service in museums is concerned, we found that there is a significant difference between local authority museum directors and those of the other two sectors. While nearly 65 per cent of the first group have been in museums for over ten years, only 34 per cent have in the national, and 36 per cent have in the non-public sectors. However, for those with over twenty years service, the pattern evens out between the national and local authority museums to around 20 per cent. Nevertheless, it is possible to suggest (although further work is clearly needed here) that the local authority museums appear to be operating a more clearly defined promotion path within their sector than either of the other two, and that once in the local authority sector most directors tend not to move to either the national or independent sectors. This path appears to be easier for men to follow than women.

Looking specifically at the sexes working as full-time, paid staff within the three main categories of museums used by the Data-Base Report (Table 29.10)[10] presents two immediate observations:

Table 29.10 Women as percentage of total full-time museum workforce by type of museum

	National	*LA*	*Other*
Women (%)	14	12	14
Men (%)	86	88	86

Source: Museums Data-Base (Original Survey) (1987).
See Note 10.

- There is a remarkable consistency of employment practice between all three types.

- 87 per cent of their full-time workers are male, a figure that is far beyond any random probability. The consistency between these figures and those on directors mentioned earlier may also be recorded.

Unfortunately, the reasons underpinning this marked disparity, and its implications for museums in general, were not examined by the Data-Base. Further research is clearly needed. In the following discussions on ages, salaries and so on, this initial staffing profile should be borne firmly in mind.

Bearing in mind the observations on working ages noted at the start of the article, the age-spreads of museum workers may have an influence on the relative under-representation of women (Table 29.11).[10] When we looked at this in the Data-Base, the first observation was that this is a strong consistency between the types of museums (particularly with respect to the national museums and the private sector institutions), with approximately half the staff being younger than forty-four. Local authority museums show a marginal tendency to employ more people in the thirty-five to forty-four year age-band, but this is balanced by their slight relative underemployment of those aged between forty-five and fifty-four.

Only the non-public museums draw greater than 10 per cent of their full-time workforce from those younger than twenty-five. Excluding this last age-band, all three types appear to employ a relatively even spread of ages up to the usually accepted male retirement age (bearing in mind the sex-ratio noted above) of sixty-five.

Salary is one of the most contentious issues, particularly bearing in mind that women's earnings are only 75 per cent of those of their male counterparts. The basic data are displayed in Table 29.12,[10] where it must be remembered that all the figures relate to 1985. There is no reason to doubt that the relative picture is the same today, and the Museums Association is currently undertaking a national salaries survey.

Table 29.11 Ages of full-time paid staff by type of museum

Age-bands	National	LA	Other
16–24	8	9	13
25–34	24	24	19
35–44	20	25	20
45–54	24	18	21
55–64	23	21	20
65 or older	13	7	
Total	100	100	100

Source: Museums Data-Base (Original Survey) (1987).
See Note 10.

Table 29.12 Numbers and proportions of male and female staff within defined salary bands, 1985

Band (£)	Males		Females		Totals	Females as percentage of total
	No.	(%)	No.	(%)		
3,000 or less	82	0.9	85	4.1	167	50.9
3,000–5,000	388	4.5	238	11.4	626	38.0
5,001–7,000	6,777	77.8	1,242	59.4	8,019	15.5
7,001–9,000	678	7.8	260	12.4	938	27.7
9,001–11,000	336	3.9	155	7.4	491	31.6
11,001–13,000	169	1.9	70	3.3	239	29.3
13,001–15,000	107	1.2	19	0.9	126	15.1
15,001–17,000	98	1.1	13	0.6	111	11.7
17,001–19,000	24	0.3	5	0.2	29	17.2
19,001–21,000	15	0.2	2	0.1	17	11.8
21,000 or more	39	0.4	3	0.1	42	7.1
Totals	8,713		2,092		10,805	

Source: Museums Data-Base (Original Survey) (1987).
See Note 10.

Taking the largest single sector of employment (in absolute terms) first, it is clear that the majority of male staff in all three types is employed at salaries ranging between £5,001 and £7,000 (74% within the nationals, 82% in the local authority museums, and 78% of those within the private sector institutions). Accounting for the fact that males dominate the employment scene within museums, it is clear that these figures represent the overall picture fairly adequately, with the ancillary conclusion that private sector institutions appear to pay the lowest average salaries across the board, followed by the local authority sector. Only a small proportion of staff within each category earns more than £11,001 each year, the local authority and private sectors being observably worse in this respect than the nationals.

Concentrating on the lower salary levels for the moment (those of less than £5,000 per year), an interesting pattern emerges between the three types of museum in terms of the ratio between male and female staff, with the firm conclusion that all three types employ an average ratio of five times as many women at this level as men. When this is compared with their relative staffing numbers it is clear that not only do less women work in museums, but of those that do there is a strong tendency for them to be employed at lower salaries than their male counterparts – this is particularly the case in local authority and private sector museums. We did not find any indication in the survey (probably because we didn't look for it) that women are paid less for the same work, and took this to mean that they are employed in different operational areas. Without a survey specifically looking at this issue, unfortunately there is not much more to say.

At the higher salary bands, the patterns change slightly towards equality. However, this percentage obscures the fact that there are singularly few women at this salary level.

The main conclusions we drew from this in *Museums UK* were, therefore, that museums (irrespective of their type) employ men to a degree that far outweighs any statistical observations of chance factors, and that, given this, women are far more likely to be employed at lower salary levels when compared with men. Further, most full-time museum employees earned less than £7,000 per year in 1985 and that this was most marked in the private sector. For salaries between £7,000 and £13,000 per year, there is a tendency towards equality in pay (as a reflection of equality of employment opportunity), but the relative numbers of men and women at this level question the validity of this observation in absolute terms. At the highest salary levels, picking up the points made under the directors' profiles, women are again significantly under-represented.

Moving away from museums as institutions and into the Museums Association as the professional body of the museum world, we can compare the membership of the MA (AMA, FMA and individual) with other professional groups and trades unions.

As at the latest available figures, 57 per cent of the Fellows of the MA were men, and 51 per cent of all members are men (Table 29.13). These are remarkably low figures for both professional bodies and trade unions, even those that have not traditionally been dominated by men.

So, what general conclusions can be drawn?

First, it looks as if the position of women in museums is broadly similar to the position of working women in Britain as a whole.

Second, this implies a strong sex-bias towards men in terms of senior managerial appointments.

Third, women are relatively under-employed by museums to a degree that is out of proportion with the types of work undertaken by them as institutions.

As I stated at the beginning, unfortunately the reasons for this were not explored by the Data-Base survey: it was after all a massive data gathering exercise aimed at the institutional level, rather than at the people working in them. In *Museums UK* we concluded that specifically targeted research was needed in this area, particularly as the way in which the data clustered came as a surprise to many people.

Table 29.13 Female membership of selected professional institutes and associations, 1987

	Female (%)
Institute of Chartered Accountants	8
Chartered Insurance Institute	15
Institute of Chartered Secretaries	7
Institute of Bankers	18
Royal Institution of Chartered Surveyors	4
Royal Town Planning Institute	16
Royal Institute of British Architects	5
Institution of Chemical Engineers	5
Institution of Mechanical Engineers	1
Institute of Health Service Management	27
British Medical Association	25
Royal College of Obstetricians/Gynaecologists	36
Institute of Marketing	8
British Institute of Management	3
Institute of Personnel Management	46
Law Society	15
Museums Association	49
Average of above	16.94

Percentage of women members of selected trade unions and percentage on national executive of those unions

Union	Women (%)	Women on NatExec (%)
TGWU	16	5
AEU	10	0
NALGO	52	38
NUPE	68	42
ASTMS	26	12
NUT	73	21
COHSE	80	14

Source: Various Institutions. The Equal Opportunities Commission.
See Notes 4 and 10.

This paper first appeared in Museums Journal *89(2) (1988), pp. 55–61.*

ACKNOWLEDGEMENT

Thanks are due to Bernadette Higgins-McLoughlin for the preparation of the base data for this article.

NOTES

1   Annual Report of the Registrar General for Scotland (1985).
2   Department of Employment (1986) *Employment Gazette* 7: 318.
3   Office of Population Censuses and Surveys (1986) *Monitor*, 28 October.
4   Equal Opportunities Commission (1986) *Women and Men in Britain: A Statistical Profile*, London: HMSO: 21.
5   Department of Education and Science (1985) *Statistics in Education: School Leavers CSE and GCE 1985.*
6   Courtenay, G. (1986) 'England and Wales Youth Cohort Study: preliminary results from the 1985 survey', *Social and Community Planning and Research*.
7   Office of Population Censuses and Surveys (1986) *New Earnings Survey 1970–1986*.
8   Office of Population Censuses and Surveys (1986) *Population Trend 37*, London: HMSO.
9   Prince, D. R. and Higgins-McLoughlin, B. A. (1987) *Museums UK: The Findings of the Museums Data-Base Project*, Section 2, London: The Museums Association.
10 ibid., Section 4.
11 *Museums Yearbook*, (1988), London: The Museums Association.
12 *Museums Yearbook* (1977), London: The Museums Association.

30

Common ground
Marcia Tucker

With the final paper in this section, we return to the issue of feminism, but much more than this Marcia Tucker challenges all of us to look for the things which unite us and not only to see but also to cross the lines of gender, race and class in museum work.

I am the director of a museum of contemporary art that, for the thirteen years of its existence, has had as its premise the assumption that art practice and cultural conditions – art and its political and social contexts – are inseparable, if not one and the same.

I left New York City's Whitney Museum of American Art at the end of 1976 in a storm of controversy after eight years as its curator. Now I am one of a few women directors in the museum field, but not one who has been chosen to direct. Instead, finding virtually no place for my ideas within the existing museological framework, I chose to start a museum (although I am neither the wife nor the daughter of a Rockefeller). This makes me both privileged and marginalized at the same time, because I had to create the institution in order to work in it.

At the Institute of Fine Arts of New York University, I received training in the traditional modernist art historical mode, and for many years didn't understand that there was, or could be, a connection between my feminism and the theoretical base of my own exhibition and writing projects. Like so many other women working in museums, I though that correcting inequities – the simple inclusion of women in shows, criticism, and lectures, not to mention museum work itself – was what was needed.

This represents a historical phase of feminism in which women fought within museums to have a voice at all, while struggling within the larger arts community to find communalities on the basis of which collective action could occur. This was nearly impossible for the few women curators at the time, because feminist artists and critics for the most part were not only separatists, but also reviled women who held power as belonging to the enemy.

At that time, much feminist art and art criticism seemed to veer toward an essentialist bias: women were believed to have a different experience of the world and of their bodies and therefore to make a different – better – kind of work from that of men (that is, round open forms, pastel colours, images drawn from the experience of mothering, caring, nurturing). This was my first taste of the nature/culture dichotomy, which posits an essential female nature, and which caused alarm bells to go off, at least for me, because 'nature' implies something immutable, eternal, and unchanging, while 'culture' can be (and most often is) part of the revolution.

Working in virtually all-male institutions, those of us who tried to include more women encountered profound resistance to the idea. Recently, a colleague at an African-American museum was asked why her museum didn't show the work of any white artists. She replied, 'Well, we certainly would if we could only find some who were good enough.'

For the majority of museums in the US and for those working in positions of authority within them, women and people of colour who are 'good enough' are still virtually impossible to find. Statistics are now available that demonstrate (in part) the imbalance: there are at present 33 women in the 153-member Association of Art Museum Directors, and only three who are not white.

But withdrawing the lines between men and women, positing more fluid, open-ended notions of the social construction of sex, results in losing sight of male complicity in women's oppression and of women's oppression itself. Just as worrisome, to my mind, is the idea that men appear to be so present in feminism as to co-opt it for themselves. Recently, listening to a learned scholar arrogantly discuss his 'feminist credentials' at a panel a friend asked, 'Why can't men get involved in a critique of masculinity instead of telling us how to be feminists?'

None the less, I believe that the lines are not and cannot be simply drawn between the sexes. The reason I prefer to avoid the traditional 'us versus them' dichotomy, created by positing men on one side and women on the other, is that such dichotomies themselves are part of the western, binary system of thought and language that gives form to and solidifies inequities. Dualistic concepts of men and women, black and white, majority and minority, centre and periphery, ignore the richness of human identity and perpetuate stereotypes.

None of us chose our age, race, sex, or country of origin; these are the givens, but where we position ourselves in relation to the issues relating to them is very much a matter of choice.

Emphasis on male oppression, although it certainly represents a very real factor in women's lives, also mitigates against coalitions, which I believe are the only way that social change in our time can occur; political bonds need to be formed between female and male feminists, people of colour, gay men and lesbians, those disenfranchised by virtue of their class, and everyone else who feels marginalized in our society.

One of the major contributions women can make today is to create nonhierarchic, interactive models, which would involve what Julia Kristeva, Jane Gallop, and Gayatri Spivak, among others, have called for in their analyses of power and authority. As Gallop puts it, 'One can effectively undo authority only from the position of authority, in a way that exposes the illusion of that position without renouncing it.'

So far, it's mostly women who are interested in this strategy, and in the museum field, such a concept is virtually unknown. The organization of which I am director has been evolving a management model over many years that is based on transparency, shared knowledge and decision-making, self-criticism, and collaboration. For many reasons – among them the forty-two people on staff – this process is difficult and will continue to evolve and change for as long as the museum exists. But there are precedents, such as women's self-help collectives, community action groups, alternative schools and nursery programmes, and neighbourhood building initiatives, among others.

This is a time to acknowledge and respect our differences, but also to find our communalities across the lines of sex, race, and class positions. This must occur if we believe that the primary goal as feminists is first and foremost to effect real social change in the existing political and cultural structures.

This paper first appeared in Museum News *(July/August 1990).*

Part 5
Professionalism

31

A *new professionalism*
Neil Cossons

The inculcation of professional attitudes and the development of practices are achieved through a host of mechanisms. Not least of these are the atmosphere or 'culture' of the workplace, training and the profession's codes of practice. In this article, published over ten years ago, Neil Cossons, as the President of the Museums Association, positions the museums profession in the context of the professionalization of work, which began in the nineteenth century, and asks key questions about how the profession and museums should develop. This address prefigures a decade of extraordinary change in museums.

Since we assembled together in Manchester twelve months ago (1981) we have seen a year in which the heritage in general and museums in particular have been the focal point of unprecedented attention, from government, from the media – and in particular the press – and from people at large. Proposals to restructure the Ancient Monuments and Historic Buildings Directorate of the Department of the Environment, the Rayner Scrutiny of the Departmental Museums and the debate on precisely what sort of addition is going to grace the National Gallery have all been hotly debated alike in the columns of professional journals and newspapers. It seemed to me therefore inevitable that some of these matters should at least in part form the subject of my address to you today if only because the theme of this conference is concerned with professionalism; and museum professionals – as we are increasingly tending to call ourselves these days – are I believe faced with fundamental dilemmas about the nature of that professionalism and more significantly perhaps how they relate to society as a whole.

If we are a profession, and I believe we are, then it might be worthwhile reflecting for a moment on those characteristics which originally defined a professional because I think these colour very strongly our attitudes to many of the contemporary issues facing museums. In Britain the growth of the professions during the nineteenth century was a peculiar and significant social phenomenon closely related to the evolving class structure of a country which, although passing through an Industrial Revolution, had not experienced the political revolutions of other European states. The professions emerged through the processes of gentrification of the Victorian middle classes anxious to establish a social niche for themselves. As capitalists became landed gentlemen and men of breeding and the radical idea of active capital became submerged in the conservative concept of passive property so too, throughout the century, the old professions like law and medicine, restructured themselves to emphasize expertise and in so doing achieved enhanced status. At the same time new professions proliferated. The establishment of the Royal College of Surgeons in 1800, the Law Society in 1825, and the British Medical Association in 1856 placed these traditional secular professions on a footing of secure respectability. One after another new professions, frequently modelled on the older ones, detached themselves from the world of business and industry, commerce and trade, aspiring to use their claims of expertise and integrity to rise above the rule of the market place – civil engineers in 1818, architects in 1834, pharmacists in 1841, actuaries in 1848 and so on.

Professional men as a class, and that is exactly what they were becoming, were characterized by their comparative aloofness from the struggle for income and the indicator of professional prestige was largely determined by that distance. Writing in 1885 T. H. S. Escott[1] observed that general practitioners and solicitors had a lower occupational status than barristers and clergymen partly because they had to undergo the vulgar and degrading process of taking money from their clients. In other words the scale of professional prestige was largely determined by distance from flagrant money grubbing. As the century progressed at least some of the professions gradually matured from status professionalism to occupational professionalism and it was this latter group that museum curators joined in 1889. In the previous half century or so Britain's population had increased by 60 per cent, the numbers in the professions by more than twice that, to constitute a substantial portion of the middle class, basically anti-capitalist in attitude. Professionals provided services and intangible goods of a higher social value than the material goods whose production was the concern of the non-professional middle classes and the working class. But the occupational or vocational professions had higher ideals too, more concerned with training, standards and ethics than with the restrictive practices which had prompted George Bernard Shaw's celebrated and all-embracing condemnation, '. . . all professions are conspiracies against the laity'.

Nevertheless, professionalization did not have a single universal meaning. In many cases it did carry values more attuned to the needs of a new urbanized and industrial society – openings for talent, specialization and efficiency. In the United States this was particularly the case, but in Britain the very manner in which a profession defined itself to its members set it and them apart from the rest of society. As the historian W. D. Rubinstein observed:

> The process of incorporation, acquisition of an expensive and palatial headquarters in central London, establishment of an apprenticeship system, limitations on entries, and scheduling of fees, are all manifestly designed to 'gentrify' the profession and make it acceptable to society. This aspect of professionalization is profoundly anti-capitalist, and hence at odds with much of the rest of nineteenth century British society.[2]

In at least one important respect the Museums Association contrasts sharply with that picture!

If the nineteenth century professions were anti-capitalist in origin they soon became conservative (with a small 'c') in attitude and in this respect alone there is perhaps some universality in Shaw's conspiracy theory. But in many other respects the museums profession does not fit the traditionalist model. As an occupational and highly vocational profession the members of which are predominantly employed in the public service it has seen the need to set standards in the education and training of museum staff, in the conduct of its members and the institutions in which they work, not so much as a restrictive practice – on the contrary – but as means of ensuring that the collections which are central to the very concept of a museum are cared for in a responsible manner. In promulgating this ideal the Museums Association has always found insuperable the problem identified so perceptively by James Paton when he addressed our Annual Conference at Dublin in 1894. He saw a profession '. . . divided into two great classes: the specialist who belongs to the great public and national museums and the provincial curator who has to do everything in his own much-embracing institution'. Although today the divide between the professionals is not quite as he saw it, it nevertheless remains true that the majority of curators in national museums see no need for this Association or its educational programmes. Many of them would argue that the principles of scholarship and connoisseurship are fundamental – which must be true – but that there is no body of knowledge specific to the profession of curatorship which can be defined, categorized and regulated through a professional institution – and that, I believe, is not true. (You will note that I have chosen not to mention the divide within this Association, between the professional individual member and the representatives of our member institutions, between employee and employer. I have some sympathy for the concept of a wholly professional association but from the years that I have served on your Council in one capacity or another, I am compelled to say that it has time and again been from the institutional representatives, not the professionals, that the soundest common sense and strongest support for our professional ideals has come.)

If, as I believe to be the case, the Museums Association has over the last ten years come increasingly to be a local authority club then that seriously weakens its ability to act as a professional institution and its right to speak on behalf of museums. But, more important, without a substantial leavening of the nationals and the new independents, it is in grave danger of promoting a narrow and introvert conventional wisdom which reflects only one point of view, a kind of cultural *cordon sanitaire* excluding creativity and innovation, protecting the status quo. Such a mental quarantine will I fear result in a profession that stands in the way of change at a time when increasingly there is a growing impatience on the part of the public – an impatience with museums as they see them and a real thirst for something better.

The museums profession, perhaps against its nature, must therefore act as the promoter of creative evolution in museums and spearhead the debate not only in what museums collect and present to their public but on how they are funded and managed and on who runs them. It would be tragic if the museums profession were to sink into the slough of despond which has engulfed so many professions, particularly in the public service, in recent years. Architects are perhaps at last emerging with renewed self-confidence from the abyss which they dug for themselves in the 1960s, when much of what they created became manifestly unacceptable to the public at large. Into the void we can already see other professions disappearing – planners, and perhaps teachers – submerged in a tide of political assertion and public opinion that, for the time being at least, finds irrelevant their carefully cultivated professional values, ideals and aspirations.

That as a profession we are ill-equipped to embrace radical ideas, let alone adequately to justify our present policies and practices, is well illustrated by reactions to the Rayner Scrutiny of the Science and Victoria and Albert Museums and, before it, the proposals for restructuring the Ancient Monuments and Historic Buildings Directorate of the Department of the Environment.

In both cases the government was overtly looking for a more 'commercial' solution to the protection and presentation of cultural assets and yet, curiously, no developed arguments emerged, even from Rayner, to relate this desire to a definable market. Having said this, Rayner at least posed questions of the two museums in order to find out what they did and why. If the question 'for whom' was asked there is no evidence of any reply. And it is this question of the quality of the replies that makes Rayner such an intriguing document; for if he misses the point about the role of the two museums does it mean that he was asking the wrong questions – in which case he should have been told – or was he given unsatisfactory answers to those which he did ask? If he appears to make unsupported assertions do we condemn the government for its brief, Rayner for his analysis or the museums for their inability to defend and justify their current policies and management systems?

Everybody would accept that the services provided by a museum to its public are in almost every sense intangible and qualitative, but for the purposes of sound management if for no other reason there must surely be every benefit to a museum in quantifying as far as possible the range and scale of its activities and the nature of its clientele. What are its functions and their trust costs? What are the unit costs of providing the various elements of the service? Who are the clientele? What is the cost of conservation or of answering enquiries? What is the socio-economic breakdown of users and does it match the local, regional or national population? What would be the likely effect of admission charges in relation to that clientele? Would a disadvantaged section of the existing users be excluded from the museum? Would significant additional revenue be raised? Would the reduction in numbers raise the unit cost, despite the additional admissions income, to an unacceptably high level? What level would be unacceptable? There is no evidence that more than the most generalized questions were posed on these particular issues. But, had a more penetrating market analysis been conducted, would the data have been available? Do these museums know the answers? It is inevitable that museums will, to use the jargon, always be predominantly product oriented rather than market oriented; but Marks and Spencer could not survive with such a limited knowledge of its customers. Why should museums, particularly in times of limited resources (and when haven't they been limited for museums?) be any different? Why do we shy away from anything that suggests we should justify our existence in measurable terms? Does it offend our professional sensibilities or is it just in bad taste?

The twin concepts of the free admission museum providing a service to a public have a long and honourable tradition and many museum professionals – almost certainly the majority – value these particular qualities of what they and their museums aspire to provide more than any others. These characteristics are not irrevocably linked. You can and often do have one without the other. Many of those who advocate admission fees do so not from the premise that welcome revenue will be earned but that the effect of charges on curator and customer alike will substantially increase the quality of service to the public, by heightening the commitment of one and the level of demand by the other. Certainly there is ample evidence (and the press have become increasingly aware of the shortcomings of many free admission museums) that the public is increasingly unwilling to accept the disparity of approach and appeal between the museum which goes out to attract, to please and cultivate its visitors – and to charge them for the privilege – and the venerable free admission institution which offers its wares on a take it or leave it basis.

Let me illustrate the point. A few days ago with half an hour to spare I dropped into a major and very good museum at half past five. It was due to close at six. Here was a classic type of museum visit – casual, spur-of-the-moment, a supremely enjoyable micro-experience, exactly what good museums often say they are there to provide. At twenty-one minutes to six a fire bell rang continuously for several minutes, attendants shouted 'closing time', lights started to go out, doors slammed, chains and bolts rattled. No caring museum professionals were in evidence. Why should a quiet contemplative visit to an art gallery (this one charges admission) be ruined by the crackle and inconsequential chatter of personal security radios? Why should the labels be missing or the press button models be out of order? Why should the museum be closed at exactly the times most people can visit it?

Some of you will no doubt be saying what on earth has all this got to do with professional standards; but in contemplating this concept of service to a public – and the question of admission charges is of course largely irrelevant – we have come round to the true purpose of museum professionalism. When we discuss our affairs together each year, service to the public and the quality of that service rarely features to any extent in our deliberations. Despite our professed high ideals the well-being of the museum user is not often mentioned by museum curators. Professional standards will inevitably, in the minds of many, be interpreted in terms of doing the right thing to the collections, writing up the report on the summer's excavations, verifying the catalogue entries, or maintaining contact with like-minded professional colleagues. Guidelines on professional conduct are set out with succinct and admirable clarity in the *Draft Code* to be debated by this Annual Conference. But the quality of service to a public cannot be so easily defined. It depends on creativity and imagination, on sound management and the careful husbandry of resources – in short on true professionalism. It bears less relationship to availability of resources than to curatorial attitude but, I suggest, our continued failure to recognize our attitudinal shortcomings is the greatest threat to the standards of curatorial care we so firmly cherish. Without a strong and articulate body of public support there will be no profession to set standards.

I believe that Rayner, despite its shortcomings, has fulfilled a major service to museums in Britain. What we need is more not fewer scrutinies asking more penetrating questions and forcing museums out into the open, to examine their objectives, their priorities and the deployment of their resources. Equally I am compelled to the view that the best protection which we as a profession can mount for the cherished ideals of service to the public and indeed free admission will be based on a wholeheartedly commercial approach, on quantifiable data demonstrating the nature and levels of usage of our museums and their contents. Pursuing this apparent paradox further I suggest that scholarship and connoisseurship will thrive on the back of an increased popular demand from a more discriminating public, sensitive to its rights and demanding quality. The requirements of society from now until the end of the century will I believe provide remarkable opportunities for museums and the people who work in them. But the museums profession must not stand in the way of change. The collective paranoia which lies just below the surface of so many of the so-called public service professions must not act as a mechanism against radical evolution nor, worse still, as a restriction on open debate.

The already identifiable characteristics of future popular demand for museums include a strong move towards a more market oriented approach (with consequent improvements in visitor management); individualistic and participative rather than organized or passive mass spectator experiences; genuine value for money (for provider and consumer) and a real service for the social problem of leisure; family oriented facilities with things for all the family to do (including the single parent family); the encouragement of self-improvement, self-respect, self-actualization and status; membership; special programmes for old people.[3] As now, the major part of the funding will be from the various pockets of the public purse but I do not believe that – except in the case of well-established and generally large museum services – this future provision can or indeed should be provided by local authorities. The implications for the museums profession will be enormous. Education of the young curator will become increasingly important; but of even greater significance will be the demand for high-grade management skills throughout the profession. The distinction between curator, administrator and manager will become increasingly blurred as professional staff take on a higher commitment to providing a service direct to the public. The uniformed attendant will all but disappear, to be replaced by the aspiring young professional serving his (or her) time with the public in the gallery. The number of active 'professionals' should increase although the number of museums may actually fall.

There will be volunteer members of the Museums Association, some holding its Diploma, and, perhaps most important of all, a new quality of creative professionalism. The new professionalism will be more attuned to the needs of the public than to regulating the activities of its membership; but it will be based nevertheless on a firm core of scholarship and sound management training.

This paper first appeared in Museums Association Conference Papers 1982, *London: Museums Association.*

NOTES

1 T. H. S. Escott (1885) *England: Her People, Polity and Pursuits*, 355–6.
2 W. D. Rubinstein (1977) 'Wealth, elites and class structure in Britain', *Past and Present* 76 (August): 122.
3 Based in part on F. Kinsman (1979) *UK Leisure Markets: Survey and Forecasts to 1985*, Staniland Hall Associates Ltd.

32

Scholarship or self-indulgence?

Neil Cossons

In a more recent article Neil Cossons, as Director of the Science Museum, questioned some of the value systems of curatorial practice. The paper was given as part of a seminar on scholarship in museums which sought to explore whether the higher public profile of museums and greater commitment to visitors, especially within national museums, were prejudicing accepted standards of research and scholarship.

This conference has been promoted on the hypothesis that scholarship in museums is under threat. Before discussing briefly the issues peculiar to the Science Museum I want to raise a number of points of a more general nature which address the myth and the reality of that threat, for there is, I believe, a notable lack of clarity on the part of outside observers and curators themselves on what are the causes and possibly the consequences of a reduction in the scholarly role of museums.

The Museums and Galleries Commission 1988 Report *The National Museums* finds that 'in every national museum, in every field, scholarship and the associated excellence of curatorial standards are perceived as being increasingly under threat'.[1] This is because 'shortage of money, the downward pressure on staff numbers, the extra time curators need to spend on managerial tasks, and their move to service functions, are seen as combining to erode the time they have for scholarly activities'.

The RSA's press release for this conference had a more rhetorical style. Is scholarship in danger of being sacrificed to the demands of 'storage . . . conservation . . . and of popularization . . .?' Is the 'controversy . . .' 'a necessary consequence of government under-funding or the result of a quite separate thrust towards treating the command structure of a museum as though it were identical to that of a business? Should the scholar–curator still play the central role in a museum or should he be no more important than the full-time manager, the conservationist, the accounts and the marketing man?'

Debates on museums are often problematical. They can generate more heat than light. They are usually conducted – as is the case today – by the people who work in them; the museum fraternity in communion with itself – yet again. When I was invited to speak and was sent a draft programme I expressed my dismay at the super-abundance of art historians – art history is not synonymous with scholarship in museums, although some of the former is associated with some of the latter.

Nor is the scholarship carried out *by* museums their only scholarship. An important part of our job is to make our collections available to be interrogated and interpreted by the scholarly community at large. That means sound collections management systems, first-class documentation, accessible stores, many of the things we have not been too good at in the past. It also means a friendly open-door policy on the part of curators. What would be the contribution to the accumulated corpus of museum scholarship if we were to place a higher priority on promoting a more widespread use of our collections? This would certainly consume more curatorial time, but would we be using our collections to better purpose? Perhaps the next RSA conference on scholarship in museums should be exclusively for the people we seek to serve – those who use and visit our collections. It is at our peril that we ignore our critics, worse still our customers.

That we have an increasing number of critics and customers is good. Museums have been outstandingly successful in the last twenty years. They have also undergone fundamental change. Some of those who argue that scholarship in museums is under threat put the blame on precisely that fundamental change. My argument is the exact opposite. I believe that it is only by managing change and using it creatively that we will protect scholarship – and not simply protect it but allow it to regenerate.

To make the point clear let us look at the nature of the changes that have taken place in recent years. The most self-evident is that museums are bigger and better and that there are more of them. There are substantially more people employed in museums now than there were twenty-five or thirty years ago. That huge growth, most of which took place during the 1970s, was as dramatic in the long-established, and in particular the larger museums, as it was in the new ones.

There were a number of characteristics in common. First, although there was a modest increase in the number of curators, the rest multiplied at a much greater rate. Conservators, designers, educational and interpretive staff, administrators and managers have radically altered the population pattern. No longer do curators hold a majority of the 'sweat equity' in our great museums. There has been a significant demographic shift in the internal balance of power. (In galleries the position may be somewhat different.)

Second, that growth was unplanned, unmanaged and largely opportunistic, especially in national museums where management skills were rare and undervalued. By the mid-1970s many large museums were grossly overstaffed in the technical sense that salaries and wages were consuming an inordinate proportion of the museum's resources. And, as we all know, what a museum provides is governed primarily by its available resources not by the scale of the demand for its services. They are resource limited not demand led. As I have said elsewhere, too many people on the payroll produce paralysis.[2] More than a decade earlier, in 1964, I think, I remember Alan Warhurst, then Director of Bristol City Museum, in a Museums Association Diploma Course, stating that staff costs should on no account exceed 65–70 per cent of the museum's budget, otherwise morale would drop and there would be insufficient liquidity in the museum to allow the people you were paying to do the job you were paying them for.

Most of the national museums – there were notable exceptions – chose not to heed that lesson, even if they heard it; the inevitability of the outcome was self-evident long before cash-limited grant-in-aid funding made the situation critical. In short, museums had too many people in ill-defined roles and unmanaged situations, competing for insufficient resources and under pressure from an increasingly demanding and discriminating public to do more and better. Some of the jobs curators had done were now being carried out by others. A classic process of the specialization and division of labour was taking place. Many of the new staff, conservators in particular, came with new skills and a new professionalism into situations of catastrophic backlog. They were instantly indispensable.

Throughout this period scholar–curators repeatedly emphasized that they were the people who knew about and had responsibility for collections. But with increased visibility and accountability inadequacies in the quality of physical management of collections became apparent. The competence of curators was brought into question and this has undoubtedly, and perhaps unjustifiably, affected their credibility as scholars. In 1983 one national museum director, Dr Basil Greenhill of the National Maritime Museum,[3] went so far as to forecast the extinction of curators and their replacement by conservators. Failure to put in place proper documentation procedures, poor quality handling of loans, inadequate provision and management of stores and a general lack of competence in an area where professional standards are well known and clearly defined, all led to a questioning of the curator's role. There is no magic about the physical care of museum collections. We all know what has to be done.

Museums had become larger, increasingly complex and, I suggest, they had outgrown their management systems, such as they were. They were also beginning to suffer the effects of their own success. With the growth in the scale and number of museums, superb new galleries and exhibitions and the huge increase in the size of their audience came a higher public and political profile. New museums captured and captivated a new public: one thinks for example of the National Museum of Photography, Film and Television in Bradford. The word 'museum' was reinterpreted in the minds of many people.

Museums in the last quarter century have moved from twilight to spotlight. They have political as well as cultural significance. They are perceived to have values more far-reaching and perhaps less altruistic than they once did. They provide economic benefits; their presence impacts upon leisure and tourism as well as education and enlightenment.

The question of who should run these museums and how has moved from the professional domain to the public stage. For the first time museums are having to be accountable for their actions. A *laissez-faire*, administrative style of management has, inevitably, had to give way to something that offered a higher degree of certainty, in which value for money and performance, both for the institutions themselves and their staff, began to feature. Public exposure has revealed the inadequacies which have existed in these museums for many years. The role of the curator has come increasingly into question, among curators themselves, and among the increasing numbers of professional staff with other skills with whom they now have to share their work.

So, this is the context of change within which museum scholarship takes place. Where is the threat? It is not in the change but in the failure to manage that change. And that's what I mean by self-indulgence. Scholars and scholarship have to be, and have to want to be, part of the process of running the whole institution; they cannot stand aside from it. They delude themselves if they believe the museum will look after them if they do not put some effort into the overall well-being of the museum. The question of management by whom and of whom is crucial. Many scholars believe their voices are not heard, others regard management as a pollution of the purity of scholarship. As a result both feel miserable. How can the contribution *they* make be properly assimilated into the dynamic of the whole institution?

I believe that good scholarship is the energy source of the museum. But scholarship and the museum cannot survive or fulfil their real potential without sound corporate management. One of the problems has been that to have reached the position of keeper of a curatorial department in one of our great museums was to be singularly unqualified to run the institution. To be expert in content was one thing, to manage the process was another. This does not mean that all scholars have to be managers but they do have to be managed.

One of the current myths is that museums have been taken over by a new breed of non-museums managers. At first sight this might appear to be true. Of the thirteen appointments of new directors of British national museums and galleries in the last decade only one has been by internal promotion of a keeper of a curatorial department. One other has seen a curatorial head appointed to the directorship of another museum.

But let us look at that evidence a little more closely. Of the remaining eleven, seven were already directors of other museums (and all had significant and substantial museum experience), two were scholars from outside the museum world, one was a librarian promoted internally, and only one was a museum administrator, again promoted internally. Despite the perceived threat of a 'managerial' takeover of Britain's major museums, when compared with the previous generation of directors, there has been a significant increase in the amount of pre-existing museum experience that these new people have brought with them. And, although I acknowledge that it is difficult to measure, I would suggest that overall they are no less scholars. Most have a record of scholarly achievement although the opportunity to keep it alive as director of a large modern museum is perhaps more limited than once it would have been.

Only in the field of small to medium-sized local authority museums, and to some extent in independent museums, has there been any significant transfer of power and responsibility to managers with no museum background. Nowhere can I find evidence to support the statement in the RSA's press release that there is a 'thrust towards treating the command structure of a museum as though it were *identical to that of a business*' (my italics). There is undoubtedly however a strong move towards *dirigiste* management which, I suspect, is here to stay.

Let me turn now to the impact of underfunding. Is this the threat to scholarship? The editorial in this September's *Apollo*[4] implores the Prime Minister to 'reconsider how those much-vaunted "Victorian values" to which she has alluded can now be applied, in emulation of the past, to our national museums and galleries. A start could be made with a *return to adequate central funding*' (my italics). When was this? Have we already created a mythology of a golden age when museums had sufficient public funds to carry out their tasks? In the twenty-nine years that I have worked in museums I can remember no such period. Museums have always been short of money and the problems of decay and deterioration have been with us for years. The roof of the V & A may or may not be a victim of Thatcherism but is a monument to half a century or more of public neglect. Scholarship and shortage of money seem to have lived quite happily together for years.

In searching for other threats to scholarship popularization is also being put in the dock. Like good taste it is difficult to define but most people know it when they see it. You either like it or you don't. But there is nothing, I believe, inherently threatening to the scholarly standards of the museum if it chooses to present its collections in a popular manner, in a way which its public understands, finds relevant to its own experience, appealing and stimulating to the imagination. Rather the reverse. Good popularization needs high-grade scholarship, from people who not only know their collections but can interpret them to the public. But scholars do sometimes need expert help in the process of interpretation and they should not be ashamed of that. Not all scholar–curators are luminaries whose command of the vivid metaphor, whose ability to place themselves in the minds of their visitors, is as developed as their knowledge of the collections they have in their care.

In some areas, most notably in the natural sciences, such is the nature and complexity of the interpretive process that specialists have been employed to do it. Here is yet another of the curator's traditional roles being nibbled away as the result of increased specialization. Interpretation also implies some knowledge and understanding of the audience to whom we are speaking. This too is perceived by those of a more fundamentalist turn of mind to pose a threat. But the concepts of Freeman Tilden[5] and others applied in, for example, United States National Parks and protected natural habitats and archaeological sites throughout the world, have had a profound effect upon the way the public views its surroundings and its past. It is inevitable that these trends should invade museums.

Many of the newer museums have embraced modern interpretive techniques with enthusiasm and in doing so attracted a new public to our doors. The ignorant sometimes use the term 'Disneyfication' to describe this process. They could do well to look more closely. If one lays aside the product, the process is extraordinarily interesting. Indeed, as Benjamin Woolley has suggested,[6] not without a little irony, the way Disney World is run is perhaps as close as we will get to the real ideals of Rousseau and Marx. No one is in authority but there is no anarchy. Management can even poke fun at itself and still survive.

But there are also deeper cultural divides in which public assumptions and attitudes are overwhelmingly important in determining what we do and how we do it. Janet Daley summed it up in *The Independent*:[7]

> the director of the Victoria and Albert Museum . . . argued forcibly for a more accessible image for her museum. The 'ace caff with quite a nice museum attached' advertising campaign and her exhibitions for non-specialists had brought a deluge of criticism. Shrieks of 'crass' and 'downmarket' reverberated around South Kensington. Walking past the Science Museum the other day, I noticed its latest advertising poster, which shows a lavatory cistern tank with an old-fashioned pull chain. The text above the picture reads: 'In 1939 Ladislao Biro designed the ballpoint pen. In 1908 William Hoover put his name to the vacuum cleaner, and in 1900 . . .' And there emblazoned on the red cistern are the words: 'Crapper's Valveless Waste Preventer'. Can one envisage the Tate advertising its Constables with the slogan: 'If you thought hay was just for rolling in . . .'? Why should the V & A invoke such flak when it strains the bounds of solemnity and purism, while its neighbours . . . can be facetious, even prurient and – most significantly – openly democratic? The reasons seem to me to go to the heart of British attitudes towards science and the arts. When Mrs Esteve-Coll proposes contextual settings for objects and perhaps even an active element in exhibitions, she is berated for turning the museum into a historical theme park. But walking into the newly redesigned Science Museum, I was engulfed in a sea of hands-on exhibits bleeping and blooping at me like so many Space Invader machines. No one apparently is offended at the idea that a science museum should be didactic because, I would suggest, there is no shame attached in British society to knowing nothing about science. . . . Science . . . is for schoolchildren, something one grows out of with maturity and the coming of civilised tastes. C. P. Snow had it wrong. It is not so much that the arts and the sciences are two cultures as that science is not part of culture at all and so this country remains chronically at odds with the twentieth century.

And that brings me to scholarship in the Science Museum. But first let me sum up the arguments so far. Essentially what I am saying is that it is not change in itself that is threatening scholarship. The threat, I suggest, has come progressively and over a number of years from *laissez-faire* management and an unwillingness on the part of scholar–curators to participate positively and constructively in shaping change. Society has thrust many of these changes upon museums; specialization and professionalization of staff functions have been inevitable consequences. Curators are having to learn to share with people who have other essential skills to offer the museum. Add the demand for accountability and the anxieties and sensitivities of scholars start to become understandable. How museums handle the future of scholarship must be a central part of their strategy. This is what we are doing about it.

The National Museum of Science and Industry, of which the Science Museum in London, the National Railway Museum in York, and the National Museum of Photography, Film and Television in Bradford form major parts, holds the most comprehensive collections on science, technology and medicine anywhere in the world. These reflect the history of the first industrial nation, the material evidence of the emergence of modern scientific and industrial man. The Science Museum may not be the British Museum but perhaps, more than any other, it is the museum of the British. Its collections come down to today. An increasing proportion are post-1960 in date, some are acquired new, straight from the manufacturer.

But its origins, unlike that of most museums, do not lie in collections, but in the aim to 'increase the means of industrial education and to extend the influence of science and art on productive industry'. Today we carry forward the twin goals of promoting the public understanding of science and technology – a contemporary interpretation of Prince Albert's vision – and revealing the truths of our great collections. In many cases of course the two are synonymous.

Scholarship in the National Museum of Science and Industry has some similarities with what goes on in other institutions but, I suspect, the differences are both more numerous and more profound. Connoisseurship[8] – the process of aesthetic discrimination – has a limited but perhaps underestimated value to us; as a structure for acquisition, hardly at all, but here and there as a path towards attribution and authentication it has its place. Our curators, like any others, must have a visceral belief in and understanding of the object.

The sort of anxiety, however, voiced recently by Jeffrey Spier[9] about the objectivity of scientific analysis is largely irrelevant to us. His belief that 'scientific studies . . . often appear to be invoked by archaeologists as a desperate appeal to the unattainable, "objective" result', itself has a certain Luddite charm. Nor are we notably afflicted by the dead hand of high cash values. Connoisseurship, attribution and the high cost of art must bring into question the independence of some types of museum scholarship. Freedom of thought is still open to curators in the Science Museum. Again, nor does Nicholas Serota's assertion that 'Acquisitions are the lifeblood of any museum'[10] ring true in our context. Acquisitions are the lifeblood of some curators, yes. But they are also the largely unquestioned legacy of the profession. For the majority of museums, the Science Museum included, acquisition is not the engine of their scholarship. It is relevant but not necessarily central to the work they do.

But acquisition is something to which we are giving increasing attention in order to develop policies that are attainable, relevant, and will leave our successors with some form of valid record. We collect against the moving target of rapid scientific and technological change. So the curators of what we already have may well not be the experts in what we want.

If we take computing as a simple example, the term 'antiquity' relates to a period in the 1940s and early attempts to use thermionic valves to perform mathematical calculations. And yet early computers are now rare, and some are unique. As Doron Swade, the Curator of Computing at the Science Museum, has pointed out,[11] 'the first days of widespread computing are still within living memory'; 'several generations of technology have been compressed into the span of a single professional lifetime'. There is a resistance, too, to believing that computers have a history. We suffer from the problems of 'recency', a language in which 'cutting-edge', 'leading-edge' and 'new technology' feature frequently in descriptions of contemporary events. Swade suggests that there may therefore be 'an unconscious reluctance to acknowledge that computing has a past. Doing so would surrender to our forebears some of our achievement and diminish our claim to the pioneering heroism endorsed by the prevailing cultural climate.'[12]

The ambiguities of the past pale into insignificance when we are confronted by collecting from the present. And the present poses real issues for the scholar–curator. The Science Museum may be the National Museum of How Things Work which, in a simpler and perhaps more unquestioning age let it reveal the truths of ingenious mechanical devices. But today we collect contraceptive pills, we have the first genetically engineered mice in our collections, we have galleries on nuclear power and exhibitions on the irradiation of food. Our policies are to press forward more actively into the field of contemporary science and technology. It is a frighteningly open-ended proposition; it will put new demands on the Museum as an institution of scholarship.

In setting the scene for a renewal of our investment in scholarship the Museum has undergone a major structural reformation in the last four years. Five Divisions, drawn up largely on functional lines, cover Collections Management, Research and Information, Public Services, Marketing, and Resource Management. Each is headed by an Assistant Director, of equal status and authority. The Heads of the York and Bradford museums have similar standing and these seven form the Museum's management team. The operational structure of the National Railway Museum and the National Museum of Photography, Film and Television reflect in miniature the South Kensington format. The equal status of these Assistant Directors is, I believe, an essential requirement for determining balanced policies and for operational harmony.

The collections are held in the Collections Management Division which is broken down into three subject-based groups – science, technology and life sciences – occupied by specialist curators. In addition there is a Projects Group, responsible for all project management and operation within the Division and elsewhere in the Museum, and a Services Group responsible for documentation, storage and conservation. A central plank of this reorganization has been to release the subject group curators from non-collection-based activities and to allow them time and facilities for research. The group heads are Curators A, their specialist curators C and D, and junior curatorial together with secretarial support staff have been provided for them.

At this point it is worth mentioning that there are peculiar problems of developing a cadre of scholarly curatorial staff. The research work of the Museum's curators is largely concerned with the history of science, technology and medicine, including contemporary history. There are no first degrees in these subjects and postgraduate opportunities are limited or nonexistent. This is no Courtauld or Institute of Archaeology. Further, most graduates with science, engineering or medical qualifications do not have their sights set on a career in museums and are not trained as historians. Equally, most historians and archaeologists have little background in the history of science. Recruitment of curators has therefore been something of a haphazard business, some joining in mid-career from industry, very few from academic backgrounds, the rest coming in as new graduates or postgraduates and working their way in a rather unstructured manner up the system.

We believe, therefore, that we have to grow our own. We have to find and attract high-grade graduates and provide them with a good quality training scheme. This will last two years and provide a thorough background in the work of the Museum in all its aspects, allowing progressively a higher degree of specialization. Those with interests in collections will have the opportunity to specialize in curatorial work, others may progress towards other Divisions. The first six graduates were recruited two weeks ago. Training of all staff will occupy about 5 per cent of their time.

Current curatorial research includes, for example, work on the history of British rocketry, the development of the electrical industry from the consumer end between the 1880s and the 1920s, the history of biotechnology, the interrelated technological and commercial history of laser barcode checkouts, the development of high performance piston aero engines, the construction of Charles Babbage's second difference engine – to coincide with the bicentenary of his birth in 1991 – and the development of the science of ship hull design. Catalogues on the Wellcome radiology collection, the George III collection of scientific instruments and the plastics collection and microscopes are in hand and we are looking at issues affecting value, authenticity and originality as they relate to early motor vehicles and the problems associated with operating them.

The second major strand of our research activity is new. It has its roots in the anxiety expressed increasingly in recent years about the relationship between science, technology and society.[13] This concern about the public understanding of science found its first significant expression in a Royal Society Working Party Report[14] which catalysed several new initiatives, including a research programme funded by the Economic and Social Research Council and a range of practical activities under the auspices of the Committee on the Public Understanding of Science (COPUS) of which the Science Museum is a member.

Why should we care about public understanding of science? Durant and Thomas[15] have identified a range of different arguments that have been formulated in response to this question. There are three key ones. They range from the cultural (science is the outstanding feature of modern western civilization; it is the thing our culture does best) to the practical (science makes our culture work and is itself overwhelmingly affected, for good and ill, by cultural attitudes towards it) and the political (to make effective and responsible decisions in a democracy in which science and technology play such a central role demands an adequate level of public understanding).

This question of the public's perception and understanding of science and technology goes back to the origins of the Science Museum in the aftermath of the Great Exhibition. Current concerns provide compelling reasons why we should readdress this issue. They have led us to launch our new public understanding of science initiative. It is being carried out jointly with our neighbours, Imperial College of Science, Technology and Medicine, and it has a number of key objectives: first, to advance our understanding of public perceptions of science; second, to improve our knowledge of the effectiveness of formal and informal education, the mass media and science museums and science centres in enhancing the public understanding of science; and third, to apply the fruits of research in both of these areas to the vital task of raising public awareness and appreciation of the pivotal part played by science in the modern world.

In 1988 the Museum appointed Dr John Durant as Head of Research and Information Services, a post held jointly with Imperial College where he is the first Professor in the Public Understanding of Science and Technology. More recently, the Museum has created the first in what is envisaged to become a series of post-doctoral Research Fellowships in Public Understanding of Science; and the College (with the help of the

Leverhulme Trust) has established a University Lectureship in Science Communication. Our plans are now well advanced for a new, one-year Master of Science course in the College which will serve both to further our scholarly work in this area and to train the science communicators (including, of course, Science Museum staff) of the future.

The strategic management of research in the National Museum of Science and Industry is conducted through the Research Committee which includes senior staff of the Museum and five outsiders, academics in the field and a science journalist. This establishes the broad parameters within which we see our scholarly activities taking place. Over time it will take an increasingly pro-active role defining key areas in which we will wish to concentrate our efforts. We are keen to sharpen the peer group view of our work and generate a real and creative tension between those working on collections (the content of the Museum) and those who concentrate upon how we use them (the process).

To conclude: in setting out to have a policy for scholarship we have had to define clearly our goals as an institution, to recognize that in our case content and process are not always the same thing. We have collections, the cultural value of which is determined by how much we know about them. We wish to grow our collections and that is only possible if we have scholar–curators who, increasingly, will need to be conversant with contemporary trends in science, technology and medicine. We have a mission to interpret – not always through our collections – and to do that we need to know much more about our audience and the broader culture within which science is viewed in British society. We believe we have a role, in conjunction with Imperial College, to work with others in changing those attitudes. Much of this we will have to generate for ourselves. We think we may even have to develop a new discipline – the history of modern technology – and encourage its growth as an academic study, and here our links with the scientific, industrial and academic community at large will be essential.

We recognize too that the work of a modern museum demands specialization in most of its fields of activity, so we are setting out to manage ourselves accordingly. We need good people and we have set about the task of growing the next generation of them. We also need to give the good people we already have the framework and opportunity to do good work. The new management structure is designed to do just that. We are making a positive forward-looking investment in high grade scholarship in order to ensure that the foundations of tomorrow's National Museum of Science and Industry are firmly laid now.

This paper first appeared in the RSA Journal *139(5415) (February 1991), pp. 184–90.*

NOTES

1 Museums and Galleries Commission (1988) *The National Museums and Galleries of the United Kingdom*, London: HMSO: 6.
2 See Neil Cossons (ed.) (1985) *The Management of Change in Museums*, London: National Maritime Museum, the proceedings of a seminar of the same title (22 November 1984), in which people from the museum community and from outside examined the issue of change in museums.
3 Basil Greenhill (1983) Address to the International Council of Museums Conference, London.
4 Editorial (1990) *Apollo* CXXXII (343) (September): 20.
5 Freeman Tilden (1957) *Interpreting Our Heritage: Principles and Practices for Visitor Services in Parks, Museums, and Historical Places*, Chapel Hill: University of North Carolina Press.
6 Benjamin Woolley, 'Of mice and men', *Listener* 124 (3182): 20.
7 Janet Daley (1989) 'The Mr Crapper approach to art', *The Independent* 25 October.
8 Charles Saumarez Smith (1989) 'The connoisseur: a short history of an idea', paper delivered at the Victoria & Albert Museum, 23 November.
9 Jeffrey Spier (1990) 'Blinded with science: the abuse of science in the detection of fake antiquities', *Burlington Magazine* CXXXII (1050) (September): 623–31.

10 Nicholas Serota (1990) Address to the Annual General Meeting of the National Art-Collections Fund, Royal Institution, 6 June.
11 Doron Swade (1990) 'Computers and antiquity', *Interdisciplinary Science Review* 15(3): 203–6.
12 ibid.: 206.
13 The Royal Society (1985) *The Public Understanding of Science*, London.
14 John Durant (1990) 'Copernicus and Conan Doyle: or, why should we care about the public understanding of science?', *Science and Public Affairs* 5(1): 7–22.
15 G. P. Thomas and J. R. Durant (1987) 'Why should we promote the public understanding of science', *Scientific Literary Papers*: 1–4.

33

Scholarship and the public

Neil MacGregor

At the same conference at which Neil Cossons gave the previous paper, Neil MacGregor, Director of the National Gallery, London, questioned the importance of scholarship in relation to the service offered to the public. MacGregor repudiates the polarity of view about sholarship in museums and looks at its positive contribution to the work and ambitions of the National Gallery.

I should like to begin rather indecorously by disagreeing with one of the last questioners. You, Madam, said you were a customer of the national museums. I want to disagree very much; you are not a customer, you are an owner. I think it is essential to put the whole of this discussion into the context of what *we* are doing with *your* museums. I want to come back to that later on, but perhaps I may be excused for challenging you right away.

As Director of the National Gallery I must say that I feel at a certain disadvantage hearing my colleagues both at home and abroad talk with such lucidity about the aims of their institutions. When Wolf-Dieter Dube talks about the edict of William I of Prussia that established the rights and the duties of those who would carry out scholarly work, when Michel Laclotte talks about the series of *lois cadres* which lay down the basis on which French museums operate, I think wistfully of the rather confused Treasury Minutes of 1824, clearly an accident forced on a no less confused government because the Austrians had unexpectedly repaid part of their war debt, through which the British government bought the Angerstein Collection under the mistaken belief that they were setting up a new department of the British Museum. It was nearly a decade before that confusion was resolved, and it is really only accident that we are not all run by David Wilson!

But the accident, as happens not infrequently in England, produced something rather special. David Wilson, in his admirable book, *British Museum, Purpose and Politics*, says, in a striking phrase, that the British Museum is a 'back-street museum'. I do not think he means that in a Soho sense, but he does mean that it is not on a great public thoroughfare. And by contrast – and this time very consciously and very deliberately – the National Gallery was set up in the busiest, most polluted area of London. It was set up on the recommendation of Peel that it should be in the very gangway of London, right in the middle, so that as many people as possible should be able to get to it, so that the public should be able to enjoy *their* pictures. The question of public accessibility has been central to the existence of the National Gallery from the moment it was rather inadvertently created.

It has been observed – I think with reference to the Arian Heresy – that all great controversies depend on both sides sharing one false premise. And in the case of today's controversy – the controversy alluded to by Neil Cossons, that there is a choice that museums have to make between scholarship and popularity – I think this is entirely true, because I feel that polarity is nonexistent.

The Trustees of the National Gallery addressed this problem in this year's *Annual Report*, published four months ago. Talking of the exhibition of Italian fourteenth-century painting, they wrote:

> The Exhibition demonstrated incontrovertibly that scholarship and public access are not, as has sometimes been asserted, alternatives between which museums and galleries must choose. Rather it is scholarship which adds a new dimension to accessibility. In consequence, we believe it is essential that scholarship remain a major priority if we are to serve the ever larger public we expect in the next few years.

And as a result of that they approved the appointment of several new curators.

I think it is worth dwelling for a moment on that – that scholarship is a way of making our collection accessible – and I am conscious that our collection is, of course, different from many of the other collections that are being discussed. We are a small collection of paintings and I would not want for a moment to undervalue the aesthetic response and the aesthetic enjoyment which many of the public – most of the public, I hope – get from those pictures. But it raises a wider question than that, because the access that we want to offer is a full one, a rich one, and I think that is a difficult matter.

I want to begin by suggesting that it is very important that we should not underestimate our public. The great success of the Open University since the 1960s has demonstrated the very widespread thirst among the general public for serious information and serious scholarship. The most recent development that I know of in this field, the pioneering Ford Project, which Ford of Great Britain have set up for their employees' development scheme, providing free education during worktime, has produced a startling take-up for the strictly and severely academic subjects. I think we can then assume that we do have a public which wants to be seriously addressed and – we should not be ashamed to say it – a public which needs to be seriously addressed if a public collection is to be properly explored.

The great enterprise of exploring the past through the physical remnants of the past is one that few of us would embark on single-handed. We have tried, especially this year in the National Gallery, to take a very particular approach to presenting scholarship to our public as a way of allowing the public to discover and to possess their collection. We have organized three separate exhibitions. The first was the Trecento Exhibition, *Art in the Making*, which was a physical examination of panel painting in fourteenth-century Italy. I think it is fair to say that it was a work of pioneering scholarship. The catalogue was a highly scientific publication and, in many areas, it broke new ground. It was among the most successful exhibitions that the Gallery has ever put on. Over 160,000 people came to look at pictures which, I think we would all agree, are among the most difficult in the National Gallery collection. They are pictures which, because of the subject-matter, because of the style, are extremely inaccessible. And yet a certain kind of scientific approach clearly allowed a great deal of interest, a great deal of enjoyment. In that area I think one can say that scholarship helped the public reach part of the collection that other approaches did not. And I can say with confidence, because we have been monitoring it, that since that exhibition the public time spent in the Early Italian rooms has remained materially higher.

The second exhibition of the year was, in a different way, about museum-based scholarship. It was an attribution exercise on the two versions of the Caspar David Friedrich landscape, of which we bought the one we believed to be the original. The aim was, again quite simply, to present to the public all the information available to the curator–scholar before having to make a decision – the drawings that are relevant, comparative paintings – and to leave the public themselves to come to the conclusion, to make the decisions themselves.

The third exhibition was a smaller exhibition of two paintings by Goya which we brought from the Prado, the intention being to put them beside the Velázquez *Rokeby Venus*, demonstrating in physical terms the thesis put forward in an article in the *Burlington Magazine* which proved that they had for a time hung together and that Goya's paintings were, in a direct sense, a response to Velázquez.

All three exhibitions were great popular successes. All three exhibitions, I think, demonstrate a particular phenomenon. We hear a great deal at the moment of the trickle-down effect of wealth, but I think we can say with confidence that the trickle-down effect of scholarship is very, very fast and very, very effective. All these exhibitions could happily have appeared in the *Burlington Magazine*, and all of them contrived to bring in a new public and to bring them back.

I should like to stress that the scholarship for these exhibitions was not conceived as scholarship for an exhibition. It was scholarship related intrinsically to the purpose of the National Gallery, and which was then presented to the public. It is important to stress that, because I think I would disagree with Wolf-Dieter Dube that 'research is the museum'. Our research has to be accountable to the public, and I think it is part of a greater purpose. Our purpose in our scholarship must be better to conserve the collections and, above all, better to allow the public to enjoy and to understand. I think the notion of curatorial scholarly accountability in museums is a very important one. We have tried regularly at the Gallery to have curators lecture to the public, explaining why they hang in a particular way; explaining how else the picture could be hung; explaining to the public what it is that they have been working at.

But if museums are not *for* scholarship – and I do not think they are – then what are they for? In this country they were set up very consciously on the model of private collections or cabinets, places of study. Gentleman scholars did of course emerge, but gentleman owners had their private collections of antiquities, of paintings, of natural history, in order themselves to form their own judgement, to refine their own taste and to understand better their place in the whole scheme of things, both natural and man-made – and that was the eighteenth-century ideal of private collections, based on the belief that possession of the past enables you to take possession of the future.

I believe our job in the National Gallery – and the function of scholarship in the National Gallery – is to enable the public to move around the past with confidence. They need the confidence that there are fixed points, individual objects which have been identified, dated, established; and various routes around those fixed points which they can follow and from which, if they like, pursue others. The process is, in a general sense, one of education, but I think in a sense it is not one of learning. If I could parody a famous Enlightenment *mot*, the great Goethe comment that in reading Winckelmann we do not learn anything, we become something, I think that the point for the public of museums is not that the public should learn something but that they should become something. What should they become? Heirs to the past, heirs to the collections which they own, deciding for themselves what they are going to do with it, what it means for them now and what it may mean for them in the future.

Most, I think, will want to use the collections personally, in locating themselves in the natural world, in examining their own or others' behaviour, in pondering the fate of individuals in society. These people need to be able to find the fixed points and the routes that the scholars have provided. But ultimately the exploration, the taking possession, has to be a personal one. There can be no doubt that we have to move on our own through the collections. We have ultimately to make our own decisions. I think that the role, then, of the scholars or the curators is not to put themselves between the public and the objects, not in any very elaborate sense to explain the objects, but to exhort the visitor to a direct experience, to an unmediated vision.

We hope, when the Sainsbury Wing opens, that we will offer to the public for the first time ever a possibility to explore the entire collection through interactive video. A great deal of scholarly input has already taken place. The entire collection has been put onto an image-retrieval system. Various kinds of information, various kinds of approach, will be available for the individual to choose from. But it will – and I think it is right that it will – be hard work, and this is where I would most disagree with what Neil was saying earlier. Neil Cossons suggested that the threat to scholarship, if there is one – and I do firmly believe there is one – comes not from change imposed by the government but from the reluctance of curators to take part constructively in that change. I believe that the threat to scholarship comes from an assumption that the enterprise of exploring the past is, or can be, an easy one. It is related, I think, to the much-aired notion of short attention span, of a society which, in the memorable title of a recent book, is amusing itself to death. Investigating the past is not a venture to be entered into lightly or wantonly. Although I believe it to be an enjoyable venture, it is one that requires a great deal of very hard work by every person who takes part.

The belief that it could be easy, the belief that it could be packaged, amusing, money-making, is not, of course, a new one. It is not a product of unprecedented financial stringency. Nor is it a product of a more sophisticated awareness of what our public wants. It is a misunderstanding of the nature of the endeavour which, as one would imagine, has already been well documented in the past; documented, I think perhaps best of all, and strikingly parodied in the 1860s, very shortly after the South Kensington museums were set up, by George Eliot in the first draft of her novel *Felix Holt*. It is a novel of quite alarming contemporaneity. There is a great deal of deploring the recent disappearance of the pound note: Treeby Magna, a fledgling spa in Loamshire, decides that it has to raise its visitor profile, to be more customer friendly, and it decides in terms that would be extremely familiar to us today to indulge in a little private health provision, to promote itself as a spa – and to set up a museum. George Eliot writes:

> An excellent guidebook and descriptive cards, surmounted by vignettes, were printed, and Treeby Magna became conscious of certain facts in its own history of which it had previously been in contented ignorance. Its castle, among the most remarkable of English ruins, had had every traditional honour that could belong to an English castle. Plantagenets had held wassail in it. The Houses of York and Lancaster had contended for it. And only the dullest mind could remain unthrilled by the probable conjecture that the cruel tyrant, Richard III, had slept in it. . . . Several articles in rusty iron dug up in the vicinity were deposited in a small pavilion near the Pump Room, and with a larger number of mugs, baskets and pincushions inscribed as 'Presents from Treeby' formed a museum. In short, every inducement was offered to visitors who combined gout . . . with a passion for antiquarian hypothesis, a general decay of the vital processes with a tendency to purchase superflous small wares and make inexpensive presents.

You will be pleased to know that the museum of Treeby Magna failed instantly. Thank you.

This paper first appeared in Museum Management & Curatorship 9(4) (December 1990), pp. 361–6.

34

The ongoing pursuit of professional status

Stephen Weil

Critical to the development of any profession is the recognition it gets and the form this takes. In particular, the workforce has to see itself as a profession and be conscious of how both individual and collective responsibility is developed.

In this paper, Stephen Weil considers the progress made in museum work, especially in the light of statements on professional conduct, and assesses whether the pursuit of professionalism has had a positive effect on museum developments.

Early in the nineteenth century – first in Great Britain and then spreading to the United States – a new phenomenon appeared in the workplace. Sociologists now call it 'professionalization'. It was a process by which a group of workers who were engaged in a common occupation could, though their own effort, achieve public recognition that their work constituted a distinct 'profession' and that each of them – as a practitioner of that profession – was entitled to the special respect that is due a 'professional'. Whereas only physicians, lawyers, and the clergy had been accorded such status in the early 1800s, by the early 1900s we find that architects, nurses, and librarians – among others – had all succeeded in achieving professional recognition in either Britain or the United States, or both.

In the years since, this process has continued at an accelerated pace. Occupational groups that span the gamut from airline pilots to zookeepers have engaged in a quest for professional identification.[1] For the members of these groups, the reward has often justified the struggle. In an open society, professionalism has the power to confer upon its practitioners some of that same elevated prestige that might elsewhere be obtained only by the accumulation of wealth or through aristocratic birth. What it has offered – and continues to offer – is what sociologist Magali Sarfatti Larson has called the 'novel possibility of gaining status through work'.[2]

Among those who have struggled for professional identification in the United States are American museum workers. The professionalism they have sought is not just the simple professionalism of those who are paid for their work as distinct from amateurs or volunteers who are not. It has been the richer, far more complex professionalism of belonging to what is recognized by the public to be a 'profession'.

Some believe that American museum workers have already succeeded in achieving this status. Others doubt that they ever can. Most, including myself, think that significant progress has been made but that much remains to be done. I think that almost everybody, however, would agree that many important improvements in American museums themselves have come about as a by-product of this struggle by museum workers to gain professional identification.

In Webster's *Third New International Dictionary*, a 'profession' is defined as:

> A calling requiring specialized knowledge and often long and intensive preparation including instruction in skills and methods as well as in the scientific, historical, or scholarly principles underlying such skills and methods, maintaining by force of organization or concerted opinion high standards of achievement and conduct, and committing its members to continued study and to a kind of work which has for its prime purpose the rendering of a public service.

To this dictionary definition, most sociologists would add the attribute of autonomy and the observation that, in the most highly evolved professions such as medicine and law, the practitioners of the profession may themselves actually prescribe and monitor the preparatory training for the field, control the entry of new practitioners, and not only promulgate standards of achievement and conduct but also enforce these standards by imposing sanctions upon those who violate them.

In the official literature of the American museum field, it has long been taken for granted that museum work is *already* well recognized as a single and distinct 'profession' and that, accordingly, those who work in museums are, ipso facto, 'professionals'. The International Council of Museums (ICOM) similarly assumes that the existence of a 'museum professional' is a given. In Article 5 of the ICOM *Statutes* it defines this profession to consist of: 'all the personnel of museums . . . having received a specialized technical or academic training or possessing an equivalent practical experience, and respecting a fundamental code of professional ethics'.

Those who doubt that museum work can ever be recognized as a distinct profession focus chiefly on the problem of diversity – the diversity of disciplines *among* museums and the diversity of the knowledge and skills required *within* any particular museum. In a closely reasoned paper delivered at the annual meeting of the American Association of Museums (AAM) in Detroit in 1985, my colleague Wilcomb E. Washburn questioned whether there really was *any* unique body of knowledge or set of skills that could be found in museums of every discipline and which could provide the unifying basis for a single profession.[3] In essence, he asked how a botanist in a natural history museum could be linked to the exhibits designer in a history museum, or how either of them could be linked to the development officer of an art museum, as members of the same profession.

Whether the inherent diversity of museum work is such that it can never be classified as a single profession may not, however, be wholly relevant. More to the point, I think, is our understanding of how beneficial an impact this pursuit of professionalism has had and can continue to have on our museums themselves. As one American museum worker has pointed out, professionalism should not properly be thought of as an end in itself but, rather, as a 'spiritual behaviour through which we seek to accomplish larger purposes'.[4] In the end, it must of course be those 'larger purposes', and not the enhancement of individual status, that museum work is about. With that as a background, let us now see what has thus far been accomplished in this pursuit.

In acquiring the various attitudes, structures, and practices that distinguish a professionalized occupation from mere employment, museum workers in the United States have been eminently successful with respect to at least four goals: first, in having developed the attitude that they follow a calling which has for its prime purpose the rendering of a public service; second, in their establishment and maintenance of a variety of strong – albeit not necessarily well-co-ordinated – national, regional, and local organizations to deal directly with professional concerns; third, in having created an institutional accreditation programme that emphasizes high standards of achievement; and fourth, in having promulgated standards of ethical conduct applicable both to the museum field as a whole and to the various specialities within it.

Particularly striking is the degree to which museum work has come to be regarded as altruistic – the sense that museum employees are not working merely for wages but are following a calling intended to benefit other individuals and the community at large. Also striking has been the proliferation and growth of the various organizations that museum workers have joined to strive together for common goals. Beginning with the establishment of the AAM in 1906, there are today more than eighty different state, regional, disciplinary, or occupationally specialized associations, councils, societies, and committees to which museums and/or museum workers may belong.

Among the more evolved professions, however, such professional associations are generally expected to fulfil a number of other roles as well: to prescribe and monitor the academic training required for entry into the field, to provide programmes of continuing education, to publish scholarly research, to promulgate and enforce standards of achievement and conduct, and to represent and defend the political interests of their constituent members.

The record of museum associations in fulfilling these other roles has been decidedly mixed. Where they have been most successful is in their political role – they have served as skilled and vigorous legislative advocates for museums – and in their promulgation of standards of achievement and conduct. Where they have been less successful, however, is in devising ways to enforce these standards, especially standards of conduct.

The standards of achievement are to be found in the programme of institutional accreditation which the AAM initiated in 1970. By combining a rigorous process of self-examination with peer reviews conducted by on-site visiting committees, the accreditation programme seeks to assure that museums adhere to 'attainable professional standards of quality and performance'.[5] Virtually all of those most familiar with this programme agree that these 'attainable professional standards' have been steadily rising during the seventeen years since the programme's inception.

The AAM has also been active in promulgating standards of conduct. These have taken the form of codes of ethics. The first of these was a *Code of Ethics for Museum Workers* that the AAM adopted in 1925.[6] Interestingly, the words 'profession' or 'professional' appear nowhere in it. Of the various codes promulgated in the years since, the most widely known is *Museum Ethics* (1978). As evidence that the way museum workers think about themselves had changed during the fifty years between these two AAM codes, consider that – in the latter – references to the 'profession' and 'professionalism' abound.

If those, then, are some of the things that we who work in American museums have accomplished in our pursuit of professionalism, where have we failed and how might these failures be remedied? Those evident failures, it seems to me, relate to the question of individual autonomy, to the supervision of preparatory training, and to the enforcement of ethical standards.

Autonomy has traditionally been considered one of the attributes of a professional. Our very sense of a professional is that such a person relies primarily on his or her own expertise and seasoned judgement in coming to a decision. Here, though, we encounter a difficulty. Even if we concede that there already *is* a museum profession, it is not one which

– like medicine or law – can be practised alone. Museum work can only be performed in an organizational setting. Can a curator, who must necessarily work under the immediate authority of a director and/or other senior staff as well as the remote authority of a lay board of trustees or other governing structure, truly be autonomous?

The AAM's 1978 ethics code sought to answer this in the affirmative. It provided:

> Responsibility for the final decisions will normally rest with the museum administration and all employees are expected to support these decisions: but no staff member can be required to reverse, alter or suppress his professional judgment in order to conform to a management decision.[7]

What this fails to acknowledge is the swiftness with which a non-tenured employee who consistently fails to conform to management decisions may become a former employee. This tension between professional autonomy and organizational structure is not unique to museums. The problem of the salaried professional is a pervasive twentieth-century phenomenon. The physician employed in a drug-testing programme for a pharmaceutical company cannot expect to exercise the same authority and responsibility as does a doctor in private practice. And the curator who works in a museum simply cannot be given any formal grant of autonomy that would transcend the museum's organizational needs.

When we turn to the question of whether museum studies programmes are the best – or even an adequate – preparation for working in a museum, the fact that strikes one immediately is that many – perhaps even a majority – of those who hold responsible positions in American museums have never had any specific academic training in museology. They are largely cultural historians or botanists or art historians who learned about museum work by working in museums.

The heart of the dictionary definition of a profession is that it requires a 'specialized knowledge' that its practitioners hold in common. Here we must return to the diversity problem raised earlier by Washburn. Once we separate out the discipline-based knowledge of history, science, or art held by our directors, curators, registrars, and educators and the theory-based technical expertise of our conservators, accountants, and graphic designers, what remains left to be called museology? Something, certainly – some of it to do with such practical matters as tidiness (keeping track of things, and keeping them in good repair) and much of it to do with community service – but is this body of knowledge extensive enough or sufficiently profound to require its own course of study? Might not this remaining museological balance be readily bundled into a compact one- or two-semester course entitled 'Introduction to Museum Methods and Practices' and offered as an adjunct to graduate-level discipline studies?

Is it possible that, in the intensity of our desire to be considered a profession, we have simply assumed the existence of a body of theoretical knowledge that is not really there?[8] The question is an important one. While our aspirations toward professionalism may be at stake, at even greater critical risk are the thousands of dollars and years of time that students eager to work in museums might far better spend in discipline-based programmes instead of in 'museum studies'. If broader training – most particularly training in management – were subsequently needed, mid-career programmes might be the best vehicle for that.

The final question, then, and perhaps the most important of all, is whether those of us who work in museums can ever attain that degree of professionalism at which we might play a major role not merely in prescribing standards of achievement and conduct for our field but in enforcing these as well. This, after all, has been one of the ultimate goals of every profession – to transfer the control of the work one does away from those who may not fully understand or appreciate it and give it, instead, to a group of one's colleagues who share a common training, practical experience, and set of sympathetic values.

Whether a hypothetically offending museum could be disciplined by removing its accreditation and suspending it from AAM membership is by no means clear. The AAM's Constitution and Bylaws provide only the limited right to withdraw membership from those individuals or institutions who use their membership 'to work for purposes inconsistent with the aims' of the AAM or who have not paid their dues.[9] For any lesser disciplinary sanctions such as reprimand or censure, there are no provisions at all.

The exercise of formal police power by an association group is beyond question a matter of considerable legal complexity. Equally clear is that there are many informal means by which the museum field enforces its standards over both the individuals and institutions within it. A high degree of 'colleague consciousness' is another of the attributes often ascribed to professionals, and for museum workers who aspire to such a status the impact of peer pressure can be an important deterrent against breaching standards of achievement or conduct. None the less, it seems to me unthinkable that we can ever advance the pursuit of professionalism very much further in museums unless and until we begin to deal squarely with this issue of enforcement.

In the end, of course, whether the claim of American museum workers to be professionals will be honoured by anyone but themselves must depend not upon their own image of themselves but upon the public's. Is the work they do perceived to be unique? Are they considered competent to be entrusted with the execution of tasks that the public thinks important?

Prior to the beginning of this century, the great prestige that was accorded to those who practised the learned professions – medicine, law, and theology – was not grounded merely on the fact that they were 'professionals'. It was based upon the awesome magnitude of the matters with which they regularly dealt: life, death, liberty, and salvation. We deal with lesser things. While some greater public recognition of our efforts would certainly be gratifying, it might none the less be wise for us to keep our claims proportionate.

Our gratification aside, however, would a greater public understanding of the distinctive nature of museum work have some other importance? I think it would. Such an understanding could, in turn, lead to a more sensitive public recognition of the distinctive nature of museums themselves. The most common public view of museums is that they are either dusty depositories for things that are dead or places of recreation that might provide for an afternoon's entertainment. Rare has been any broad public understanding that museums might also be – that they might even primarily be – socially relevant institutions with the skills to collect, preserve, and exhibit objects in ways that not only deepen our understanding of the past but also enrich our lives and enhance in powerful ways our ability to shape a better future for ourselves, our descendants, and our communities. These may not be immediate matters of life or death, but neither are they unimportant.

Here, then, is where our pursuit of professionalism might legitimately end: with the realization that our quest for professional recognition may or may not ever be successful but that the by-products of this effort are both positive and extremely important. Those by-products are, first, to the extent that, in our pursuit of professional status, we apply ever-increasing standards of achievement and conduct to the work we do, then – at the same time – we are helping to move the museums that we serve toward their fullest potential. And, second, in seeking to draw the public's attention to the value of this work, we also stimulate a broader understanding of how significant a role museums might play in making better, richer lives for all of us, both as individuals and as members of a community.

If we are able to do these things, then whether or not we ever achieve the status of 'professionals' might, to my thinking, be beside the point. We will still have served a larger purpose.

This paper first appeared in Museum News 67(2) (1988), pp. 30–4.

NOTES

1 Harold Wilensky (1964) 'The professionalization of everyone?', *The American Journal of Sociology*, September: 137.
2 (1977) *The Rise of Professionalism: A Sociological Analysis*, Berkeley, California: University of California Press: 5.
3 Subsequently published in *Museum News* in December 1985, as 'Professionalizing the muses': 18–25ff.
4 Scott Swank (1985) 'Peer review: what's in it for you?', *Museum News* December: 32–5.
5 *Professional Standards for Museum Accreditation*, Washington, DC: American Association of Museums (1978): 8.
6 Reproduced in Marilyn Phelan (1982) *Museums and the Law*, Nashville, Tennessee: American Association for State and Local History: 252–7.
7 *Museum Ethics*, Washington, DC: American Association of Museums (1978): 23.
8 For a pertinent discussion, see the paper by Geoffrey D. Lewis in *Museological Working Papers*, *No. 1*, Stockholm, Sweden: ICOM Committee for Museology (1980): 27.
9 American Association of Museums Constitution, Article III, Section 7; Bylaws, Chapter 1, Section 3.

35

Ethics: constructing a code

Robert MacDonald

No code of ethical behaviour can be of real value unless it is subject to careful review and, if necessary, revision. Times and priorities change and museum agendas are rewritten: ethical concerns will inevitably shift as a result. Not only will the content have to change, but also maybe the tone of the document. Hitherto, most codes have been written to declare preferred procedures or to control the actions of the workforce through a form of 'regulation'. It is, however, possible to write a code which inspires and fosters a positive attitude to work, drawing on the 'tenets of the faith' about museums and their potential. This was shown in the 'Madison Code' of 1924 (see p. 265).

In 1987, the American Association of Museums started work on a new code of ethics. In this article, Robert MacDonald, Director of the Museum of the City of New York, reflects on the processes involved in creating such a document. The code arrived at is included in this volume.

In 1987, when the American Association of Museums set out to create a code of ethics, it did not know how formidable a task it had set itself. Five years later, after great efforts by a large number of professionals and much spirited, at times forceful, but always informative debate, a code is in place. Even now, however, two key elements continue to be debated. To best understand AAM's *Code of Ethics*, and what was intended by its creation, it is necessary to know how it evolved to its present stage of development.

Sixty-two years had passed since the association adopted its first code, the 1925 *Code of Ethics for Museum Workers*. In 1978, the association published *Museum Ethics* which, while not a code, presented the current museum thinking on such matters as collection care and the relationships among governing authorities, directors, and staff. The 1925 code had been long forgotten, and while the 1978 statement served the community well and was often used as a model for professional activities, AAM realized that the American museum community needed to codify its understanding of ethics and establish mechanisms that would encourage adherence to ethical principles in the operations of America's museums. The impetus to create an enforceable code had come from the museum profession. There were discussions at meetings of regional museum associations, AAM's Standing Professional Committees and its Accreditation Commission, as well as comments from the association's affiliated organizations. Driving the desire to create an American code was the work of the International Council of Museums, which adopted its *Code of Professional Ethics* in 1986.

Another factor was the recognition that museums and the society they served were rapidly changing. The success of American museums in attracting new and larger audiences, the phenomenal growth of the art market, concern for the environment and for cultural heritages, an educational system at risk, and the occasional 'museum scandal' were bringing renewed attention to museums from the press, government at all levels, and the public. American society was also experiencing revolutionary changes. Innovative technologies were altering the way Americans communicated. New corporate and individual wealth were influencing institutions such as museums. The democratic process had produced new political interest groups and fresh demands of and from elected and appointed officials. New political forces included women, minorities, homosexuals, environmentalists, and religious fundamentalists. These and other factors brought increased pressure on the seemingly tranquil world of museums.

Museums and the museum profession were aware of these challenges. In 1984 AAM published *Museums for a New Century*, a report in which the Commission on Museums for a New Century analysed the factors that promised to influence museums as they approached the next millennium. Among the commission's most important findings were the need for museums to continue their tradition of public service as collectors, preservers, and learning resources, and for AAM to establish programmes that would foster that effort.

In 1986, as the newly elected president of AAM, I appointed an Ethics Committee to undertake the work of preparing an ethics code for America's museums. The committee first met during the association's 1987 annual meeting in San Francisco. It was an inauspicious beginning. The committee, composed of forty individuals representing all segments of the museum community, spent its first meeting attempting to define 'ethics'. They consulted dictionaries, referred to legal treatises, and debated meanings. Subsequent meetings of the committee saw little advance in developing an ethics code. It became apparent that while a committee of forty talented and experienced museum people could raise and discuss a myriad of complex issues, it would be impossible for a group of this size to write the code. At the recommendation of the committee's co-chairs, Patterson Williams of the Denver Art Museum and Alan Ullberg of the Smithsonian Institution, it was agreed that a task force would be appointed and charged with the responsibility of formulating drafts that could be reviewed and critiqued by the larger committee and others.

Following discussions with Joel N. Bloom, my successor as AAM president, an Ethics Task Force was formed and given the responsibility of preparing drafts that could be reviewed by the larger committee and by representatives of institutions and museum disciplines. Joel Bloom and I made joint appointments to the Ethics Task Force and agreed to serve as co-chairs. Kenneth Starr and Thomas W. Leavitt, both former presidents of the AAM, accepted the invitation to serve as members, as did AAM's treasurer and future president, Ellsworth H. Brown. Marie C. Malaro, director of the Graduate Programme in Museum Studies at The George Washington University and a lawyer, provided a legal perspective for the task force during its deliberations. Unlike the original committee, the Ethics Task Force was not designed to be representative of the museum community, professional disciplines, sizes, regions, trustees, or volunteers. It was designed to accomplish its assignment by having a small, experienced group prepare working drafts for review by the diverse community the code was intended to serve.

The task force began its work with members selecting topics on which they prepared 'white papers' that were reviewed by the other members of the task force. The topics selected were governance, collections, public accountability, and implementation. A background paper on the history of museum ethics was also drafted. These papers, along with information on existing ethics codes of museum disciplines and other professional organizations compiled by Patricia E. Williams and her staff at AAM, provided the basis of the task force's discussions over the next ten months.

Early in its deliberations the task force concluded that, while only individuals could be ethical, only institutions had the capacity to regulate the museum-related behaviour of their governing authorities, staffs, and volunteers. The code would therefore be addressed to the non-profit institutional members of AAM. The task force also recognized that for the code to be meaningful it needed to be enforceable. Enforcement would have to be voluntary and achieved by making adherence to an application of the code a condition of non-profit, institutional membership in the association. This approach to implementing the code would require the discussion of ethical issues among those working on the member museums' behalf and within the context of each museum's mission, history, and resources. The ethics code could provide the framework for advancing the standards and self-regulation of America's museums, the primary goal of the task force.

The concept of 'public trust' became the focus of early debate, with the task force's legal advisors preferring the narrow, legal definition of the term and the non-lawyers favouring the broader concept of stewardship and public confidence. The discussion over the notion of 'trust' led the task force to understand that a code of ethics for museums was not a legal document written for attorneys or the courts, although the final document would have an effect on the interpretation of the law. The code would instead be directed to the museum community and, because it dealt with ethics, would be more than a guide for avoiding legal liability. It would set a standard higher than the law and be based on fundamental values held by the majority of the museum community. But what are those values? And how could they be articulated to a diverse population of institutions and professional disciplines?

The task force's discussions of these issues led its members to understand that museum ethics are not practices dictated by a 'higher authority'. Rather they are the traditional concepts and perspectives that have been developed over more than a century and a half in the experience of America's museums. These values are articulated in the writings of America's museum founders, our professional predecessors, and in the conventions maintained by the majority of the contemporary museum profession and their institutions. The members of the task force sought to reflect what they understood to be these widely held traditional values and tenets. There were lively debates over professional canons and traditions, but as the task force members gained insight into the historical and contemporary approaches to a variety of museum issues a consensus developed.

The task force members met with AAM's Accreditation Commission to discuss areas of commonality and distinction among ethics, standards, and practices. They consulted individual members of AAM and representatives from other associations. The association's Executive Committee was briefed and asked for comments, and Ann Hofstra Grogg was engaged as editor to begin consolidating the task force's work and forging a document that would be rational, practicable, and readable.

Believing that the document should be educative, the task force developed a section on practices intended to act as a guide to assist museums in applying the code to their own institutional settings. Task force members presented several of the 'model' practices at an American Law Institute–American Bar Association annual conference on legal matters related to museums. Additional critiques of the task force's work evolved through formal and informal discussions held at meetings of the six regional museum associations. A first draft was reviewed by the association's Executive Committee. Following this review the draft was mailed to all institutional members of AAM, presidents of regional associations, the chairs of Standing Professional Committees, and directors of the association's affiliated organizations. The draft was also presented to the AAM Council for discussion and suggested revisions.

Not surprisingly, the responses were immediate, varied, and in some cases forceful. While most respondents praised the substance of the effort, there were strong criticisms of the practices section and vigorous objections to the implementation section. Armed with the comments and recommendations of the reviewers, the task force returned to its deliberations. In a series of meetings in the spring of 1991, the members refined both their thinking and the draft code.

A particular area of contention was the question of a museum's use of funds earned through the disposal of collections. There are ardently held positions on both sides of the issue. The task force reviewed the matter in the context of historic convictions about the character of a museum's custody of collections, the position of the ICOM code on the issue, and recent attempts by some museums and accounting agencies to view collections as convertible assets. The task force recognized that in many instances museum boards have the legal right to use funds earned through disposal of collections as they deem proper. Relying on the responses to the earlier drafts and their understanding that ethics called for a standard higher than the law, the majority of the task force concluded that the traditional restrictions on the use of such funds for acquisition should be maintained. Using wording that paralleled the ICOM code, this section stated that disposal of collections should be 'solely for the advancement of the museum's mission' and that 'proceeds from the sale of collection materials is restricted to the acquisition of collections'.

In this new draft, now called the *Code of Ethics for Museums*, the practices section of the earlier document was dropped, and the implementation section was completely revised. By deleting the list of practices, the task force hoped to avoid confusion between commonly held ethical principles and recommendations of specific techniques for applying those principles. The implementation section was simplified in recognition of the need to separate the code's content from its administration. It would be left to the AAM governing authority, the elected Board of Directors (formerly Council), to develop and approve detailed and equitable administrative procedures within the framework provided by the code. Central to meeting this responsibility would be the creation of an Ethics Commission and programmes that would assist the association's non-profit institutional members in developing their own codes. After several revisions the second draft was shared with the Executive Committee and mailed to the recipients of the first draft for review.

The Ethics Task Force recognized that the code it was recommending was an imperfect document. Some would view the code as too weak, others would see it as too strong. There would be those who felt that it was not the role of AAM to require the association's non-profit, institutional members to subscribe to the code and develop their own institutional codes in accordance with the *Code of Ethics for Museums*. But the task force believed that it had articulated the commonly held values of the vast majority of American museums of differing sizes, disciplines, and missions. That collective wisdom had been defined through the inclusive process of review and comment that was an essential part of the process from the initiation of the effort in 1987.

The members of the task force believed that the application of the *Code of Ethics for Museums* on the institutional level would be as important as the code's contents. The development by museums throughout the United States of institutional ethics codes conforming to the AAM document would call for the formal discussion of ethical issues by trustees, staffs, and volunteers in institutions that wished to be members of AAM. The substantive work of self-regulation and the advancement of ethical practices by America's museums would be accomplished through the process of the institutional members of AAM applying the code to their operations.

A final draft of the *Code of Ethics for Museums* was presented to the Executive Committee and Board of Directors of the AAM for debate and action at the association's annual meeting in Denver on 18 and 19 May 1991. There were some protests, occasionally vigorous, over the requirement that all non-profit institutions wishing to be members of AAM be required to subscribe to the document and implement their own institutional codes over a five-year period. But the majority of the museum community's elected representatives agreed with the code's canons and the belief that, if museums did not regulate themselves, others, such as government, would.

The *Code of Ethics for Museums* was adopted by AAM's Board of Directors by a vote of 31 to 4. The approved code called for the creation by AAM of an Ethics Commission, the members of which would be nominated by the association's president and confirmed by the Board of Directors. The Ethics Commission would be responsible for establishing programmes of information, education, and assistance to museums in developing their own ethics codes and for periodically reviewing the code and recommending refinements and revisions to the association's Board of Directors. Under procedures to be established by the Board of Directors, the Ethics Commission would review alleged violations of the *Code of Ethics for Museums* and recommend to the board's Executive Committee that non-profit institutional members determined to be in violation of the code have their AAM membership withdrawn.

The code provides for the application of the American museum community's collective experience to the refinement of the understanding of museum ethics in the coming years through the work of the Ethics Commission. By adopting and implementing the code AAM continues its purpose, established in 1906, to advance museum work through self-regulation. Museums that subscribe to the *Code of Ethics for Museums* and develop their own institutional codes will confirm the canon of public service as the foundation of their activities and further their contributions to a democratic society.

This paper first appeared in Museum News *(May/June 1992), pp. 62–5.*

Part 6
Codes of ethical conduct

This section contains four very different codes of conduct for museum professionals:

H. L. Madison (1925) 'Tentative code of museum ethics, published for the twentieth annual meeting of the American Association of Museums', *Museums Journal* 25: 19–23.

American Association of Museums (1991) *Code of Ethics for Museums*.

ICOM (1987) *Code of Professional Ethics*.

Museums Association (1991) *Code of Conduct for Museum Professionals*.

These four codes are different both in their tone and their content. It is well worth comparing and contrasting them from a number of standpoints. It is also useful to have in mind a range of questions when reading each one:

- *Who is this code aimed at or written for?*
- *How do the authors intend the code to work?*
- *What has been included?*
- *What has been omitted?*
- *How are the priorities set?*
- *What weighting is given to the different elements?*
- *What form of language has been used?*
- *How is this document supposed to work within a museum?*
- *Would I be able to use it?*

36

Tentative code of museum ethics

H. L. Madison

PUBLISHED FOR DISCUSSION AT THE TWENTIETH ANNUAL MEETING OF THE AMERICAN ASSOCIATION OF MUSEUMS, ST LOUIS, MISSOURI, 17–21 MAY 1925

(This tentative code has been drafted by Harold L. Madison, Chairman of the Committee on Ethics of The American Association of Museums. It is printed for scrutiny of the museum profession and especially for discussion at the Twentieth Annual Meeting of the Association.)

Museums, in the broadest sense, are institutions which hold their possessions in trust for mankind and for the future welfare of the race. Their value is in direct proportion to the service they render the emotional and intellectual life of the people.

The life of the museum worker, whether he be an humble laborer or a responsible trustee, is essentially one of service. His conduct rests on a threefold ethical basis.

1 Devotion to the cause he serves.
2 Faith in the unselfish motives of his co-workers.
3 Honor based on a high sense of justice as the controlling motive of his thoughts and actions.

RELATIONSHIPS WITH THE PUBLIC

Courtesy

A museum worker will always be courteous to the visitor, thoughtful even to the extent of great personal inconvenience upon occasion. It may be helpful to remember that one is in a sense the host to a visiting guest.

Service

A museum worker will always give his best service to the public. Every member, in so doing, approximates most fully the ideals and purposes for which the museum stands. This service may be performed indirectly or by direct contact with the people. He will at no time allow jealousy to prevent him from transferring a call to a colleague, if by so doing, better and more proper service can be rendered.

Business dealings

The maintenance of a museum involves business relationships with many different persons including such individuals as lecturers, architects, lawyers and physicians.

No museum official or worker may honorably accept any commission, gift or tip which may be offered by a business concern as an inducement to do business with it. Only the museum itself is entitled to the discounts customarily allowed on a large volume of business or for prompt payment of bills.

Business independence

A museum should avoid any business relationship which shall put it under any obligation, financial or otherwise, to deal exclusively with any particular person or concern, but should rather base its business dealings on quality of goods, promptness of service, and fairness of price. In the long run a museum will prosper if it keeps its business dealings clearly separated from its public support regardless of the source from which it may be derived.

A museum may feel free to ask or accept service of a non-professional lecturer, but it should pay a suitable fee to him whose livelihood in part or whole is derived from his lecture service.

The public

He who represents the public should be slow to demand a service which will be freely given, should be mindful of the fact that any unnecessary time occupied in serving him reduces the amount and quality of service the museum may render all.

RELATIONSHIPS AMONG MUSEUMS

The relationships among museums is essentially one between presidents, trustees or directors

Employees

A museum may not properly offer a position to an employee of another museum with which it has regular and intimate relations without having first notified the director of its intentions so to do. If, however, an employee of a museum shall apply for a position to another museum, that museum shall not be under any obligation to confer with the museum by which the applicant is then employed; the obligation in such cases resting with the employee.

A museum shall regard the advancement of an employee qualified to assume larger responsibilities as a matter of first importance, both from the point of view of the welfare of the employee and the cause of museums, and if it is unable for financial or other reasons to offer the enlarged opportunity, it not only should put nothing in the way of that employee going elsewhere, but if the occasion should arise, it may encourage such an employee to make application for a better position which it knows to be open.

Collection and acquisition

If a museum has under negotiation the acceptance of a gift or the purchase of an object or collection of objects, another museum knowing of such negotiations may not with honor make an offer, either for whole or part of the collection, until the first museum has reached a decision in the matter. On occasion where two or more museums may be interested in the purchase of a collection in whole or in part, the highest ethical standards shall require that they co-operate through correspondence, conference or otherwise, toward the consummation of the purchase. None of the above shall apply to auction sales or where objects are offered to the first purchaser or under no restrictions.

Explorations

Where two or more museums conduct explorations in the same region for the same kind of material, they not only duplicate effort but needlessly expend funds. It is highly desirable that museums establish an intimate co-operative practice in the matter of fieldwork so that an exploration party may have financial support from a number of institutions with freedom to carry on exhaustive exploration in its chosen field, making collections in such quantities that all museums contributing to the work may have representative collections, while that museum which has the work in charge may retain the rarer finds. It shall be considered unethical for a museum not to report every specimen collected to the museums concerned. The material should be placed where it will be of greatest value to science or to art or to history and to mankind.

Collections and exchanges

Museums should co-operate by exchange, sale or otherwise, so that a very rare object or specimen may be placed where it can best be studied and kept in association with closely related objects. A museum should not 'corner the market' by refusing to dispose of duplicate specimens to other museums. It, however, should not release valuable specimens until after they have been studied and it should make those studies as promptly as possible so that an early distribution of material may be made.

Duplication of effort

Two or more museums should not attempt to do the same service for the same community. They should so arrange the work that the effort of one should not duplicate that of the other and it should be considered dishonorable for a museum, knowing the tentative plans of another museum, to take any action whatsoever to forestall or prevent the carrying out of such plans unless it shall be clearly in the interest of the public so to do, and then not until the matter has been discussed between the two museums, and, if possible, an agreement reached as to division of labor. The most honorable action which one museum may take toward the work of another is that of sympathetic understanding and hearty co-operation.

Information

A museum will always give willingly and courteously, in so far as its rules and regulations will permit, any information regarding its finances, methods and researches, which may be asked of it by another museum. That museum to which such information has been given shall make use of it only for its own individual needs, it being dishonorable for it to make use of such information either for publication or for money except by permission. A free exchange of ideas and facts between museums is highly desirable if museums are to render their best service to mankind.

RELATIONSHIPS OF THE DIRECTOR WITH THE TRUSTEES

Responsibility

A museum director is responsible to his trustees for the treasures within the museum, the character of the service it renders, and the expenditure of the funds it receives. He should, therefore, expect and the trustee should grant a wide range of freedom in carrying on the work of the museum. He, in return, should make a strict accounting to the trustees at frequent intervals of the condition and activities of the museum, should make no large expenditure of finds without their approval, and should obtain their sanction to all change in policy. He should neither expect nor ask an action from his trustees until he is sure that they thoroughly understand the matter which they are asked to consider, and if the action is contrary to his wishes, he should patiently wait until conditions have changed before presenting the matter again. The trustees should be sharers with the director of his responsibilities and should earnestly endeavor to so acquaint themselves with museum matters that they may fully bear their part of the burden.

Authority

With large responsibility goes large authority. The museum director has always before him the danger that he will abuse the authority vested in him unless he temper it with wisdom, justice and sympathy. While on the one hand the trustees should trust to the judgement of the director and give sympathetic consideration to his recommendations, the director must so act as to inspire the confidence of his trustees.

An indiscreet trustee may unconsciously wreck the whole morale of the museum organization through casual conversation with curators or other workers of the museum. It is incumbent on the trustee, therefore, to be discreet in his relationships with staff members, avoiding topics which may be concerned with administrative and executive matters.

Loyalty

A director should be loyal to the trustees and the trustees loyal to the director. When this condition cannot exist it is time relations were severed. Other than the formality of his election for a term of years to the directorship, there should be no necessity for any written agreement between the director and his trustees. If either are dissatisfied, it should be recognized that his directorship be terminated upon reasonable notice.

Sincerity

A director should be absolutely sincere with his trustees. To paint a picture in too glowing terms or to minimize the importance of the matter in an attempt to mislead in order to carry one's point is never justifiable.

Tact

To say the right thing at the right time and in the right way often means the success or failure of an undertaking. This is not incompatible with frankness. The better a director knows the individual members of his Board of Trustees, the more successfully should he be able to bring museum matters to their attention.

Impartiality

It is inevitable that a director shall more frequently consult the president and other officers of his Boards of Trustees in an official capacity, but to show favoritism toward certain trustees and to ignore others will ultimately result in friction.

RELATIONSHIP OF DIRECTOR WITH THE STAFF

Duty

It is the duty of the director to see that members of his staff work under as pleasant and healthful conditions as it is possible for the museum to maintain; that they be paid a suitable salary based upon their training, length of service and faithful performance of their duty; and that they be given every opportunity for advancement within the organization or for service in some other museum.

Fairness

In any organization certain rules are absolutely necessary. In the establishment of such rules the director should not only consider the welfare of the institution, but also that of its employees. At no time should he feel justified to make a rule to cover an individual case but which would work a hardship on others. Ideally it should not be necessary to enforce fair rules but if compelled to do so, such rules should be enforced impartially and without exception.

Sympathy

A director should show sympathetic interest in the work of his staff. In dealing as he does with different individuals, he should endeavour to have a sympathetic understanding of their personalities which shall be free from sentimentality.

RELATIONSHIPS OF STAFF TO THE DIRECTOR

Loyalty

A museum employee should be loyal to the director, to the museum and to the cause it serves. Personal criticism may readily become disloyalty and it is better that an employee sever his connection with the museum than that he feel disloyal toward it or the director.

Responsibility

A museum employee is responsible for the work he is engaged to do. Habitual lateness, loafing, or the use of museum time for personal gain are forms of irresponsibility which no director should countenance and no employee should practise.

269

Respect for authority

In the last analysis, the director is the final authority. He may ask for suggestions and advice from members of the museum staff which shall help him toward a final decision, and staff members should respond to such requests with a full realization of the use to which their contribution is to be given. They should carry out to the best of their ability the plans of the director, even though those plans may not appear expedient to them. An employee's attitude toward the museum director and the museum official by whom he is employed should be one of respect for authority.

INTER-STAFF RELATIONSHIPS

Comity

Among all workers in the museum there should exist a good will and a friendliness in regard to the rights of each other.

Charity

Where many persons are working together in more or less close contact, each should have for the other a respect for his personality, his intelligence, his feelings and his work. Jealous acts, gossip, inquisitiveness, sarcasm, practical jokes while often thoughtless, are always uncharitable, selfish and often cruel.

This paper first appeared in Museums Journal *25 (1925), pp. 19–23.*

37

Code of ethics for museums
American Association of Museums

Adopted by the American Association of Museums Board of Directors on 18 May 1991.

Introduction

In 1987 the Council of the American Association of Museums (AAM) determined to revise the association's 1978 statement on ethics. The impetus for revision was recognition throughout the American museum community that the statement needed to be refined and strengthened in light of the expanded role of museums in society and a heightened awareness that the collection, preservation, and interpretation of natural and cultural heritages involve issues of significant concern to the American people.

Following a series of group discussions and commentary by members of the AAM Council, the Accreditation Commission, and museum leaders throughout the country, the president of the AAM appointed an Ethics Task Force to prepare a code of ethics. Drafts were shared with the AAM Executive Committee and Council, then twice referred to the field for comment. Hundreds of individuals and representatives of professional organizations and museums of all types and sizes submitted thoughtful critiques that were instrumental in shaping the final document. The Code of Ethics for Museums was adopted by the AAM Board of Directors (formerly the AAM Council) on 18 May 1991.

In its work, the Ethics Task Force was committed to codifying the common understanding of ethics in the museum profession and to establishing a framework within which each institution could develop its own code. For guidance, the task force looked to the tradition of museum ethics and drew inspiration from the AAM's first code of ethics, published in 1925 as *Code of Ethics for Museum Workers*, which states in its preface:

> Museums, in the broadest sense, are institutions which hold their possessions in trust for mankind and for the future welfare of the [human] race. Their value is in direct proportion to the service they render the emotional and intellectual life of the people. The life of a museum worker ... is essentially one of service.

This commitment to service derived from nineteenth-century notions of the advancement and dissemination of knowledge that inform the founding documents of America's museums. George Brown Goode, a noted zoologist and first head of the United States National Museum, declared in 1889:

> The museums of the future in this democratic land should be adapted to the needs of the mechanic, the factory operator, the day laborer, the salesman, and the clerk, as much as to those of the professional man and the man of leisure. ... In short, the public museum is, first of all, for the benefit of the public.

John Cotton Dana, an early twentieth-century museum leader and director of the Newark Museum, promoted the concept of museum work as public service in essays with titles such as 'Increasing the usefulness of museums' and 'A museum of service'. Dana believed that museums did not exist solely to gather and preserve collections. For him, they were important centers of enlightenment.

By the 1940s, Theodore Low, a strong proponent of museum education, detected a new concentration in the museum profession on scholarship and methodology. These concerns are reflected in *Museum Ethics*, published by the AAM in 1978, which elaborated on relationships among staff, management and governing authority.

During the 1980s, Americans grew increasingly sensitive to the nation's cultural pluralism, concerned about the global environment, and vigilant regarding public institutions. Rapid technological change, new public policies relating to non-profit corporations, a troubled educational system, shifting patterns of private and public wealth, and increased financial pressures all called for a sharper delineation of museums' ethical responsibilities. In 1984 the AAM's Commission on Museums for a New Century placed renewed emphasis on public service and education, and in 1986 the code of ethics adopted by the International Council of Museums (ICOM) put service to society at the center of museum responsibilities. ICOM defines museums as institutions 'in the service of society and of its development' and holds that 'employment by a museum, whether publicly or privately supported, is a public trust involving great responsibility'.

The Code of Ethics for Museums that follows confirms the commitment to professional standards of the 1978 statement on ethics by placing it in the context of the traditional values that have always guided America's museums and were so eloquently expressed in the 1925 code. This new code is informed by a renewed emphasis on the historic American concepts of museums as public trusts and museum work as service to society.

This code also marks a significant departure, however. For the first time in the history of the American Association of Museums, it includes provisions for implementation. In initiating implementation, the AAM recognizes that a code of ethics cannot be meaningful or effective without adequate means of encouraging adherence. It is also recognized that, while the AAM cannot directly regulate the ethical behavior of individuals, it can encourage member museums to do so. This code provides a framework. Elaborating that framework is a task best assumed by individual museums.

Thus, as of 1 January 1992, each non-profit museum member of the American Association of Museums must, as a condition of membership, subscribe to the AAM Code of Ethics for Museums. Subsequently, these museums must set about framing their own institutional codes of ethics, which are to be in conformance with the AAM code and to expand on it through the elaboration of specific practices. This requirement is placed on these member institutions in the belief that engaging the governing authority, staff and volunteers in applying the AAM code to institutional settings will stimulate the development and maintenance of sound policies and procedures necessary to understanding and ensuring ethical behavior by institutions and by all who work for them or on their behalf.

On 1 January 1992, an Ethics Commission will begin operation. Nominated by the president and confirmed by the AAM Board of Directors, it will have as its first responsibility the development of informational and educational programs about ethics, to assist museums in elaborating their own institutional codes. The Ethics Commission's second task will be the development of procedures for implementation, to be brought to the Board of Directors for approval.

No later than 1 January 1997 (the exact date to be determined by the AAM Board of Directors on recommendation of the Ethics Commission), each non-profit museum member of the AAM must, as a condition of membership, have its institutional code of ethics in place. On or before that date, the Ethics Commission, operating under Board-approved policies, will begin reviewing allegations of violations of the Code of Ethics for Museums by those museums that have subscribed to it. The commission may recommend to the AAM Executive Committee that the membership of institutions in clear violation of the code be withdrawn.

With these steps, the American museum community expands its continuing effort to advance museum work through self-regulation. Formal implementation promotes higher and more consistent ethical standards and assures that the Code of Ethics for Museums serves the interests of museums, their constituencies and society. The primary goal of the AAM is to encourage institutions to regulate the ethical behavior of members of their governing authority, employees, and volunteers. To this end, the Ethics Task Force envisions an array of workshops, model codes and publications. These and other forms of technical assistance will stimulate a dialogue about ethics throughout the museum community and provide guidance to museums in developing their institutional codes.

Ethical codes evolve from traditional, commonly held values. Museums in the United States were created to serve a democratic society. Although that society grows increasingly complex, museums today continue to find profound guiding values in the ethic of service. With the adoption of this Code of Ethics for Museums, non-profit institutional members of the American Association of Museums affirm the ethic of public service as the foundation of their actions and their contributions to society, present and future.

CODE OF ETHICS FOR MUSEUMS

Museums make their unique contribution to the public by collecting, preserving and interpreting the things of this world. Historically, they have owned and used natural objects, living and non-living, and all manner of human artefacts to advance knowledge and nourish the human spirit. Today the range of their special interests reflects the scope of human vision. Their missions include collecting and preserving as well as exhibiting and educating with materials not only owned but also borrowed and fabricated for these ends. Their numbers include both governmental and private museums of anthropology, art, history and natural history, aquariums, arboreta, art centers, botanical gardens, children's museums, historic sites, nature centers, planetariums, science and technology centers, and zoos. The museum universe in the United States includes both collecting and non-collecting institutions. Although diverse in their missions, they have in common their non-profit form of organization and a commitment of service to the public. Their collections and/or the objects they borrow or fabricate are the basis for research, exhibits, and programs that invite public participation.

Taken as a whole, museum collections and exhibition materials represent the world's natural and cultural common wealth. As stewards of that wealth, museums are compelled to advance an understanding of all natural forms and of the human experience. It is incumbent on museums to be resources for humankind and in all their activities to foster an informed appreciation of the rich and diverse world we have inherited. It is also incumbent upon them to preserve that inheritance for posterity.

Museums in the United States are grounded in the tradition of public service. They are organized as public trusts, holding their collections and information as a benefit for those they were established to serve. Members of their governing authority, employees and volunteers are committed to the interests of these beneficiaries.

The law provides the basic framework for museum operations. As non-profit institutions musuems comply with applicable local, state and federal laws and international conventions, as well as with the specific legal standards governing trust responsibilities, and this Code of Ethics for Museums takes that compliance as given. But legal standards are a minimum. Museums and those responsible for them must do more than avoid legal liability. They must take affirmative steps to maintain their integrity so as to warrant public confidence. They must act not only legally but also ethically. This Code of Ethics for Museums therefore outlines ethical standards that frequently exceed legal minimums.

Loyalty to the mission of the museum and to the public it serves is the essence of museum work, whether volunteer or paid. Where conflicts of interest arise – actual, potential or perceived – the duty of loyalty must never be compromised. No individual may use his or her position in a museum for personal gain or to benefit another at the expense of the museum, its mission, its reputation and the society it serves.

For museums, public service is paramount. To affirm that ethic and to elaborate its application to their governance, collections and programs, the American Association of Museums promulgates this Code of Ethics for Museums. In subscribing to this code, museums assume responsibility for the actions of members of their governing authority, employees and volunteers in the performance of museums-related duties. Museums thereby affirm their chartered purpose, ensure the prudent application of their resources, enhance their effectiveness and maintain public confidence. This collective endeavor strenghtens museum work and the contributions of museums to society, present and future.

GOVERNANCE

Museum governance, in its various forms, is a public trust responsible for the institution's service to society. The governing authority protects and enhances the museum's collections and programs and its physical, human and financial resources. It ensures that all these resources support the museum's mission, respond to the pluralism of society, and respect the diversity of the natural and cultural common wealth.

Thus the governing authority ensures that:

- All those who work for or on behalf of the museum understand and support its mission and public trust responsibilities.
- Its members understand and fulfil their trusteeship and act corporately, not as individuals.
- The museum's collections and programs and its physical, human, and financial resources are protected, maintained, and developed in support of the museum's mission.
- It is responsive to and represents the interests of society.
- It maintains a relationship with staff in which shared roles are recognized and separate responsibilities respected.
- Working relationships among trustees, employees and volunteers are based in equity and mutual respect.
- Professional standards and practices inform and guide museum operations.
- Policies are articulated and prudent oversight is practiced.
- Governance promotes the public good rather than individual financial gain.

274

COLLECTIONS

The distinctive character of museum ethics derives from the ownership, care and use of objects, specimens and living collections representing the world's natural and cultural common wealth. This stewardship of collections entails the highest public trust and carries with it the presumption of rightful ownership, permanence, care, documentation, accessibility and responsible disposal.

Thus the museum ensures that:

* Collections in its custody support its mission and public trust responsibilities.
* Collections in its custody are protected, secure, unencumbered, cared for and preserved.
* Collections in its custody are accounted for and documented.
* Access to the collections and related information is permitted and regulated.
* Acquisition, disposal and loan activities are conducted in a manner that respects the protection and preservation of natural and cultural resources and discourages illicit trade in such materials.
* Acquisition, disposal and loan activities conform to its mission and public trust responsibilities.
* Disposal of collections through sale, trade or research activities is solely for the advancement of the museum's mission, and use of proceeds from the sale of collection materials is restricted to the acquisition of collections.
* The unique and special nature of human remains and funerary and sacred objects is recognized as the basis of all decisions concerning such collections.
* Collections-related activities promote the public good rather than individual financial gain.

PROGRAMS

Museums serve society by advancing an understanding and appreciation of the natural and cultural common wealth through exhibitions, research, scholarship, publications and educational activities. These programs further the museum's mission and are responsive to the concerns, interests and needs of society.

Thus the museum ensures that:

* Programs support its mission and public trust responsibilities.
* Programs are founded on scholarship and marked by intellectual integrity.
* Programs are accessible and encourage participation of the widest possible audience consistent with its mission and resources.
* Programs respect pluralistic values, traditions and concerns.
* Revenue-producing activities and activities that involve relationships with external entities are compatible with the musuem's mission and support its public trust responsibilities.
* Programs promote the public good rather than individual financial gain.

Implementation

This Code of Ethics for Museums was adopted by the Board of Directors of the American Association of Museums on 18 May 1991. Beginning on 1 January 1992, each non-profit museum shall, upon joining the AAM or renewing its membership, subscribe to the code as a condition of membership. No later than 1 January 1997 (the exact date to be determined by the AAM Board of Directors on recommendation of the Ethics Commission), each non-profit museum member of the American Association of Museums shall also affirm, as a condition of membership, that it has adopted and promulgated its separate code of ethics, applying the Code of Ethics for Museums to its own institutional setting.

An Ethics Commission, nominated by the president of the AAM and confirmed by the Board of Directors, will be charged with three responsibilities:

- Establishing programs of information, education and assistance to guide museums in developing their own codes of ethics.
- Reviewing the Code of Ethics for Museums and periodically recommending refinements and revisions to the Board of Directors.
- Reviewing alleged violations of the Code of Ethics for Museums under procedures approved by the Board of Directors and recommending to the Executive Committee of the AAM that membership of institutions in violation be withdrawn. Final determination in such matters shall be made by the Executive Committee.

The memberships of museums that choose not to subscribe to the Code of Ethics for Museums after 1 January 1992, shall be withheld or withdrawn. Memberships of museums that are without institutional codes of ethics after 1 January 1997, shall be withheld or withdrawn.

ACKNOWLEDGMENTS

Robert R. Macdonald, president of the American Association of Museums, 1985–8, and director of the Museum of the City of New York, provided the leadership, vision and perseverance that made the Code of Ethics for Museums possible. His co-chair of the Ethics Task Force was Joel N. Bloom, AAM president, 1988–90, and president and director emeritus of the Franklin Institute Science Museum and Planetarium, Philadelphia, Pennsylvania. Other members of the task force included Ellsworth H. Brown, AAM president, 1990–2, and president and director of the Chicago Historical Society; Thomas W. Leavitt, AAM president, 1982–5, and director of the Herbert F. Johnson Museum of Art, Ithaca, New York; and Kenneth Starr, AAM president, 1978–80, and director emeritus of the Milwaukee Public Museum. Marie C. Malaro, director of the Graduate Program in Museum Studies at the George Washington University, Washington, D.C., participated in early drafting sessions and was especially helpful in presenting the legal perspective on museum ethics. AAM staff direction was provided by Patricia E. Williams, director of the AAM's Accreditation Program, assisted by Sara Dubberly, coordinator of the AAM's Technical Information Service. The project editor was Ann Hofstra Grogg.

Addendum

At its 16 November 1991 meeting, the AAM Board of Directors voted to postpone the subscription to the *Code of Ethics for Museums* for at least one year. In its motion, the Board also directed the newly appointed Ethics Commission to review the *Code of Ethics* and recommend to the Board changes in either the *Code of Ethics* or its implementation. As part of its review, the Ethics Commission will develop procedures and due processes for the withdrawal of membership from museums in violation of the *Code of Ethics* that are in accord with the association's constitution.

38

Code of professional ethics
ICOM

I PREAMBLE

The *ICOM Code of Professional Ethics* was adopted unanimously by the 15th General Assembly of ICOM meeting in Buenos Aires, Argentina on 4 November 1986.

It provides a general statement of professional ethics, respect for which is regarded as a minimum requirement to practise as a member of the museum profession. In many cases it will be possible to develop and strengthen the *Code* to meet particular national or specialized requirements and ICOM wishes to encourage this. A copy of such developments of the *Code* should be sent to the Secretary General of ICOM, Maison de l'Unesco, 1 Rue Miollis, 75732 Paris Cedex 15, France.

For the purposes of Articles 5 and 16(c) of the ICOM *Statutes*, this *Code* is deemed to be the statement of professional ethics referred to therein.

I DEFINITIONS

1.1 The International Council of Museums (ICOM)

ICOM is defined in Article 6 of its *Statutes* as 'the international, non-governmental, and professional organization representing museums and the museum profession. In this capacity it maintains close consultative and co-operative relations with UNESCO, ICOMOS, and ICCROM, and with other national, regional or international, inter-governmental or non-governmental organizations, with the authorities responsible for museums and with specialists of other disciplines.'

The primary aims of ICOM, as defined in Article 7 of the *Statutes* are:

'(a) To define, support and aid museums and the museum institution; to establish, support and reinforce the museum profession.
(b) To organize co-operation and mutual assistance between museums and between members of the museum profession in the different countries.
(c) To emphasize the importance of the role played by museums and the museum profession within each community and in the promotion of a greater knowledge and understanding among peoples.'

1.2 Museum

A Museum is defined in Article 3 of the *Statutes* of the International Council of Museums as 'a non-profitmaking, permanent institution in the service of society and of its development, and open to the public, which acquires, conserves, researches, communicates, and exhibits, for the purposes of study, education and enjoyment, material evidence of man and his environment.'

In addition to museums designated as such, ICOM recognizes (under Article 4 of the *Statutes*) that the following comply with the ICOM definition:

'(a) Conservation institutes and exhibition galleries maintained by libraries and archive centres.
(b) Natural, archaeological, and ethnographical monuments and sites and historical monuments and sites of a museum nature, for their acquisition, conservation and communication activities.
(c) Institutions displaying live specimens such as botanic and zoological gardens, acquaria, vivaria, etc.
(d) Nature reserves.
(e) Science centres and planetariums.'

1.3 The museum profession

ICOM defines the museum profession under Article 5 of the *Statutes* as consisting of all of the personnel of museums or institutions as detailed under para. 1.1 above who have received a specialized technical or academic training or who possess an equivalent practical experience, and who respect a fundamental code of professional ethics.

1.4 Governing body

The government and control of museums in terms of policy, finance and administration, etc., varies greatly from one country to another, and often from one museum to another within a country according to the legal and other national or local provisions of the particular country or institution.

In the case of many national museums the Director, Curator or other professional head of the museum may be appointed by, and directly responsible to, a Minister or a Government Department, while most local government museums are similarly governed and controlled by the appropriate local authority. In many other cases the government and control of the museum is vested in some form of independent body, such as a board of trustees, a society, a non-profit company, or even an individual.

For the purposes of this *Code* the term 'Governing Body' has been used throughout to signify the superior authority concerned with the policy, finance and administration of the museum. This may be an individual Minister or official, a Ministry, a local authority, a Board of Trustees, a Society, the Director of the museum or any other individual or body. Directors, Curators or other professional heads of the museum are responsible for the proper care and management of the museum.

II INSTITUTIONAL ETHICS

2 BASIC PRINCIPLES FOR MUSEUM GOVERNANCE

2.1 Minimum standards for museums

The governing body or other controlling authority of a museum has an ethical duty to maintain, and if possible enhance, all aspects of the museum, its collections and its services. Above all, it is the responsibility of each governing body to ensure that all of the collections in their care are adequately housed, conserved and documented.

The minimum standards in terms of finance, premises, staffing and services will vary according to the size and responsibilities of each museum. In some countries such minimum standards may be defined by law or other government regulation and in others guidance on and assessment of minimum standards is available in the form of 'Museum Accreditation' or similar schemes. Where such guidance is not available locally, it can usually be obtained from appropriate national and international organizations and experts, either directly or through the National Committee or appropriate International Committee of ICOM.

2.2 Constitution

Each museum should have a written constitution or other document setting out clearly its legal status and permanent, non-profit nature, drawn up in accordance with appropriate national laws in relation to museums, the cultural heritage, and non-profit institutions. The governing body or other controlling authority of a museum should prepare and publicize a clear statement of the aims, objectives and policies of the museum, and of the role and composition of the governing body itself.

2.3 Finance

The governing body holds the ultimate financial responsibility for the museum and for the protecting and nurturing of its various assets: the collections and related documentation, the premises, facilities and equipment, the financial assets, and the staff. It is obliged to develop and define the purposes and related policies of the institution, and to ensure that all of the museum's assets are properly and effectively used for museum purposes. Sufficient funds must be available on a regular basis, either from public or private sources, to enable the governing body to carry out and develop the work of the museum. Proper accounting procedures must be adopted and maintained in accordance with the relevant national laws and professional accountancy standards.

2.4 Premises

The board has specially strong obligations to provide accommodation giving a suitable environment for the physical security and preservation of the collections. Premises must be adequate for the museum to fulfil within its stated policy its basic functions of collection, research, storage, conservation, education and display, including staff accommodation, and should comply with all appropriate national legislation in relation to public and staff safety. Proper standards of protection should be provided against such hazards as theft, fire, flood, vandalism and deterioration, throughout the year, day and night. The special needs of disabled people should be provided for, as far as practicable, in planning and managing both buildings and facilities.

2.5 Personnel

The governing body has a special obligation to ensure that the museum has staff sufficient in both number and kind to ensure that the museum is able to meet its responsibilities. The size of the staff, and its nature (whether paid or unpaid, permanent or temporary), will depend on the size of the museum, its collections and its responsibilities. However, proper arrangements should be made for the museum to meet its obligations in relation to the care of the collections, public access and services, research, and security.

The governing body has particularly important obligations in relation to the appointment of the director of the museum, and whenever the possibility of terminating the employment of the director arises, to ensure that any such action is taken only in accordance with appropriate procedures under the legal or other constitutional arrangements and policies of the museum, and that any such staff changes are made in a professional and ethical manner, and in accordance with what is judged to be the best interests of the museum, rather than any personal or external factor or prejudice. It should also ensure that the same principles are applied in relation to any appointment, promotion, dismissal or demotion of the personnel of the museum by the director or any other senior member of staff with staffing responsibilities.

The governing body should recognize the diverse nature of the museum profession, and the wide range of specializations that it now encompasses, including conservator/restorers, scientists, museum education service personnel, registrars and computer specialists, security service managers, etc. It should ensure that the museum both makes appropriate use of such specialists where required and that such specialized personnel are properly recognized as full members of the professional staff in all respects.

Members of the museum profession require appropriate academic, technical and professional training in order to fulfil their important role in relation to the operation of the museum and the care for the heritage, and the governing body should recognize the need for, and value of, a properly qualified and trained staff, and offer adequate opportunities for further training and retraining in order to maintain an adequate and effective workforce.

A governing body should never require a member of the museum staff to act in a way that could reasonably be judged to conflict with the provisions of this *Code of Ethics*, or any national law or national code of professional ethics.

The Director or other chief professional officer of a museum should be directly responsible to, and have direct access to, the governing body in which trusteeship of the collections is vested.

2.6 Educational and community role of the museum

By definition a museum is an institution in the service of society and of its development, and is generally open to the public (even though this may be a restricted public in the case of certain very specialized museums, such as certain academic or medical museums, for example).

The museum should take every opportunity to develop its role as an educational resource used by all sections of the population or specialized group that the museum is intended to serve. Where appropriate in relation to the museum's programme and responsibilities, specialist staff with training and skills in museum education are likely to be required for this purpose.

The museum has an important duty to attract new and wider audiences within all levels of the community, locality or group that the museum aims to serve, and should offer both the general community and specific individuals and groups within it opportunities to become actively involved in the museum and to support its aims and policies.

2.7 Public access

The general public (or specialized group served, in the case of museums with a limited public role), should have access to the displays during reasonable hours and for regular periods. The museum should also offer the public reasonable access to members of staff by appointment or other arrangement, and full access to information about the collections, subject to any necessary restrictions for reasons of confidentiality or security as discussed in para. 7.3 below.

2.8 Displays, exhibitions and special activities

Subject to the primary duty of the museum to preserve unimpaired for the future the significant material that comprises the museum collections, it is the responsibility of the museum to use the collections for the creation and dissemination of new knowledge, through research, educational work, permanent displays, temporary exhibitions and other special activities. These should be in accordance with the stated policy and educational purpose of the museum,and should not compromise either the quality or the proper care of the collections. The museum should seek to ensure that information in displays and exhibitions is honest and objective and does not perpetuate myths or stereotypes.

2.9 Commercial support and sponsorship

Where it is the policy of the museum to seek and accept financial or other support from commercial or industrial organizations, or from other outside sources, great care is needed to define clearly the agreed relationship between the museum and the sponsor. Commercial support and sponsorship may involve ethical problems and the museum must ensure that the standards and objectives of the museum are not compromised by such a relationship.

2.10 Museum shops and commercial activities

Museum Shops and any other commercial activities of the museum, and any publicity relating to these, should be in accordance with a clear policy, should be relevant to the collections and the basic educational purpose of the museum, and must not compromise the quality of those collections. In the case of the manufacture and sale of replicas, reproductions or other commercial items adapted from an object in a museum's collection, all aspects of the commercial venture must be carried out in a manner that will not discredit either the integrity of the museum or the intrinsic value of the original object. Great care must be taken to identify permanently such objects for what they are, and to ensure accuracy and high quality in their manufacture. All items offered for sale should represent good value for money and should comply with all relevant national legislation.

2.11 Legal obligations

It is an important responsibility of each governing body to ensure that the museum complies fully with all legal obligations, whether in relation to national, regional or local law, international law or treaty obligations, and to any legally binding trusts or conditions relating to any aspect of the museum collections or facilities.

3 ACQUISITIONS TO MUSEUM COLLECTIONS

3.1 Collecting policies

Each museum authority should adopt and publish a written statement of its collecting policy. This policy should be reviewed from time to time, and at least once every five years.

Objects acquired should be relevant to the purpose and activities of the museum, and be accompanied by evidence of a valid legal title. Any conditions or limitations relating to an acquisition should be clearly described in an instrument of conveyance or other written documentation. Museums should not, except in very exceptional circumstances, acquire material that the museum is unlikely to be able to catalogue, conserve, store or exhibit, as appropriate, in a proper manner. Acquisitions outside the current stated policy of the museum should only be made in very exceptional circumstances, and then only after proper consideration by the governing body of the museum itself, having regard to the interests of the objects under consideration, the national or other cultural heritage and the special interests of other museums.

3.2 Acquisition of illicit material

The illicit trade in objects destined for public and private collections encourages the destruction of historic sites, local ethnic cultures, theft at both national and international levels, places at risk endangered species of flora and fauna, and contravenes the spirit of national and international patrimony. Museums should recognize the relationship between the marketplace and the initial and often destructive taking of an object for the commercial market, and must recognize that it is highly unethical for a museum to support in any way, whether directly or indirectly, that illicit market.

A museum should not acquire, whether by purchase, gift, bequest or exchange, any object unless the governing body and responsible officer are satisfied that the museum can acquire a valid title to the specimen or object in question and that in particular it has not been acquired in, or exported from, its country of origin and/or any intermediate country in which it may have been legally owned (including the museum's own country), in violation of that country's laws.

So far as biological and geological material is concerned, a museum should not acquire by any direct or indirect means any specimen that has been collected, sold or otherwise transferred in contravention of any national or international wildlife protection or natural history conservation law or treaty of the museum's own country or any other country except with the express consent of an appropriate outside legal or governmental authority.

So far as excavated material is concerned, in addition to the safeguards set out above, the museum should not acquire by purchase objects in any case where the governing body or responsible officer has reasonable cause to believe that their recovery involved the recent unscientific or international destruction or damage of ancient monuments or archeological sites, or involved a failure to disclose the finds to the owner or occupier of the land, or to the proper legal or governmental authorities.

If appropriate and feasible, the same tests as are outlined in the above four paragraphs should be applied in determining whether or not to accept loans for exhibition or other purposes.

3.3 Field study and collecting

Museums should assume a position of leadership in the effort to halt the continuing degradation of the world's natural history, archaeological, ethnographic, historic and artistic resources. Each museum should develop policies that allow it to conduct its activities within appropriate national and international laws and treaty obligations, and with a reasonable certainty that its approach is consistent with the spirit and intent of both national and international efforts to protect and enhance the cultural heritage.

Field exploration, collecting and excavation by museum workers present ethical problems that are both complex and critical. All planning for field studies and field collecting must be preceded by investigation, disclosure and consultation with both the proper authorities and any interested museums or academic institutions in the country or area of the proposed study sufficient to ascertain if the proposed activity is both legal and justifiable on academic and scientific grounds. Any field programme must be executed in such a way that all participants act legally and responsibly in acquiring specimens and data, and that they discourage by all practical means unethical, illegal and destructive practices.

3.4 Co-operation between museums in collecting policies

Each museum should recognize the need for co-operation and consultation between all museums with similar or overlapping interests and collecting policies, and should seek to consult with such other institutions both on specific acquisitions where a conflict of interest is thought possible and, more generally, on defining areas of specialization. Museums should respect the boundaries of the recognized collecting areas of other museums and should avoid acquiring material with special local connections or of special local interest from the collecting area of another museum without due notification of intent.

3.5 Conditional acquisitions and other special factors

Gifts, bequests and loans should only be accepted if they conform to the stated collecting and exhibition policies of the museum. Offers that are subject to special conditions may have to be rejected if the conditions proposed are judged to be contrary to the long-term interests of the museum and its public.

3.6 Loans to museums

Both individual loans of objects and the mounting or borrowing of loan exhibitions can have an important role in enhancing the interest and quality of a museum and its services. However, the ethical principles outlined in paras 3.1 to 3.5 above must apply to the consideration of proposed loans and loan exhibitions as to the acceptance or rejection of items offered to the permanent collections: loans should not be accepted nor exhibitions mounted if they do not have a valid educational, scientific or academic purpose.

3.7 Conflicts of interest

The collecting policy or regulations of the museum should include provisions to ensure that no person involved in the policy or management of the museum, such as a trustee or other member of a governing body, or a member of the museum staff, may compete with the museum for objects or may take advantage of privileged information received because of his or her position, and that should a conflict of interest develop between the needs of the individual and the museum, those of the museum will prevail. Special care is also required in considering any offer of an item either for sale or as a tax-benefit gift, from members of governing bodies, members of staff, or the families or close associates of these.

4 DISPOSAL OF COLLECTIONS

4.1 General presumption of permanence of collections

By definition one of the key functions of almost every kind of museum is to acquire objects and keep them for posterity. Consequently there must always be a strong presumption against the disposal of specimens to which a museum has assumed formal title. Any form of disposal, whether by donation, exchange, sale or destruction requires the exercise of a high order of curatorial judgement and should be approved by the governing body only after full expert and legal advice has been taken.

Special considerations may apply in the case of certain kinds of specialized institutions such as 'living' or 'working' museums, and some teaching and other educational museums, together with museums and other institutions displaying living specimens, such as botanical and zoological gardens and aquaria, which may find it necessary to regard at least part of their collections as 'fungible' (i.e. replaceable and renewable). However, even here there is a clear ethical obligation to ensure that the activities of the institution are not detrimental to the long-term survival of examples of the material studied, displayed or used.

4.2 Legal or other powers of disposal

The laws relating to the protection and permanence of museum collections, and to the power of museums to dispose of items from their collection vary greatly from country to country, and often from one museum to another within the same country. In some cases no disposals of any kind are permitted, except in the case of items that have been seriously damaged by natural or accidental deterioration. Elsewhere, there may be no explicit restriction on disposals under general law.

Where the museum has legal powers permitting disposals, or has acquired objects subject to conditions of disposal, the legal or other requirements and procedures must be fully complied with. Even where legal powers of disposal exist, a museum may not be completely free to dispose of items acquired: where financial assistance has been obtained from an outside source (e.g. public or private grants, donations from a Friends of the Museum organization, or private benefactor), disposal would normally require the consent of all parties who had contributed to the original purchase.

Where the original acquisition was subject to mandatory restrictions these must be observed unless it can be clearly shown that adherence to such restrictions is impossible or substantially detrimental to the institution. Even in these circumstances the museum can only be relieved from such restrictions through appropriate legal procedures.

4.3 De-accessioning policies and procedures

Where a museum has the necessary legal powers to dispose of an object the decision to sell or otherwise dispose of material from the collections should only be taken after due consideration, and such material should be offered first, by exchange, gift or private treaty sale, to other museums before sale by public auction or other means is considered. A decision to dispose of a specimen or work of art, whether by exchange, sale or destruction (in the case of an item too badly damaged or deteriorated to be restorable) should be the responsibility of the governing body of the museum, not of the curator of the collection concerned acting alone. Full records should be kept of all such decisions and the objects involved, and proper arrangements made for the preservation and/or transfer, as appropriate, of the documentation relating to the object concerned, including photographic records where practicable.

Neither members of staff, nor members of the governing bodies, nor members of their families or close associates, should ever be permitted to purchase objects that have been de-accessioned from a collection. Similarly, no such person should be permitted to appropriate in any other way items from the museum collections, even temporarily, to any personal collection or for any kind of personal use.

4.4 Return and restitution of cultural property

If a museum should come into possession of an object that can be demonstrated to have been exported or otherwise transferred in violation of the principles of the Unesco *Convention on the Means of Prohibition and Preventing the Illicit Import, Export and Transfer of Ownership of Cultural Property* (1970) and the country of origin seeks its return and demonstrates that it is part of the country's cultural heritage, the museum should, if legally free to do so, take responsible steps to co-operate in the return of the object to the country of origin.

In the case of requests for the return of cultural property to the country of origin, museums should be prepared to initiate dialogues with an open-minded attitude on the basis of scientific and professional principles (in preference to action at a governmental or political level). The possibility of developing bi-lateral or multi-lateral co-operation schemes to assist museums in countries which are considered to have lost a significant part of their cultural heritage in the development of adequate museums and museum resources should be explored.

Museums should also respect fully the terms of the *Convention for the Protection of Cultural Property in the Event of Armed Conflict* (The Hague Convention, 1954), and in support of this *Convention*, should in particular abstain from purchasing or otherwise appropriating or acquiring cultural objects from any occupied country, as these will in most cases have been illegally exported or illicitly removed.

4.5 Income from disposal of collections

Any moneys received by a governing body from the disposal of specimens or works of art should be applied solely for the purchase of additions to the museum collections.

III PROFESSIONAL CONDUCT

5 GENERAL PRINCIPLES

5.1 Ethical obligations of members of the museum profession

Employment by a museum, whether publicly or privately supported, is a public trust involving great responsibility. In all activities museum employees must act with integrity and in accordance with the most stringent ethical principles as well as the highest standards of objectivity.

An essential element of membership of a profession is the implication of both rights and obligations. Although the conduct of a professional in any area is ordinarily regulated by the basic rules of moral behaviour which govern human relationships, every occupation involves standards, as well as particular duties, responsibilities and opportunities that from time to time create the need for a statement of guiding principles. The museum professional should understand two guiding principles: first that museums are the object of a public trust whose value to the community is in direct proportion to the quality of service rendered; and, second, that intellectual ability and professional knowledge are not, in themselves, sufficient, but must be inspired by a high standard of ethical conduct.

The Director and other professional staff owe their primary professional and academic allegiance to their museum and should at all times act in accordance with the approved policies of the museum. The Director or other principal museum officer should be aware of, and bring to the notice of the governing body of the museum whenever appropriate, the terms of the *ICOM Code of Professional Ethics* and of any relevant national or regional Codes or policy statements on Museum Ethics, and should urge the governing body to comply with these. Members of the museum profession should also comply fully with the *ICOM Code* and any other Codes or statements on Museum Ethics whenever exercising the functions of the governing body under delegated powers.

5.2 Personal conduct

Loyalty to colleagues and to the employing museum is an important professional responsibility, but the ultimate loyalty must be to fundamental ethical principles and to the profession as a whole.

Applicants for any professional post should divulge frankly and in confidence all information relevant to the consideration of their applications, and if appointed should recognize that museum work is normally regarded as a full-time vocation. Even where the terms of employment do not prohibit outside employment or business interests, the Director and other senior staff should not undertake other paid employment or accept outside commissions without the express consent of the governing body of the museum.

In tendering resignations from their posts, members of the professional staff, and above all the Director, should consider carefully the needs of the museum at the time. A professional person, having recently accepted appointment, should consider seriously their professional commitment to their present post before applying for a new post elsewhere.

5.3 Private interests

While every member of any profession is entitled to a measure of personal independence, consistent with professional and staff responsibilities, in the eyes of the public no private business or professional interest of a member of the museum profession can be wholly separated from that of the professional's institution or other official affiliation, despite disclaimers that may be offered. Any museum-related activity by the individual may reflect on the institution or be attributed to it. The professional must be concerned not only with the true personal motivations and interests, but also with the way in which such actions might be constructed by the outside observer. Museum employees and others in a close relationship with them must not accept gifts, favours, loans or other dispensations or things of value that may be offered to them in connection with their duties for the museum (see also para. 8.4 below).

6. PERSONAL RESPONSIBILITY TO THE COLLECTIONS

6.1 Acquisitions to museum collections

The Director and professional staff should take all possible steps to ensure that a written collecting policy is adopted by the governing body of the museum, and is thereafter reviewed and revised as appropriate at regular intervals. This policy, as formally adopted and revised by the governing body, should form the basis of all professional decisions and recommendations in relation to acquisitions.

Negotiations concerning the acquisition of museum items from members of the general public must be conducted with scrupulous fairness to the seller or donor. No object should be deliberately or misleadingly identified or valued, to the benefit of the museum and to the detriment of the donor, owner or previous owners, in order to acquire it for the museum collections nor should be taken nor retained on loan with the deliberate intention of improperly procuring it for the collections.

6.2 Care of collections

It is an important professional responsibility to ensure that all items accepted temporarily or permanently by the museum are properly and fully documented to facilitate provenance, identification, condition and treatment. All objects accepted by the museum should be properly conserved, protected, and maintained.

Careful attention should be paid to the means of ensuring the best possible security as a protection against theft in display, working or storage areas, against accidental damage when handling objects, and against damage or theft in transit. Where it is the national or local policy to use commercial insurance arrangements, the staff should ensure that the insurance cover is adequate, especially for objects in transit and loan items, or other objects, which are not owned by the museum but which are its current responsibility.

Members of the museum profession should not delegate important curatorial, conservation, or other professional responsibilities to persons who lack the appropriate knowledge and skill, or who are inadequately supervised, in the case of trainees or approved volunteers, where such persons are allowed to assist in the care of the collections. There is also a clear duty to consult professional colleagues within or outside the museum if at any time the expertise available in a particular museum or department is insufficient to ensure the welfare of items in the collections under its care.

6.3 Conservations and restoration of collections

One of the essential ethical obligations of each member of the museum profession is to ensure the proper care and conservation of both existing and newly acquired collections and individual items for which the member of the profession and the employing institutions are responsible, and to ensure that as far as is reasonable the collections are passed on to future generations in as good and safe a condition as practicable having regard to current knowledge and resources.

In attempting to achieve this high ideal, special attention should be paid to the growing body of knowledge about preventative conservation methods and techniques, including the provision of suitable environmental protection against the known natural or artificial causes of deterioration of museum specimens and works of art.

There are often difficult decisions to be made in relation to the degree of replacement or restoration of lost or damaged parts of a specimen or work of art that may be ethically acceptable in particular circumstances. Such decisions call for proper co-operation between all with a specialized responsibility for the object, including both the curator and the conservator or restorer, and should not be decided unilaterally by one or the other acting alone.

The ethical issues involved in conservation and restoration work of many kinds are a major study in themselves, and those with special responsibilities in this area, whether as director, curator, conservator or restorer, have an important responsibility to ensure that they are familiar with these ethical issues, and with appropriate professional opinion, as expressed in some detailed ethical statements and codes produced by the conservator/restorer professional bodies.[1]

6.4 Documentation of collections

The proper recording and documentation of both new acquisitions and existing collections in accordance with appropriate standards and the internal rules and conventions of the museum is a most important professional responsibility. It is particularly important that such documentation should include details of the source of each object and the conditions of acceptance of it by the museum. In addition specimen data should be kept in a secure environment and be supported by adequate systems providing easy retrieval of the data by both the staff and by other bona fide users.

6.5 De-accessioning and disposals from the collections

No item from the collections of a museum should be disposed of except in accordance with the ethical principles summarized in the Institutional Ethics section of this *Code*, paras 4.1 to 4.4 above, and the detailed rules and procedures applying in the museum in question.

6.6 Welfare of live animals

Where museums and related institutions maintain for exhibition or research purposes live populations of animals, the health and well-being of any such creatures must be a foremost ethical consideration. It is essential that a veterinary surgeon be available for advice and for regular inspection of the animals and their living conditions. The museum should prepare a safety code for the protection of staff and visitors which has been approved by an expert in the veterinary field, and all staff must follow it in detail.

6.7 Human remains and material of ritual significance

Where a museum maintains and/or is developing collections of human remains and sacred objects these should be securely housed and carefully maintained as archival collections in scholarly institutions, and should always be available to qualified researchers and educators, but not to the morbidly curious. Research on such objects and their housing and care must be accomplished in a manner acceptable not only to fellow professionals but to those of various beliefs, including in particular members of the community, ethnic or religious groups concerned. Although it is occasionally necessary to use human remains and other sensitive material in interpretative exhibits, this must be done with tact and with respect for the feelings for human dignity held by all peoples.

6.8 Private collections

The acquiring, collecting and owning of objects of a kind collected by a museum by a member of the museum profession for a personal collection may not in itself be unethical, and may be regarded as a valuable way of enhancing professional knowledge and judgement. However, serious dangers are implicit when members of the profession collect for themselves privately objects similar to those which they and others collect for their museums. In particular, no member of the museum profession should compete with their institution either in the acquisition of objects or in any personal collecting activity. Extreme care must be taken to ensure that no conflict of interest arises.

In some countries and many individual museums, members of the museum profession are not permitted to have private collections of any kind, and such rules must be respected. Even where there are no such restrictions, on appointment, a member of the museum profession with a private collection should provide the governing body with a description of it, and a statement of the collecting policy being pursued, and any consequent agreement between the curator and the governing body concerning the private collection must be scrupulously kept. (See also para. 8.4 below.)

7 PERSONAL RESPONSIBILITY TO THE PUBLIC

7.1 Upholding professional standards

In the interests of the public as well as the profession, members of the museum profession should observe accepted standards and laws, uphold the dignity and honour of their profession and accept its self-imposed disciplines. They should do their part to safeguard the public against illegal or unethical professional conduct, and should use appropriate opportunities to inform and educate the public in the aims, purposes and aspirations of the profession in order to develop a better public understanding of the purposes and responsibilities of museums and of the profession.

7.2 Relations with the general public

Members of the museum profession should deal with the public efficiently and courteously at all times, and should in particular deal promptly with all correspondence and enquiries. Subject to the requirements of confidentiality in a particular case, they should share their expertise in all professional fields in dealing with enquiries, subject to due acknowledgement, from both the general public and specialist enquirers, allowing bona fide researchers properly controlled but, so far as possible, full access to any material or documentation in their care, even when this is the subject of personal research or special field of interest.

7.3 Confidentiality

Members of the museum profession must protect all confidential information relating to the source of material owned by or loaned to the museum, as well as information concerning the security arrangements of the museum, or the security arrangements of private collections or any place visited in the course of official duties. Confidentiality must also be respected in relation to any item brought to the museum for identification and, without specific authority from the owner, information on such an item should not be passed to another museum, to a dealer, or to any other person (subject to any legal obligation to assist the police or other proper authorities in investigating possible stolen or illicitly acquired or transferred property).

There is a special responsibility to respect the personal confidences contained in oral history or other personal material. Investigators using recording devices such as cameras or tape recorders or the technique of oral interviewing should take special care to protect their data, and persons investigated, photographed or interviewed should have the right to remain anonymous if they so choose. This right should be respected where it has been specifically promised. Where there is no clear understanding to the contrary, the primary responsibility of the investigator is to ensure that no information is revealed that might harm the informant or his or her community. Subjects under study should understand the capacities of cameras, tape recorders and other machines used, and should be free to accept or reject their use.

8 PERSONAL RESPONSIBILITY TO COLLEAGUES AND THE PROFESSION

8.1 Professional relationships

Relationships between members of the museum profession should always be courteous, both in public and private. Differences of opinion should not be expressed in a personalized fashion. Notwithstanding this general rule, members of the profession may properly object to proposals or practices which may have a damaging effect on a museum or museums, or the profession.

8.2 Professional co-operation

Members of the museum profession have an obligation, subject to due acknowledgement, to share their knowledge and experience with their colleagues and with scholars and students in relevant fields. They should show their appreciation and respect to those from whom they have learned and should present without thought of personal gain such advancements in techniques and experience which may be of benefit to others.

The training of personnel in the specialized activities involved in museum work is of great importance in the development of the profession and all should accept responsibility, where appropriate, in the training of colleagues. Members of the profession who in their official appointment have under their direction junior staff, trainees, students and assistants undertaking formal or informal professional training, should give these the benefit of their experience and knowledge, and should also treat them with the consideration and respect customary among members of the profession.

Members of the profession form working relationships in the course of their duties with numerous other people, both professional and otherwise, within and outside the museum in which they are employed. They are expected to conduct these relationships with courtesy and fair-mindedness and to render their professional services to others efficiently and at a high standard.

8.3 Dealing

No member of the museum profession should participate in any dealing (buying or selling for profit), in objects similar or related to the objects collected by the employing museum. Dealing by museum employees at any level of responsibility in objects that are collected by any other museum can also present serious problems even if there is no risk of direct conflict with the employing museum, and should be permitted only if, after all disclosure and review by the governing body of the employing museum or designated senior officer, explicit permission is granted, with or without conditions.

Article 14 of the ICOM *Statutes* provides that in no circumstance shall individual or institutional membership be accorded to anyone who, for reasons of commercial profit, buys or sells cultural property.

8.4 Other potential conflicts of interest

Generally, members of the museum profession should refrain from all acts or activities which may be construed as a conflict of interest. Museum professionals by virtue of their knowledge, experience and contacts are frequently offered opportunities, such as advisory and consultancy services, teaching, writing and broadcasting opportunities, or requests for valuations, in a personal capacity. Even where the national law and the individual's conditions of employment permit such activities, these may appear in the eyes of colleagues, the employing authority, or the general public, to create a conflict of interest. In such situations all legal and employment contract conditions must be scrupulously followed, and in the event of any potential conflict arising or being suggested, the matter should be reported immediately to an appropriate superior officer or the museum governing body, and steps must be taken to eliminate the potential conflict of interest.

Even where the conditions of employment permit any kind of outside activity, and there appears to be no risk of any conflict of interest, great care should be taken to ensure that such outside interests do not interfere in any way with the proper discharge of official duties and responsibilities.

8.5 Authentication, valuation and illicit material

Members of the museum profession are encouraged to share their professional knowledge and expertise with both professional colleagues and the general public (see para. 7.2 above).

However, written certificates of authenticity or valuation (appraisals) should not be given, and opinions on the monetary value of objects should only be given on official request from other museums or competent legal, governmental or other responsible public authorities.

Members of the museum profession should not identify or otherwise authenticate objects where they have reason to believe or suspect that these have been illegally or illicitly acquired, transferred, imported or exported.

They should recognize that it is highly unethical for museums or the museum profession to support either directly or indirectly the illicit trade in cultural or natural objects (see para. 3.2 above), and under no circumstances should they act in a way that could be regarded as benefiting such illicit trade in any way, directly or indirectly. Where there is reason to believe or suspect illicit or illegal transfer, import or export, the competent authorities should be notified.

8.6 Unprofessional conduct

Every member of the museum profession should be conversant with both any national or local laws, and any conditions of employment, concerning corrupt practices, and should at all times avoid situations which could rightly or wrongly be construed as corrupt or improper conduct of any kind. In particular no museum official should accept any gift, hospitality, or any form of reward from any dealer, auctioneer or other person as an improper inducement in respect of the purchase or disposal of museum items.

Also, in order to avoid any suspicion of corruption, a museum professional should not recommend any particular dealer, auctioneer or other person to a member of the public, nor should the official accept any 'special price' or discount for personal purchases from any dealer with whom either the professional or employing museum has a professional relationship.

NOTE

1 'The conservator–restorer: a definition of the profession', *ICOM News* 39(1), 1986: 5–6.

39

Code of conduct for museum professionals
Museums Association

INTRODUCTION

1.1 This Code is concerned with the ethical conduct of Museum Professionals, who are defined as persons working in museums and art galleries, or in organizations directly related to them on a regular basis, whether paid or unpaid, and whether full- or part-time, but whose status is recognized by the institution's governing body.

1.2 All persons employed in a museum in a professional capacity have a duty of care to the collections and to the provision of services to the public. This Code, therefore, includes not only curators, collection managers and conservators who have the primary responsibility for collections, but also all others who are involved in the work of the museum, and who may have their own professional bodies and codes of practice.

1.3 It is essential that all those working in museums should have a proper understanding of the principles involved, and the code is therefore to be interpreted in the light of individual duties, but having regard always to the best interests of the museum and the museum service as a whole.

1.4 The duty of trusteeship is vested in the governing body of the museum. Museum professionals are in a contractual relationship to the governing body whatever the capacity in which they are working for it.

1.5 The Association urges specialist groups to produce and regularly update guidelines for their members on the best current practice in their specialist areas, and which may be endorsed by the Association.

1.6 This Code assumes that museum professionals will ensure that their activities accord with at least the minimum standards set out in *Guidelines for a Registration Scheme for Museums in the United Kingdom* (Museums and Galleries Commission), their Guidelines for Specialist Collections and that they comply with the best national and international practice.

1.7 This Code further assumes that museum professionals will undertake their duties and conduct their professional relationships in accordance with the principles of equal opportunities and other policies adopted by the Museums Association.

2 GENERAL MANAGEMENT PRINCIPLES

2.1 **Rule** Museum professionals must manage resources responsibly to achieve the highest quality of care and service. This will include advising on the formulation of objectives, and then striving to achieve targets. These policies and targets should be regularly reviewed and revised by the governing body, and should always be consistent with the *Code of Practice for Museum Authorities*.

2.2 **Rule** Museum professionals must recognize that the success of the museum depends upon a variety of skills, and must be prepared to work together with colleagues, volunteers and outside specialists to achieve this end.

Guideline For example, the planning of displays will be most effective if the various aspects, such as conservation, accessibility and education are taken into account in the planning stage. There is also a valuable sense of corporate achievement.

2.3 **Rule** Museum professionals should be prepared to participate in the evaluation of their work and to take the results into account in future plans.

Guideline Effective communication is a two-way process. Only by encouraging and analysing feedback from the public which the museum exists to serve, can the success of services be evaluated. Consideration should also be given to quality as well as to popular response.

2.4 **Rule** Museum professionals who are responsible for other staff must ensure that opportunities for training are provided for staff development, and should advise the governing body of the need for such training.

2.5 **Rule** Museum professionals must be aware of, and comply with, relevant law which affects their work and conditions of service. They must ensure that it is obeyed and that, where appropriate, their governing bodies are apprised of their obligations under the law.

3 MANAGEMENT AND CARE OF COLLECTIONS

3.1 **Rule** Museum professionals must care for the museum's existing collections and, where relevant, acquire material for their development in accordance with a properly researched, approved, and regularly updated collection management policy.

Guideline The collections are the very core of a museum's role and existence. The integrity and development of the collections are therefore prime responsibilities of the museum professional.

In reviewing the collection management policy museum professionals should ensure that the following factors are taken into account: the role of the museum in relation to the public it serves; the nature, condition and quality of the existing collections: the nature, purpose and use of the material it seeks to preserve and interpret; the resources available for the proper long-term management of that material, including conservation, documentation and access; and the inter-relationship of the museum with other museums by virtue of geographical location or subject specialism.

An acquisition policy should, where appropriate, take into account the need for handling and loan service material. Such material may form part of the core collections of the museum or may be managed as a separate educational resource. Careful judgement must be exercised in this respect, since material managed in a separate handling or loan collection may be put to different uses and may not necessarily be preserved indefinitely.

Where the museum is involved in fieldwork, it may not be unethical for surplus material to be collected in excess of the museum's requirements, but, such material should only be collected with due regard to the conservation requirements in that subject area, and with the intention of transferring the excess material to appropriate institutions.

When a major legacy or a mixed lot at auction might contain material inconsistent with the collection management policy, loans or transfers to other museums should be given priority.

3.2 **Rule** Museum professionals must take every practicable step fully to protect all the items in their care so as to minimize physical deterioration, whether on display, in store, in transit, used in handling or loan collections subject to research or conservation, or on loan to or from the museum.

Guideline Museum professionals must be aware of the actions needed for the proper care, and conservation of objects. Curatorial and conservation staff have a corporate responsibility for treatment methods, records, and the nature and extent of restorations.

3.3 **Rule** Museum professionals must establish, maintain and regularly revise, in consultation with the appropriate specialists, safeguards against fire, theft, flood and other hazards, and procedures to secure the collections in emergency. They must apprise the governing body of the recommendations made and ensure that all safeguards and procedures subsequently adopted are enforced.

Guideline The dangers of fire and theft are easily recognized but precautions against flood are frequently overlooked. Consideration should also be given to making provision for a major crisis such as a crashed airliner or civil disorder, so that staff are properly conversant with what is expected of them. Every effort should be made to protect the collections but in no circumstances should the lives of individuals be put at risk.

Careless or deliberate disclosure of information regarding safeguards against theft, or details of transportation can also put not only objects but persons at risk.

3.4 **Rule** Museum professionals must ensure that all objects within their care are recorded to conform with the *Guidelines for a Registration Scheme.*

Guideline Museum professionals are accountable for all the objects in their charge and proper documentation is essential for audit as well as management purposes. The scientific or cultural value of any object is in direct proportion to the data associated with it, and hence a secure link between the two is of fundamental importance.

3.5 **Rule** Museum professionals must uphold the principles that there is always a strong presumption against the disposal of objects to which a museum has assumed formal title.

Guideline Any form of disposal, whether by donation, exchange, sale or destruction should only be recommended to a governing body after appropriate curatorial specialist, and, if necessary, legal advice has been taken.

Guidance on the disposal of collections is contained in *Guidelines for a Registration Scheme.* Subject to legal considerations, the long-term loan of objects to other museums may be a satisfactory way of dealing with items which are under consideration for disposal. The recipient museum professional must take care that the provisions of such loan or transfer of material between museums are in accordance with the *Guidelines* and any existing conditions.

The best means of disposal is by transfer to another registered museum, since there is the presumption that museum collections are held for the public benefit. This may be achieved by formal transfer of ownership, or, if that is not legally possible or undesirable for other reasons, then by loan for a finite but renewable term. Formal transfer of ownership to another museum should be achieved preferably by exchange or gift, or failing that, by private treaty sale. Disposal to non-museum bodies, commercial concerns or individuals by sale or other means should be considered only as a line of last resort. Where a museum proposes to dispose of objects in contravention of the *Guidelines* it would be unethical for other museums to encourage such disposal.

3.6 **Rule** Museum professionals must not delegate specialist functions relating to care of collections without adequate professional supervision.

Guideline In particular, acquisition, documentation, conservation and disposal procedures must be under the direct supervision of a museum professional suitably qualified to undertake such work.

3.7 **Rule** Museum professionals must not treat the collections as personal property or assume exclusive rights of research or publication.

Guideline For security or other reasons, access to certain items may occasionally need to be restricted, but such circumstances should be regarded as exceptional and museum professionals should make every effort to overcome them.

3.8 **Rule** Research undertaken by museum professionals as part of their prescribed duties must relate to the collections, functions or agreed research programme of their institution.

Guideline Museum professionals, having direct access to the collections for which they are responsible, are best placed to study them in depth, and thus should be prepared to take advantage of the privilege and opportunity to make a positive contribution to knowledge in their chosen discipline.

The balance struck between research and other responsibilities should accord with the policy and objectives of the museum. Unpublished results of a museum professional's research or research notes should be protected from plagiarism during the reasonable term of completion, but in principle the results should be publically available wherever possible.

3.9 **Rule** Museum professionals have a duty to seek appropriate expert advice when personal expertise or that of immediate colleagues is insufficient.

Guideline Few museums are likely to contain all the expertise necessary for complete identification or conservation of every object in their collections or for decisions regarding such matters as security. Relevant advice should be sought from the Museums and Galleries Commission, other national or regional institutions, Area Museum Councils, universities, specialist groups or individual specialists.

3.10 **Rule** Where a museum maintains live animals the museum professional responsible must ensure their health and well-being in accordance with the appropriate legislation and best practice. The breeding of certain animals should be in accordance with the regulations laid down by relevant breed societies.

It is essential that a veterinary surgeon be available for advice and for regular inspection of the animals and their living conditions.

The museum must prepare and follow in detail a safety code which has been approved by an expert in the veterinary field for the protection of staff and visitors.

Guideline The introduction of living animals into the museum environment extends the range of curatorial responsibility considerably, and museum professionals must ensure that all the necessary provisions for animal welfare are made. High standards of hygiene must be maintained as a precaution against infestation and disease for both humans and livestock. Stress can be caused to animals through the behaviour of visitors, and the barriers between one and the other must be effective and secure.

Museum professionals must also be prepared to care for stock continuously, even when the museum is closed.

3.11   **Rule** Where a museum or building housing a museum is isolated as a result of industrial action, the care and maintenance of the collections and/or livestock remains the primary ethical responsibility of museum professionals.

Guideline When an industrial dispute affects the conduct of a museum professional's duties, provision must be made for the safeguarding of the collections. Should the labour of an individual be withdrawn, provision should be made as if the museum were being closed in the normal way. Any maintenance work needed to prevent damage or harm to the collections should not be interrupted.

Museum professionals should inform the relevant trade unions of the nature of their responsibilities and seek agreement with them in advance of any proposed industrial action.

3.12   **Rule** Museum professionals must not evaluate, accept on loan or acquire by any means an object which there is good reason to believe was acquired by its owner in contravention of the *UNESCO Convention on the Means of Prohibiting and Preventing the Illicit Import, Export and Transfer of Ownership of Cultural Property 1970*, or by any other illegal means. This Convention has not yet been ratified by the British government but is supported by the Museums Association.

Guideline When considering acquiring imported objects, museum professionals should take reasonable steps to ascertain the relevant laws, regulations and procedures of the country or countries of origin.

4   MANAGEMENT AND CARE OF ENVIRONMENTAL RECORDS AND ACCESSIBILITY OF DATA

4.1   **Rule** Museum professionals must ensure as far as possible the accuracy of museum records relating to the collections and the local historic, cultural or natural environment and provide reasonable access to such records.

Guideline In principle museum records are maintained for public use but museum professionals should exercise caution where there is good reason to believe that unrestricted access to information might lead to the abuse of significant sites or sensitive material.

Confidentiality in relation to the identity of lenders, donors, etc. must also be maintained where it is demanded.

4.2 **Rule** Museum professionals must be aware of the implications of becoming involved, in their professional capacity, with any public pressure group or lobbying faction, since this might call into question their professional objectivity.

If an issue arises which in their professional judgement would have a detrimental effect on a sensitive site, they should make their reservations known in writing to the appropriate persons or organizations.

5 RESPONSIBILITIES AND SERVICES TO THE PUBLIC

5.1 **Rule** Museum professionals must uphold the fundamental principle of museums that the collections are maintained for the public benefit, and the implication of non-discriminatory public access which this carries.

Guideline Museum professionals should ensure that equal opportunity of access is afforded to all and be mindful of the principles of equal opportunities in all their undertakings. They should ensure that, wherever possible, the collections are made available to those with disabilities, and that exhibitions and activities are designed with a variety of disabilities in mind.

The issues of equal opportunity relate to the particular access needs of a wide range of potential user groups. Through consultation with; and participation by user and community groups, museum professionals should assess their requirements and formulate a policy for the governing body to develop services to meet these needs.

5.2 **Rule** Museum professionals must ensure that objects on public display, with all forms of accompanying information should present a clear, accurate and objective exposition, and should never deliberately mislead.

Guideline Interpretation in its broadest sense is one of the core activities of a museum. This principle applies also to books and information published or otherwise disseminated by the museum, and to any educational activities, where the quality, objectivity and accuracy of information should be ensured.

Great sensitivity should be exercised when presenting contemporary cultural issues or social history. Museum professionals must clearly understand the point where professional judgement ends and personal bias begins.

From time to time, however, exhibitions will be set up by the museum or received on loan which develop a particular point of view. In such cases it is a museum professional's duty to ensure that this is made clear. The same conditions apply to educational programmes, publications and interviews.

5.3 **Rule** Museum professionals should be aware of the positive contribution that a museum shop, cafe, restaurant or other trading activities can make to the revenue generation and the interpretive role of the museum.

Guideline A careful balance must be maintained between the needs of revenue generation and the provision of services to visitors; the museum professional must be continually concerned that only goods of quality and reliable publications are offered for sale.

Whether or not trading activities are contracted to a commercial concern, museum professionals should ensure that the museum has the right to recommend stock or to veto merchandise on ethical grounds and that this right forms part of any formal contract.

There should be a strong presumption against the sale of historic artefacts or natural objects, as this may be confused in the public mind with material in the collections, and with the purpose of the museum itself.

All replicas of museum objects should be clearly marked in a permanent manner.

In the case of a cafe or restaurant museum professionals must ensure that their design and location preclude the generation of atmospheric conditions which might affect the conservation of the collections and avoid any conflict of alternative use.

5.4 **Rule** Museum professionals must ensure that when museum premises are let to non-museum concerns the collections are not put at risk. The same applies to loans of objects to non-museum premises.

5.5 **Rule** Museum professionals must ensure that, where special sales are held to raise funds for the museum it is made clear to the public that the sale does not include items from the museum's collections.

Guideline In general it is not advisable to hold such sales on museum premises in order to avoid public misinterpretation. Museum professionals should try to avoid being personally involved in the sale of objects.

5.6 **Rule** The museum professional must conduct the acquisition of museum items from the public with scrupulous fairness to the seller or donor.

Guideline In the case of a dealer or auction house, the normal conditions apply. However, in the case of members of the general public it would be improper to take advantage of their unawareness of the nature or value of the objects offered. Where an object is of considerable financial value the museum professional should advise the owner that the opinion of an independent qualified valuer should be sought before a price is agreed. Where a proposed gift is of considerable value the museum professional should also inform the owner should they not previously be aware of the fact.

Where it is the intention that an object offered as a gift is to be used primarily for educational activities such as handling or loan collections or for purposes of demonstration, this should be made clear to the donor at the time of acquisition.

Care should be exercised before donations are accepted from minors. In all cases the parents or legal guardians of the donor should be asked for their consent to the gift after the museum professional has explained to them the significance of the proposed donation. Tactful handling of these situations is essential, the young person should not be discouraged, but equally the legal title must be clear.

5.7 **Rule** Where an identification service is provided by the museum the relevant museum professional has a duty to identify an object submitted by a member of the public. Significant facts must not be witheld or deliberately misleading information given. In the event of the professional having insufficient specialized knowledge, this should also be stated.

Guideline The provision of an identification service can be a fruitful source of acquisitions and afford useful contributions to knowledge, as well as developing the museum's image in the local community.

Museum professionals should be objective about their own capabilities, and seek advice when needed.

5.8 **Rule** A museum professional must not reveal information imparted in confidence during the course of professional duty.

5.9 **Rule** Museum professionals must be aware that the curation of human remains and material of religious significance can be a sensitive issue. A number of interested parties may claim rights over such material. These include actual and cultural descendants, legal owners and the worldwide scientific community. Museum professionals should inform themselves of the concerns of these interest groups when considering the management and display of such sensitive material.

Guideline Despite the general obligations of access to collections (5.1), it may be appropriate to restrict access to certain specified sacred items where unrestricted access may cause offence to actual or cultural descendants. This may include the provision of separate storage facilities.

There have been a number of guidelines produced for the curation of human remains and sacred material, including *Museum Ethnographers Group Professional Guidelines Concerning the Storage, Display, Interpretation and Return of Human Remains in Ethnographical Collections in the United Kingdom Museums* (1991) and *The Vermillion Accord: Human Remains*; World Archaeological Congress (World Archaeological Bulletin, November 1989) and the ICOM Code of Professional Ethics section 6.7.

Governing bodies and museum professionals should therefore consider all ethical and legal implications before continuing the active or passive acquisition of human remains. Requests concerning the appropriate return of particular human remains must be resolved by individual museums on a case by case basis. This will involve the consideration of ownership, cultural significance, the scientific, educational and historical importance of the material, the cultural and religious values of the interested individuals or groups, the strength of their relationship to the remains in question, and the long-term fate of the items under consideration.

All requests should be accorded respect and treated sensitively.

5.10 **Rule** Museum professionals must ensure that in giving professional advice on any matter, such advice is consistent with good practice and given impartially.

5.11 **Rule** Museum professionals may not delegate responsibility for services to the public to persons who lack appropriate knowledge or skill.

Guideline A museum professional must maintain control of essential public service functions. In particular the design of educational programmes and planning of educational materials and the training of museum teachers, guides, interpreters or volunteers must be undertaken by a museum professional or under their supervision.

6 PERSONAL ACTIVITIES

6.1 **Rule** Museum professionals must at all times carry out their duties to the best of their abilities and with due regard to codes of practice in their discipline.

6.2 **Rule** Museum professionals must not collect for themselves in competition with their employing institution. On appointment, museum professionals with private collections must inform the governing body of their scope and collecting policy. Any agreement between them must be scrupulously kept thereafter.

Guideline It is not unethical for museum professionals to own or collect objects and it is recognized that this can enhance professional knowledge. However, extreme care must be taken to ensure that no conflict arises with the collecting policy of the employing institution. Indeed, museum professionals are advised to eschew personal collections, mindful that the best opportunity for an object to be preserved for the public is in a museum.

Staff members who collect for museums on expeditions should only engage in private collecting if:

a The collecting is incidental and the time involved is reasonable.
b Pertinent conditions and laws are observed.

Museum professionals occupy a position of trust; this implies that they will discharge their responsibilities always giving precedence to the interests of the institution over individual interests.

Museum professionals should also be aware that they are part of a wider community concerned with the preservation of the national and international heritage, and that their actions affect the reputation of their profession worldwide.

6.3 **Rule** Museum professionals may on no account solicit a personal gift, loan or bequest from a member of the public.

6.4 **Rule** Museum professionals must neither solicit nor accept a gift of significant value either directly or indirectly from an artist, craftsperson or other originator of artefacts or their agent with whom the professional has come in contact through any kind of collaboration, either actual or planned involving the institution.

Guideline The same principle identified under 6.2 applies. It is not uncommon for the organizer of an exhibition to be offered a work as a personal token of gratitude by the originator. Careful judgement must be exercised in dealing with such a situation so as to ensure that the act is not misinterpreted. The safest course, therefore, is to accept the gift on behalf of the institution, thereby putting the integrity of the individual beyond question.

6.5 **Rule** Museum professionals must not deal (buy or sell for profit) in material covered by the institution's collecting policy.

Guideline The professional should also be aware that such dealing might affect other institutions, and it is thus best avoided altogether.

6.6 **Rule** Museum professionals must not undertake authentication and identification for personal gain outside the course of normal duties, with the intention of establishing the market value of an object, without the consent of the governing body. It should then be undertaken with the highest standards of academic objectivity.

Guideline In some countries professional rules totally prohibit museum professionals from such activities. In order to maintain an unimpeachable image the practice is best avoided. Specifically, a museum professional should never become involved in an identification or authentication when there is a possibility that the object might be sold to any museum or fund with which that professional is associated.

A museum professional could face legal proceedings for negligence if advice is given which proved to be erroneous.

6.7 **Rule** Museum professionals should refrain from putting a market value on objects for commercial purposes.

Guideline Museum professionals are not normally qualified to undertake valuations and must therefore be aware of any implications of using employment for personal gain. This does not include the valuation of the museum's collection for insurance purposes.

6.8 **Rule** Museum professionals must obtain the consent of the governing body before undertaking private work from which regular additional remuneration may accrue, such as publication, lecturing, authorship, consultancy and contributions to the media.

Guideline This matter is usually covered by contracts of employment and such activities should not be allowed to take precedence over, or conflict with, official duties and responsibilities.

7 RELATIONSHIP WITH COMMERCIAL ORGANIZATIONS

7.1 **Rule** Museum professionals should ensure that, as far as practicable, when working with other professionals, the relevant codes of practice are mutually respected.

Guideline Many commercial organizations operate to professional or trade codes of practice. Where appropriate the museum professional should obtain copies of such codes to ensure that proper practices are observed on both sides to their mutual benefit.

7.2 **Rule** A museum professional must never accept from a commercial organization any personal gift or favour which might subsequently be interpreted as an inducement to trade with that organization.

Guideline Paragraph 9882 of the *Civil Service Pay and Conditions of Service Code* offers a useful guide on this matter. 'The behaviour of officers as regards the acceptance of gifts, hospitality, etc., should be governed by the following general guidance. The conduct of a civil servant should not foster the suspicion of a conflict of interest. Officers should therefore always have in mind the need not to give the impression to any member of the public, or organization with whom they deal, or to their colleagues, that they may be influenced by any gift or consideration to show favour or disfavour to any person or organization whilst acting in an official capacity. An officer must not, either directly or indirectly, accept any gift, reward or benefit from any member of the public or organization with whom he/she has been brought in contact by reason of his/her official duties. The only exceptions to this rule are as follows:

a   Isolated gifts of a trivial character or inexpensive seasonal gifts (such as calendars).

b   Conventional hospitality, provided it is normal and reasonable in the circumstances. In considering what is normal and reasonable, regard should be had:

i   to the degree of narrow personal involvement. There is, of course, no objection to the acceptance of, for example, an invitation to an annual dinner of a large trade association or similar body with which a department is in much day-to-day contact; or of working lunches (provided the frequency is reasonable) in the course of official visits;

ii   to the usual conventions of returning hospitality, at least to some degree. The isolated acceptance of, for example, a meal would not offend the rule, whereas acceptance of frequent or regular invitations to lunch or dinner on a wholly one-sided basis even on a small scale might give rise to a breach of the standard required.

When in doubt, the museum professional should consult a senior officer or the chair of the governing body, and the decision should be recorded.

7.3   **Rule**   A museum professional must ensure that the standards and objectives of the museum are not compromised in any matter of commercial sponsorship.

Guideline   Museum professionals should ensure that the precise terms of the sponsorship are agreed in writing before the project begins, in order to avoid any subsequent friction. Sponsors normally and rightly expect evidence of recognition for their assistance.

Museum professionals are also advised that in certain instances the products or activities of an intending sponsor may be open to popular criticism, and care should therefore be taken to ensure that the governing body is fully informed of the circumstances and its approval obtained.

7.4   **Rule**   A museum professional must ensure that information for the media, or publicity in any form is factually accurate and well presented, and presents the museum in the best possible light.

Guideline   Museum professionals and governing bodies should recognize that the media are trained to approach news from a personal standpoint. There is nothing wrong in communicating information in this way provided the rule is followed.

Ethical problems might arise if, for example, a museum professional was asked to take part in a discussion on a topical issue, and in such cases the approval of a senior officer or the governing body should be obtained in advance. The presence of museum staff can be of great advantage to the museum provided the opinions expressed are objectively presented.

8   RELATIONSHIP WITH PROFESSIONAL COLLEAGUES

8.1   **Rule**   A museum professional's relationship with professional colleagues should always be courteous, both in public and private. Differences of professional opinion can be robustly expressed but never in a gratuitously personalized fashion.

Guideline   Care must be taken to avoid discourtesy by word or gesture and the museum professional should also be aware that more subtle kinds of behaviour can cause as much, or more offence. All museum professionals in positions of

303

authority carry a concomitant responsibility to pay due respect to the feelings of others, especially to junior staff, who should be included in discussions relating to their roles in the museum wherever practicable, and whose problems should be addressed with patience and impartiality.

Museum professionals should take particular care to avoid any dispute coming to public notice so as to bring discredit on the persons concerned and the profession at large. Where a point of professional principle cannot be resolved internally, the arbitration of the President of the Museums Association or a nominee should be sought.

8.2 **Rule** Museum professionals, especially when working outside their own area of expertise, must consult other professionals either within the museum or outside.

Guideline Personal considerations should never be allowed to inhibit proper collaboration. Museum professionals should always be open to consultation.

8.3 **Rule** Where acquisition policies, collecting areas or other activities overlap, the museum professionals concerned should draft mutually satisfactory agreements, which should then be submitted to respective governing bodies for approval. Where it is likely that there may be a difference of opinion over the acquisition of an object, museum professionals should make every effort to see that the matter is amicably resolved.

8.4 **Rule** Museum professionals must conduct working relationships with people within and outside the museum with courtesy and fair-mindedness, and render professional services to others of a high standard.

Part 7
Institutional standards

40

Setting standards for museums
Museums and Galleries Commission

Central features of museum provision in the 1980s and 1990s have been the setting of targets in key areas of provision and the measurement of performance. It is no longer good enough for museums just to be well run. They now have to be seen to be well run. As a result, in most forms of museums, performance measurement of one sort or another is common practice. In 1991, the Office of Arts and Libraries set out the performance indicators it wanted the national museums and galleries to use. In the same year, the Audit Commission completed its guide for the auditing of local authority museums. The private sector, although under no compulsion, have found it good business practice to use indicators to assess performance, and use those best suited to the priorities of their institution.

The Museums and Galleries Commission has done a great deal to generate an awareness of the standards museums could and should be achieving in key areas of their work. This paper summarizes their work in this regard.

The Museums and Galleries Commission (MGC) has been advising the government on museum affairs throughout the United Kingdom since 1931. Increasingly, this advisory role has extended to the provision of advice to museums and, in recent years, to the translation of expert advice into a range of published standards and guidelines. Standards development is now a key element of the MGC's remit from government and our other activities, such as grant-giving, are strongly geared to assisting museums to meet agreed standards.

WHY IS THERE A NEED FOR MUSEUM STANDARDS?

Museums in the UK are very diverse in their size and nature and they are run by a wide variety of different bodies: government; local authorities; universities; and charities. Apart from national museums, there is no statutory responsibility for museum provision. Without a formal infrastructure for museums the MGC considers it has a particular responsibility to ensure that advice on good practice is available at a national level and that all bodies concerned with museums are aware of this. Long experience has also made it clear that museums themselves require and value access to external standards when setting their own objectives.

Museums currently face many problems. All have been affected by the economic recession and some are struggling to survive. The forthcoming changes in the structure of local government are producing uncertainty. It is particularly important at this time that standards should be defined and made highly visible.

The existence of the Registration Scheme, which carries the MGC's minimum standards for museums, has already been invaluable in assisting museums facing serious financial cuts. More positively, our standards form the basis of advice which the MGC is providing on a wide range of topical issues.

WHAT STANDARDS?

Standards which touch in some way on the activity of museums are set by a wide range of bodies such as the Health and Safety Executive, the British Standards Institute, and the Audit Commission. The MGC sees itself as having special responsibility for setting standards for the core activities, such as collections management, which distinguish museums from other kinds of organizations. We also draw on those standards in related sectors, such as education, training and tourism, to provide guidance which is appropriate to museums.

MGC STANDARDS AND GUIDELINES

Below is a summary of the standards which the MGC has already published and those which we plan to publish over the next two years. Although some are titled 'Standards' and others 'Guidelines', they are all part of the same family of MGC standards.

Guidelines for a Registration Scheme for museums in the UK

The MGC's minimum standards for museums are outlined in these Guidelines first issued in 1988. By 1993 the great majority of museums has adopted these standards in the process of applying to be registered with the MGC. Registration provides general eligibility for funding available through the MGC and the ten Area Museum Councils. Revised guidelines for a second phase of the scheme, due to be implemented from 1995, will be published for consultation in the second half of 1993. It is envisaged that registration will continue to represent the minimum standards which all museums should achieve.

Standards in the museum care of collections

This is a series of publications outlining standards in the care of different classes of museum collection. They represent current professional views of best practice and, as such, we recognize that not all museums will be able to reach them immediately. However, they are standards which museums should aspire to and the MGC's grant schemes will help to promote them. Current and planned publications are *Standards in the Museum Care of*:

1 *Archaeological Collections*, published 1992.
2 *Biological Collections*, published 1993.
3 *Geological Collections*, due August 1993.
4 *Industrial and Social History Collections: larger objects and working exhibits*, due Spring 1994.
5 *Musical Instrument Collections*, due 1994.
6 *Photograph Collections*, due 1994.

7   *Costume and Textile Collections*, due 1995.
8   *Ethnographic Collections*, due 1995.

Other titles will be added in due course.

Environmental management guidelines

This comprehensive publication from the MGC's Conservation Unit will support the standards for the care of individual collections. It will reflect the greatly increased emphasis which is now placed on preventive conservation as an essential complement to remedial conservation. It will also offer museums detailed guidance on devising an environmental strategy to suit their particular needs and circumstances. Due for publication in autumn 1993.

Quality of service in museums and galleries: customer care in museums, guidelines on implementation 1992

These Guidelines expand upon *The National Tourist Board's Code of Practice for Visitor Attractions* by setting out ways in which museums can achieve quality of service. They are designed to help with the forward planning process and the setting of performance indicators.

Guidelines on disability for museums and galleries (jointly with the Museums Association) 1992

Starting from the premise that people with disabilities have the right to derive the same benefits from museums as others, these guidelines recommend the preparation of a disability policy and action plan. They provide guidance about the issues to be addressed and how disability policies and action plans should be implemented. During 1993 the MGC will publish a disability resource directory for museums which will provide useful information to supplement these Guidelines.

Standards for travelling exhibitions

These Standards are currently being developed by an expert group and will be published in March 1994 on the commonly agreed rules which should be followed by those generating exhibitions and those borrowing them. They will be complemented by more detailed guidance in a manual to be published by the Travelling Exhibitions Group.

Documentation

It is relevant in this context to mention the work of the Museum Documentation Association (MDA) which is funded by the MGC. The MDA published a data standard for museums in 1991. It is now taking the lead in developing national documentation standards covering both data and procedures for collection management. These will be published in Spring 1994. Further information is available from the Standards Manager at the MDA, Lincoln House, 347 Cherry Hinton Road, Cambridge, CBI 4DH. Telephone: 0223 242848.

Further information

For further information concerning the MGC's standards development programme please contact:

The Professional Services Section
Museums & Galleries Commission
16 Queen Anne's Gate, London SW1H 9AA.
Telephone: 071 233 4200.

For information about publications please contact the Information Unit at the same address.

41

Registration Scheme for museums and galleries in the United Kingdom. Second phase: Draft for Consultation

Museums and Galleries Commission

The system of registering all museums which had reached set criteria was brought in by the Museums and Galleries Commission (MGC) in 1988. It has had a significant impact on museum standards in the UK. It has lifted awareness of collection management and encouraged museums to upgrade the documentation of their collections. It has also helped many museums in the private sector to revise their constitutions, so that their collections and long-term well-being are better secured. Of especial note, the scheme has had a marked influence on the way museums perceive themselves, and has brought both pride in accomplishment and an enhanced sense of professional identity.

The scheme is now entering its second phase and the document that follows is the discussion paper from which the future scheme will be developed. It extends the minimum standards set out in the first scheme.

INTRODUCTION

All concerned with museums and galleries agree that the museum Registration Scheme has been an outstanding success. More than that, it has been hailed as one of the most significant developments for UK museums in this century. It has assisted in raising standards in a number of key areas, such as the documentation of collections and access to professional curatorial advice; it has stimulated individual museums to assess how they are operating or to tackle long-standing problems, and it has encouraged greater co-operation and sharing of expertise between museums themselves. Between 1988 and 1993 over 1,500 museums had voluntarily applied to join the scheme and had demonstrated that they met the standards involved or were actively working towards them.

The requirements of registration

Registration is a minimum standards scheme, and addresses a number of fundamental questions which the public and funding authorities are right to ask of museums. The key requirements of registration are:

- Accordance with the Museums Association's definition of a museum or, if appropriate, the MGC's definition of a 'national' museum (see 1 and 2 below)

- An acceptable constitution (see Guidelines 1.0 below).
- A statement of purpose and key objectives (this is proposed as a new requirement from 1995: see Guidelines 2.0 below).
- Provision of an acceptable statement of collections management policy (see Guidelines 3.0 below).
- Provision of a range of public services and visitor facilities appropriate to the nature, scale and location of the museum (see Guidelines 4.0 below)
- Access to professional curatorial advice (see Guidelines 5.0 below).
- An acceptable financial basis, and compliance with all legal, planning and safety requirements (see Guidelines 6.0 and 7.0 below).

The benefits of registration are:

- **The opportunity for a museum to publicize itself as an organization which provides a basic range of services for the benefit of its visitors and other users.**

There are over 2,000 museums in the UK and they are enormously diverse in terms of their size, the nature of their collections, funding and organization. There are no statutory provisions, beyond those relating to the national museums, which determine how they should be established and operated. Through its wide acceptance museum registration now provides a recognized national minimum standard for museums, enabling them to demonstrate, whatever their size and nature, a shared ethical basis and a common framework of operation.

- **The fostering of confidence among potential providers of material for a museum's collections that a registered museum is, in principle, a suitable repository.**

All the museums on the MGC's Museums Register exist to provide a public benefit, and it is therefore important to disseminate the message to the general public, whether visitors, benefactors, or donors, that a Registered Museum has a long-term, public purpose, is a non-profit distributing organization, and has undertaken to manage and use its collections in a responsible manner. Now that the scheme is well established, the MGC is taking steps to promote it to the public in this way, at national and regional levels, and through publicity material available for use in individual museums.

- **Eligibility for MGC and Area Museum Council (AMC) grant-aid and subsidized services.**

On a practical level, the MGC's Museums Register determines basic eligibility for grant-aid and subsidized services provided by the MGC and AMCs, helping to ensure that the public funding which is available to assist museums in their development is used in an effective and responsible way.

- **The fostering of confidence among other funding agencies that a registered museum is, in principle, worthy of support.**

The scheme already has the acknowledged support of a wide range of other bodies and funding agencies. It now forms, for example, one of the Audit Commission's recommended criteria for auditing local authority museums services and for local authority support for independent museums. The MGC will continue to promote the Museums Register to funding agencies as a guide to institutions which are basically worthy of support.

THE SECOND PHASE OF REGISTRATION

Timetable

From the outset of the scheme in 1988 it was agreed that museums would periodically be asked to re-register with the MGC, both to provide updated information and to enable standards to be monitored. It was originally envisaged that museums would resubmit a full application at least every five years. That timetable has been modified in the light of local government reorganization and the re-registration programme is now likely to commence in 1995. In the interim we are seeking through consultation to establish how, if at all, the Guidelines should be amended or extended. We aim to publish the agreed Guidelines during 1994 so that museums will have plenty of time to familiarize themselves with the criteria and prepare to meet them. On this basis re-registration should be a simple process for most museums.

Registration remains a minimum standards scheme

We have determined that museum registration will remain a minimum standards scheme to enable it to continue to embrace museums of widely different scale and resources. This factor has been crucial to its success to date. As a complement to the Registration Scheme, the MGC is defining the higher standards to which museums should aspire through a range of publications on aspects of collections management and service to the public. This 'best practice' advice is promoted in a variety of ways, for example through the grant-making activity of the MGC and AMCs.

Proposed development of the scheme

In the second phase of registration we propose therefore that the *key requirements* should essentially remain the same as in the first phase. They are on the whole standards which it is possible to assess objectively. There are many important areas of museum work, particularly in the area of provision of service to the public, where it is more difficult to establish objective minimum standards of operation which can be applied to museums of all kinds. We nevertheless believe that there are two reasons why it is right to ask museums to provide more detailed information on these areas: first to enable the Registration Committee to assess whether the level of activity seems appropriate to the nature and scale of the institution concerned and to make recommendations accordingly, and second to encourage a more rounded assessment of their activities by museums themselves. These revised Guidelines are therefore more comprehensive than those published in 1988, and the accompanying application form contains a more detailed range of questions. We believe that many museums will be able to answer most of these questions by reference to existing forward plans or collections management plans, and we will encourage the submission of such plans in support of applications.

The importance of planning

Museums are not static institutions: they continue to develop their collections and to respond to growing or new audiences. The resources of time and money may not necessarily increase; they may even decline. In these circumstances, the maintenance of collections and effective public services will require particularly careful planning. Museums also operate in a changing world in which it is increasingly important that they demonstrate a clear sense of purpose and direction to funding authorities and organizations,

313

and to sponsors and benefactors. The best way to prepare to meet all these challenges is through a well-thought-out written plan which:

- Defines the museum's purpose.
- Outlines its present situation.
- Indicates what needs to be maintained, changed or developed.
- Considers how and when these objectives could be realized.
- Enables a museum to measure its achievements.
- Enables a museum to demonstrate its achievements.

The MGC strongly recommends that museums should have such plans. Some Area Museum Councils already make, and others are planning to make, the possession of forward plans and collections management plans a requirement for their grant-aid.

Forward plans are not here being proposed as mandatory for registration, because it is felt that some (particularly small) museums may not find it easy to respond to such a requirement within the timetable for applying for re-registration. It *is* proposed, however, that museums should be required to submit a statement of purpose and key aims and objectives. Moreover the questions on the application form have been framed to yield a body of basic planning information, which we hope will encourage and stimulate museums without forward plans to go on to produce one.

DEFINITIONS USED AND THE SCOPE OF THE SCHEME

1 Definition of a museum

1 The definition used is that adopted by the UK Museums Association in 1984 which is:

A museum is an institution which collects, documents, preserves, exhibits and interprets material evidence and associated information for the public benefit.

The following guidelines will apply when interpreting this definition for the purposes of the registration scheme.

a. *Institution* implies an establishment which has a formal governing instrument and a long-term purpose. Museums and collections privately owned by individuals are not eligible for registration (see also Guidelines 1.0 and 6.0 below).

b. *Collects* embraces all means of acquisition. It should also imply the museum's possession of, or intention to acquire, permanent collections in relation to its stated objectives (see also Guidelines 3.1 and 3.2 below).

c. *Documents* emphasizes the obligation to maintain records (see also Guidelines 3.3 below).

d. *Preserves* includes all aspects of conservation and security (see also Guidelines 3.4 below).

e. *Exhibits* confirms the expectation of visitors that they will be able to see at least a representative selection of objects in the collections. It should also imply that the museum opens to the public at appropriate times and for reasonable periods of time (see also Guidelines 4.0 below).

f. *Interprets* covers such diverse fields as display, education, research and publication (see also Guidelines 4.0 below).

g. *Material* indicates something that is tangible, while evidence indicates its authenticity as the 'real thing'.

h. *Associated information* represents the knowledge which prevents a museum object

314

being merely a curio and also includes all records relating to its past history, acquisition and subsequent usage.

i. *For the public benefit* is deliberately open-ended and is intended to reflect the current thinking, both within the museum profession and outside it, that museums are the servants of society. It also implies that a museum should not be a profit-distributing organization, i.e. it should not distribute profits to shareholders (see also Guidelines 6.0 below).

2 Definition of a 'national' museum

1 Some museums are 'national' by virtue of status conferred through legislation, and are directly funded by government. Other museums not so constituted or funded may choose to style themselves 'national' in order to reflect a pre-eminent role to which they aspire in the interpretation of a particular subject. It may seem an easy option for museums to adopt a 'national' title, and it is certainly an attractive choice in terms of marketing the institution, but it is less straightforward to fulfil this role properly in practice. *The MGC believes that the public has the right to expect more than minimum standards of a museum making a claim to be 'national'.*

2 To be eligible for registration, therefore, a museum wishing to use the word 'national' or equivalent in its title (see below for list of terms) should, as well as meeting all the requirements of the Registration Scheme, conform with the points listed below:

   a. The policy and practice of the museum should be to collect a range of objects of national importance and associated information in its particular fields, and these collections should be subject to appropriate standards of care.
   b. It should already have a substantial collection in relation to its stated objectives and the museum's display policy should reflect the full range of its collections.
   c. It should be able to provide professional and authoritative expertise and advice over its whole field to the public, to other museums, and to national and local government.
   d. It should provide study and research facilities for the public.
   e. It should offer visitor services of a quality appropriate to a museum purporting to provide a national facility.

3 The following names should be regarded as equivalent to 'national' and therefore subject to the above-mentioned criteria: International; World; Nation; Europe; European; United Kingdom; Great Britain; Britain; British; England; English; Scotland; Scottish; Wales; Welsh; Ulster; Northern Ireland; Northern Irish.

3 Institutions ineligible for independent registration

The following categories of institution will not normally be deemed eligible for registration unless they form part of a broadly based museum service which conforms with the registration guidelines:

- Science centres and planetaria.
- Natural and archaeological sites, and historical and industrial buildings and sites, not having associated museum collections.
- Institutions displaying live specimens, e.g. zoos, aquaria and botanical gardens.
- Educational loan services.
- Record offices and libraries.
- Venues for temporary exhibitions.

- Biological and environmental records centres.
- Archaeological sites and monuments record centres.
- Sound, film and photographic archives.

4 Organizations ineligible for museum registration but eligible for MGC and/or AMC funding

1 The following types of organization providing specialist services of repute for museums will be eligible for financial support from the MGC and/or AMCs notwithstanding their ineligibility for museum registration:

- District and county-wide, regional and nationwide museum advisory services.
- Reputable conservation services, which should normally be registered with MGC's Conservation Unit.
- Reputable museum-related training institutions.
- Reputable research establishments.

2 Record offices and libraries are eligible to receive grants from the V & A/MGC and PRISM Purchase Grant Funds, despite their ineligibility for museum registration.

THE GUIDELINES

1 Constitution

1.1 The following constitutions are deemed acceptable:

a. Those based on an Act of Parliament.
b. Those based on a Royal Charter.
c. Those based on Local Government Acts and forming the subject of a local authority resolution.
d. Those based on the formal decision of a University Council, Senate or Court.
e. Those based on an acceptable memorandum and articles of a company with charitable status limited by guarantee and with no share capital.
f. Those based on an acceptable deed of trust of a charitable trust.
g. Any constitution which is charitable, which meets the criteria set out in this document, including the non-distribution of profits, and which is acceptable to the MGC.

1.2 It may be that a museum's collections are owned by one body but managed by another body under contract, for example a regimental museum trust which has placed its collections on loan to a local authority museum. The acquisition and disposal policy relating to the collection must be approved by the owning body and any other body which collects on behalf of the owning body. *In such cases details should be provided concerning the constitution of each body (including copies of constitutional documents where appropriate) as well as information about the terms of the contract or agreement between them.*

1.3 *Information should be provided about the museum's managing committee if this is not the same as its governing body.* This should include the name of the committee and an outline of how it relates to the governing body, if this is not obvious. An example might be the terms of reference of a University Collections Committee.

2 Statement of purpose and key objectives

2.1 *Museums should provide a statement of their purpose (mission statement) and of the key aims and objectives which stem from this.* These may not be necessarily be the simple equivalent of the statement of purpose in a museum's constitutional document. They may be submitted by reference to a copy of the museum's forward plan, which should have been formally approved by the governing body. If the museum does not have a forward plan, these statements should be provided on the application form, and confirmation should be given that they have been approved by the museum's governing body.

3 Collections management

> A museum is an institution which collects, documents, and preserves . . . material evidence and associated information for the public benefit.

Registered museums act as long-term guardians of collections which are in the public domain. This section outlines the minimum standards which should govern collecting and the management of collections. Information may be submitted on the application form, or by reference to a separate collections management plan.

3.1 Existing collections

Details should be provided of the museum's existing collections, including information about any significant elements of the collections which are on loan.

3.2 Acquisition and disposal policy

A copy of the museum's most recent acquisition and disposal policy should be provided. This should be formally approved by the governing body. Evidence of formal approval should be supplied in the form of a signed committee minute signed by a properly authorized person.

3.2.1 The policy should include:

a. A description of the existing collections.
b. The criteria governing future collecting policy, including the subjects or themes for collecting.
c. The period of time and/or geographical area to which collecting pertains.
d. The limitations on collecting imposed by such factors as inadequate staffing, storage, or conservation resources.
e. Reference to the acquisition policies of other museums collecting in the same or related areas or subject fields, so as to demonstrate awareness of the need to avoid unnecessary duplication and waste of resources.

3.2.2 The acquisition policy should be published and reviewed from time to time, at least once every five years, and the date when the policy is next due for review should be noted in the document. Acquisitions outside the current stated policy should only be made in very exceptional circumstances, and then only after proper consideration by the governing body of the museum itself, having regard to the interests of other museums. The MGC should be notified of any changes to the acquisition policy, and the implications of any such changes for the future of existing collections.

3.2.3 *Sub-paragraphs a. to h. inclusive, or equivalent wording, should be incorporated within the policy (b and c may be omitted if they are not relevant to the museum's fields of acquisition).* These paragraphs are based upon the UK Museums Association's *Code of Practice for Museum Authorities* (1987), and are those used in the first phase of registration:

a. The museum will not acquire, whether by purchase, gift, bequest, or exchange, any object or specimen unless the governing body or responsible officer is satisfied that the museum can acquire a valid title to the item in question, and that in particular it has not been acquired in, or exported from, its country of origin (or any intermediate country in which it may have been legally owned) in violation of that country's laws. (For the purposes of this paragraph 'country of origin' includes the United Kingdom.)

b. So far as biological and geological material is concerned, the museum will not acquire by any direct or indirect means any specimen that has been collected, sold or otherwise transferred in contravention of any national or international wildlife protection or natural history conservation law or treaty of the United Kingdom or any other country, except with the express consent of an appropriate outside authority (e.g. a British court in the case of a specimen seized from a third party under the Protection of Birds Acts).

c. So far as British or foreign archaeological antiquities (including excavated ceramics) are concerned, in addition to the safeguards under sub-paragraph c. above, the museum will not acquire by purchase objects in any case where the governing body or responsible officer has reasonable cause to believe that the circumstances of their recovery involved the recent unscientific or intentional destruction or damage of ancient monuments or other known archaelogical sites, or involved a failure to disclose the finds to the owner or occupier of the land, or to the proper authorities in the case of a possible Treasure Trove (England, Wales and Northern Ireland) or Bona Vacantia (Scotland).

d. By definition a museum has a long-term purpose and should possess (or intend to acquire) permanent collections in relation to its stated objectives. The governing body accepts the principle that there is a *strong presumption* against the disposal of any items in the museum's collection except as set out below.

e. In those cases where the museum is legally free to dispose of an item (if this is in doubt, advice will be sought) it is agreed that any decision to sell or otherwise dispose of material from the collections will be taken only after due consideration. Decisions to dispose of items will not be made with the principal aim of generating funds. Once a decision to dispose of an item has been taken, priority will be given to retaining the item within the public domain and with this in view it will be offered first, by exchange, gift or sale to registered museums before sale to other interested individuals or organizations is considered.

f. In cases in which an arrangement for the exchange, gift or sale of material is not being made with an individual registered museum, the museum community at large will be advised of the intention to dispose of material. This will normally be through an announcement in the Museums Association's *Museums Journal* and/or other appropriate professional journal. The announcement will indicate the number and nature of the speciemens or objects involved, and the basis on which the material will be transferred to another institution. A period of at least two months will be allowed for an interest in acquiring the material to be expressed.

g. A decision to dispose of a specimen or object, whether by exchange, sale, gift or destruction (in the case of an item too badly damaged or deteriorated to be of any use for the purposes of the collections), will be the responsibility of the governing body of the museum acting on the advice of professional curatorial staff, and not of the curator of the collection acting alone. Full records will be kept of all such decisions and the items involved and proper arrangements made for the preservation and/or transfer, as appropriate, of the documentation relating to the items concerned, including photographic records where practicable.

h. Any monies received by the museum governing body from the disposal of items will be applied for the benefit of the collections. This should normally mean the purchase of further acquisitions but in exceptional cases improvements relating to the care of collections may be justifiable. Advice on these cases may be sought from the MGC.

3.2.3 A museum's governing body, acting on the advice of professional curatorial staff, may take a decision to return human remains to a country or people of origin. This is entirely a matter for individual museums to consider, taking into account the ethical and legal implications, however it is recognized and accepted that it would be inappropriate to apply the procedure outlined in paragraphs e. and f. in such cases.

3.2.4 Where a museum holds or intends to acquire archives, its governing body must take account of, and where appropriate adopt, the *Code of Practice on Archives for Museums in the United Kingdom*** agreed by the Standing Conference on Museums and Archives, and published by MGC in 1990 (NB currently undergoing amendment to take account of Scottish arrangements) and it should aim to meet the standards outlined in the Royal Commission on Historical Manuscripts' *Standards for Record Repositories* (1990).

3.3 Documentation

3.3.1 *Information should be provided about how the museum documents its collections. The records listed below should be maintained as a minimum.* They are deemed to be those necessary to enable museums to fulfil their fundamental responsibilities for collections and the information associated with them. The principles are that a museum should know at any time exactly for what items it is legally responsible (this includes loans as well as permanent collections), and where each item is located. Documentation must also enable the unique information linked with individual objects to be preserved, and there should be appropriate methods to enable this information to be readily retrieved. It is recognized that the format of such records will differ between museums according to the nature and size of their collections, but each museum should be able to demonstrate that these broad principles are reflected in its documentation procedures.

a. *Entry and exit records*: a record should be kept of all items deposited in the museum, whether on the basis of enquiries, loans or potential acquisitions.
b. *Movement records*: similarly, a record should be maintained of the location and movement of items within the museum.
c. *Accession records*: each museum should maintain an accession register which records the formal acceptance of items into the museum's permanent collection, allocates a permanent identity number, and provides sufficient information for collections management purposes.
d. *Security copy of accession records*: a second copy of the museum's accession records should be kept off-site. Where accession information is wholly computerized it should be supported by a copy of key accession information produced in an alternative medium which meets proven archival standards.

e. *Marking and labelling*: each accessioned item or, where appropriate, group of items should be marked or labelled with its permanent identity number, with due consideration for conservation needs.

f. *Information retrieval*: each museum should maintain appropriate indexes or equivalent information retrieval facilities. The accession register provides a method of retrieving information about items in the collection by their identity number: there must be at least one other method of retrieving information.

g. *Loan records*: museums should maintain records of all loans, whether incoming or outgoing. Long loans should be subject to fixed terms which should be periodically reviewed. The term 'permanent loan' is ambiguous and should be avoided.

3.3.2 *If documentation of the collection has not been completed as set out above, museums should provide details of their plans to eliminate backlogs within a stated timescale.*

3.4 Care of collections

3.4.1 Conservation

Each museum should aim to display, store and handle its collections in such a way as to minimize the risk of damage through environmental factors. It should have regular access to professional conservation advice, to ensure that it can develop informed policies and procedures relating to the preventive and remedial conservation of its collections. Remedial conservation work should normally be carried out under the supervision of a qualified conservator.

Where deficiencies are identified, whether in the condition of individual items or collections, or in the conditions in which collections are housed and used, the museum should plan to institute improvements over time, and on the basis of priority, and these objectives should be reflected in its plan.

Museums should provide information concerning their conservation plans and priorities, including details of the specialist conservation advice which is normally available to them.

3.4.2 Security and risk management

Museums should assess the risks to their collections from such threats as fire, water, theft and vandalism, and should take appropriate steps to meet these, seeking specialist advice as necessary. This will include such measures as the identification of particularly vulnerable collections, the installation of physical protection and alarm systems, staff invigilation, key security systems, inventory check procedures, and insurance arrangements. Where problems are identified, museums should make an assessment of additional requirements and should plan to meet these within an appropriate timescale. (Risks to the safety of museum staff and visitors must also be considered; see also 7.0 below.)

3.4.3 Disaster planning

Each museum should aim to develop a written procedure, or Disaster Plan, for the protection and rescue of the collection in the event of emergencies, such as thefts, fire, flood or other catastrophes. *Museums should indicate whether they have drawn up such plans or are considering doing so.*

4 Public services

A museum is an institution which . . . exhibits and interprets material evidence and associated information for the public benefit.

Registered museums exist to provide a public benefit, not only through the long-term preservation of their collections, but also through the active interpretation and communication of the information and knowledge which they represent. Education, in its broadest sense, is central to a museum's purpose. Each museum must provide some public services including, at any time, an exhibition of at least a representative selection of items from its collections. The museum should be open to the public at appropriate times and for reasonable periods and should provide visitor facilities appropriate to the nature and scale of the institution. It should also plan, to the best of its ability, to provide public services and visitor facilities which encourage and permit access and use by all sections of the public.

4.1 Interpretation

Details should be provided of services in the following areas, including reference to future plans:

a. Permanent exhibitions.
b. Temporary exhibitions.
c. Research and publication.
d. Events, lectures, etc.
e. Any other form of interpretation used, e.g. working exhibits, demonstrations, film, drama, guide/interpreters, etc.

4.2 Education

Each museum should assess its educational role and activities, taking into account its current and potential audiences, and the type of education provision, formal and informal, which its collections, staffing and resources enable it to offer.

Details should be provided of the museum's educational work and the specialist professional guidance (if any) which it receives in this field.

4.3 Other public services

Details should be provided of any other public services, e.g. enquiry and identification service, or the maintainance of regional archaelogical, biological or geological site records.

4.4 Visitor facilities and care

Details should be provided of the museum's visitor facilities and of the steps it has taken, or plans to take, to ensure good standards of visitor care.

A museum should provide or have available in the immediate vicinity a reasonable range of visitor facilities appropriate to the scale, location and nature of the museum, and should aim to manage and staff the museum so as to provide good standards of visitor care, cleanliness, courtesy, and maintenance to ensure visitor safety and comfort. The National Tourist Board's *Code of Practice for Visitor Attractions* is commended to all museums, and the MGC's publication *Quality of Service in Museums and Galleries** provide guidance on how this should be implemented in a museum context. It is also recommended that museums should take account of the 'Principles of public service' outlined in the government's white paper *The Citizens' Charter* (1991).

4.5 Access

Details should be provided of the museum's arrangements for public access, including opening hours.

Museums should regularly review the level of access they offer, taking into account existing and potential users, and the need to cater for people with disabilities or other special needs. Constraints to access, whether physical (such as limited opening hours, or the nature of the site, building or collection) or intellectual (such as the level of difficulty of language used in labelling) should be assessed, and the museum should plan to mitigate these constraints wherever possible. The MGC's *Guidelines on Disability for Museums and Galleries** are commended to all museums as a framework for developing policies and plans in this area.

4.6 Marketing

Museums should have a clear picture of the particular sections of the public at which they are aiming their services and should develop a strategy to assist in reaching these users. They should regularly assess whether this strategy is working successfully. *Details should be provided.*

5 Staffing

5.1 A museum's governing body has a special obligation to ensure that there are staff, whether paid or voluntary, sufficient in both number and kind to ensure that the museum is able to meet its responsibilities. Proper arrangements should be made for the museum to meet its obligations in relation to the care of the collections, public access, research, education and security. The size of the staff and its nature will depend on the size of the museum, its collections and its responsibilities. *Museums should provide details of the nature and number of their staff, whether paid or unpaid, temporary or permanent.*

5.2 Curatorial advice

Information should be provided concerning the museum's access to professional curatorial advice. The following factors should be taken into account:

a. As a minimum, a museum's governing body should normally have the services of a professionally trained and/or experienced curator. *Details should be provided.*
b. There should be an efficient line of communication between the senior museum professional and the appropriate committee of the museum's governing body. MGC would normally expect that the senior museum professional is, at the least, allowed direct access to the appropriate committee when museum policy is discussed. *Details of these arrangements should be provided.*
c. In the case of a *small* museum which does not have the services of a professionally trained and/or experienced curator, the museum's governing body should make arrangements to receive advice from a Curatorial Advisor on a regular basis. This person should be formally appointed by the museum's governing body. It is expected that a museum which has a Curatorial Advisor will seek his or her advice in preparing its application for registration, and the Advisor should also countersign the application form. Curatorial Advisors should also provide a brief report as part of the museum's annual registration return.
    Details should be provided of the Curatorial Advisor's name and their training and/or experience. Evidence of their appointment in the form of a signed and dated committee minute should also be provided.

5.3 Staff training and development

Each museum should assess and keep under review the training needs of all its staff, whether paid or voluntary. Each museum should aim to develop its own training policy and plan to make resources available to implement it. *Details should be provided of current arrangements and future plans.*

6 Financial management

6.1 A museum should be able to demonstrate that it has a sound financial basis. It should be sufficiently well supported and financially viable irrespective of any valuation placed on the items in its collection. In no circumstances should those items be mortgaged or in any way offered as security for any loan. Items given to the museum for its collection should not be capitalized in accounts, and the value of items purchased for the collection should be written off in the year of acquisition. The foregoing advice should also apply to any historic buildings owned by the museum which form an essential part of what the museum exists to preserve and interpret. This policy is in line with the recommendations of the Accounting Standards Board.

6.2 *Local authority and university museums should provide copies of their current annual museum budget and the budget for the previous year. Museums constituted as charities should submit audited accounts for two years* in the form required by the Charities Act 1992 (England and Wales), the Charities Accounts (Scotland) Regulations 1992, and/or the Companies Acts 1985–9. They should include an income and expenditure account and balance sheet, and should be presented in a way which distinguishes between operating and development costs. The accounting practice and conventions described in the *Statement of Recommended Practice 2: Accounting by Charities* (1988), issued by the Accounting Standards Board, are strongly recommended.

6.3 Museums should also aim, as far as possible within any constraints posed by their governing bodies budgeting arrangements, to plan their income and expenditure for at least one year in advance, and ideally for longer. This will involve an assessment of all forms of income that can be predicted for the year(s) in question, together with an estimate of what the museum will need to spend over the same period, taking into account its fixed commitments and the activities and projects it wishes to pursue. Budget estimates should reflect the key activities within the museum.

6.4 Museums should state whether the buildings or sites housing the museum's collections are the freehold of the governing body, or whether they are held under lease, or other arrangements. *Where premises are leased, details of the lessor (e.g. local authority, charity, private company or individual) and the period of the lease should be provided.*

7 Legal, planning and safety requirements

7.1 *Museum governing bodies are required to undertake that they have ensured and will continue to ensure that all relevant legal, safety and planning requirements are complied with.*

NOTE

* Free copies available on request from the MGC, 16 Queen Anne's Gate, London SW1H 9AA.

42

No objects, no money, no venue, no problem

Fred Dunning

One of the interesting problems that arose from the Registration Scheme hinges on the definition of a museum. Of those applications which were rejected, a significant proportion were deemed not to be museums in the terms laid out in the Museums Association's definition. For example, they may have exhibitions but no collections, or collections with no exhibitions venue or programme.

The registration of Jorvik, based on the Coppergate excavations in York, presented particular difficulties and gave rise to much discussion. Fred Dunning in this paper looks at the issues involved.

The Jorvik Viking Centre (JVC) was established by York Archaeological Trust (YAT) in 1984 to display its Coppergate excavations in the centre of York. Jorvik is famous for its Time Car Journey, a recreation of the habitations, figures, sights, sounds and smells of a Viking river port. There is also a formal museum display of Coppergate finds. Visitor numbers average over 875,000 per annum. YAT's Archaeological Resource Centre (ARC), opened in 1990, is aimed mainly at schoolchildren who participate in discovery activities modelled on practical archaeological methods. YAT also engages in other traditional museum activities, including curation, conservation, publication at popular and academic level, and exhibition design.

Without doubt, if Jorvik and the ARC had been part of an established local authority museum service which owned the displayed finds, they would have been registered without hesitation. The difficulty with YAT's application was that the Coppergate finds were owned not by YAT but by York City Council, the site owners. York City Council had arranged for finds on their property to go to the Yorkshire Museum on long loan (twenty-five years initially) for curation and storage. A representative selection of finds was lent by the Yorkshire Museum for display in the JVC. The public ownership of this collection is secure beyond doubt and no one would wish to disturb the harmonious symbiotic relationship that exists between YAT (the discoverers and present custodians), York City Council (the owners) and North Yorkshire County Council's Yorkshire Museum (the curators).

Guidelines governing registration follow the Museums Association's definition of a museum. The implication of guideline 7b is that a museum should possess, or intend to acquire, 'substantial permanent collections'. Since registration began in 1988, a number of cases have arisen where institutions have been loaned sizeable collections by local authorities or by private individuals. The Museums and Galleries Commission (MGC) has no rooted objection to loans so long as they are subject to legally binding, written remain in the public domain; if this is in serious doubt, registration will not be forth-coming. Though the registration committee is wary of applications from theme park heritage experiences, Jorvik's chief attraction, the Time Car Journey, was immaterial to YAT's eligibility for registration which focused on the question of ownership of the displayed collections. Of course, if there had been no displayed collection at Jorvik and if the ARC's educational activities were not artefact-based, the application would not have stood a chance.

YAT's first application came before the MGC registration committee in March 1992. It was rejected by three votes to two. Yorkshire and Humberside Museums Council had adopted a position of benevolent neutrality but the committee ruled YAT ineligible. However, the MGC indicated in its notification of the result that it would be prepared to re-examine the application in the light of YAT's response. A meeting was accordingly arranged by the MGC in York between the registration committee chairs, MGC officers and YAT officers, with the director of the Yorkshire Museum present.

Meanwhile the application was discussed at the June review meeting in London, attend-ed by fourteen of the twenty-one registration committee members. The majority of those at the meeting were, it would be fair to say, undecided. Several spoke firmly against reg-istration, mainly on the familiar grounds that Jorvik was more a heritage experience than a museum while YAT, as an archaeological trust passing its finds to a registered museum, would not normally be considered for registration. Those in favour of regis-tration felt Jorvik was regarded as a museum and would be registered without question if the collections belonged to YAT rather than being on loan. YAT engaged in many other activities traditionally associated with a museum and moreover had discovered the objects in the first place. Uppermost in some members' minds was the thought of the damage that might be done to the MGC's registration initiative by a seemingly bureau-cratic, legalistic decision. At the conclusion of the debate, members were asked to sub-mit their views after the findings of the York meeting were circulated.

The MGC delegation to the York meeting was greatly impressed by the scale and quality of YAT's activities, all of which were firmly collections-based. Of particular note were the conservation facilities, and the quality and range of interpretive activities. As a result, a clear majority of registration committee members favoured registration of YAT. Against were Val Bott, Michael Fopp, Catherine Wilson and Alan Warhurst, although the latter two subsequently decided to go along with the majority, doubtless with reservations.

YAT's formal reapplication came up before the registration committee in July 1992 and, in spite of spirited opposition from Herbert Coutts and Anne Partington-Omar, YAT's application finally succeeded. Two committee members suggested that the MGC must now reconsider guideline 7b, the definition of a museum.

Some had expressed fears of a flood of applications from highly unsuitable theme park heritage experiences following this precedent. But the MGC thinks that few could demonstrate the kind of relationship Jorvik has with the Yorkshire Museum, nor would many be under the wing of an exemplary archaeological service of the calibre of YAT. As ever, each case will be considered on its merits.

This paper first appeared in Museums Journal *(February 1993), p. 22.*

43

Guidelines on disability and quality of service for museums and galleries in the United Kingdom
Museums and Galleries Commission

The Museums and Galleries Commission and the Museums Association do a great deal to influence museum standards. As has been seen in Chapter 40, the Museums and Galleries Commission in particular publishes both guidelines and codes of practice in a number of different areas. By way of an example of this work, the following are the MGC's guidelines on provision for the disabled in museums and the quality of service to be given to visitors. They serve as a standard against which current provision can be assessed and future developments planned.

GUIDELINES ON DISABILITY FOR MUSEUMS AND GALLERIES IN THE UNITED KINGDOM
Museums and Galleries Commission

Notes

The Guidelines are applicable to all museums and galleries, regardless of size, collection, funding or management structure.

These Guidelines use the social definition of disability: that society disables people by putting barriers in their way. These range from physical and communication barriers to those of attitude. Formerly, disabled people were defined by their medical condition or 'impairment', and the term 'handicap' was used to refer to the relationship between them and their environment.

In these Guidelines the term 'museum' is used to subsume 'gallery'.

'The museum's governing body' refers to the controlling body for the museum, e.g. a committee of the local authority or board of trustees. The term 'museum' refers to the museum management.

The term 'staff' refers to paid and volunteer staff.

These Guidelines have been produced by the Museums and Galleries Commission following consultation with museum and disability organizations. They are endorsed by The Museums Association. Copies of the Guidelines are available on request in large print, braille and on tape.

A Resource File will be available from the Museums and Galleries Commission. The File will provide information which will help museums to undertake the work set out in the Guidelines.

Introduction

Museums serve the public interest and are for the public benefit. Everyone has rights and particular needs and expects equitable treatment. Museums should strive to meet these in the services they provide.

Disabled people have the right to derive the same benefits from museums as others. Since disabled people comprise over 10 per cent of the population, museums will wish to meet their needs, as far as practicable, and to see that their management structures and services reflect this commitment.

The aim of these Guidelines is to help museums to meet the needs of all their users – actual and potential, visitors and staff. They treat each issue in this context.

The Guidelines provide a basis on which every museum, in the light of its circumstances, can develop a policy on disability and decide the actions required to give effect to that policy. Once the policy is given effect, services will be enhanced for all users, whether or not they are disabled people.

These Guidelines will also assist museums to meet any requirements in respect of provision for disabled people set by the Museums and Galleries Commission, the Area Museum Councils and other museum funding agencies.

Some museums will wish to develop their policies on disability in the wider context of equal opportunities. These Guidelines do not attempt to cover the whole range of equal opportunity issues but sources of initial advice are indicated in the MGC Disability Resource File.

Policy and procedure

1.1 The museum's governing body should seek to ensure that disabled people have equal opportunities for appointment to that body, and that action is taken to enable people to be identified for such appointments on equal opportunity principles.

1.2 The museum should prepare a written Disability Policy based on these Guidelines setting out its policy on provision for disabled people as staff and visitors.

1.3 The Disability Policy should incorporate a procedure for regular consultation with disabled people and disability organizations, in order to assist in designing, improving and developing the provision of services and the recruitment and employment of disabled people. Consultation procedures should be incorporated into all work covered by these Guidelines.

1.4 The Disability Policy, should incorporate provision for inviting suggestions and responding to complaints, and for regular review in the light of experience.

1.5 Those museums with a single policy covering all aspects of equal opportunities, or that are part of a local authority which has an equal opportunities policy, should ensure that it fully covers the points set out in these Guidelines.

1.6 The museum should also prepare an Action Plan, with timetable and budget requirements, setting out the order in which work will be undertaken to fulfil the museum's

Disability Policy. The Action Plan may form part of the museum's forward plan but should be available for public scrutiny.

1.7 Work on preparing, implementing and monitoring the Disability Policy and Action Plan should be co-ordinated by a designated senior member of staff, working (except in small museums) with a staff working party which is fully representative of all the museum's functional areas, e.g. education and conservation.

1.8 The Disability Policy and Action Plan should be endorsed by the museum governing body, published and made available to staff and contractors, clients and public.

1.9 Information about the Disability Policy and the implementation of the Action Plan should be provided in the museum's annual report or equivalent publication. The implications of the Disability Policy and Action Plan should be taken into account when preparing development plans, annual work programmes, budgets, marketing strategies, specifications for building works and in setting performance indicators.

Employment and training

2.1 It will be necessary for staff involved in preparing the Disability Policy and Action Plan to receive some initial training about disability and how it relates to each functional area of the museum's work.

2.2 Disability Equality Training should be an integral part of training for those involved in all stages of recruitment, job appraisals and career development, and those responsible for monitoring and reviewing these procedures.

2.3 All staff and members of the governing body should receive training to ensure that they are aware of their responsibilities in fulfilling the Disability Policy, and this should be included in the induction training of all staff.

2.4 Aspects of the Disability Policy and Action Plan which relate to specific areas of the museum's service should form part of the training of the relevant staff group, e.g. curators and designers should be trained in applying guidance to the design of displays.

2.5 Staff responsible for advising visitors about the museum's services should be informed of arrangements for facilitating access to the museum and its services and collections, and should be trained in how to provide help. These considerations should also form part of 'Customer Care' training where the aim should be to be welcoming and supportive to disabled people without being patronising.

2.6 All staff should undertake regular refresher training to provide feedback on the implementation of Disability Policy, to maintain levels of awareness and to disseminate new developments and procedures.

2.7 The museum should establish written procedures to ensure that recruitment, employment procedures and practices and staff benefits and conditions of service seek to encourage and support disabled people to achieve equal opportunity for recruitment, employment, training and promotion. It should also introduce a system for monitoring and reviewing these procedures.

2.8 Adherence to the Disability Policy should form part of all service contracts and contracts of employment whether staff and volunteers are directly employed or subcontracted. This applies to all areas of the museum service.

2.9 Job descriptions, contracts and appraisal procedures should incorporate the post-holders' responsibilities in fulfilling the museum's Disability Policy and Action Plan.

Collections and premises

3.1 Parking and set down facilities for disabled people should be available whether on site or by arrangement off site.

3.2 Ways should be sought to enable disabled people to achieve intellectual, physical and sensory access to the collections as well as to facilities such as shop, lecture room, cafeteria and toilets. For collections this can be achieved by means of an alternative or supplementary method of presentation. Segregated provision should be avoided except where disabled people prefer it.

3.3 Where physical access to a display, store or research area poses severe problems, ways should be sought to enable the user to gain some experience of that section of the collection.

3.4 The same consideration should be given to making provision for disabled staff so that they are not precluded from fulfilling the necessary requirements of their post.

3.5 Where appropriate, collecting policies should take account of the work of disabled people in accordance with equal opportunities principles; and displays should recognize their role in society in a positive way.

3.6 Pricing policies, e.g. for admission or rental, should take account of any reduction in the visit experience due to the nature of the disability, the need for a companion or the restrictions of the site, building or displays. Reducing charges does not absolve the museum from demonstrating every effort to overcome these restrictions.

3.7 Where museum premises are made available to outside organizations and groups, this should be conditional on their applying the museum's Disability Policy in particular on providing information to facilitate access to and use of the museum.

3.8 The museum should seek to provide equal opportunities for disabled people to mount exhibitions or hold events on museum premises.

Information

4.1 In producing publicity material, publications such as guidebooks, audio tours, programmes of events and educational material, thought should be given to the needs of different user groups, and to different ways of presenting the information and disseminating it to disabled people and those that may have contact with them.

4.2 All publicity, information and advertisements should, wherever feasible, give details of addresses, opening times, travel and parking arrangements, charges, precise information to help people with different types of disability, and a telephone number for specific enquiries. Where space is limited, a minimum requirement is that symbols or wording are used to indicate how full information can be obtained.

4.3 The provision of facilities or services of help to disabled people and their companions should be clearly indicated by signs in and around the museum.

4.4 At the entrance and enquiry points a 'front-of-house' check-list of information should be available for staff, setting out the facts on physical access, equipment and provision for disabled people. The list should be updated regularly: it should be made available to local organizations concerned with museums and disabled people, and provided to members of the public on request.

Links with the community

5.1 The museum should develop its links with other agencies in the community, such as arts, leisure, education, social services, health, transport and disability organizations in order to promote initiatives that will benefit disabled people. This work is often best undertaken in conjunction with other local museum and arts organizations to enable research costs to be shared and resources maximized.

5.2 Community outreach programmes should be devised to introduce disabled people and their companions to the museum, its collections and facilities.

Responding to policy changes

6.1 Legislative changes, especially in areas of building design and use, social services and special educational needs, should be monitored for their implications for museum services.

QUALITY OF SERVICE IN MUSEUMS AND GALLERIES
Museums and Galleries Commission

Introduction

The National Tourist Board's *Code of Practice for Visitor Attractions* is mandatory for membership of a tourist board. It is very proper in spirit, and very elastic in interpretation. The Museums and Galleries Commission encourages every museum to adopt it, and to exceed it. The guidelines published here amplify the code and place it in a museum context. They are not mandatory, but they do indicate the quality of service which every museum should be aiming at. The guidelines set out ways in which this quality is to be achieved and are designed to help with the forward planning process and the setting of performance indicators. Throughout the document, the word museum is taken to mean 'museums and/or galleries'.

Public service is in the bloodstream of museums. However, putting the customer at the centre of that public service provision is more difficult to achieve. Lack of market research is responsible for some of this failure. Two reports have highlighted good customer care as an essential ingredient for success. The Audit Commission's *The Road to Wigan Pier*, HMSO, 1991:

> Scholarship and conservation are essential to a museum. Without them displays, though lively, may be superficial and uninformed and may even be misleading or incorrect. But scholarship and conservation have little point if people do not visit a museum or use its services.

In 1991, the then Office of Arts and Libraries produced a report, *The Development of Performance Indicators for the National Museums*. Commenting on the requirement for feedback on users' perceptions of the museums, it stated:

> Spending money on service provision is of little value if the level, mix and quality of service is at odds with the requirements and preferences of those for whom the service has been provided and whose needs it has been agreed should be met.

This report has resulted in a survey of customer care in five of the national museums by the National Audit Office, due for publication in early 1993.

In preparing these guidelines, the MGC has been mindful of the vastly different characteristics of museums in the UK. Wide consultation has taken place within and around the profession. These standards have emerged from the profession, based upon the experience and aspirations of those within it. By their nature they are set at a higher level of attainment than most museums can achieve today. We are confident however that they are set at a level which the customer of the 1990s expects and wishes to find. Those customers will quite naturally make comparisons between what they find in museums and what they are offered in the wider leisure sector.

The word 'customer' has been used advisedly. Museums give service to more people than those who actually visit. Contact occurs in writing and by telephone. Also, even when a museum is admission-free, a museum user may have contributed through rates or taxes, or may have spent time and money in reaching the museum. A transaction, takes place, even if indirectly.

The word 'access' is intended to be used in its broadest sense, relating to both physical and intellectual access. Relating to this, you will find a recommendation to museums to make their visitors feel 'welcome'. This is not an exhortation to introduce a 'have-a-nice-day' approach, but to create an atmosphere in which visitors feel comfortable and able to enjoy, learn and, if appropriate, ask questions.

National code of practice for visitor attractions

The following National Tourist Board's code is a broad one, which most museums should be able to adopt.

The owners and management have undertaken:

1   To describe accurately to all visitors and prospective visitors the amenities, facilities and services provided in any advertisement, brochure or any other printed means, and to indicate on all such promotional material any significant restrictions on entry.
2   To display clearly at public entry points any charges for entry (including service charges and taxes where applicable) and whether there are any additional charges for individual attractions.
3   To manage and, where appropriate, staff the Attraction in such a way as to maintain a high standard of customer care, cleanliness, courtesy and maintenance to ensure visitor safety, comfort and service.
4   Where appropriate to the nature, scale and location of the Attraction, to provide adequate toilet facilities, coach and car parking and catering arrangements.
5   To give due consideration to access and other provision for people with impaired mobility and for others with special needs, and to make suitable provision where practicable.
6   To deal promptly and courteously with all enquiries, requests, reservations, correspondence and complaints from visitors.
7   To provide public liability insurance or comparable arrangement and to comply with all applicable planning, safety and other statutory requirements.

In the museum context, there must obviously be a new first point, embodied in the MGC/Museums Association definition and code of practice:

> To collect, document, preserve, exhibit and interpret material evidence and associated information for the public benefit.

Thereafter, the customer would expect much the same standard of service as he or she receives in other parts of the leisure sector. What does this mean in terms of measurable performance? The following (guidelines) give a basis for both planning and assessment of an acceptable quality of service in museums.

Guidelines on quality of service in museums

The management should undertake the following:

Museum practice

1   To meet the minimum standards of the MGC's Registration Scheme.

Collections management

1   Each museum should publish its acquisition and disposal policy.
2   Each museum should document its collections sufficiently to ensure that its ethical responsibilities towards donors of items are fulfilled, and that information about its collections can be made readily accessible to users.
3   Each museum should aim to promote knowledge of the existence of its collections, particularly its research collections, whether through publicity information, scholarly publication, or sharing collections data with other institutions where customers are likely to seek it.
4   There should be arrangements to provide access to the collections for study purposes. These arrangements should be notified through public information material and on-site signs.
5   Public benefit should be enhanced by publication of scholarly research findings. If museums have a formal research policy this should be made publicly known.
6   Items left for opinion should be accorded the same standards of care as items in the museum's permanent collection. Appropriate entry records should be maintained and the depositor should be given a copy as a receipt.

Customer care policy

1   Each museum should have a considered, written customer care policy.[1] If the Code cannot be fully complied with, the policy should indicate how improvements are to be introduced.
2   Implementation should be monitored continuously and policy should be reviewed annually.
3   The needs of customers should be taken into account in all relevant job descriptions.
4   Every museum should conduct regular research with different customer groups to establish both their requirements and their perceptions of the existing service, including the standard of care provided by staff, and to use this information in planning.
5   Suggestions from customers should be responded to promptly and courteously.

Access

1   As far as regulations allow, each museum should be well signposted from major approach routes, and clearly identified upon arrival.
2   MGC Guidelines on Disability for Museums and Galleries should be adopted.
3   Every effort should be made to give the greatest opportunity to all customers, adopting the principle that no one is denied access on the basis of age, creed, race, sex,

physical or mental capability. This will mean reviewing or formulating a policy on equal opportunities.

4   Details of the nearest car and coach parking available should be given in public information material.

5   Details of available public transport to the site should be given in public information material.

6   Opening hours should be based on user needs, and necessary closures on public holidays should be made clear in advance.

7   Telephone and written enquiries should be dealt with courteously and promptly.

8   The special needs of pre-booked groups should be catered for in every way that site and facilities permit.

Marketing

1   Market research is a requirement, and should be based on customers of all types.

2   Each museum should have a marketing strategy which takes account of customer needs and aspirations within their forward plan.[2]

3   Where admission charges apply there should be a customer-conscious pricing policy, with appropriate concessions.

4   Public information material should accurately describe the nature of the experience offered to visitors; opening and closing times; admission and concessionary charges; any restrictions on entry, such as any requirement to pre-book groups; difficulty of access for the elderly, very young, or infirm; and any extra charges which may apply for supplementary activities.

Display and education

1   Each museum should provide display areas which interpret the collections and issues relevant to the museum, in ways which are interesting and enjoyable to museum visitors.

2   Each museum should use information gathered through visitor research to inform its display and education provision.

3   Physical differences between visitors such as height, eyesight, etc. should be accommodated wherever possible.

4   Account should be taken of intellectual differences between visitors.

5   Consideration should be given to language requirements.

6   Provision of further interpretation of the collection should be made, through education services, events and outreach programmes.

7   Appropriate facilities and support should be provided for group visits (pre-booked if required).

8   Consideration should be given to the diverse cultural traditions of existing and potential visitors.

Training

1   Each museum should have and implement a regularly reviewed training policy for paid and voluntary staff which includes customer care.

2   Museums should state their commitment to customer care at entry points.

3   Training should provide effective preparation for dealing with all visitors in a courteous and helpful way.

4   Training should also provide effective preparation for dealing with written and telephone enquiries and complaints in a courteous and helpful way.

5   All staff should receive training in how to implement the museum's fire evacuation procedures and other disaster plans.

Museum support

1   Museums management should involve all staff, particularly front-of-house staff, in a continuous process of reviewing and identifying opportunities to improve structures, procedures and practices relating to quality of service.

2   All staff, particularly front-of-house staff, should receive all the information they need to do their work well, at the time and in the fashion that best meets their needs.

3   Effective two-way communication should be in place to encourage feedback from all staff into policy and practice, and to ensure they are kept informed about the result of their suggestions.

4   Effective personnel services have a role to play in creating the right environment for good customer care.

On-site care

1   Each museum should make every visitor feel welcome.

2   Any admission charges and concessions should be clearly displayed.

3   Public information should be readily available, and up to date.

4   Orientation and direction-finding should be provided.

5   Assistance and information should be readily available to all visitors, including wheelchair and pushchair users and to people with mobility, hearing and sight problems.

6   An adequate number of clean, functioning, attractive, and regularly·inspected public lavatories should be provided and signposted where circumstances allow. Where they do not, information should be readily available as to the whereabouts of the nearest facilities.

7   Facilities for baby-care should be provided and signposted, where circumtances allow. These should be available for both male and female visitors.

8   Clean, attractive catering services should be provided where appropriate and where circumstances allow.

9   An attractive, well-stocked shop will be an enhancement to the visit.

10   The site should generally provide people with a comfortable level of temperature, humidity and cleanliness.

11   Circulation and seating should take into account visitors' stamina, levels of attendance, and time needed to do justice to the displays.

12   Lighting should be adequate for comfort and safety, and where dim for conservation reasons explanation should be given.

13   Equipment failure should be attended to promptly.

14   Closures of any part of the building should be explained in writing.

15   The personal appearance of museum staff should be appropriate to the standards set by the museums.

16   There should be an easy-to-use complaints procedure, readily available.

17   Provisions must be made to deal with emergencies such as fire, flood and other disasters. The fire regulations for public buildings as amended in 1993 should be complied with, and all members of staff should understand their duties in respect of objects, visitors and their own safety.

Safety

1   Each museum must comply with all relevant health and safety and other statutory requirements, including provision of public liability insurance, or a comparable arrangement in the case of publicly funded bodies.

2 Consideration should be given to additional measures for the comfort and safety of visitors, such as warning and explanatory notices, extra handrails, etc.
3 First aid must be available for employees under the HSE Approved Code of Practice (ACOP) HMSO, ISBN 0118855360. In museums this service should be extended to volunteers and visitors.
4 Visitors' personal possessions, such as coats, bags and umbrellas, should be handled and stored carefully and safely.

Monitoring and Evaluation

1 Each museum should have a mechanism for monitoring its effectiveness in customer care. Such monitoring should be regular enough for potential problems to be resolved and potential opportunities to be exploited. This will usually mean annually, and will encompass market research.
2 An easy-to-use system for customer comments should be provided.
3 All staff should be encouraged to give their views on what is helping and hindering the museum in reaching its objectives of constantly improving the quality and standard of customer care.

NOTES

1 A framework for policy is provided in these guidelines.
2 Guidance on how to prepare a marketing policy is given in the MGC publication *The Museum Marketing Handbook*.

44

Code of practice for museum authorities
Museums Association

In the 1970s, when the Museums Association was developing its approach to the ethical basis of curatorial work, it was recognized that two codes would be necessary: one which addressed the responsibilities of the individual, the other the responsibilities of the institution. As a consequence, museums in the UK now have access to both.

The following is the institutional code which, at the time of writing, is being revised. It is proposed that in its new form it will include material from the Guidelines for Museum Committee Members, *published by the Museums Association in 1990.*

Many museums in the UK formally recognize this document and use it as the basis for their policy and development plans.

1 INTRODUCTION

1.1 The Museums Association was founded in 1889 as an organization comprising and representing museums and art galleries and the staff who work in them, both in the British Isles and overseas. Thus it has both Institutional and Personal Members. Membership is open also to persons connected with, or interested in, museums, who are not professionally engaged in museum work, and to certain classes of institutions which do not themselves own museums, but which are in some way connected with the Museums Service.

1.2 The principal aims of the Association are to promote the establishment and better administration of museums and galleries and to improve the qualifications and status of members of museum staffs. It furthers these aims by the arrangement of conferences and meetings, by the collection and reporting of information about museums in its publications, including *Museums Journal* (published monthly), *Museums Yearbook* (annual), and other literature, and by the organization of professional and technical training which leads to recognized qualifications for museum staff.

1.3 It represents the interests of museums and the museum profession with governmental and other outside bodies, whether public or private, national or foreign. It maintains links with UNESCO and the International Council of Museums and collaborates with the Museums and Galleries Commission, the Arts Council, the Council for British Archaeology, the Local Authority Associations, the Countryside Commission and similar organizations in related fields of study. The Association works closely with the Area Museum Councils which provide, with the aid of central government grant-in-aid, technical and advisory services to museums in their areas, with the regional Museums Federations, and with the specialist professional groups in affiliation.

1.4 Throughout its existence the Association has offered guidance to all charged with the specific function of trusteeship of museums and art galleries, an essential part of the heritage, on practical, ethical and professional matters relating to the management of museums and the care and development of their collections. Over the past ten years in particular, guidance has been issued on a wide range of important topics, and in the light of the developing policy of the Association this Code of Practice for Museum Authorities adopted by the Annual General Meeting of the Association of 16 July 1977 and amended by the Annual General Meeting on 24 July 1987, is now commended to boards of trustees, local authorities, museum committees, senior staff and others involved in the management of museums and art galleries.

2 DEFINITION OF A MUSEUM

'A museum is an institution which collects, documents, preserves, exhibits and interprets material evidence and associated information for the public benefit.'

Explanation

Every effort has been made to include all the basic functions of a museum in as few words as possible. 'Institution' implies a formalized establishment which has a long-term purpose. 'Collects' embraces all means of acquisition. 'Documents' emphasizes the need to maintain records. 'Preserves' includes all aspects of conservation and security. 'Exhibits' confirms the expectation of visitors that they will be able to see at least a representative selection of the objects in the collections. 'Interprets' is taken to cover such diverse fields as display, education, research and publication. 'Material' indicates something that is tangible, while 'Evidence' guarantees its authenticity as the 'real thing'. 'Associated information' represents the knowledge which prevents a museum object being merely a curio, and also includes all records relating to its past history, acquisition and subsequent usage. 'For the public benefit' is deliberately open ended and is intended to reflect the current thinking, both within our profession and outside it, that museums are the servants of society.

3 BASIC PRINCIPLES FOR MUSEUM GOVERNANCE

3.1 The governing body or other controlling authority of a museum has an ethical duty to maintain, and if possible enhance, all aspects of the museum, its collections and its services. Above all, it is the responsibility of each governing body to ensure that all of the collections in their care are adequately housed, conserved and documented. The minimum standards in terms of finance, premises, staffing and services will vary according to the size and responsibility of each museum. Guidance on these can be obtained from the Museums and Galleries Commission, the Area Museum Councils, the Museums Association and various specialist professional bodies and groups.

3.2 Each museum should have a written constitution or other document setting out clearly its legal status and permanent, non-profit nature, drawn up in accordance with appropriate national laws in relation to museums, the cultural heritage and non-profit institutions. The governing body or other controlling authority of a museum should prepare and publicise a clear statement of the aims, objectives and policies of the museum and of the role and composition of the governing body itself.

3.3 The governing body holds the ultimate financial responsibility for the museum and for the protecting and nurturing of its various assets: the collections and related documentation, the premises, facilities and equipment, the financial assets and the staff. It is obliged to develop and define the purposes and related policies of the institution, and ensure that all of the museum's assets are properly and effectively used for museum purposes. Sufficient funds must be available on a regular basis, either from public or private sources, to enable the governing body to carry out and develop the work of the museum. Proper accounting procedures must be adopted and maintained in accordance with the relevant national laws and professional accountancy standards.

3.4 The governing body has specially strong obligations to provide accommodation giving a suitable environment for the physical security and preservation of the collections. Premises must be adequate for the museum to fulfil within its stated policy its basic functions of collection, research, storage, conservation, education and display, including staff accommodation, and should comply with all appropriate national legislation in relation to public and staff safety. Proper standards of protection should be provided against such hazards as theft, fire, flood, vandalism and deterioration, throughout the year, day and night. The special needs of disabled people should be provided for, as far as practicable, in planning and managing both buildings and facilities.

3.5 The governing body has a special obligation to ensure that the museum has staff sufficient in both number and kind to ensure that the museum is able to meet its responsibilities. The size of the staff, and its nature (whether paid or unpaid, permanent or temporary), will depend on the size of the museum, its collections and its responsibilities. However, proper arrangements should be made for the museum to meet its obligations in relation to the care of the collections, public access and services, research and security.

The governing body has particularly important obligations in relation to the appointment of the director of the museum, and whenever the possibility of terminating the employment of the director arises, to ensure that any such action is taken only in accordance with appropriate procedures under the legal or other constitutional arrangements and policies of the museum, and that any such staff changes are made in a professional and ethical manner, and in accordance with what is judged to be the best interests of the museum, rather than any personal or external factor or prejudice. It should also ensure that the same principles are applied in relation to any appointment, promotion, dismissal or demotion of the personnel of the museum by the director or any other senior member of staff with staffing responsibilities.

The governing body should recognize the diverse nature of the museum profession and the wide range of specializations that it now encompasses, including conservator/restorers, scientists, museum education service personnel, registrars and computer specialists, security service managers, etc. It should ensure that the museum both makes appropriate use of such specialists where required and that such specialised personnel are properly recognized as full members of the professional staff in all respects. Members of the museum profession require appropriate academic, technical and professional training in order to fulfil their important role in relation to the operation of the museum and the care for the heritage, and the governing body should recognize the need for, and value of, a properly qualified and trained staff, and offer adequate opportunities for further training and retraining in order to maintain an adequate and effective workforce. The director or other chief professional officer of a museum should be directly responsible to, and have direct access to, the governing body in which trusteeship of the collections is vested.

3.6 By definition a museum is an institution in the service of society and of its development, and is generally open to the public (even though this may be a restricted public in the case of certain very specialized museums, such as certain academic or medical museums, for example).

The museum should take every opportunity to develop its role as an educational resource used by all sections of the population or specialized group that the museum is intended to serve. Where appropriate in relation to the museum's programme and responsibilities specialist staff with training and skills in museum education are likely to be required for this purpose.

The museum has an important duty to attract new and wider audiences within all levels of the community, locality or group that the museum aims to serve, and should offer both the general community and specific individuals and groups within it opportunities to be actively involved in the museum and to support its aims and policies.

3.7 The general public (or specialized group served, in the case of museums with a limited public role) should have access to the displays during reasonable hours and for regular periods. The museum should also offer the public reasonable access to members of staff by appointment or other arrangement and full access to information about the collections, subject to any necessary restrictions for reasons of confidentiality or security.

3.8 Subject to the primary duty of the museum to preserve unimpaired for the future the significant material that comprises the museum collections, it is the responsibility of the museum to use the collections for the creation and dissemination of new knowledge, through research, educational work, permanent displays, temporary exhibitions and other special activities. These should be in accordance with the stated policy and educational purpose of the museum, and should not compromise either the quality or the proper care of the collections. The museum should seek to ensure that information in display and exhibitions is honest and objective and does not perpetuate myths or stereotypes.

3.9 Where it is the policy of the museum to seek and accept financial or other support from commercial or industrial organizations, or from other outside sources, great care is needed to define clearly the agreed relationship between the museum and the sponsor. Commercial support and sponsorship may involve ethical problems and the museum must ensure that the standards and objectives of the museum are not compromised by such a relationship.

3.10 Museum shops and any other commercial activities of the museum, and any publicity relating to these, should be in accordance with a clear policy, should be relevant to the collections and the basic educational purpose of the museum, and must not compromise the quality of those collections. In the case of the manufacture and sale of replicas, reproductions or other commercial items adapted from an object in a museum's collection, all aspects of the commercial venture must be carried out in a manner that will not discredit either the integrity of the museum or the intrinsic value of the original object. Great care must be taken to identify permanently such objects for what they are, and to ensure accuracy and high quality in their manufacture. All items offered for sale should represent good value for money and should comply with all relevant national legislation.

3.11 It is an important responsibility of each governing body to ensure that the museum complies fully with all legal obligations, whether in relation to national, regional or local law, international law or treaty obligations, and to any legally binding trusts or conditions relating to any aspect of the museum collections or facilities.

4 ACQUISITIONS TO MUSEUM AND ART GALLERY COLLECTIONS

4.1 The Museums Association has been actively co-operating for many years with UNESCO and the International Council of Museums and fully supports international efforts to control and eliminate international trafficking in stolen and illegally exported works of art, antiquities and other museum objects.

4.2 The United Kingdom already has treaty obligations under the 'European Convention on the Protection of the Archaeological Heritage' adopted in March 1973 (Cmnd. 5224) but in addition the Association supports the principle of the much wider UNESCO 'Convention of the Means of Prohibiting and Preventing the Illicit Import, Export and Transfer of Ownership of Cultural Property', 1970, and will continue to press the United Kingdom government to ratify and enact the 'Convention'.

4.3 The Association considers it essential that notwithstanding the fact that the UNESCO 'Convention' has not yet been ratified by the United Kingdom each museum should comply with the terms and ethical principles of the 'Convention' so far as these are applicable to an individual museum authority.

4.4 Each museum authority should adopt and publish a written statement of its acquisitions policy. This policy should be reviewed from time to time, at least once every five years. Acquisitions outside the current stated policy should only be made in very exceptional circumstances, and then only after proper consideration by the governing body of the museum itself, having regard to the interest of other museums.

4.5 A museum should not acquire, whether by purchase, gift, bequest or exchange, any work of art or object unless the governing body or responsible officer as appropriate is satisfied that the museum can acquire a valid title to the specimen in question and that in particular it has not been acquired in, or exported from, its country of origin (and/or any intermediate country in which it may have been legally owned) in violation of that country's laws. (For the purpose of this paragraph 'country of origin' shall include the United Kingdom.)

4.6 So far as biological and geological material is concerned a museum should not acquire by any direct or indirect means any specimen that has been collected, sold or otherwise transferred in contravention of any national or international wildlife protection or natural history conservation law or treaty of the United Kingdom or any other country except with the express consent of an appropriate outside authority (e.g. a British court in the case of a specimen seized from a third party under the Protection of Birds Acts).

4.7 So far as British or foreign archaeological antiquities (including excavated ceramics) are concerned, in addition to the safeguards under para. 4.5 above, the museum should not acquire by purchase objects in any case where the governing body or responsible officer has reasonable cause to believe that the circumstances of their recovery involved the recent unscientific or intentional destruction or damage of ancient monuments or other known archaeological sites, or involved a failure to disclose the finds to the owner or occupier of the land, or to the proper authorities in the case of possible Treasure Trove (in England and Wales) or Bona Vacantia (Scotland).

4.8 Special attention is drawn to Articles 6(2)(a) and 6(2)(b) of the European Convention on the Protection of the Archaeological Heritage:

2 Each Contracting Party undertakes specifically:

a As regards museums and other similar institutions whose acquisition policy is under State control, to take the necessary measures to avoid their acquiring archaeological objects suspected, for a specific reason, of having originated from clandestine excavations or of coming unlawfully from official excavations.

b As regards museums and other similar institutions, situated in the territory of a Contracting Party but enjoying freedom from state control in their acquisition policy: (i) to transmit the text of this Convention, and (ii) to spare no effort to obtain the support of the said museums and institutions for the principles set out in the preceding paragraph.

4.9 If appropriate and feasible the same tests as are outlined in the above four paragraphs should be applied in determining whether to accept loans for exhibition or other purposes.

4.10 Each museum authority should recognize the need for co-operation and consultation between all museums and galleries, both national and provincial, with similar or overlapping interests and collecting policies and should seek to consult with such other institutions both on specific acquisitions where a conflict of interest is thought possible and, more generally, on defining areas of specialization.

4.11 If a museum should in future come into the possession of an object that can be demonstrated to have been exported or otherwise transferred in violation of the principles of the UNESCO 'Convention' and the country of origin seeks its return and demonstrates that it is part of the country's cultural heritage, the museum should, if legally free to do so, take responsible steps to co-operate in the return of the object to the country of origin.

4.12 Special attention is drawn to the following statement issued in May 1972:

The Standing Commission on Museums and Galleries, in consultation with the British Academy, the British Museum and the Museums Association (representing the other relevant museums in the United Kingdom), having considered the UNESCO Convention on the Means of Prohibiting and Preventing the Illicit Import, Export and Transfer of Ownership of Cultural Property, adopted in Paris in November 1970, and the aims underlying it, declare that:

(i) they attach the highest importance to preventing the destruction of the records of man's past and the despoliation of archaeological and other historical sites;

(ii) they recognize the importance, in the scientific and scholarly study and inter-change of archaeological and other cultural material, of mutual confidence and assistance between countries concerned and will do everything in their power to promote it;

(iii) they affirm that it is and will continue to be the practice of museums and galleries in the United Kingdom that they do not and will not knowingly acquire any antiquities or other cultural material which they have reason to believe has been exported in contravention of the current laws of the country of origin.

4.13 Many museums and galleries have experienced great difficulty from time to time because of special conditions and restrictions on items in their collections (e.g. that items will be permanently displayed, shown in separate rooms, etc.). The Associa-tion does not recommend the acceptance of a gift or bequest to which any special conditions apply (except for conditions intended to assure the permanent protec-tion of the item in the collection, such as restrictions on any legal power of dis-posal that the museum or gallery may have). The use of the term 'permanent loan' has no legal status.

4.14 The collecting policy or regulations of the museum should include provisions to ensure that no person involved in the policy or management of the museum, such as a trustee or other member of a governing body, or a member of the museums staff may compete with the museum for objects or may take advantage of privi-leged information received because of his or her position, and that should a con-flict of interest develop between the needs of the individual and the museum, those of the museum will prevail. Special care is also required in considering any offer of an item either for sale or as a tax-benefit gift, from members of governing bodies, members of staff or the families or close associates of these.

5 DISPOSAL OF COLLECTIONS

5.1 The definition of a museum in para. 2 makes it clear that it is a key function of a museum or art gallery to acquire objects and/or works of art and to keep them for posterity. Consequently there must be a strong presumption against the disposal of any items in the collections of a museum.

5.2 A number of the most important national museums and galleries are governed under Acts of Parliament which specifically prohibit the disposal of items in the collections and, even where this is not the case, various severe restrictions are placed on the powers to dispose of items from the museum or gallery.

5.3 So far as local authority and private trust museums and galleries are concerned, attention is drawn to the important advice on the legal position included in the 'Report of the Committee of Enquiry into the Sale of Works of Art by Public Bodies' (HMSO, 1964) as follows:

The basic principle upon which the law rests is that when private persons give property for public purposes the Crown undertakes to see that it is devoted to the purposes intended by the donor, and to no others. When a work of art is given to a museum or gallery for general exhibition, the public thereby acquires rights in the object concerned and these rights cannot be set aside. The authori-ties of the museum or gallery are not the owners of such an object in the ordinary sense of the word: they are merely responsible, under the authority of the Courts, for carrying out the intentions of the donor. They cannot sell the object unless authorized to do so by the Courts or by the Charity Commissioners or the Minister of Education on behalf of the Courts, because they have themselves nothing to sell. If they attempt a sale in breach of trust it is the function of the Attorney General to enforce the trust and protect the rights of the public in the object by taking proceedings in the 'Chancery Division.'

5.4 It should also be stressed that even where general powers of disposal exist a museum or art gallery may not be completely free to dispose of items purchased where financial assistance has been obtained from an outside source (for example central government grant-in-aid, National Art-Collections Fund, Friends of the Museum organization or a private benefactor) disposal would require the consent of all parties who had contributed to the purchase.

5.5 In those cases where a museum is free to dispose of an item (e.g. by virtue of a local Act of Parliament or of permission from the High Court or the Charity Commissioners) any decision to sell or dispose of material from the collections should be taken only after due consideration, and such material should be offered first, by exchange, gift or private treaty sale, to other museums before sale by public auction is considered.

5.6 In cases in which an arrangement for the exchange, gift or private treaty sale of material is not being made with an individual museum, the museum community at large must be advised of the intention to dispose of material through an announcement in *Museums Journal*. The announcement must indicate the number of specimens involved, the prime objects concerned and the basis on which the material would be transferred to another institution. A period of at least two months must be allowed for an interest in acquiring the material to be expressed.

5.7 A decision to dispose of a specimen or work of art, whether by exchange, sale ordestruction (in the case of an item too badly damaged or deteriorated to be restorable), should be the responsibility of the governing body of the museum acting on the advice of professional curatorial staff and not of the curator of the collection concerned acting alone. Full records should be kept of all such decisions and the specimens involved and proper arrangements made for the preservation and/or transfer, as appropriate, of the documentation relating to the object concerned, including photographic records where practicable.

5.8 Any monies received by a governing body from the disposal of specimens or works of art should be applied solely for the purchase of additions to the museum or art gallery collections.

6 MUSEUM ORGANIZATION

6.1 Over a period of more than fifty years a series of independent reports have consistently supported the view of the Museums Association that the curator or director of a museum or art gallery should be directly responsible and have direct access to the governing body in which trusteeship of the collections is vested.

6.2 The Wright Committee, in its Report to the Minister for the Arts (Provincial Museums and Galleries, HMSO, 1973) discussed the Bains 'Report on the Management and Structure of the New Local Authorities' and stated:

12.2 We have seen and heard of a good many cases in which museums, even if they are provided with professionally qualified staff, are administered by librarians. We discuss in Chapter 6 the levels of training and expertise required of a museum curator, and consider that curatorial decisions within museums should be taken by staff who possess such expertise. Despite the valuable links which can be forged between libraries and museums we believe that efficiency is generally better served, if museums are administered separately.

12.3 In any case we are convinced by the argument for a museum director or curator having direct access to the appropriate committee, at least when estimates are presented and museum policy discussed. Even if for administrative purposes the director is a subordinate of some other officer this should always be made possible.

6.3 The Museums Association considers that precisely the same criteria should apply in other circumstances (e.g. where the museum or gallery is part of a local authority recreation department or, indeed, a part only of the activities of a more general charitable trust). The Association is of the firm opinion that the only means of ensuring efficient operation and development of the service is for the curator/director to be a chief officer with direct access to the governing body and, in any case, regardless of the status of the most senior professional, the following minimum standards should apply.

a. A competently trained and qualified Curator should be responsible for the services and staff of the museum and/or art gallery.
b. The Curator should be responsible for compiling reports and submitting them in person to the governing body or committee.
c. The Curator should be responsible for preparing and controlling annual estimates and participating in their presentation to the governing body or committee.
d. The Curator should be concerned with a preparation of capital development schemes and the submission of agreed capital estimates to the governing body.
e. A properly qualified Curator should be paid at a salary commensurate with her/his specialized qualifications, professional experience and the responsibilities she/he has for the collections which are normally of high monetary, artistic or scientific value.

7 RESPONSIBILITY TO THE CURATOR

The employing body should pursue a policy that allows the curator to act in accordance with the *Code of Conduct for Museum Curators*. The employing body should never require the curator to act in a way that would reasonably be judged to conflict with the provisions of her/his professional Code.

45

Performance assessment in museums

Penny Spencer *et al.* and Giulia Ajmone Marsan

In the final two papers, experienced museum people assess how performance assessment works in museums and point to likely ways of developing museum standards in the future.

FEEL THE WIDTH
Penny Spencer, Mike Pye and Stuart Davies

Over the past few years, performance measurement has become part of the managerial language of museums and art galleries. A recent survey of local authority museums revealed that one-third of them claim to use perfomance indicators regularly (although another third never use them!). Measuring performance is a key plank in the government's desire to keep tabs on the efficiency and value for money of services subsidized by the national or local taxpayer. This line has been strongly promoted by the National Audit Office, the Audit Commission for England and Wales and the Accounts Commission for Scotland.

Performance measurement even affects independent museums that depend on public subsidies. Indeed, many local authorities have set more stringent performance targets for those to whom they give grants than for their own services. Furthermore, those who give grants or offer sponsorship (whether to public or independent bodies) increasingly want to measure the return on their 'investment'. Indicators are also being used for internal management within public sector organizations, to help determine the best application of decreasing resources.

Recent initiatives in this area go one step further. Attempts are now being made to establish a small number of indicators which are clear enough to allow citizens (those who pay for the subsidy of public services) to judge for themselves whether or not they are getting value for money. This is one of the key features of John Major's Citizens Charter. Under the Local Government Act 1992, the Audit Commission must list performance indicators which every local authority in England and Wales will be obliged to report annually. The commission's initial list became effective on 1 April 1993 and data is now being gathered with a view to publishing (probably in the local press) information for 1993/94 at the end of 1994. Draft indicators were proposed for museums and galleries in September 1992 (see *Museums Journal* October 1992: 9). At the point the Museums Association (MA) decided to collect responses to the commission's proposals and investigate the whole issue of performance measurement. As it turned out, the commission decided not to pursue indicators in some parts of local authority services, including museums (see *Museums Journal* January 1993: 9). Nevertheless, the MA continued its analysis in an attempt to establish a list of indicators which met Audit Commission requirements and seemed 'acceptable' to the museum community.

Measuring the measures

There is no shortage of possible performance indicators for museums and galleries: over one hundred have already been published (see further reading). However, most of these are designed for internal management purposes and do not satisfy the criteria for Citizen's Charter indicators which, according to the Audit Commission, should:

- Interest citizens.
- Deal with cost, economy and efficiency, as well as quality and effectiveness.
- Support useful comparisons over time and between authorities.
- Deal with the main services provided by local government.
- Focus on the performance of individual authorities.
- Be reasonably acceptable without laying down new norms or standards.
- Avoid incentives to distort.
- Use information which is cheap and easy to collect.

The Local Government Act envisaged that each service activity (of which 'museums' was expected to be one) would need about five indicators covering:

- Amount of service provided.
- Use made of the service.
- Quality or effectiveness.
- Cost to the taxpayer.
- Value for money.

Few indicators meet all the Citizen's Charter criteria and many present problems of collection or interpretation. Most museum accounting systems seem incapable either of allocating costs to specific activities or of allowing comparison between museums and across time. There are also problems of definition: when is an exhibition temporary? How do you define (never mind identify and record) a 'user'? It is easier to construct a 'resource' indicator based on total expenditure and number of users but there are still interpretation problems. There is, after all, a very fine line between efficiency and under-resourcing. The lack of readily available data about museums is a further handicap.

Measuring 'quality' is a particular problem, as the Audit Commission recognizes in its own discussion documents. It now seems accepted that the most appropriate way forward is by some sort of standardized market research formula which asks users to react to the service provided. The commission has promised to investigate this but the MA should again prepare recommendations in advance.

Performance measurement is valid only if the organization has clearly stated aims, objectives or goals that can be measured. It is not an end in itself. Performance may also be assessed qualitatively. The only real merit of quantitative measures is that they may be comparable but even then league tables may not be good guides to efficiency and effectiveness. Indeed they may be more useful to governments seeking new ways of allocating resources than to citizens wishing to be better informed about how their taxes are spent.

An MA working party considered all these issues and finally settled on nine indicators: six relating to the services provided by museums and three 'resource' or 'context' indicators which give an indication of the size and scope of an individual museum service (see below). These proposed draft Citizen's Charter indicators are being forwarded to the Audit Commission for their comments.

REFERENCES

Ian Walden (1992) 'Qualities and quantities', *Museums Journal* January: 27–8.

Museums Association, 'Guidelines on performance management', in *Museums Yearbook*, 1991/2 onwards.

Peter Ames (1991) 'Measuring museums' merits', in G. Kavanagh (ed.) *The Museums Profession: Internal and External Relations*, Leicester: Leicester University Press: 59–69.

Peter Jackson (1991) 'Performance indicators: promises and pitfalls', in S. Pearce (ed.) *New Research in Museum Studies*, vol. 2, *Museum Economics and the Community*: 41–64.

Office of Arts and Libraries (1991) *Report on the Development of Performance Indicators for the National Museums and Galleries*, London: Department of National Heritage.

N. Nicholson (1992) *Performance Indicators: An Introductory Guide*, Local Government Management Board.

Performance jargon

Performance indicators: any types of information which help to judge how well a service is being delivered, how successfully it is meeting the needs it is supposed to meet and what it costs. Performance indicators can be descriptions as well as statistics. Achievement of full registration is not a statistic but it may be an important indicator of a successful service

Performance measures: another term for performance indicators but usually only statistical ones.

Effectiveness: is the service doing what it is supposed to do?

Efficiency: doing things right. Is the required standard of service being provided at the lowest cost?

Inputs: the human, financial and technological resources put into a service.

Outputs: the results achieved by the service.

Outcomes: do the outputs reflect the overall aims and objectives of the service? You may allocate a budget to produce exhibitions and create a wonderful Edwardian costume exhibition, but if the objective of the service is to interpret local archaeology then the desired outcome has not been achieved.

Museums Association proposed Citizens Charter performance indicators

1 Amount of service provided

These are context indicators that give some idea of the size and scope of the museum service and its resources.

1.1 Number of staff (in full-time equivalents) working in management and administration, curatorial posts and visitor services.

1.2 Square metres of space used for public displays, trading operations, storage and offices.

1.3 Number of specimens/groups of specimens in social history, archaeology, ethnography, geology, biology, art, etc.

2 Use made of the service

2.1 Total annual attendance per square metre of public space (multiplied by) total number of hours open.

An indication of the capacity and accessibility of public gallery space (the total number of square metres available over the year). The equation takes into account the varying size of museums and the variable opening hours and should produce a figure which is comparable across services.

2.2 Number of users per employee (in full-time equivalents).

This equation should include all users: enquiries (telephone, written, in person), researchers (ditto), visitors, school parties, school loans users, attendance at lectures and events (in-house or outreach), etc. It should also include all staff: curatorial, administration, attendants, technical, shop, etc.

3 Quality

3.1 Registration Status (full, provisional or not registered).

The Registration Scheme provides a simple measure of quality through the achievement of minimum standards.

4 Cost to taxpayer

4.1 Net expenditure per head of the local authority's population.

The principle adopted here is that museum services are provided for the benefit of all citizens, even if they are not visitors or users.

4.2 Income as a proportion of gross costs.

'Income' here means earned income or grants from outside the local authority. Independent museums or local authority trust museums would inevitably show a better 'performance' here, since they would include local authority grants as income.

5 Value for money

5.1 Ratio of market-generated income to public-sector funding.

As with 4.2 this indicates how much income the museum is attracting but also shows the balance between the income derived from users (through admissions, sales, sponsorship, etc.) and that provided by local authorities, area museum councils, the Museums and Galleries Commission, etc.

MEASURE THE ECSTACY
Giulia Ajmone Marsan

'Ah, the ecstasy and the agony!' This exclamation from a curator encapsulates the National Museums and Galleries' (NMG) experience with performance indicators. In the early 1990s, the then Office of Arts and Libraries (OAL) introduced indicators on the basis of a report by consultants Coopers & Lybrand that identified two groups of indicators, one for NMG internal use and one to show to the OAL – the so-called 'group one' of nineteen indicators (see table).

Some remain sceptical about the value of performance indicators. A British Museum curator insists: 'They do not make any difference: we were doing our job well before and will carry on doing it equally well now that they have been introduced.' Christopher Brown, chief curator of the National Gallery, observes: 'We are very much in the public eye, almost continously under scrutiny. We feel we are in more of a fish bowl than an ivory tower. We are also involved in a continuous monitoring process, reporting monthly to the trustees about our activities and drawing up a report annually.' In this context performance indicators do not appear to have brought about a managerial revolution.

Others feel that if indicators are integrated into the corporate planning system they can be useful as a management tool for individual museums to assess what has been done, to set realistic targets and to examine whether they have been achieved. Gwyn Miles, surveyor of collections at the Victoria and Albert Museum (V & A), explains: 'The value of performance indicators lies in the fact that through them you are prevented from making flabby statements about what you do.' Chris Jones, British Museum head of administration, agrees that they help to keep the museum on course: 'For instance, we have always worked towards keeping open as many galleries as possible; now there is a proper count and this induces better discipline.' In 1991 the museum achieved 95.6 per cent of open galleries days against the objective set in the corporate plan to keep open to the public 100 per cent of galleries, excluding those that were being refurbished.

Introducing the performance measurement system initially involved much hard work and also a change in approach. This was particularly true for larger institutions and those that did not already have thorough internal review procedures. Robert Bud, head of life and environmental sciences at the Science Museum, points out: 'When a museum does not think of itself in terms of systems and numbers, performance measurement involves a change in corporate culture.'

More or better

He warns quality is much more difficult to measure than quantity and that 'it is wrong to think in merely quantitative terms'. Visitor surveys can be used to assess public service and display quality. Robin Cole-Hamilton, V&A head of public affairs, is pleased that 'the museum now has a robust system to measure visitor satisfaction', but he does recognize its limitations: 'It is possible to find out what visitors are looking for in a display. But measuring the type of experience visitors have is more difficult.' Michael Cowdy, National Gallery director of administration, agrees: 'We are aiming at conducting a visitor survey every two years but it provides a broad-brush assessment only.'

Museums are quick to point out that it is crucial how figures are interpreted and in particular that more is not necessarily better. Miles stresses: 'Numbers by themselves are of little significance. For instance, in the case of loans the V&A felt that insufficient care and time was devoted to them and therefore decided to look more carefully at the kind of exhibition they were loaned to, how many people would be expected to visit it and whether the loan procedures were meticulously followed.' In 1992 the British Museum had 6.7 million visitors, compared to 5.4 million in 1991. 'The museum might actually want to reduce the number of visitors,' says Jones, 'given the strain on services and resources.' In any case, an increase in the number of visitors does not necessarily reflect an improved museum service. It may be a result of the flow of foreign tourists or changes in school curricula requirements. However, the expected number of visitors can be usefully worked into the targets to improve facilities.

The relevance of other indicators is also in question. Some museums do not consider indicator 2 – expenditure per user – very useful, because the balance of home and foreign visitors varies between institutions, and the cost of the service rendered depends on what is curated, in what state it is and – crucially – on the condition of the building.

Family discipline

Another way of assessing museum performance is the peer review. So far only the Science Museum has participated in such a study, looking at acquisitions, conservation, documentation, storage, galleries and exhibitions, scholarship, customer care and management. It intends to do so regularly on a five-year cycle. But peer reviews have their difficulties. 'They are like parental discipline – either brutal or non-existent,' says Bud. The choice of assessors is crucial if they are to strike the right balance.

The team at the Science Museum, appropriately headed by Otto Mayr, director of the Deutsches Museum in Munich, did not mince its words and the experience was very stressful. Preparing the review involved an immense amount of work. Bud adds: 'If the practice were universal, it would be very expensive in terms of opportunity cost. If museums spent on peer review what the Science Museum has spent, the total would go a long way towards buying the *Three Graces*.'

Now the British Museum is considering bringing in a team of international assessors – possibly the director of the Louvre, sponsors and trustees – with written terms of reference to look at one aspect of the collection at a time, intending over a decade to cover a number of areas. On the other hand the National Gallery feels that a peer review would be very cumbersome for a relatively transparent, small institution with only seven curators.

Comparative intentions

The Department of National Heritage (DNH), the enlarged OAL, as the sponsoring government department, wants assurance that it is getting value for money and that the NMGs know what they are doing and where they are going. But beyond this, it is not entirely clear what intentions DNH has. The V&A complains that it had no specific response to its submissions: 'In 1991 we enclosed with the indicators fourteen appendices but had no reaction. In 1992 we forwarded simply one page of numbers and again had no reaction.' At the British Museum Chris Jones says more generally: 'Response from the DNH was interesting and appeared fairly positive in the grant that followed for the year 1992–93.' The National Gallery says: 'Every year we discuss our corporate plan with the department but we do not expect a detailed reaction to the indicators.' It is understood that DNH uses the information provided by indicators only in an 'indirect way, not in a specific one, in negotiations with the Treasury', according to a former special advisor.

Table 45.1

	Performance component	*Indicator area*
1	Access and use	Movement in user numbers by category
2	Access and use	Expenditure per user
3	Access and use	New loans made
4	Visitor care/display	Visitor satisfaction
5	Visitor care/display	Gallery days: availability *v.* plan
6	Display	Achievement of display programme objective (institution specifies)
7	Access/display/visitor care	Visitor flow
8	Collection management	Achievement of specified collection management objectives for corporate planning period
9	Collection management/ scholarship	View of assessors
10	Scholarship	Scholarly outputs *v.* plan
11	Scholarship	Citations/critical review/other impact assessment
12	Building management	Major projects: variance in actual time and cost *v.* plan
13	Building management	Ratio of planned to unplanned maintenance
14	Building management	Compliance with fire standards
15	Building management	Accident levels
16	Income generation and financial management	increase in self-generated income by type
17	Income generation and financial management	Ratio of self-generated income to grant-in-aid
18	Income generation and financial management	Salaries as percentage of running costs, grant-in-aid
19	Human resource management	Achievement of training programme objectives

Note: National museums and galleries submit nineteen 'group one' perfomance indicators to the Department of National Heritage each year. Many of them do not allow direct comparison between institutions, making league tables impossible.

Source: Report on the Development of Perfomance Indicators for the National Museums and Galleries (Office of Arts and Libraries, 1991).

When indicators were first introduced, the emphasis was on finding a way to assess the performance of individual institutions over time. The purpose was to develop a system which mapped out how an institution served the public, to complement financial data. This was also intended to function as an early warning system identifying emerging problems. In implementing the system, individual museums have defined and adapted performance indicators to fit their own needs and DNH recognizes that a considerable degree of tailoring was necessary.

But there are now signs that the emphasis is shifting towards comparing performance between institutions. Bud warns: 'Now, in a different climate and with increasingly tight budgetary constraints, beneath the rhetoric of devolution there appears to be a move towards centralization which would involve tightening up the definitions of performance indicators in order to allow comparisons.' DNH is asking NMGs to single out around six key objectives and related indicators, and to establish a hierarchy among them. For instance, the sixth objective of the BM corporate plan for the period 1994–97 is to begin to use space vacated by the British Library. It sets as target the opening in September 1994 of a Mexican gallery in a room off the north end of the King's Library.

A DNH spokesperson insists that it would like to avoid constructing a mechanistic league table and judging the national museums by numbers. The DNH admits that it would like to be able to make comparisons, while recognizing that it is not easy to do so in a meaningful and fair way.

DNH is thus giving conflicting signals, provoking speculation about its real intentions. It is legitimate to ask whether its request for a short list of prioritized indicators represents a step towards constructing NMG league tables. Discussions on the matter have been protracted: this may be significant. Some museums, like the V&A, are reluctant to produce a short-list, regarding it as too simplistic a representation of museum activities. Others, like the BM, have put forward a series of broad objectives tailored to their own activities, rather than closely modelled on those of group one of the OAL report.

These factors may explain the length of the discussion. But DNH may be making continued efforts to persuade NMGs to adopt to some extent uniform objectives so their performance can be compared. .

The long-awaited National Audit Office (NAO) report into customer care and marketing – the British Museum, the Natural History Museum, the Science Museum, the National Portrait Gallery – may confirm this shift in emphasis. According to an NAO spokesperson, the draft report says that performance indicators should be quantifiable and have a common format to allow comparison between institutions, where appropriate. Publication of the final report (expected as *Museums Journal* goes to press) will mark a major step forward in the current debate. If it calls for comparisons, museums are likely to argue that the recommendation is misguided.

This paper first appeared in Museums Journal *(July 1993), pp. 27–8, 29–30.*

Further reading

Ambrose, T. M. (ed.) (1987) *Education in Museums; Museums in Education*, Edinburgh: HMSO/SMC.

Ambrose, T. M. (ed.) (1988) *Working with Museums*, Edinburgh: HMSO/SMC.

Ambrose, T. M. (ed.) (1991) *Money, Money, Money & Museums*, Edinburgh: HMSO/SMC.

Ambrose, T. M. (1993) *Managing New Museums. A Guide to Good Practice*, Edinburgh: HMSO/SMC.

Ambrose, T. M. and Paine, C. (1993) *Museum Basics*, London: Routledge.

Ambrose, T. M. and Runyard, S. (eds) (1991) *Forward Planning. A Basic Guide for Museums, Galleries and Heritage Organizations*, London: Routledge.

American Association of Museums (1992) *Excellence and Equity: Education and the Public Dimension of Museums*, Washington.

Audit Commission (1991) *The Road to Wigan Pier? Managing Local Authority Museums and Art Galleries*, London: HMSO.

Falk, J. and Dierking, L. (1992) *The Museum Experience*, Washington: Whaleback Books.

Hooper-Greenhill, E. (1992) *Museums and the Shaping of Knowledge*, London: Routledge.

Hudson, K. (1987) *Museums of Influence: The Pioneers of the Last 200 Years*, Cambridge: Cambridge University Press.

Hudson, K. and Nichols, A. (1989) *Cambridge Guide to the Museums of Britain and Ireland*, Cambridge: Cambridge University Press.

Hudson, K. and Nichols, A. (1991) *Cambridge Guide to the Museums of Europe*, Cambridge: Cambridge University Press.

Karp, I. and Lavine, S. D. (1991) *Exhibiting Cultures, the Poetics and Politics of Museum Display*, Washington: Smithsonian Institution Press.

Karp, I. and Lavine, S. D. (1992) *Museums and Communities. The Politics of Public Culture*, Washington: Smithsonian Institution Press.

Kavanagh, G. (ed.) (1991) *Museum Languages: Objects and Texts*, Leicester: Leicester University Press.

Kavanagh, G. (ed.) (1991) *The Museums Profession: Internal and External Relations*, Leicester: Leicester University Press.

Lewis, J. (1990) *Art, Culture and Enterprise. The Politics of Art and the Cultural Industries*, London: Routledge.

Lord, G. D. and Lord, B. (eds) (1992) *The Manual of Museum Planning*, Manchester: MSI/HMSO.

Lumley, R. (ed.) (1988) *The Museum Time Machine*, London: Methuen/Routledge.

Montaner, J. M. (1990) *New Museums*, London: Architectural and Design Press.

Pearce, S. M. (ed.) (1988) *Museum Studies in Material Culture*, Leicester: Leicester University Press.

Pearce, S. M. (ed.) (1991) *Museum Economics and the Community*, London: Athlone Press.

Pearce, S. M. (ed.) (1992) *Museums and Europe 1992*, London: Athlone Press.

Roberts, J. (1990) *Postmodernism, Politics and Art*, Manchester: Manchester University Press.

Thompson, J. M. A. *et al.* (eds) (1992) *Manual of Curatorship: A Guide to Museum Practice*, London Museums Association/Butterworths.

Vergo, P. (ed.) (1989) *The New Museology*, London: Reaktion Books.

Weil, S. (1985) *Beauty and the Beasts. On Museums, Art, the Law, and the Market*, Washington: Smithsonian Institution Press.

Weil, S. (1990) *Rethinking the Museum and Other Meditations*, Washington: Smithsonian Institution Press.

Index